MARX'S *CAPITAL* AND CAPITALISM; MARKETS IN A SOCIALIST ALTERNATIVE

RESEARCH IN POLITICAL ECONOMY

Series Editor: Paul Zarembka

RESEARCH IN POLITICAL ECONOMY VOLUME 19

MARX'S *CAPITAL* AND CAPITALISM; MARKETS IN A SOCIALIST ALTERNATIVE

EDITED BY

PAUL ZAREMBKA

Department of Economics, State University of New York, Buffalo, USA

2001

JAI

An Imprint of Elsevier Science

Amsterdam – London – New York – Oxford – Paris – Shannon – Tokyo

ELSEVIER SCIENCE Ltd
The Boulevard, Langford Lane
Kidlington, Oxford OX5 1GB, UK

First edition 2001

Library of Congress Cataloging in Publication Data
A catalog record from the Library of Congress has been applied for.

British Library Cataloguing in Publication Data
A catalogue record from the British Library has been applied for.

ISBN: 0-7623-0838-9

⊗ The paper used in this publication meets the requirements of ANSI/NISO Z39.48-1992 (Permanence of Paper).
Printed in The Netherlands.

CONTENTS

LIST OF CONTRIBUTORS *vii*

I. SIEBER'S READING OF *CAPITAL*, VOLUME 1; MARX ON SIEBER

NIKOLAI SIEBER AND KARL MARX
James D. White *3*

MARX'S THEORY OF VALUE AND MONEY
Nikolai Ivanovich Sieber (1871), translated by
Rakhiya Mananova and James D. White from
David Ricardo's Theory of Value and Capital in
Connection with the Latest Contributions and
Interpretations *17*

THE SPECTRAL REALITY OF VALUE:
SIEBER, MARX, AND COMMODITY FETISHISM
David Norman Smith *47*

II. POLITICAL ECONOMY OF CAPITALISM AND OF A SOCIALIST ALTERNATIVE

CAPITAL ACCUMULATION AND THE COMPOSITION
OF CAPITAL
Alfredo Saad-Filho *69*

CRITERIA OF TECHNICAL CHOICE AND EVOLUTION
OF TECHNICAL CHANGE
Cheol-Soo Park *87*

ON THE POLITICAL ECONOMY OF SOCIALISM:
AGAINST THE REGULATION OF SOCIAL RELATIONS
BY MARKETS
Martijn Konings *107*

III. IDEOLOGY

ALIENATION, IDEOLOGY AND FETISHISM
Thierry Suchère   157

THE WORLD AS A GAME IN SRAFFA AND
WITTGENSTEIN: A CASE STUDY IN MODERN
BOURGEOIS IDEOLOGY
Jørgen Sandemose   173

STALINIST IDEOLOGICAL FORMATION:
ABSOLUTE GENERAL SECRETARY AND THE
PROLETARIAN FETISH
Charles Bettelheim, translated by A. D. Bhogle   233

Sponsor's Preface *by Ranganayakamma*

LIST OF CONTRIBUTORS

Martijn Konings

Deparment of Political Science, York University, Canada

Cheol-Soo Park

Department of Economics, New School University, USA

Ranganayakamma

Sweet Home Publications, Hyderabad, India

Alfredo Saad-Filho

Department of Development Studies, SOAS, University of London, UK

Jørgen Sandemose

Department of Philosophy, University of Oslo, Norway

David N. Smith

Department of Sociology, University of Kansas, USA

Thierry Suchère

Institut Universitaire de Technologie du Havre, France

James D White

Department of Central & East European Studies, University of Glasgow, Scotland

PART I.

SIEBER'S READING OF *CAPITAL*, VOLUME 1; MARX ON SIEBER

NIKOLAI SIEBER AND
KARL MARX

James D. White

Of all the commentaries written on Marx's economic ideas, that of Nikolai Sieber is practically unique in being endorsed by Marx himself. In the Postscript to the second edition of *Das Kapital* Marx stated:

> Already in 1871 Mr N.Sieber (Ziber), Professor of Political Economy at the University of Kiev in his book *Teoriya tsennosti i kapitala D. Rikardo* (*D. Ricardo's Theory of Value and Capital*, etc.) referred to my theory of value, money and capital in its general outlines as a necessary sequel to the teachings of Smith and Ricardo. What surprises the Western European reader on reading this excellent work is the consistent comprehension it shows of the purely theoretical standpoint (Marx, 1872, p. 818).

As Marx was not apt to bestow credit lightly, this judgement on Sieber's book was praise indeed. Even more compelling evidence of Marx's regard for Sieber came seven years later, in 1879, when, commenting on a book by Adolf Wagner, Marx noted:

> Mr Wagner could have discovered, both from *Das Kapital* and from Sieber's work (if he knew Russian) the difference between me and Ricardo, who in fact concerned himself with labour only as a *measure of value-magnitude* and on that account found no connection between his theory of value and the essence of money (*Marx Engels Werke*, 1962, p. 358).

In this note, which was not intended for publication and therefore reflected his genuine opinion, Marx implied that on the question under discussion Sieber's work was comparable to his own. In view of Marx's attitude to it, Sieber's work is clearly of great significance for students of Marx's economic thought. Despite this, Sieber is not well known and none of his writings have appeared

Marx's *Capital* and Capitalism; Markets in a Socialist Alternative,
Research in Political Economy, Volume 19, pages 3–16.
Copyright © 2001 by Elsevier Science Ltd.
All rights of reproduction in any form reserved.
ISBN: 0-7623-0838-9

in English translation. The present paper sets out to explain who Sieber was and to place his work in the context of the history of Russian Marxism. It also attempts to place Marx's reception of Sieber in the evolution of Marx's economic thought.

Nikolai Ivanovich Sieber was born on March 10 (22) 1844 in the village of Sudak in the Crimea. His father was a Swiss who had settled in Russia, his mother being a Ukrainian of French descent (Ianzhul, 1894, p. 581). (The spelling 'Ziber' is the Russian transliteration of Sieber). Although Sieber was brought up in Russia and thought of himself as a Russian, he remained a Swiss subject throughout his life. He was educated at the high school in Simferopol and entered the law faculty of Kiev University in 1863. In Russian universities at that time economics was a subject that was often taught as part of a law degree, and it was in this way that Sieber began his economic studies. He was fortunate to have as his teacher Nikolai Bunge, who later became the Minister of Finance under Alexander III (Kleinbort, 1923). Bunge was an adherent of the Smith and Ricardo school, but was also very receptive to the latest developments in economic thinking. He exercised a strong influence on Sieber and fostered his interest in economics. Sieber graduated from Kiev University in 1866, and, encouraged by Bunge, decided to embark on an academic career, and to specialise in the study of political economy.

Sieber's postgraduate studies had to be postponed for a year, however, as he had to wait for a grant to become available. Consequently, for eight months Sieber worked as an arbiter of the peace (*mirovoi posrednik*) in the province of Volhynia before returning to Kiev University. The function of a *mirovoi posrednik* was to implement at a local level the peasant reform which had been promulgated by Alexander II in 1861, and see to it that relations between the newly liberated peasants and the landowners were settled peaceably. When Sieber took up the post, peasant allotments were being readjusted in the aftermath of the Polish uprising of 1863. In order to win over the peasants in the South Western provinces to its side, the Russian government had revised the terms of the 1861 legislation giving the peasants more generous land allotments and on more favourable terms (Zaionchkovskii, 1968, p. 214). Sieber was involved in putting the amended agrarian legislation into effect. The first-hand experience of working in the countryside could not but give him an insight into the workings of peasant communities – something which he was later to write about extensively.

Discussions surrounding the peasant reform had formed an important element in Russia's intellectual climate of the 1860s. It was the general opinion that liberating the serfs was the first step towards Russia's developing a capitalist economy, like those of advanced countries of the West. The framers of the

1861 legislation had no doubts that Russia was destined to have a capitalist future; they only feared that capitalism would be introduced too precipitously and destabilise the country. As a result, built into the reform legislation were measures specifically designed to slow down the development of capitalism. Peasant communities were to be preserved intact to impede peasant mobility. It was expected, however, that in the long term these peasant communes would be dissolved by the inroads of the capitalist economy. One of the few voices to be raised in protest at this scheme of things was that of Nikolai Chernyshevskii, who deplored the projected demise of Russian peasant collectivism and the emergence of an economic system based on selfish individualism. Chernyshevskii was critical of the peasant reform and of the capitalist economic system which it was intended to introduce. He wrote extensively on the subject during the 1860s, one of his main works being a critique of classical economics which took the form of a commentary on John Stuart Mill's *Elements of Political Economy*. Marx was familiar with Chernyshevskii's work and in the same Postscript to the second edition of *Das Kapital* as he had praised Sieber's book he commented very favourably on Chernyshevskii's work on Mill.

In 1868 Sieber took his master's examination and returned to Kiev University to commence his postgraduate studies. The master's examination was an oral one, and on this occasion the examiner was Bunge, who asked him to outline the economic theory of Karl Marx, whose book had just appeared. Sieber had assimilated Marx's ideas and gave a good account of himself at the examination. He then proceeded to work on his master's dissertation, which set out to show how Marx's ideas were an elaboration on the ideas of the classical economists. The dissertation, entitled, *David Ricardo's Theory of Value and Capital in Connection with the Latest Contributions and Interpretations* was presented in 1871 and published in Kiev in the same year (Ziber, 1871). It appeared a year before Nikolai Danielson and Herman Lopatin's translation of the first volume of *Das Kapital* into Russian, and was therefore the first introduction to Marx's ideas for the Russian-speaking public.

After a study trip abroad, Sieber took up a teaching post in Kiev University, and in 1873 was awarded the chair of Political Economy and Statistics. His tenure of the post, however, was brief, for, in 1875 he resigned from the university in protest at the dismissal of his colleague, the historian Mikhail Dragomanov, for promoting Ukrainian national identity. Sieber left Russia and settled in Switzerland, from where he continued his academic work and sent articles to be published in Russian periodicals (Ovsianiko-Kulikovskii, 1923, p. 145).

No doubt encouraged by Marx's favourable response to his dissertation, in 1874 Sieber began to publish a series of articles in the journal *Znanie*

(Knowledge) under the general title 'Karl Marx's Economic Theory'. At the beginning of March 1874, Danielson wrote to Marx informing him of this fact, quoting Sieber's statement that the object of the series was to 'popularize the economic theories of the author and analyze them critically'. Danielson had found the articles highly commendable and was passing them on to Marx via Lopatin (*K. Marks, F. Engel's i revoliutsionnaia Rossiia*, 1967, p. 311). The series in fact continued to appear sporadically in *Znanie* until 1877, and when that journal was closed down the series was resumed in *Slovo* (The Word) during 1878. The four articles which appeared in Slovo were incorporated into a revised edition of *David Ricardo's Theory of Value and Capital* and the resulting work published in 1885 under the new title of *David Ricardo and Karl Marx in their Socio-Economic Investigations* (Ziber, 1885).

Among Marx's published notes there is reference only to the first of Sieber's articles in *Znanie*. It contains the sole point of criticism Marx found to make of the article in question. This concerned Sieber's defence of Marx against Karl Rössler, a German reviewer of *Das Kapital*, who had demanded to know why it should be that 'the food in the stomach of a worker should be the source of surplus value, whereas the food eaten by a horse or an ox should not'. To this Sieber had replied that the subject of Marx's investigation had been human society and not the society of domestic animals; therefore it had been concerned only with the kind of surplus value produced by human beings. On this explanation Marx commented:

> The answer, which Sieber does not find, is that because in the one case the food produces human labour power (people), and in the other – not. The value of things is nothing other than the relation in which people are to each other, one which they have as the expression of expended human labour power. Mr Rössler obviously thinks: if a horse works longer than is necessary for the production of its (labour power) horse-power, then it creates value just as a worker would who worked 12 instead of 6 hours. The same could be said of any machine (Marx, 1927, p. 61).

This error, as it happened, was one that Sieber would later correct in articles written in Marx's defence.

Sieber was to act not just as the popularizer of Marx's works in Russia, but also their champion. He took up his pen to counter the attacks on *Das Kapital* by two critics who approached Marx's book from the point of view of classical liberal economics, Yu. G. Zhukovskii and B. N. Chicherin. In 1877 Zhukovskii, a follower of Ricardo, published a lengthy review of Marx's *Kapital* in the journal *Vestnik Evropy* (European Herald). Zhukovskii raised several objections to Marx's work. As far as methodology was concerned, he had the impression that Marx was still very much influenced by Hegel, so that his approach was formalistic, paying insufficient attention to the actual content of economic affairs. Nor could Zhukovskii believe Marx's contention that only human labour created surplus value. He was of the opinion that anything which bore fruit, be it a tree, livestock or the earth, all were capable of providing exchange value. For Zhukovskii one of the main sources of value was Nature. He thought too, that Marx's account of the origins of capitalism, the expropriation of the peasants and the formation of a proletariat, had a fortuitous quality about it; Marx had traced the beginnings of capitalism in Europe to the liberation of the peasantry without land, but this clearly implied that in other places, if the peasants were not so liberated, then capitalism would not develop (Zhukovskii, 1877, pp. 67–72).

Sieber's reply appeared in the journal *Otechestvennye zapiski* (Annals of the Fatherland) in November 1877. In regard to Zhukovskii's objections to Marx's philosophical approach, Sieber conceded that Marx would have done no harm by 'reducing somewhat the dialectical side of his exposition'. (Ziber, 1959b, p. 562) But, on the other hand, Sieber pointed out, in the case of value, the metaphysical approach was necessary, because in capitalist society perceptions of value were metaphysical. Marx's treatment of the subject duly reflected this fact. Sieber then explained how exchange-value represented the essential unity of humanity through the prism of the division of labour and the fragmentation of society (Ziber, 1959b, p. 564). In response to Zhukovskii's idea that exchange value was created not only by human labour, but also by Nature, Sieber emphasised that it was human labour which constituted the sole source of exchange value, something, he added, that Zhukovskii as an authority on David Ricardo, ought to know full well. Sieber was eager to defend Marx against Zhukovskii's charge that he had presented the origins of capitalism as a fortuitous event rather than as a Natural process and quoted from the Russian translation of *Kapital* one of the few passages in which Marx suggested that the development of capitalism was a universal and necessary phenomenon.

In the following year the liberal historian, philosopher and political thinker, Boris Chicherin published an article attacking Marx's *Kapital* in the journal *Sbornik gosudarstvennykh znanii* (Compendium of Statecraft) (Chicherin, 1999). The article was couched in much the same terms as Zhukovskii's had been, and when he replied to Chicherin in *Slovo* in February 1879 (Ziber, 1879), Sieber could note that both critics shared some key misapprehensions. In a passage which brought out the metaphysical character of exchange value, he observed:

> But to people it *appears* as though things exchange themselves one for another, that things themselves have exchange value, etc. and that the labour embodied in the thing given is reflected in the thing received. Here lies the whole groundlessness of the refutations of Mr Chicherin, and before him of Mr Zhukovskii, that neither the one nor the other could

understand, or wanted to understand, as he should the circumstance that Marx presents to the reader the whole doctrine of value and its forms not on his own behalf, but as the peculiar way people at a given stage of social development necessarily understand their mutual relations, based on the social division of labour. In fact, every exchange value, every reflection or expression of it, etc. represents nothing but a myth, while what exists is only socially-divided labour, which by force of the unity of human nature, seeks for itself unification and finds it in the strange and monstrous form of commodities and money (Ziber, 1900, p. 697).

Marx followed Sieber's literary output closely, and Danielson sent him the journals in which articles by Sieber appeared, including Sieber's polemics with Zhukovskii and Chicherin. Marx had certainly read Sieber's article against Zhukovskii, and possibly that against Chicherin. Sieber was not the only defender of Marx's *Kapital* against Zhukovskii. The editor of *Otechestvennye zapiski*, N. K. Mikhailovskii, who had written a favourable review of the Russian translation of *Das Kapital* in 1872, also wrote an article in reply to Zhukovskii's criticisms. Mikhailovskii's defence of Marx, however, was not without its reservations; it deplored the implication of Marx's 'historico-philosophical theories' that Russia would have to endure the horrors of capitalism, 'the maiming of women and children' so that the kind of collectivist society that already existed in Russia could be created. This seemed to Mikhailovskii illogical and unnecessary. Mikhailovskii's article appeared in *Otechestvennye zapiski* in October 1877 under the title of 'Karl Marx before the Tribunal of Mr. Zhukovskii'. Danielson sent this article to Marx along with Sieber's replies to Zhukovskii and Chicherin. On 15 November 1878 Marx wrote to Danielson:

> Of the polemics of Chicherin and other people against me, I have seen nothing, save what you sent me in 1877 (one article of Sieber, and the other, I think of Michailoff[skii], both in the "Fatherlandish Annals", in reply to that queer would-be Encyclopedist Mr. Zhukovskii) (Marx & Engels, 1991, p. 343).

Marx drafted a reply to Mikhailovskii, denying that he had any such 'historico-philosophical theory', repudiating the idea that the growth of capitalism was inevitable in Russia and conceding that the founding of socialism on the Russian peasant commune was possible and desirable (Marx & Engels, 1965, pp. 311–313). One important factor in Marx's decision not to send the letter was that Sieber had argued the very opposite, that the development of capitalism was universal. Sieber's view in this respect was subsequently to become the prevalent one among Marx's followers in Russia, Plekhanov and Lenin in particular.

From the late 1870s Sieber began to turn his attention to the study of primitive communities. It was a preoccupation which emerged from his commentaries on Marx's economics, especially from the parts of *Das Kapital* which were devoted to the subject of cooperation, one of Sieber's own early interests. Sieber explained the relevance of the study of primitive communes for Marx's economics in 'The Theory of Social Cooperation', an article in *Slovo* in 1876, which later became a chapter in *David Ricardo and Karl Marx*. In Sieber's view, economists had given insufficient attention to the fact that the theory of cooperation in the broad sense of the term was the theory of society itself. Because of this, cooperation outweighed in importance all other economic questions (Ziber, 1937, p. 538).

In noting the absence of a historical dimension in Marx's treatment of capital, Sieber observed:

> One can only regret that the author of *Das Kapital*, not wishing to broaden the scope of his task, should have limited himself to studying the forms of labour combination and the movement of these forms within capitalist society alone. That is why we do not find in his work an account of the social cooperation at previous stages of economic development. Even the feudal handicraft order, which gave rise to capitalist manufacture, is passed over in silence. And yet it is precisely the knowledge of this order which is of enormous importance for giving the necessary understanding of the capitalist modes of the succeeding period. It is to be hoped that someone else will undertake the beneficent work of filling where necessary this and other gaps left by Marx in the great series of changing forms of social cooperation (Ziber, 1937, p. 360).

Sieber even suggested what kind of sources could be used for the purpose. 'What a mass of material', he remarked, 'having a bearing . . . on the relations of production of hunting, fishing, and nomadic peoples, lie buried in countless travellers' tales' (Ziber, 1937, p. 377). This was the kind of material Sieber himself was to employ when he embarked on his study of pre-capitalist forms of social cooperation, *Studies in the History of Primitive Economic Culture*, published in 1883.

Sieber's book appeared too late for Marx to have read, but there is every reason to suppose that Marx was familiar with at least its main arguments. In his memoirs the Russian economist N.A.Kablukov stated:

> In the second half of 1880 I lived in London, studying every day in the library of the British Museum and spending some time in the company of N. I. Sieber, who was then working on his book *Studies in the History of Primitive Economic Culture*, on which we talked a great deal. I went with him several times to visit K. Marx and F. Engels, who made us very welcome and introduced us to their families (*Russkie sovremenniki o K.Markse i F.Engel'se*, 1969, p. 78).

Marx himself referred to these meetings. In a letter to Danielson dated 19 February 1881, he wrote: 'Last month we had several Russian visitors including Professor Sieber (he has now gone to Zurich) and Mr Kablukov (from Moscow). They worked for whole days at a time in the British Museum' (Marx & Engels,

1992, p. 64). It is likely that Sieber discussed his work on primitive communities with Marx, who at that time had an immediate interest in the subject, as he was in the process of drafting a reply to Vera Zasulich, who had written to him inquiring if he considered the development of capitalism to be inevitable in Russia.

Marx replied to Zasulich as he had to Mikhailovskii, that Russia might well avoid capitalism if the country's present economic policies were changed. In that case socialism in Russia could be based on the peasant commune. Sieber's own attitude to this question was quite unambiguous. He regarded the peasant commune as a pathetic relic of the past, doomed to destruction. He associated Russia's progress, economic, political and cultural with the development of capitalism on the European pattern. In reviewing V. P. Vorontsov's book *The Fate of Capitalism in Russia* (1882), which warned that the development of capitalism might dispossess the peasants without turning them into proletarians and leaving them with no means of livelihood, Sieber agreed that the plight of the Russian peasants was deplorable, but that capitalism was a necessary stage in the 'general development of civilisation'. If there were no displacement of people from the countryside to the towns, the concentration of population, the building of railways etc., Russia would still be in the same condition as it had been in the reign of Ivan the Terrible (Ziber, 1959a, p. 673). Sieber was quoted as saying that 'Until the peasant is refined in the factory boiler nothing good will come of him' (Mikhailovskii, 1909, p. 327).

Although Sieber believed that the development of capitalism in Russia was inevitable and that the peasant commune would not long survive, he was deeply interested in the way the commune had evolved and how it would eventually dissolve and give way to capitalist relations. As one can see from the drafts of his letter to Vera Zasulich and from the notes he made for his studies of the Russian economy, Marx too from about 1870 onwards viewed the emergence of capitalist relations in this way. The following generation of Russian disciples of Marx, however, including Plekhanov and Lenin, disregarded the peasant commune entirely, considering it to be a preoccupation of the 'Narodniki'. Lenin's major work on the Russian economy, *The Development of Capitalism in Russia* (1899) is the most obvious example of this kind of approach (Lenin, 1960).

Sieber was not himself a participant in the Russian revolutionary movement, and he was rather dismissive of the revolutionary groups with which he was familiar, the followers of Lavrov, Bakunin and Tkachev. According to his friend Ovsianiko-Kulikovskii, Sieber's attitude was that they were 'good people, but that they hadn't the slightest clue about scientific socialism or political economy' (Ovsianiko-Kulikovskii, 1923, p. 146). Sieber abhorred terrorism, but understood why people resorted to it. On the other hand, he was deeply disturbed by the political reaction in Russia following the assassination of Alexander II, and even in his Swiss exile, felt himself threatened by it. Moreover, he was irked by attacks on socialism, and felt impelled to come to its defence. His polemics with Zhukovskii and Chicherin were inspired by this kind of sentiment. (Ovsianiko-Kulikovskii, 1923, p. 146).

In 1884 Sieber fell ill with a degenerative disease, and returned to his family in the Ukraine. He died in Yalta in 1888 aged 44 (Kleinbort, 1923, pp. 18–19). The brevity of Sieber's life is one factor that ensured that he did not receive the recognition he deserved as the pioneer of Marxism in Russia. In this respect he was to be overshadowed by Plekhanov, who subtly undermined Sieber's significance by suggesting that he did not understand dialectics, a verdict which became enshrined in Soviet doctrine. Sieber's reputation in the Soviet Union was also clouded because he belonged to the Ukraine and not Russia proper, so that the honour of producing the first Marxist in the Russian Empire went to the Ukraine rather than to Russia (Ziber, 1937, p. XLIV).

Nevertheless, Sieber's influence was considerable; it was from Sieber that Plekhanov, Lenin and much of the revolutionary generation in Russia learnt their Marxism. Sieber's work, particularly his *David Ricardo's Theory of Value and Capital* provided an excellent introduction to Marx's thinking, and smoothed the passage to reading *Das Kapital* itself. This is still true of Sieber's book, and in this respect it is much to be regretted that Sieber's work has not been more familiar to students of Marxism in the West.

On reading Sieber's dissertation it is difficult not to agree with Marx's verdict on it; Sieber really does have an excellent grasp of the theoretical aspects of Marx's work, and his exposition of it is a considerable achievement. One has to remember that Sieber was working from the first German edition of *Das Kapital*, which is much more Hegelian than the much simplified second edition of 1872 and subsequent editions. In summarizing the first section of Marx's book he had to negotiate some very complex terminology and concepts. He did this adroitly, so that whereas most of the philosophy is excised in Sieber's account, the essence of what the philosophical element conveyed is retained. Sieber himself remarked that he thought the philosophical dimension unnecessary:

This brief extract from the first chapter of Marx's work and the appendix to it at the end of the book contains, if I am not mistaken, the most essential features of the author's doctrine of value and the general properties of money. The peculiar language and the quite laconic manner of expression does little to facilitate the comprehension of his ideas, and in some cases has led to the accusation that he employs a metaphysical approach to the investigation of value. With the exception of a few places in the chapter where perhaps some statements are indeed made which do not really correspond to the truth, the accusation seems to me unjust. As far as the *theory* itself is concerned, Marx's method is the deductive method of the whole English school, and both its faults and its merits are those shared by the best of the theoretical economists (Ziber, 1871, pp. 169–170).

This was the passage from which Marx quoted (selectively) in his Postscript to the second edition of *Das Kapital*.

Sieber not only summarized Marx's first chapter, but went on to elaborate on Marx's ideas and to illustrate these with examples. It is this aspect of Sieber's work which testifies to his profound comprehension of Marx's arguments. He not only could expound Marx's theory, but explain its interconnections and ramifications. Sieber's insight came in the first place from his extensive knowledge of the classical economists, of Ricardo in particular. He was consequently able to judge in precisely what way Marx had built on the ideas of his predecessors. He could observe, for example, how Marx had modified Ricardo's labour theory of value, and in this way appreciate what contribution to economic thought Marx had made.

Sieber's book is a unique document because it is the authentic reception of Marx's work at the time of its publication. As such, it judges *Das Kapital* not in relation to anything that came after, but solely in terms of what came before. Sieber knew precisely what belonged to Smith, Ricardo and the economists of the classic school, and what belonged to Marx.

There is another advantage that Sieber had in his understanding of Marx: he did not share the individualist assumptions of the classical economists. In this respect he was like Chernyshevskii, whose commentary on J. S. Mill is a critique of the individualist standpoint. Perhaps this characteristic of Sieber is not so obvious in his *David Ricardo's Theory of Value and Capital* as it is in his later works, but, like Chernyshevskii, Sieber understood the dynamics of a society based on collectivism and cooperation as opposed to one composed of an aggregate of individuals.[1] It is highly probable that Sieber knew Chernyshevskii's work, but he was unable to refer to it because of the tsarist censorship. This is one of the themes of Marx's *Kapital*, though there, especially in the first edition, Marx approaches this question philosophically rather than sociologically. In the 1870s, however, Marx was in the process of making the transition from philosophy to sociology. It is this transition which helps explain Marx's very positive reception of Sieber's writings, despite the fact that in them Sieber was rather dismissive of the philosophical dimension of Marx's work.

Just as Marx was about to publish the first volume of *Das Kapital* he had run into serious problems with the section of his projected work which would deal with the circulation of capital. He had hitherto assumed that capital would spread throughout the world carrying all before it, but he had overlooked the fact that even in his own native Hunsrücken despite the development of capitalism, the older, collective, social and economic system still survived. Capitalism, apparently, did not necessarily erode traditional peasant society, but coexisted with it. Marx removed much of the philosophical underpinnings for his earlier view of capitalist development from the published version of *Das Kapital*, continuing the excisions in the second and French editions, and he embarked on a lengthy empirical investigation of how capital actually began to circulate. He had an excellent example to hand in Russia, which had just embarked on the capitalist road, having abolished serfdom a few years earlier. In 1870 Marx learnt Russian and got down to the serious job of collecting materials on Russian economic development (White, 1996).

Just at the time Marx was becoming interested in Russia, Russia was becoming interested in Marx. Marx, after all, was the economist par excellence who had studied the dynamics of the capitalist system, and whose findings were of great relevance to Russians. The interest in Marx was greatest among the adherents of Chernyshevskii. To this category belonged Danielson and Lopatin, the translators of *Das Kapital* into Russian; it was they who were chiefly responsible for supplying Marx with publications on the economic situation in Russia. They also acquainted him with the writings of Chernyshevskii, which Marx greatly appreciated. It was also through Danielson and Lopatin that Marx received Sieber's book *David Ricardo's Theory of Value and of Capital.*

Marx was deeply impressed by Sieber's book, and it is significant that the only marginal note which he made was a criticism of a highly specialised order. Sieber had referred to Boisguillbert's advocacy of stable prices, and had noted the apparent contradiction that the same writer should state that it mattered little in general whether prices were high or low. Here Marx wrote: 'Sieber forgets that Boisguillbert in fact is speaking about the raising of agricultural prices, brought about by fiscal measures, etc.' In the Postscript to the second edition of *Das Kapital*, (which appeared in instalments between 1872 and 1873) Marx made public his appreciation of Sieber's work. Presumably through Lopatin, who visited him in London, Marx had learnt some personal details about Sieber, and knew that he was at the time of writing Professor of Political Economy at Kiev University.

Marx's reception of Sieber's work is of great significance for how one understands Marx's system. In particular it provides material with which to evaluate Lenin's dictum that 'It is impossible to understand Marx's *Das Kapital*, and especially its first chapter, without having thoroughly studied and understood the whole of Hegel's *Logic*.' (Lenin, 1961, p. 180) Clearly this proposition is untrue, because Sieber understood the chapter in question to the satisfaction of its author without having any special familiarity with Hegelian philosophy.

Sieber's exposition of Marx, in fact, meticulously strips out the Hegelian framework from *Das Kapital* to give a coherent and comprehensible account of Marx's arguments. Marx himself would go through a similar procedure in the second edition of his work. In this respect Sieber's commentary on Marx not only has a profound appreciation of the theoretical aspects of *Das Kapital*, but also anticipates the direction that that theory would take.

REFERENCES

Chicherin, B. N. (1999). Marx. In: G. M. Hamburg (Ed.), *Liberty, Equality and the Market: Essays by B. N. Chicherin* (pp. 321–350). Yale University Press, New Haven and London.

Ianzhul, V. (1894). Ziber. In: F. A. Brockgauz & I. A. Efron (Eds), *Entsiklopedicheskii Slovar,'* 12A. St Petersburg, 581–582.

Marks, K. (1967). *F. Engel's i revoliutsionnaia Rossiia*, Moscow.

Kleinbort, L. M. (1923). *Nikolai Ivanovich Ziber*. Kolos, Petrograd.

Lenin, V. I. (1960). The Development of Capitalism in Russia. *Collected Works, 3*. Foreign Languages Publishing House, Moscow.

Lenin, V. I. (1961). *Collected Works, 38*. Foreign Languages Publishing House, Moscow.

Marx Engels Werke, 19. (1962). Dietz Verlag, Berlin.

Marx, K. (1872). *Das Kapital*, 2nd. Otto Meissner, Hamburg.

Marx, K. (1927). Iz chernovoi tetradi K. Marksa. *Letopisi Marksizma, 4*, 56–62.

Marx, K., & Engels, F. (1965). *Selected Correspondence*. Progress Publishers, Moscow.

Marx, K., & Engels, F. (1991). *Collected Works, 45*. Lawrence & Wishart, London.

Marx, K., & Engels, F. (1992). *Collected Works, 46*. Lawrence & Wishart, London.

Mikhailovskii, N. K. (1909). *Polnoe sobranie sochinenii, 7*. M M Stasiulevich, St Petersburg.

Ovsianiko-Kulikovskii, D. N. (1923). *Vospominaniia*. Vremia, St Petersburg.

Russkie sovremenniki o K.Markse i F.Engel'se (1969). Moscow.

White, J. D. (1996). *Karl Marx and the Intellectual Origins of Dialectical Materialism*. Macmillan, Basingstoke and London.

Zaionchkovskii, P. A. (1968). *Otmena krepostnogo prava v Rossii*. Prosveshchenie, Moscow.

Zhukovskii, I. G. (1877). Karl Marks i ego kniga o kapitale. *Vestnik Evropy, 5*, 64–105.

Ziber, N. I. (1871). *Teoriia tsenosti i kapitala D. Rikardo v sviazi s pozdneishimi dopolneniiami i raz"iasneniiami*. Kiev.

Ziber, N. I. (1879). B. Chicherin contra K. Marks. (Kritika kritiki). *Slovo*, February, 63–101.

Ziber, N. I. (1885). *David Rikardo i Karl Marks v ikh obshchestvenno-ekonomicheskikh issledovaniiakh*. I D Sytin, St Petersburg.

Ziber, N. I. (1900). Nemetskie ekonomisty skvoz' ochki g. B. Chicherina. In: *Sobranie Sochinenii, 2*. Izdatel,' St Petersburg.

Ziber, N. I. (1937). *David Rikardo i Karl Marks v ikh obshchestvenno-ekonomicheskikh issledovaniiakh*. Sotsekgiz, Moscow.

Ziber, N. I. (1959a). *Izbrannye ekonomicheskie proizvedeniia, 2*. Sotsekgiz, Moscow.

Ziber, N. I. (1959b). *Izbrannye ekonomicheskie proizvedeniia, 1*. Sotsekgiz, Moscow.

DAVID RICARDO'S THEORY OF VALUE AND CAPITAL IN CONNECTION WITH THE LATEST CONTRIBUTIONS AND INTERPRETATIONS

Contents

I   On Value in General and its Constituent Elements

II   The Doctrine of Value of Ricardo, His Predecessors and Some of His Successors

III   Costs of Production and Demand and Supply

IV   K. Marx's Theory of Value and Capital

V   The Concept of Capital

VI   On the Origins and Accumulation of Capital

VII   On Fixed and Circulating Capital

Nikolai Ivanovich Sieber's edition 1871 edition–Teoriia tsennosti i kapitala D. Rikardo v sviazi s pozdneishimi dopolneniiami i raz"iasneniami. Published in Kiev.

DAVID RICARDO AND KARL MARX IN THEIR SOCIO-ECONOMIC INVESTIGATIONS

Contents

I On Value in General and its Constituent Elements [Corresponds to Chapter I in the 1871 edition with some minor textual changes].

II The Doctrine of Value of Ricardo, His Predecessors and Some of His Successors [Corresponds to Chapter II in the 1871 edition with some minor textual changes].

III Costs of Production and Demand and Supply [Corresponds almost exactly to Chapter III in the 1871 edition].

IV Marx's Theory of Value and Capital [This chapter is much expanded and follows the exposition given in the second edition of Marx's *Das Kapital*].

V   The Concept of Capital [Corresponds to Chapter V in the 1871 edition; only the final paragraph has been changed].

VI   On the Origins and Saving of Capital [In the title the word 'accumulation' [*uvelichenie*] has been changed to 'saving' [*sberezhenie*]; otherwise identical to Chapter VI in the 1871 edition].

VII   On the Causes for the Production of Pure Income From Capital or on the Value of Labor Power [The content of this chapter corresponds closely to that of Chapter VII in the 1871 edition entitled 'On Fixed and Circulating Capital'].

VIII   Constant and Variable Capital. Simple and Complex Social Cooperation [First published as 'Marx's Economic Theory. I. The Theory of Social Cooperation', *Slovo*, January 1878].

IX   The Analysis of the Theory of Social Cooperation [First published as 'Marx's Economic Theory. II. Large-Scale Industry'. *Slovo*, March 1878].

X   Machines and Large-scale Industry [First published as 'Marx's Economic Theory. III. An Evaluation of the Theory of Machines', *Slovo*, July 1878].

XI   The Theory of Capital Accumulation and the Capitalist Law of Population [First published as 'Marx's Economic Theory. IV. The theory of capital accumulation and the capitalist law of population, *Slovo*, September 1878].

XII   An Analysis of the Theory of Capitalist Accumulation and the Refutation of Malthus's Theory.

Nikolai Ivanovich Siebers's 1885 edition–David Rikardo i Karl Marks v ikh obshchestvenno-ekonomichaskikh issledovaniiakh. Published in St Petersburg.

MARX'S THEORY OF VALUE AND MONEY

Nikolai Ivanovich Sieber (1871),
translated by Rakhiya Mananova and James D. White
from *David Ricardo's Theory of Value and Capital in Connection with the Latest Contributions and Interpretations*

Having already devoted sufficient space and time to explaining the different peculiarities represented by the question of value, we, nevertheless, have still not arrived at a solution of the point of this question, which, it would seem, should be the first and most important of all – what exactly is value? We have sufficiently oriented ourselves in the material relating to this question to have all the grounds for rejecting the vast majority of those definitions of value which we adduced at the beginning of the first chapter. Neither use-value, nor the degree of utility, nor the relationship between services and so on, can satisfy us further. However, only a short step separates the approach to the question of the Smith-Ricardo school from the definition of the subject, which left nothing to be desired in terms of clarity, precision and certitude. The credit for discovering such a definition, together with a number of important additions to the theory under discussion, should be given to the German economist K. Marx. The exposition and critique of his ideas on value and money will constitute the subject of the present chapter.

Marx's *Capital* and Capitalism; Markets in a Socialist Alternative,
Research in Political Economy, Volume 19, pages 17–45.
Copyright © 2001 by Elsevier Science Ltd.
All rights of reproduction in any form reserved.
ISBN: 0-7623-0838-9

The commodity, Marx says,[1] is first and foremost an object, a thing, which satisfies a need of one kind or another, indirectly or directly, whether its origin is in the stomach or in the fantasy. If it is useful to people, every object has use-value. Use-value constitutes the material content of wealth, whatever its *social form* may be. That *social form of wealth*, which we shall have to examine, is *exchange value*. Exchange value appears first of all as a quantitative relationship, the proportion in which use-values of one kind are exchanged for use-values of another kind, a relationship which constantly changes with place and time. That is why exchange value appears to be something accidental, and at the same time something inherent in the commodity. In fact, a single commodity can be exchanged with other commodities in the most varied proportions; but nevertheless its exchange-value remains unaltered, whether it is expressed in x silk or y gold. The exchange relation of two commodities can be represented by an equation; e.g. one quarter of wheat = a cwt of iron. What does this equation signify? It means that two different things have one and the same exchange value. Consequently, both are equal to some third thing, which is neither the one nor the other. Each of the things, in so far as they are exchange values, can, independently of each other, be reduced to this third thing. Exchange relations show immediately that exchange value is something distinct from use-value. It is characterized precisely by the abstraction from use-value. In relation to exchange-value all good things are equally worthy, so long as they exist in their proper proportions. Commodities can be regarded simply *as values*, *irrespective* of exchange relations, or *of the forms in which they appear as exchange values. The value of a commodity is nothing other than the labor materialized in it.* The unit of measurement of labor is simple average labor, whose character changes by country and cultural epoch, but in any given society represents a definite magnitude. More complex labor is simple labor raised to a higher power or compound labor. The *measure of a commodity's value* is determined by measuring the *quantity of labor* contained in it. The quantity of labor itself is measured by its temporal duration, e.g. an hour, a day and so on. *Only socially necessary labor time* constitutes value. If this were not the case, then the more clumsy and indolent the worker, then the more valuable his product would be, because more of his labor time would be spent on its completion. Socially necessary labor time is determined by the socially normal condition of production and the social average level of competence and intensity of labor. After the introduction of the steam-driven loom in England, for example, a given quantity of yarn was turned into cloth twice as rapidly as before. The hand-weaver needed the same labor time as before, but the product of his individual labor-hour now represented only one half of a social labor hour, and sank, accordingly, to half its earlier value. Thus, the quantum of the value of a good is determined by the quantity of socially necessary labor or labor time expended on its production. A given commodity, in this respect, counts as an *average* sample of its own kind. As values, all commodities represent particular masses of coagulated labor-time. But necessary labor-time changes with every alteration in the productive power of labor. This latter is determined, among other things, by the average level of competence of the workers, the level of development of science and its technological applicability, the social combination of the process of production, the quantity and efficacy of the means of production, and natural relationships. One and the same quantity of labor is contained, after clement weather, in 8 bushels of wheat, after inclement, in 4. The very same quantity of labor provides more metals in richly laden mines than in poor ones.

A thing can have a use-value but not exchange value; for example an object collected where no labor is involved. A thing can be useful and be a product of labor without being a commodity; for example, something created to satisfy one's own needs, but not someone else's. In order to produce a commodity one must produce not only use-value, but also use-values for others, social use-values. Just as a commodity has a two-sided character, use-value and exchange-value; so the labor contained in the commodity also bears a two-sided character. Consider two commodities: a coat and linen, the former, say, has twice the value of the latter; so 10 yards of linen = w, the coat = 2w. A coat is a use-value which satisfies a particular need. In order to produce it, a particular kind of purposeful productive activity is required, and this activity is determined in accordance with its aim, mode of operation, object, means and result of production. For the sake of brevity, we shall refer to this activity as useful labor. Just as coat and linen are qualitatively different use-values, so too are the deployments of labor expended on their production: tailoring and weaving. If these qualitative differences did not exist between products and types of labor, exchange could not take place; nobody would exchange a coat for a coat. In the totality of various use-values there appears a totality of varying deployments of useful labor – the social division of labor. This is the precondition for the existence of commodity production, but commodity production is not the precondition for the social division of labor. In the peasant commune of ancient India labor was socially divided, but the products were not commodities. In every factory labor is systematically divided, but the workers do not exchange their individual products among themselves. Only products of those deployments of private labor which are self-sufficient and independent of one another confront one another as commodities.

Let us now turn from the use-value of a commodity to its exchange-value. As values, a coat and linen are things of equal substance, objective expressions of labor of one and the same kind. But tailoring and weaving are qualitatively different kinds of labor; both constitute productive expenditure of human muscles, brain, nerves, and in this sense are united in the one concept of *human* labor. They are merely two different forms of expending human labor power. Between the simple labor power of a day-laborer and the skilled labor power of the tailor there is only a quantitative difference. If, for example, a coat represents the product of one working day of a tailor, it has the same value as the product of two working days of a farm laborer. The various proportions, in which different kinds of labor are reduced to simple labor as their unit of measurement, are established by a social process that goes on behind the backs of the producers; and these proportions therefore appear to the producers in this or that magnitude of their income. For the sake of simplicity, we shall henceforth view every form of complex labor as simple labor, by which we shall save ourselves the trouble of reducing the former to the latter. Just as, in viewing the coat and the linen as values, we abstract from their different use-values, so, in the case of the labor represented by those values, we abstract from the difference between the useful forms, of which one is tailoring and the other is weaving. Tailoring and weaving are formative elements in the use-values of a coat and linen, precisely because they *differ* in quality; but on the other hand, they are formative elements in the value of the coat and the linen as a result of the fact that their particular qualities have been abstracted from, and there remains only one thing, *common to both* and equal to both, the quality of human labor. Although an increase in the amount of use-value represents an increase in material wealth, nevertheless a rise in material wealth may correspond to a fall in the magnitude of its value. This contradictory movement arises out of the twofold character of labor. Productive power is naturally nothing other than the productive power of *useful*, concrete, *labor*. Therefore, any change in it has no affect upon the *labor representing value*. The same labor performed for the same length of time always yields the same amount of value, however the productive force might change. But labor provides different quantities of goods, use-values, during equal periods of time; more, if productivity rises; less, if it falls. It may happen that two coats contain less labor than one coat did formerly, or vice versa. From the foregoing it follows that, although a commodity does not contain two different kinds of labor, the same labor is specified in a differing and even in a contradictory manner, in accordance with whether it is spoken of in terms of the use-value of a commodity, as a product of labor, or as the value of commodities. In order to become a value, a commodity has to be a use-value, just as labor has to be in the first place useful labor before it can be considered as an expression of human labor-power, of human labor.

Let us turn to an analysis of the value *form*. Let us take two quanta of commodities which cost the same amount of labor time, consequently, two equal *magnitudes* of value; e.g. 40 yards of linen = 2 coats, or 40 yards of linen have the price of two coats. We observe that the value of the linen is expressed in a specific quantum of coats. *The value* of a commodity, thus represented in the *use-value* of another commodity is the *relative value* of the first commodity. The relative value of a commodity can change, though its value remains constant, and vice versa. Thus, the value of linen changes with the increase or decrease in the labor time necessary for its production, whereas the value of the coats remains unchanged. It follows that the relative value of commodity A, as expressed in commodity B, rises and falls in inverse relation to the value of commodity A, while the value of commodity B remains the same. On the other hand, if the value of linen remains unchanged, the value of coats changes when the demand for the production of coats rises and falls. Consequently, with one and the same value for commodity A, its relative value expressed in commodity B rises and falls in inverse proportion to the change of price in commodity B. Then, the demand for the quantities of labor necessary for the production of the linen and the coat can vary simultaneously, in the same direction and in the same proportion. The changes in values can be revealed in such a case only when they are compared with the third commodity, whose value remains constant. Finally, the time necessary for the production of the linen and the coat may vary in the same direction, but to an unequal degree, or in the opposite directions, and so on. The influence of all possible combinations on the relative value of commodities can be explained with reference to the definitions given above. We have investigated relative value from the quantitative side. Let us now look at its form. We observed that an object possessing the form of a commodity must have a twofold form, the form of use-value and the form of exchange-value. The first is the *natural* form of commodity; the second is the *social* form.

The form of a commodity's value is expressed in the relation of commodities to each other. Let us consider the simplest example of this relation, that between *two* commodities. In the equation 20 yards of linen = 1 coat, the linen expresses its value in a commodity different from itself, namely a coat – the coat, on the other hand, serves as the material for such an expression; the first appears in its relative value-form, the second in the equivalent-form. Both forms complement each other as indivisible constituents of value, but at the same time they are polar opposites to each other. A commodity situated in one of them, presupposes the existence of another commodity in another form and cannot be in both forms at the same time. Certainly, in the expression 20 yards of linen = 1 coat, the linen has the relative form of value for the owner of the linen; the coat has the same form for the owner of the coat; from the point of view of the former the equivalent is the coat, from the point of view of the latter the equivalent is the linen. Hence, it turns out as if both these commodities have both forms simultaneously; but it should be noted that here we are dealing with, firstly, two persons, and secondly, with two different expressions of value. By means of the relative expression, the value of a commodity acquires a form different from its use-value. The commodity's use-form is linen. It acquires its value-form in its *relation of equality* with the coat. Moreover, being a value of a definite magnitude, the linen is measured quantitatively by means of that proportion in which another commodity is equated with it. If a commodity has an equivalent form, it means that it possesses the form of immediate exchangeability with another commodity. To appear as a value relative to another commodity it needs no form different from its immediate, natural form. But the commodity becomes an equivalent only in the exchange relation. In itself the commodity is simply a useful thing, a use-value.

Let us consider the following example. A loaf of sugar, being a body, possesses weight; but we cannot determine this weight other than through equating it with the weight of another body – a piece of iron, whose weight has been determined beforehand. The natural form of iron in itself just as little constitutes a form which displays weight as does the form of sugar. But on establishing a weight relation with sugar, a quantity of iron takes on a form which indicates the weight of the sugar. Likewise, in our expression, the coat confronts the linen *only* as a value. Whatever object serves as an equivalent to the linen, it serves as an embodiment of abstract human labor, but only in so far as, being an equivalent, this object represents the crystallisation of concrete useful labour: tailoring, farming, mining, etc. Serving as an equivalent, a product has an immediately social form, i.e. the form of immediate exchangeability or the value of another commodity, because it represents the product of independent *private* labor – a constituent of the *social* division of labor. The simple relative form of a commodity corresponds to the *single* equivalent form of another commodity. Thus, the coat possesses the equivalent-form, or the form of immediate exchangeability, only in relation to linen alone. When the linen enters into a value-relation with this or that other commodity, there arise different simple expressions of value. Thus, there appears the *expanded* value-form: 20 yards of the linen = 1 coat, or 10 pounds of tea, or 40 pounds of coffee, etc. The value of one commodity – the linen – is now represented in all elements of the whole totality of commodities and appears as a real value for the first time, i.e. as human labor *in general*. With this labour every kind of human labor is now equated, whatever natural form it might possess – a coat, wheat, iron or gold. The linen acquires a social relation not just with a single commodity, but with the whole world of commodities. But each of the commodity-equivalents represents in this case nothing more than a special equivalent, excluding all others. If together with the linen, we place other commodities, then each of them would have its own special series of equivalents. Both the natural form and the concrete useful labor, contained in each equivalent, are only special forms, and not the general form in which universal human labor manifests itself. But each of the equations we have adduced also contains within itself its opposite, identical to it; namely: 1 coat = 20 yards linen, 10 pounds of tea = 20 yards of linen, 40 pounds of coffee = 20 yards of linen and so on. Thus, the *general* form of value appears:

1 coat	=	
10 lb tea	=	
40 lb coffee	=	20 yards of linen
etc.	=	

Each of these commodities now expresses its value in a single commodity, one which is common to other commodities. In this case the linen serves all the commodities as a common shape, as a value equivalent and in this form possesses a common, social form. Only in taking on a general character can the value form correspond fully to the concept of value. In this form all commodities appear as undifferentiated, homogeneous, human labor, i.e. they are *qualitatively* equated. At the same time, as we can see from the expression, they are also equated *quantitatively*; if 10 lb. tea = 20 yards of linen and 40 lb. coffee also = 20 yards of linen, then 10 lb. tea = 40 lb. coffee. Or in each 4 lb. of coffee there is embodied as much labor as in 1 lb. of tea. The private and concrete labor contained in the linen becomes a labor in the immediate general, social, form, the form of equality with every other labor. In the form of *simple* relative value the polarity between it and the equivalent form has been manifested purely formally. If we reverse the order, the equivalent takes the place of a relative value, and the relative value takes the place of the equivalent. In the *second* form only one commodity has fully developed its relative form of value, while all the others serve as its equivalents. Finally, in the third form the whole world of commodities possesses the universal-social, relative value form, in so far as, all commodities comprising it are excluded from the equivalent form, or from the form of immediate exchangeability. A commodity only acquires its universal equivalent form when it is excluded as an equivalent from all other commodities. In the historical development of the commodity's form, first one commodity then another acquired the form of univèrsal equivalent. But as soon as such a commodity appeared the relative value-form of other commodities took on an objective stability and universal social recognition. The specific commodity, whose form is the general equivalent form becomes the money commodity, or functions as money.

Let us suppose that this commodity is gold, in which case *it* will take a place of the linen in our last equation and will distinguish itself from the linen by its specific natural form, acknowledged by society as an equivalent form. Gold confronts the other commodities not before it has become a commodity. Like all other commodities it has functioned initially as that simple equivalent in individual acts of exchange, as that particular equivalent alongside other commodity-equivalents. Gradually it began to function as the universal equivalent, of course in a more or less broad sphere. The simple expression of the relative value of a commodity, linen, for example, in the money commodity – gold – is the price form. The price form of the linen is therefore: 20 yards of linen = 2 ounces of gold, or, if 2 ounces of gold when coined are worth 2 pounds sterling, then 20 yards of linen are worth 2 pounds sterling.

The obscure character of the commodity does not arise from its use-value. There is nothing enigmatic in the fact that, by his activity, man changes the forms of natural material in such a way as to achieve beneficial results. In itself exchange-value is just as little paradoxical. However different the useful kinds of labor, or productive activities may be, it is a *physiological* truth that they are functions of a specifically human organism, as opposed to other types of organism, and that every such function, whatever may be its content or form, is the application of the human brain, muscles, nerves and so on. As for the determinations of the amount of value by means of the quantity of labor, this too is easily distinguished from the quality of labor. Finally, it is also quite clear that when people work for each other, their labor assumes a social form. Robinson Crusoe on his island satisfied his different needs by means of various types of labor. But, despite this, he knew full well that all these different types constitute only different forms of activity of one and the same Robinson, different modes of *human* labor. If he kept a journal, he would doubtless note down in it how much labor-time he had to spend on the production of this or that article. All the relationships between Robinson and these objects are completely simple and transparent, but nevertheless they contain all the essential determinants of value. Let us put in Robinson's place an association of free people, working with the means of production held in common, and expending their individual labor-power as social labor power. All the determinations of Robinson's labor are repeated here on a social plane. But the products of Robinson's labor were for him exclusively personal products, articles of use for him, whereas the common product is a social product. Part of it must be divided among the participants in production. The manner of this division will vary according to the particular kind of social production organization itself and the corresponding historical level of social development of the producers. As a parallel with commodity production, we shall suppose that the share of each individual producer is determined by his labor-time. In such a case, the labor-time would play a double role. Its socially planned distribution establishes the correct proportion between the various labor functions and the various needs, and, in addition, it would serve as a measure of the amount of the common product which is due to each individual producer. The social relationships of people to their labor remain completely simple, in production as well as in distribution. Whence comes the puzzling character of the product when it takes on the *form of a commodity*?

People relate their various types of labor to each other as human labour by relating their *products* to one another as values. The personal relationship is concealed in the objectified form. In order to relate their products to each other as commodities, people are compelled to equate their different types of labor to universal human labor. They do this unconsciously, but they do it by reducing the material thing to the abstraction of value. This is a natural, instinctive operation of the brain, which necessarily grows out of the particular mode of material production and the relationships in which it places people. As far as the amount of value is concerned, private labors, which function independently of each other, but as constituent elements of the social division of labor closely connected to each other, are constantly reduced to their socially-proportional measure by the fact that their labor-time necessary for production acts as a natural law (like the law of gravity), regulating the fortuitous and perpetually fluctuating exchange relations of products. The determination of the amount of value by labor-time is therefore concealed by the apparent motions in the relative value of commodities. The producers' own social movement takes on, for them, the form of a movement of things, under whose control they are, instead of their being in control of the movement. Finally, as far as the value form is concerned, it should be noted that it is precisely this form which veils with its objective husk the social relationships of private workers and social determinations of private labors. When we say that a coat, boots, etc. relate to linen as universal incarnations of abstract human labor, the obscurity of this expression is obvious. Nevertheless, when producers of the coat, boots, etc. relate these commodities to the linen as a universal equivalent, then social relation of their individual labors appears to them in just this distorted form. Forms like these represent categories of definite historically-defined social means of production. Private producers enter into social contact by means of individual product-objects. The social relations of their labors exist and manifest themselves not as the social relations of people to their works, but as material relations of people or the social relations of things. Thus, the mysterious character of the commodity stems from the fact that social determinations of private labors appear to their private producers as socially-natural determinations of the products of labor, and that the social-production relations of *persons* appear as the *social* relations of things to each other and to persons. Relations of private workers to the social collective labor are *reified* and appear to them in the form of objects.

Money represents the necessary product of the exchange process of commodities. The internal contradiction of a commodity as a use-value and an exchange-value, as a product of useful private labor and as a social embodiment of abstract labor – is resolved only provided that it appears not only as commodity but also as money. Just as there takes place the transformation of the products of labor into commodities, in the same way there is a transformation of commodities into money. Both processes occur only gradually. The mutual relationship of the *alienation of things*, representing use-value *only* for a buyer does not take place for the members of a community in the form of a patriarchal family, an ancient Indian commune, an Inca state, etc. The exchange of commodities begins where communities have their boundaries, at their points of contact with other communities or with their members. The quantitative exchange-relation is at first a purely fortuitous one; but the constant repetition of exchange makes it a normal social process and in the course of time, some portion of the products at the point of production itself begins to be designated exclusively for exchange. With the increase in the number and diversity of commodities entering into the exchange process, the need grows for an instrument of exchange, whose form would be independent of the individual needs of the exchanging parties. The social, equivalent, form of such a third commodity, an instrument of exchange, originally shifts from one commodity to another, later remaining for an extended period with one particular commodity. The money form comes to be attached either to the most important articles of exchange from outside, which are in fact the most natural forms of the manifestation of the exchange-value of local products, or to the object of utility which forms the chief element of indigenous alienable wealth (cattle among nomads). As the local boundaries expand, the value of commodities becomes more and more the incarnation of *human labor in general*, and its money form begins to extend to those commodities, which, by nature are capable of carrying out the social function of the universal equivalent. Only a material whose every sample possesses the same *uniform* quality can be the form of appearance of value or abstract human labor. On the other hand, since the difference between the magnitudes of value is purely quantitative, the money commodity must also be capable of purely quantitative division, i.e. *divisible* at will and able to be reassembled from its component parts. Gold and silver possess these properties by nature. The money commodity acquires a dual use-value. Alongside its *special use-value* as a simple commodity (gold for the manufacture of luxury items), the money commodity also acquires a *formal use-value*, arising out of its specific social function. The process of exchange gives to the commodity which it has converted into money not its value but its specific value-form. Confusion between these two concepts has misled some writers (Galiani, Locke) into maintaining that the value of gold and silver is imaginary. As money can, in certain functions, be replaced by symbols representing it, this has given rise to another misapprehension: that money itself is a mere symbol (de Forbonnais, Montesquieu). The value of money is determined, like that of any other commodity, by the amount of labor-time expended on its production, and is expressed in the quantity of any other commodity in which the same amount of labor-time is contained. This establishing of its relative value occurs at the source of its production by means of barter. As soon as gold enters into the exchange process as money, its value is already given. Being the universal relative expression of value of other commodities, gold functions with regard to the latter as a measure of value. Because all commodities, as values, are objectified human labor, all of them taken together can be measured by some third commodity, that is by money.[2] A change in the value of gold does not prevent its being a measure of value. This change affects all commodities simultaneously, thus leaving their mutual relative values unaltered. Price is the money-name for the labour-time objectified in a commodity, originally related to the weight of metal. Socially necessary labor-time of the same magnitude is expressed in one quarter of wheat and two pounds sterling. But sometimes the price may not coincide with the value and even be in qualitative contradiction with it, i.e. it can apply to the things that are not commodities in themselves. Things like, for example, conscience, honor, etc. can be alienated for money from their owners and in that way, acquire the form of commodities in their price. Thus, an object can, formally speaking, have a price without having a value. But where we find such an imaginary price form for important production relationships, e.g. what the price of land is (although land to which no human labour has been deployed does not have any value), there a more profound analysis constantly discloses a real value relation or a relation derived from a real one, concealed beneath the imaginary form.

A commodity's exchange process consists in two opposite yet mutually complementary metamorphoses: the transformation of the commodity into money and the re-conversion of the money into a commodity. The two phases of this metamorphosis nevertheless constitute the trading transaction of the commodity-owners – selling, or the exchange of the commodity for money, and buying, or the exchange of the money for a commodity – and the unity of the two acts: selling in order to buy. The process of exchange has the following form: Commodity-Money-Commodity; by its material content, the movement is Commodity-Commodity, the exchange of social labors, with which the whole process is concluded. As a result of the social division of labor his own product serves its owner only as exchange-value, as a universal equivalent. But the commodity acquires a universal *social* equivalent form *only* by being converted into money, and that money is in someone else's pocket. To draw it out, the commodity must be a use-value for the owner of the money; the labor expended on it must be of a socially useful form, be a constituent element in the social division of labor. But the division of labor is a natural production organization, a web that has been woven behind the backs of the producers of commodities. Today the product satisfies a social need; tomorrow it may perhaps be displaced wholly or in part by another product of the same kind. Let us assume that the given product does retain its use-value for others, and that money is paid for it. Now we have to ask: How much money? No doubt, the answer is already anticipated in the price of the commodity, which gives expression to the magnitude of its value. We leave out of consideration here any possible subjective errors in calculation by the owner of the commodity, which will be corrected objectively in the market. The producer has to spend on his product only a socially necessary quantity of labor-time. But what was yesterday socially necessary labor-time ceases to be so today. Finally, if every example of the product contains socially necessary time, then the whole mass of the product may contain superfluously expended labor-time: if the market's stomach cannot digest the whole quantity of linen at the price of 2 shillings a yard, this proves that too much labor-time has been expended on its manufacture. The quantitative division of the social productive organism is just as fortuitous in its nature as the qualitative one. The owners of commodities observe that the same division of labor which turns them into independent private producers also makes the social process of production and the relations of the individual producers to each other within that process independent of the producers themselves; they also see that the independence of persons from each other is supplemented by their all-round dependence on things.

Conditioned by the division of labor, the product of labor is converted into a commodity and thereby *makes necessary its conversion into money*. But one and the same process is sale – from the point of view of the product owner, and purchase – from the viewpoint of the owner of the money. The *first* metamorphosis of the commodity is its transformation from the commodity-form into money, which at the same time comprises the *second*, opposite metamorphosis of another commodity, its transformation out of the money form, which it had hitherto taken on, into the commodity form.[3] The *second* metamorphosis of a commodity is its transformation from a money, back into a commodity form. This represents the whole sum of the *first* metamorphoses of the other commodities, a sum because the producer of the commodity sells only a single commodity in large quantities and buys numerous commodities to satisfy his own various needs.[4] As one and the same commodity successively passes through the two inverse phases (the transformation from a commodity into money and from money into a commodity) the same owner of the commodity changes his role from seller to buyer. The circulation of commodities differs from the direct exchange of products not only in form, but also in essence. We have only to look at the foregoing to see this. The weaver of linen, for example, has undoubtedly exchanged his linen for a Bible, i.e. his own commodity for someone else's. But this phenomenon is true only for him.

The Bible owner had no intention of exchanging his Bible for linen, just as the weaver of linen did not know that his linen had been used to exchange for wheat. Firstly, the exchange of commodities breaks through all the individual and local limitations of the immediate exchange of products. Secondly, there develops a whole network of social-natural dependencies, beyond the control of the persons involved in exchange. The weaver is only in a position to sell his linen, because the peasant has already sold his wheat. The owner of the Bible is able to sell his Bible on condition that the weaver has sold his linen, and so on. Unlike direct exchange, the process of circulation does not conclude once the use-values have changed places and changed hands. The money does not vanish, although it has dropped out of the series of metamorphoses undergone by a commodity. It always occupies the place, left vacant in circulation by other commodities.

Nothing could be more foolish than the doctrine that because every sale is a purchase, and every purchase is a sale, the circulation of commodities necessarily implies an equilibrium between sales and purchases. One would have to prove that every seller brings his own buyer to the market. Sale and purchase are one identical act, considered as the exchange relation between the seller and the buyer, but as the action of one and the same person they are two polar-opposite acts. Since the first metamorphosis of a commodity is at once a sale and a purchase, it is an independent process in itself. The buyer has the commodity, the seller has the money, i.e. a commodity which remains in a form capable of circulating, whether it reappears on the market at an earlier or later date. As a consequence of this, circulation broke through all local and individual limits of the direct exchange of products, and it did this by splitting up the direct identity between the exchange of one's own and someone else's products into the two antithetical elements of *sale* and *purchase*. These mutually independent and antithetical processes form a movement of their internal unity through their external antitheses. As soon as external independence and the internal dependence slightly diverge from one another, the unity disintegrates into crisis.

This brief extract from the first chapter of Marx's work and the appendix to it at the end of the book contains, if I am not mistaken, the most essential features of the author's doctrine of value and the general properties of money. The peculiar language and the quite laconic manner of expression does little to facilitate the comprehension of his ideas, and in some cases has led to the accusation that he employs a metaphysical approach to the investigation of value. With the exception of a few places in the chapter where perhaps some statements are indeed made which do not really correspond to the truth, the accusation seems to me unjust. As far as the *theory* itself is concerned, Marx's method is the deductive method of the whole English school, and both its faults and its merits are those shared by the best of the theoretical economists.

With regard to the general properties of money, Marx develops the concepts of money as a means of circulation and a token of value, as an instrument of payment, as a means of accumulating wealth, and so on. The interpretation of the first of these functions, as far as we can see, represents only a minor departure from the view on the matter of Ricardo and some of his followers, and, moreover, lies outside the confines of our investigation. The second and third functions of money, corresponding to the questions of credit and the accumulation of money capitals, embrace and area of those comparatively specialised phenomena, which we do not wish to consider here, since we intend to examine the theory of money only in so far as it serves as a step towards the general theory of capital.

As for Marx's theory of value and his general theory of money, here, in my opinion, is contained the following new and important scientific propositions, which impart to Ricardo's theory a fuller and more complete form, and also endorse its validity with new proofs.

The doctrine of the economists who recognise labour as the most important regulator of exchange ratios has succeeded in giving to value, as we have already had occasion to remark, a firm and enduring objective basis, having shown that the *relative* magnitude of exchange is determined by comparison with of *absolute* quantities of labour, contained in each of the products exchanged. Although the majority of these theoreticians, for example MacCulloch,[5] J. S. Mill and often Ricardo himself, speak mainly of exchange *relations*, within which, in their opinion, the whole question of exchange revolves, nevertheless they all show clearly that prior to the establishment of this or that exchange relationship there are present *absolute* factors for comparison, namely the quantities of labour which are embodied in the products. The following statement by Ricardo leaves no room for doubt in this respect: "According to M. Say,[6] if the labour expended on producing cloth were to double, and consequently cloth was to exchange for double the quantity of commodities for which it is exchanged before, it would be doubled in value, to which I give my fullest assent: but if there were any peculiar facility in producing the commodities, and no increased difficulty in producing cloth, and cloth should in consequence exchange *as before* for double the quantity of commodities, M. Say would still maintain that cloth had doubled in value, whereas according to my view of the subject, he should say, that cloth retained its former value, and those particular commodities had fallen to half their former value." Thus we observe that the doctrine of the school is in no way contradicted by the fact that the exchange value of one and the same product can be expressed in two different quantities of another product (where the technique remains unchanged, and where the technique has changed in the production of the other commodity) and remains in these circumstances unaltered, due solely to the fact that the quantity of labour embodied in the first product has not been subject to change. But hence it clearly follows that the definition of value most commonly given by this school, namely: "value is the quantity of a product which is received in exchange", does not embrace all the peculiarities of the phenomenon and must be changed or emended. If the value of a product does not change, irrespective of whether or not a greater quantity of another product is received for it in exchange, with the proviso that the level of technique in the production of this latter product has changed, then it is obvious that value and this quantity are not synonymous.

If one examines any act of exchange then we will find, as Marx did, that it represents the kind of equality of two exchanged products, in which each of them is equal to the other because each of them is equal to some third product. Thus, *the equality* of products turns out to be something outside the products themselves, and at the same time it completely coincides with the characteristics of the exchange act, which is the mutual substitution of two non-identical products. Whether there are many or few products on this or that side of the exchange act, the exchange takes place only if these quantities are equal in terms of the labour or labour time contained in them. Therefore, it is insufficient to say that the measure of exchange of the exchanged products, *value*, in the usual sense of this word for the school, corresponds to the measure of labour, or is *regulated by labour*. Labour, and not the product, is the basic element of the relationship. Labour itself is value, Marx says. In other words, labour is the only *social* creator of those proportions in which acts of exchange take place.

Thus to labour is attributed the role not just of regulator, but also of creator of measures of exchange. This definition of value has an important scientific significance precisely because it reconciles completely views on value both in isolated and in exchange economies. If the elements of value and the most important of them – labour – are present in an isolated economy, if an exchange economy does not introduce any essential changes into this sphere in terms of the content of the relationship, then it is obvious that one cannot speak of *exchange* value, as something distinct or even opposed to use-value or utility. What is distinct from use-value, and to a certain degree, opposed to it, is not *exchange* value, but value *in general*, i.e. labour in a definite form. Labour in this form – abstract, general, equal in all spheres – even exists in Robinsonades and in every other isolated economy. But the exchange economy differs from the latter by the fact that labour acquires in it this universal form, making it social labour precisely by means of exchange. Every specialised labour of a separate branch of the social division of labour is rendered social, i.e. carries out its function, only on condition that it finds its expression in a product of another specialised labour, which takes the form of *exchange* value. Exchange value is therefore only a *form* of labour, taken on by the latter in an exchange economy. Labour finds such a form in the useful qualities of another product, in use-value.

Before proceeding to a more detailed examination of these definitions, we shall say a few words about the importance of the concept of socially necessary labour time. Only such time, says Marx, i.e. time 'determined by the given socially-normal conditions of production and the social average level of competence and intensity of labour', creates value. The introduction into science of this concept once and for all eliminates any possibility of discussing the question of value within those narrow, atomistic, confines in which very many economists speak of it: once and for all the ground is cut from under the feet of those objections to Ricardo's theory (Walras, Bastiat, Macleod, etc.), who try to show its falsity in specific instances of exchange. No diamond found on the street, no butter, transported twenty times from one place to another and back again, are in any position to shake in future the truth that the measures of exchange are determined *in general* in accordance with labour, expended on the production of products. A product may cost a single producer at a certain time more than it costs an average producer on an average number of occasions, but in exchange it can only charge for itself not more, but only as much of another product as the average product would. The value of a specific product is aligned here with the average value; but only the latter can be considered a social value and can serve as the first and foremost subject of the study of value in general. A product may cost less, but until this relative cheapness of production has become social the owner of the product enjoys on the market a certain advantage, which also does not infringe the law of the average, social value, because it is a special, individual phenomenon. A product may not be a product in the usual sense of this word, but an individual chance occurrence; historical peculiarities can make it a product of the social division of labour, impart value to it, align it with real social values, for example, the product of labour of a prostitute, the product of labour of a civil servant who takes bribes, etc. But the correct combination of those methods of study about which we spoke in its due place, determines with precision the role and significance of each of these types of value, allotting them to a separate category and subjecting them to special investigation. Average value is studied in average place and in average time; specific value is studied in those special factors and in those specific spheres, when and where they arise. The investigation of the first type of value precedes the second type, because it relates to a more general phenomenon. The two types are never found in combination in any respect.

Let us now look more closely at the distinction Marx draws between concrete and abstract labour and the implications which arise from this. Before entering into an explanation of the concepts of these two things, Marx speaks, as we have seen, about certain properties of the *commodity*. The first of these properties, he says, is that every commodity satisfies some need or other, has use-value. But this is the most general property of the commodity. A commodity must possess use-value not for its owner, but for other people. Moreover, it also has a social form – exchange value.

The school of Ricardo, i.e. Ricardo himself and his immediate predecessors and followers, for the most part paid very little attention to the general conditions of exchange. A number of writers beginning with Steuart spoke of the division of labour in society and tried to define the social benefits deriving from it. But with regard to exchange, this principle was usually understood as implying that each of the partners in exchange produced a product for himself and only used the surplus for exchange.[7] This view on the produce of more advanced economies, which regards the exchange phenomena of the modern economy in the same simple form as primitive exchange has, e.g. the surpluses of hunting, fishing and herding, violates in the most essential way the cardinal principle of modern economic society. This principle is – the kind of division of labour which ensures that not only private economies do not produce a product exclusively for themselves, exchanging only what is surplus to their own requirements, but, on the contrary, the portion of the product required by its producer is either completely insignificant, or is not produced at all. This circumstance is closely connected with the enormous success of modern economic technique, which makes it impossible for separate economies to produce in any way other than applying the most economic methods, including – the most minute division of labour. The reason for introducing increasingly important improvements into economic activity consists in the necessity to produce more and more products as cheaply as possible, thereby opening up more and more new markets. The motives for the urge to make more and cheaper products can be is explained only with the help of the theory of capital. But the fact this urge exists is sufficient to explain why, parallel with the introduction of various kinds of technical improvement, there is an increasing degree of the division of labour not only within individual workshops and factories, but also in the society of independent economies. This division, taken together with the perfection of machines, tools, means of production, means of communication, etc. are powerful lever to make the product cheaper. The social combination of the production process serves as a source for an additional force of production, all of which is transferred to the surplus product, without being included in the reckoning of its value. Such is the general consequence of the social division of labour and the division of labour in the separate branches of industry. In relation to exchange, the first kind of division brings with it the mutual substitution of products produced by individual economies in the exclusive ways of satisfying other people's needs. In this sense the social division of labour is the totality of the different concrete types of labour, which fulfil their function only provided that each of them takes on the form of a product which corresponds to someone else's needs, and is exchanged for another product. Such are the universal conditions of exchange, by means of which the question of use- and exchange-values can be satisfactorily resolved. The differences between concrete types of labour serve as a source for that qualitative difference between products, without which exchange would be inconceivable. But the same exchange also requires a quantitative similarity and finds it in the equality of quantities of labour, abstracted from their concrete properties and representing universal human labour – the exercise of the brain, muscles, nerves, etc. Ricardo's school had this kind of labour in mind when they spoke of the regulator of exchange ratios; but it did not go further, did not enter into the distinction between special types of labour, which provide the material for the conception of universal labour and serve as a basis for establishing the formula for value. Smith, Ricardo and J. S. Mill also speak of the different types of labour, about the difficulties of making comparisons between these and so on. All of them come to the conclusion that, in spite of the considerable difficulties, practice manages somehow to make these comparisons, albeit in a rough and ready fashion. But these differences between labour are not those about which Marx speaks. Here is understood labour which demands different degrees of skill, different kinds of training, etc. Similarity and difference between kinds of labour, satisfying identical or differing needs, represents from this point of view no more than a secondary phenomenon. Marx, on the other hand, is concerned exclusively with distinctions in the types of labour in relation to the properties of needs, with those of their differences which determine exchange. Such concrete types of labour constitute use value. Abstract, or universal-human labour, serves to constitute the exchange-value of things. But labour of the latter type does not at once acquire such a form in people's minds, nor does exchange value acquire at once its fullest expression.

The first or simple form of exchange value is that relative value, which represents the measure of human labour materialised in a commodity, expressed in the use-value of one commodity or another or in a number of units (poods, arshins, and so on) of this latter, corresponding to a certain number of units of concrete labour expended on its production. By means of this form of value the product acquires an aspect different from its use-value. The labour expended in the product takes on a universal form and begins to bear a dual character. But neither exchange-value nor labour acquire at this stage the forms which will distinguish them subsequently. Equally, neither has the product yet completely become a commodity. In every act of exchange one special product serves as an equivalent, material for expressing exchange-value. The proportions established as a result of this are purely fortuitous, and, moreover, the products cannot be compared amongst themselves independently of their equivalents. These are the first timid steps of a social economy on the way to developing exchange transactions. But due to increasingly frequent instructive circuits of exchange, the exchange-value of a commodity begins to find an expression for itself not in a single chance commodity-equivalent, but in a whole range of such commodities. Such, for example is the trade of the Bedouin and the nomadic Indians who, in the words of Roscher, in exchange for oil acquire almost all foreign commodities. Salt in the Sahara, rubber in the Indian desert, furs in Siberia, all play the same part. With regard to the owners of foreign commodities, all these things have the significance of real equivalents for showing the exchange-value of their commodities. But with regard to the nomads and Bedouin, a great variety of foreign commodities serve as their equivalents of value. Nevertheless, the commodities serve as special equivalents for the value of butter, salt, furs, etc. If, for example, a Bedouin sold, in addition to butter, the surplus of his flocks, then he would have to carry out the whole operation of comparing the values of his livestock and the commodities on offer from scratch, because there are no features in common for comparison between livestock and butter. Salt, butter, etc. already represent their exchange-value in a more perfect form than a commodity which has only one equivalent; the labour which is materialised in them already bears a more universally-human character; they come closer in their properties to the commodity in general. Nevertheless, they still have to pass through one, extremely important, stage in order to become fully a value, abstract labour, a commodity. When *all* the commodities display their values in some single commodity, then their exchange-value serves as the expression of really universal-human labour, then they fully become commodities. In finding a universal token for comparison between particular commodities and an equivalent, economies acquire the possibility of comparing particular commodities as well. With the help of the universal equivalent – money – the product acquires a truly social form and serves social needs. Commodities become equal qualitatively, from the viewpoint of abstract labour, which finds for itself a universal expression, and quantitatively, from the point of view of the quantity of this labour.

The private and concrete labour which is contained in money takes on a immediately social form, having made itself equal with every other kind of labour. All other commodities, which represent their value in money, do not serve as socialised immediately-social labour. Difference in useful qualities alone does not transform products into commodities. "If", Marx says, "a peasant family produces for its own use, linen, butter or wheat, then in relation to the family these things are no more than various articles of family use, but are by no means commodities". "If the labour", he continues,

> were immediately social labour, then the products would acquire the character of a common product *for their producers*, but not the character of commodities for each other. The social form of the commodity is its relation to other commodities as *equal labour*, i.e. as *human labour in general*, whatever its concrete forms may be. In every social form of labour the labours of different individuals are related to each other as human labours, but here this relationship itself is the *specific* social form of labour. *None of these private labours* in its natural form *possess* this specifically *social form* of abstract *labour*, just as little as the commodity in its natural form possesses the *social form* of value. However, by virtue of the fact that the natural form of one commodity becomes the universal equivalent-form, since all other commodities relate themselves to this natural form as the form in which it displays its own value, *the concrete labour which created this commodity becomes* the universal form in which abstract human labour appears, or *labour in its immediately-social form*. Since particular private labours are not immediately social, they all acquire a social character only in a contradictory way, by all being equated to one exclusive kind of private labour (31–33).

We are confronted with the important distinctions which exist on the one hand between isolated and social economies, and on the other by between the ordinary commodity and money. At the end of the first chapter and in the pages that followed we drew the reader's attention to the fact that in isolated economies all the elements of value are present, and that the role of combined economies with the division of labour is expressed in relation to these elements solely in the fact that here value is defined and manifests itself. Now we can add to this, that it is precisely here that *exchange* value emerges, i.e. the special means of expressing human labour in a product belonging to another branch of industry. This difference concerns first and foremost, not the content of relationships, but their form, but nevertheless it has a very great significance. It alone is capable of illuminating the phenomenon that in the combination of economies with the division of labour "the personal relation between people is concealed by a reified form". In relating the products of their labour to each other as commodities, people in fact compare only the different labours, finding a common expression for them in human labour. But this relationship is masked by the relationship of products amongst themselves. "The producers' own social movement possesses for them the form of a movement of things, under whose control they are, instead of the producers themselves being in control of the things". According to J. B. Say[8] "Exchange has been regarded as the foundation of social wealth, whereas in fact it adds absolutely nothing to it . . . There exist many varieties of wealth, which are produced and even distributed without the help of exchange."

"When a big Kentucky landowner", Say asserts, "distributes within his family bread from his own lands and meat from his own herds, when he makes someone weave and sew at his home wool and cotton for his own use, when he preserves apricots for making a homemade drink, he himself and people belonging to his household, produce and consume wealth that were not at all exposed to exchange." Certainly, we cannot state after Say that exchange does not take place at all in an isolated economy like this. Everywhere that people live and work together, a type of division of labour is established, the limits of which in the most extreme case, by age, sex and other natural differences between individuals. When distributing the product between members of Say's landowner's family or between the members of a commune, because the roles of producer and consumer of the products in one and the same person do not coincide, it is likely that a type of exchange will take place. But in this exchange will any attention be paid to the relation *between product units*, which constitute the outcome of the activities of different people? Marx thinks that there would not, and as we see it, we have to agree with him in this respect. In fact, labor can also serve as a criterion for comparison of participation shares in the common product of different people in an isolated economy, but in circumstances like this it is compared *directly*, without a relation both between product units and between the latter and a universal equivalent. In a society in which labor is divided into separate economies and where, firstly, every separate economy enters into exchange relations with the other economies by imparting to the product the character of a commodity, and, secondly, where a certain average regularity and planned character of the economic order are attained solely by an endless series of checks and evaluations. Labor becomes social necessarily through the mediacy of the relationship between it and its products and necessarily through the mediacy of the universal equivalent. Here the relation between products is hidden by the relations between separate labours, and thus appears in the form of relative value; there the relation between separate labours, although it makes itself manifest, but remains immediate. Here every separate type of labor does not have an immediate social form, but must yet acquire it by the transformation into such a product which by the nature of its relations has acquired a form that is suitable for comparing the exchange proportions of all other products. There, every labor bears an immediately social form, i.e. form directly suitable for comparison with other labours of the same kind. In relation to the isolated economy the word "value" can mean only labor; in relation to a number of economies with the division of labor it means labor expressed in a number of units of another product, and acquires the designation "relative". In its highest form, represented by money, it is exchange-value. Owen's "labor money," i.e. sheets of paper serving as certificates that their bearer had performed a certain amount of work, are no more money, Marx says, than theater tickets. Such certificates define only the individual part played by a producer in the common labor and in the common product. It presupposes the existence of immediately social labor in a society in which all the products are sold, i.e. have their designated purpose only in the form of commodities. The commodity form is inconceivable without the existence of a special kind of *product*, in whose use-value or natural form the labour contained in all other products is expressed.

The other important distinction concerns money and ordinary commodities. As we do not have an opportunity to speak in detail about the development of the concept of money by various economists, we shall confine ourselves to some brief remarks on the relationship of the new theory to some of the earlier ones. The reaction to mercantilism, which acknowledged money as the sole or the most important form of wealth, was expressed in the works of the dominant school by a denial that money had properties not to be found in other commodities. This position was just as one-sided as the mercantilists' exaggeration of the relative significance of money. Let us look, for example, at what J. S. Mill, whose opinion on the subject can be considered as one of the most pervasive, says about the significance of money. "Great as the difference would be between a country with money, and a country altogether without it, it would be only one of convenience; a saving of time and trouble, like grinding by water power instead of by hand, or (to use Adam Smith's illustration) like the benefit derived from roads; and to mistake money for wealth is the same sort of error as to mistake the highway, which may be the easiest way of getting to your house or lands, for the house and lands themselves."[9] But having belittled in this way the relative role of money, Mill adds: "Money, being an instrument of an important public and private purpose, is rightly regarded as a wealth; but everything else which serves any human purpose, and which nature does not afford gratuitously, is wealth also." In another place [10] Mill states that "in the absence of money, a tailor who had nothing but coats, might starve before he could find any person having bread to sell who wanted a coat." Thus, money is only an insignificant matter of convenience; money is wealth; without money members of society would be exposed to danger of dying of starvation. Inescapably, one or other of these statements is wrong, and we have reason to think that it is the first one. But, irrespective of these contradictions, let us pause for a moment to consider the concept of the word "wealth". The question of what exactly wealth is and what it is not, serves in political economy together with many other questions, as an example of the extent to which people are apt to take the name of something for the thing itself, and in discussing what kind of meaning should be attached to a given term, they lose sight of the reality and its demands, or adjust it to some more or less accidental designations. In turning to the source of definitions and characteristics, to the economic phenomena themselves, it can be easily observed that one kind of things is obtained by means of labor, while another kind is acquired by people for nothing. The distinction between these two types of thing is an essential and important one because only articles of the first type serve as a source of relations between the *society* of people and things, and also between the members of *society* in regard to things.

As to the things of the second type, they enter into relations only with individual persons. Social economy has to do exclusively with social relations and so, naturally, leaves relations of the second type outside its consideration. It is appropriate to give a special name to the articles obtained with the help of labor, e.g. "wealth." On examining more closely the peculiarities of the articles that are given this name we cannot but see that although they all serve human needs, they do not do so in the same way. Some of them are instruments of production in the real sense; they serve human purposes indirectly. Others are articles of utility which support human existence at a certain constant or increasingly high level, and fulfil their purpose by being used directly. To which of these categories should one assign money; and should one assign it to any of them at all? In the opinion of some economists, money is a means of production; but in opinion of others it is partly an instrument of production, and partly an article of consumption, and so on. In fact, money cannot be assigned to either of these categories, but comprises a type of wealth of its own, which has its origin in the specific need of a society with the division of economic labor, for a universal equivalent for the heterogeneous, independent, types of labor. The form of money, of course, is acquired by one of the types of *wealth* mentioned above, and it is acquired without fail by such an article, because otherwise money would be deprived of one of its most essential properties, namely the property to serve as the material for expressing the value of all the other articles of wealth. But once it has taken on this form, the product acquires as many specific qualities, as correspond to its new functions. And, conversely, divests itself of its original property of serving as an article of consumption in its true sense, directly or indirectly. Thus, there are no grounds at all to assign it to those categories mentioned above. What do these qualities consist in; how do they arise; how do they demarcate the various functions of money between themselves? These are the questions which can be more profitably taken up by an investigator, that the refutation of mercantilist doctrines that have long ago lost any credibility. Therefore, it is somewhat unjust, Roscher says,[11] that "most recent economists have not paid sufficient attention to the qualities by which money differs from the rest of commodities", and that "in this respect one cannot regard the semi-mercantilist theories of Ganilh and St. Chaman as completely lacking in sense."

We cannot agree with J. S. Mill when he says that a country which has a currency differs from one that does not have it at all only by the fact that in the former circulation is more *convenient*, that there is a gain in time and the difficulties are lessened. We know that logically this is untrue (following the same method of drawing distinctions that Mill elucidates so admirably in his inductive logic). To suppose that two countries could be equal in all respects except for the presence or absence of money is a misconception, because money is not something accidental, something introduced only for the sake of greater convenience, a unit of a socio-economic system, but, on the contrary, it is an indispensable, completely integral link in any developed social division of labor. We assume that Marx's foregoing analysis as well as our interpretation of his work has sufficiently demonstrated that a profound and many-sided division of labor is impossible without money, for otherwise the products manufactured by the various concrete types of labor would be deprived of any possibility of being exchanged for one other, and to find for themselves the kind of market which is necessary when one produces in order to satisfy the needs of other people. Only within very strict limits and only where the surplus over one's own requirements are alienated, are individual acts of change possible, which do not have recourse to the universal equivalent. But production for the market has long displaced production for oneself in the most developed economies of Europe.

Thus, there is not any possibility of comparing, after Mill, two such systems, of which one is completely inconceivable without money, and the other is just as inconceivable with it. The social functions of money constituting its particularity in relation to other commodities should be defined by means of investigation rather other than those resorted to by Mill which, moreover, turn out to be not just to facilitate circulation and diminish difficulties. Mill's argument that a tailor would die of hunger in absence of money and so on, does as little in elucidating the essence of the matter. It is true that the tailor would die, but he would also die if he did not have bread and other things; and one cannot say that a feature of money is that it has many things attached to it. In a society with labor divided into separate economies only the owner of money represents a person possessing the product in immediately exchangeable form; while the owner of any other product satisfies his needs only by first changing his product into money. Having divided immediate exchange into two opposing phases – purchase and sale, the introduction of money has the consequence that the product of a separate economy, entering into each of these phases, manifested its value in money, in other words – every purchase is at the same time a sale, i.e. the adoption by an individual commodity of the money form indispensable to it.[12] This is an economic fact and its characteristic features are contained to a certain extent in the phrase of Mill's that we cited. But beyond the description of the fact there should be an explanation of it, but such an explanation is to be found neither in Mill nor in any other economist other than Marx.

Ricardo and all his school clearly understand that, like any other commodity, money is not exchanged other than in accordance with the quantity of labor contained in it. Thus, for example, in the chapter about currency and banks Ricardo says about this subject the following:[13] "Gold and silver, like all other commodities, are valuable only in proportion to the quantity of labor necessary to produce them and bring them to market. Gold is about fifteen times dearer than silver, not because there is a greater demand for it, nor because the supply of silver is fifteen times greater than that of gold, but solely because fifteen times the quantity of labor is necessary to procure a given quantity of it. (Smith, Say and Storch adhered to an opposing opinion.)" But neither Ricardo himself nor his followers, being concerned as they were solely with investigations into the magnitude of value and conditions upon which it depended, paid any attention to the qualitative difference between the labor contained in money and that contained in other products, and did not notice that only labor of the first type was labor of the directly social form. By the identification and elaboration on these important distinctions, Marx provides an explanation for the afore-mentioned economic fact and in so doing makes an important contribution to economic science. The money form, he says, is indispensable for every commodity, because only by manifesting itself in monetary material can each concrete type of *labor* become a social labor.

We cannot say that social character of money has completely escaped the notice of the writers, who along with the study of other economic questions, investigate the general characteristic features of the universal equivalent. Their attention was mostly attracted by the function of money as a criterion of value, the property of money to be directly a product or a commodity, and not only the representative of value, the quantitative relationship of commodities and money as an instrument of circulation.[14] But occasionally space was given to the question of the more general and basic properties of money. Thus, for example, we find the following relating here to the opinion in Storch:[15] "If we disregard the value which the material used in its production may have, money as such does not have direct value (use- or utility-value) for anyone in isolation; no one can use it for oneself; everyone seeks it only with the object of exchanging it for other things . . . Only money alone can always remain a commodity and never become a provision . . . Everywhere where there is consumption, there have to be consumers; but who are the consumers of money? Society taken as a whole . . . Money has direct value only for society, but in society it has exchange value for every individual person." J. B. Say[16] expresses the same idea in equally general terms: "Currency satisfies everyone's needs, because there is hardly a person who does not have to buy. If I produce silk fabrics or elegant furniture my products will not be needed by everyone; but no one can do without exchanging the values he possesses for a commodity equally suitable for all purchases, because it is essential to all sellers, as there are not any sellers who will not subsequently become buyers." The author of *Nouveaux principes d'économie politique*[17] also points out a characteristic social property of money. "Money," he says, "represents the only wealth that does not increase due to circulation, and is not eliminated in consumption. It always emerges unchanged whether out of the hands of the person who has used it to advantage or out of the hands of one who has squandered it on his pleasure." Money plays the part of an intermediary between sides, entering into a contract, as a thing which everyone needs and by means of which everyone finds whatever is of immediate use. The property of money to serve without being consumed was noticed by Law,[18] who, among other things, taught that "currency is a not a value commodities are exchanged for," but that "it is a value by means of which commodities are exchanged." Designations such as *"marchandise universelle," "marchandise banale," "produit préferé"* and so on are also intended to show the social characteristic of money and the source of its origin. But all these and similar descriptions and differentiations are deficient in the sense that, disregarding the inner nature of a phenomenon, they expound on its external features. It is not sufficient to know that money functions in a society with the division of labor, being transferred from hand to hand, and that there is no one who did not need to buy or sell. We still have to form an opinion on why money connects all the links in the chain of the division of labor together, by what properties it accomplishes its purpose. Divisibility, flexibility, great value in small volume, as well as many other similar properties, usually adduced by economists, are attributes not of money as such, but of precious metals. Whatever object in society carries out the function of money, in every case it acts as the incarnation of universal human labor as distinct from the concrete types of labor contained in all other economic objects. Precious metals differ from other objects chosen to carry out the aforementioned functions only by the fact that they are better suited to these functions in their natural form. In this regard an important role is played by the homogeneity and divisibility of gold and silver. The first of these properties satisfies the requirement of a universal equivalent, which requires identical material to represent different types of labor; and the second property corresponds to the function of value measurement.

We mentioned above that being preoccupied with the analysis of the measure of value, economists have concentrated most of their attention on the quantitative sides of the problem of money. Smith, Ricardo, the two Mills and a great many other authors have constantly evaded the question of the form of value, and dealt exclusively in their investigations with its magnitude and the factors on which it depends. The elucidation of the functions of money serves as a criterion for value; research on how much money is required for commodity circulation, what part is played in this regard by the velocity of money circulation, what influence amount of money has on value of money and commodities and so on: these represent the most important content of both special treatises on money and those sections in general works on economics which are devoted to this subject. Hence, it is no wonder that the formal side of the question, namely the determination of those specific particularities which characterize monetary exchange in economies with the division of labor, and upon which Marx concentrated his research, was ignored by the economists. We do not consider it appropriate to enter into a detailed analysis of the relationship of his theory to earlier ones, fearing to go beyond the objectives which form the basis of the present work.

NOTES

1. *Das Kapital*, Chapter I.
2. The question why money does not itself directly represent labor-time, so that, for example, a piece of paper may represent, for instance, x hours' labor, simply arises from the question why in conditions of *commodity* production, *every product* of labor must

take the form of a commodity. The concept of a commodity presupposes the concept of its twofold character, as a commodity and as money. Owen's labor money is no more money than a theater ticket is. Owen presupposes *immediately* socialized labor, i.e. a form of production diametrically opposed to the form of commodity production. The certification that labor has been carried out merely establishes individual part played by the producer in the common labour and his *individual right* to partake in a certain portion of the common product.

3. By the sale, for example, of linen, the opposite movement is concluded, which began with the sale, for example, of wheat. C-M (linen-money), which is the first phase of the movement C-M-C (linen-money-Bible) is at the same time M-C (money-linen), the second phase of another movement C-M-C (wheat-money-linen).

4. With the purchase of some goods by the weaver, who has already sold his linen, are concluded a whole series of *first* metamorphoses for the owners of these commodities, which have now been converted into money. C-M, the second phase of the movement C-M-C (linen-money-Bible) is at the same time C-M, the first phase of another movement C-M-C (Bible-money-wine). Here "Bible" stands for the whole totality of purchases.

5. "The capacity of exchanging for or buying other things is inherent in all commodities which, at the same time that they are in demand, are not spontaneous productions; but it can neither be manifested nor appreciated except when they are compared with each other . . . No article or product can have any exchangeable value, except in relation to something else that is, or may be, exchanged for it. We may as well talk about absolute height or absolute depth, as about absolute value." MacCulloch, *Principles*, pp. 291–292.

6. *Oeuvres complètes*, p. 256.

7. See, for example, Adam Smith, *The Wealth of Nations*, Ch. IV: "The greater part of a person's wants is supplied by exchanging that surplus part of the produce of his own labor, which is over and above his own consumption, for such parts of the produce of other men's labor as he has occasion for." J. Mill, *Eleménts d'économie politique*, p. 85: "Supposons que deux hommes aient *plus qu'il ne leur est necessaire*, l'un, par exemple, de vivres et l'autre de drap, et que le premier désire plus de drap qu'il n'en nossède, et le second plus de vivres; ce sera un grand avantage pour tous deux que de pouvoir échanger une portion des vivres de l'un contre une portion du drap de l'autre. *Il en est ainsi dans tout autre cas.* MacCulloch, *Principles of Political Economy*, etc., p. 92: "But the facility of exchanging, or the circumstance of being able readily to barter *the surplus produce of our own labour* for such parts of the surplus produce of other peoples' labour as we may desire to obtain and they may choose to part with, is not the only advantage of the separation of employments." J. S. Mill *The Elements of Political Economy*, Vol. I, p. 157 "A set of workers producing more food than they need for themselves can exchange the surplus with another set of workers, who produce more clothes than they need for themselves." But in the chapter on international trade, Vol. II, p. 103, J. S. Mill following Ricardo disputes Adam Smith's opinion on this subject which was that international trade opens up a market for the surplus produce of a country. "These expressions," Mill says, "suggest ideas inconsistent with a clear conception of the phenomenon. These expression, 'surplus produce' seems to imply that a country is under some kind of necessity of producing the corn or cloth which it exports; so that the portion which it does not consume, if not wanted and consumed elsewhere, would either be produced in sheer waste, if it was not in demand and was not consumed abroad . . . The country produces in excess of its own wants . . . as the cheapest mode

of supplying itself with other things." The author does not notice that the same objection regarding vagueness of expression applies equally well to the term "surplus produce which finds a market within the country." And here as well as in international trade, the words "surplus produce" suggest the inconsistent idea that the parties have a necessity to manufacture a product for the market, and that it would be fatal if this there were no demand for it. Products are produced here too only because it is the cheapest mode of supplying oneself with the other products.

8. See note to p. 6 of *Oeuvres complèttes*, "Ricardo".

9. *Principles*, Vol. I, pp. 10–11.

10. *Principles*, Vol. II, p. 4.

11. *Principes d'économie politique*, Vol. I, p. 276.

12. "Toute vente est achat." Quesnay, *Dialogues sur le commerce et les travaux des artisans*, p.170.

13. *Oeuvres complètes.*, Chapter XXVII, p. 323.

14. Incidentally, we leave aside also Ricardo's theory on relation between the quantity and the value of money and other commodities, on the basis of which, with the help of some other supplementary concepts he constructed the theory on "economic and stable money circulation"; the development of this side of the question of money is not so closely linked with the general theory of capital that we have to dwell upon it.

15. *Cours d'économie politique*, Vol. III, pp. 3 ff.

16. *Cours d'économie pratique*, Vol. III, p. 3 ff.

17. Sismondi, *Nouveaux principes*, Vol. II, pp. 2–3.

18. *Considérations sur le numéraire et le commerce.*

THE SPECTRAL REALITY OF VALUE: SIEBER, MARX, AND COMMODITY FETISHISM

David Norman Smith

ABSTRACT

No interpreter of Marx's Capital *has been as highly esteemed by Marx or as little noticed as Nikolai Ivanovich Sieber. Yet Sieber's contribution has been overlooked by almost all of the participants in the innumerable debates sparked by* Capital. *This is not only a failure of exegesis, but significant as well, since Sieber's work, in fact, is a valuable coda to* Capital. *Several aspects of Marx's theory which remain obscure to many critics can be better grasped in the light of Sieber's exposition.*

No commentator on Karl Marx's *Capital* has been as highly esteemed by Marx or as little remembered as Nikolai Ivanovich Sieber. Sieber's Russian-language dissertation on value (1871), which focused primarily on Ricardo and Marx, won Marx's ardent praise. Said Marx: "As early as 1871, N. Sieber, Professor of Political Economy in the University of Kiev, in his work *David Ricardo's Theory of Value and Capital*, referred to my theory of value, money and capital as in its essentials a necessary sequel to the teaching of Smith and Ricardo. What astonishes the Western European who reads this excellent work is the author's solid and consistent grasp of the purely theoretical position" ([1873]

Marx's *Capital* and Capitalism; Markets in a Socialist Alternative,
Research in Political Economy, Volume 19, pages 47–66.
Copyright © 2001 by Elsevier Science Ltd.
All rights of reproduction in any form reserved.
ISBN: 0-7623-0838-9

1976, p. 99).[1] Later, in his reply to an influential critic, Marx cited Sieber as an authority on the difference between Marxian and Ricardian value-theory: "Mr. Wagner could have acquainted himself with the difference between Ricardo and me not only from *Capital* but (if he knew Russian) from Sieber's work . . ." ([1879] 1976, p. 204).

Strangely, however, Sieber's contribution to the elucidation of Marxian value-theory has been almost entirely neglected. In the unceasing storms that have swirled around *Capital* for well over a century, almost nothing has been learned from the commentary most warmly endorsed by Marx. This is unfortunate, not only in principle (as mute witness to the exegetic limitations of traditional scholarship) but in substance as well, since Sieber's contribution, in fact, is a valuable coda to *Capital*. Several aspects of Marx's theory which remain obscure to many critics can be better understood in the light of Sieber's exposition.

What follows, then, is a brief overview of Sieber's life and work, intended to facilitate insight into what Sieber called the "exposition and critique" of Marx's theory ([1871] 2001). Only a few previous works have attempted this. The most notable of these include Soviet-era studies of Russian intellectual history (Kleinbort, 1923; Reuel, 1937, 1956); a roughly equivalent recent effort to claim Sieber for Ukrainian intellectual history (Koropeckyj, 1990, 1984; cf. Horkina, 1994); and two brief recent studies, one of which emphasizes Sieber's influence on Russo-Marxist determinism (White, 1996) while the second probes Sieber's connection to contemporary neo-Ricardianism (Scazzieri, 1987).[2]

So far, few if any scholars have offered careful readings of the central facet of Sieber's work that Marx found "astonishing" and commendable – namely, his interpretation of Marx's value-theory "in its essentials." That, above all, is what I seek here. But first, to put Sieber's contribution in context, I will probe his life; trace the arc of his thought and influence (above all in connection with the Russo-Marxist philosophy of history); and sketch the intellectual backdrop against which Sieber's reading of Marx stands out in bold relief.

I. SIEBER'S LIFE, SCHOLARSHIP, AND POLITICS

Many aspects of Sieber's life remain obscure. Of Swiss and French descent, Sieber was born in 1844, in the Ukrainian community of Sudak in the Crimea. Raised and educated in the Ukraine, Sieber entered Kiev University in 1864, where he studied political economy under Nikolai Kh. Bunge.[3] After receiving his law degree in 1866, Sieber spent eight months as a volunteer judicial mediator working with the peasants in Volhynia province (Kleinbort, 1923,

p. 13; Scazzieri, 1987, p. 26; Koropeckyj, 1990, p. 215 n. 81). In 1869, after returning to Kiev University, he was elected chair of the Kiev cooperative society (Koropeckyj, 1984, p. 202, n. 191) and published a pamphlet on cooperative societies (Ziber, 1869). An article on rent published the next year (Ziber, 1870) prefigured some of the themes in his dissertation on Ricardo and Marx (Ziber, 1871), which appeared both in the Kiev University journal (in monthly installments) and in book form.

In 1873, after touring Europe – where he visited factories and cooperatives and attended classes with economists such as F. A. Lange in Zurich [Billington, 1958, p. 190, Note H) and Knies in Heidelberg (Koropeckyj, 1990, p. 200) – Sieber returned to Kiev to accept the chair in political economy and statistics. That same year he published the first installment of his Russian edition of Ricardo's works (Ziber, ed., 1873). He also published an essay on Ricardo (Ziber, 1873) and, a year later, an essay on labor costs (Ziber, 1875a).

Sieber remained in Kiev only two years. When, in 1875, his Kiev colleague Mykhailo Drahomanov was fired from the university as a Ukrainian "separatist" at the direct order of Tsar Alexander II, Sieber resigned in protest. Drahomanov was then, and until his death 20 years later, the guiding spirit of the Ukrainian left. Neither a "separatist" nor a nationalist, Drahomanov represented a unique mix of anti-imperial federalism, constitutionalism, civil libertarianism, and what he called "non-authoritarian" socialism in which sympathy for the working class played a central part (Rudnytsky [1952] 1987, *passim*; Drahomanov [1884] 1996, pp. 171–183; Lindheim & Luckyj, 1996, pp. 22–25). Until his expulsion from Kiev, Drahomanov was a key figure in the illegal Ukrainian cultural-political organization *Kiev Hromada* (Community) and a leading contributor to the dissident journal *Kievski telegraf*. Subsequently, in Geneva, Drahomanov edited a pair of journals (*Hromada*, 1877–1882; *Volnoe slovo* [Free Word], 1883) in which he affirmed a humanist socialism sympathetic to the cultural-political aspirations of ethnic minorities and opposed to ethnocentrism.[4]

Sieber was linked to Drahomanov in each of these phases (Meijer, 1955; Geierhos, 1977). He collaborated on *Kievski telegraf*, lectured to *Kiev Hromada* women's courses and may have belonged to *Kiev Hromada* (Rusov & Volkov, 1907, pp. 155–156; Sapitsky, 1929, pp. 142, 147; both cited by Koropeckyj, 1990, p. 215, n. 81). Sieber also drafted a plan (1875b) for the collection of Ukrainian economic data at the request of the Southwest Section of the Russian Geographical Society, an organization which the imperial government outlawed in 1876 because, as Nancy Butler Hasegawa explains (1972, pp. 52–53), it was viewed as the institutional base of Ukrainian dissent.

Sieber remained close to Drahomanov in exile. Both were now in Switzerland, where Sieber taught at the University in Bern. James Billington (1958, p. 113) describes Sieber and Drahomanov as "two of the principal *zemstvo* liberals" in the late 1870s – by which he means partisans of rural self-government in imperial Russia – and Sieber was close to other leading *zemstvo* advocates as well, including Maxim Kovalevskii and Ivan Ianzhul. In the early 1880s both Sieber and Drahomanov were stalwarts of *Volnoe slovo*, and Ivan Rudnytsky finds the "very promising beginnings of a specifically Ukrainian school of socialism in the 1870s and 1880s in the pioneer work done by Drahomanov and his friends, Serhii Podolynski and Mykola Ziber" ([1958] 1987, p. 139).[5]

Just how closely Sieber and Drahomanov agreed with one another remains uncertain, however. Rudnytsky concurs that Drahomanov first learned about Marxism from Sieber, and he finds "some verisimilitude" in Zaslavsky's claim that Drahomanov, like Sieber, prefigured aspects of Russian Marxism ([1952] 1987, p. 225). But beyond this nothing is yet certain. Sieber's articles in *Volnoe Slovo* have not yet been reported in detail, and many other facts relevant to his association with Drahomanov remain obscure.

The same is true of Sieber's links to Marxism. Several writers have called Sieber's outlook "purely scientific" and conclude, on this ground, that even his embrace of Marxism was "apolitical" (Dan, [1946] 1970, p. 188). But the evidence offered for this conclusion is scant, and (in my opinion) contradictory. Sieber was deeply critical of capitalism and (as some of the evidence suggests) he may have been far more militant than Dan believed. He wrote often on contemporary politics and society (see Ziber, 1876a, 1876b, 1877a, 1878c, 1879a, 1880, 1882a, 1883b). But until further research is completed, we will simply remain unclear about the tendency of Sieber's commitments.

Sieber's links to Marx, however, are quite clear. Marx was quick to learn about the 1871 dissertation, which he praised as early as 1873 in the *Nachwort* to the second edition of *Capital*. (And note that Marx refers to Sieber here as a Kiev professor, showing current knowledge of Sieber's status.) Marx's friends Danielson and Kovalevskii kept him abreast of most of Sieber's later Marxian writings – including, most notably, Sieber's essays on Marx's economic theory (1876–1878) and his replies (1877b, 1879b) to critiques of *Capital* by Yurii Zhukovskii (1877) and Boris Chicherin (1878). Kovalevskii, in turn, gave Sieber copies of Marx's writings (including texts on Dühring and Bakunin) which he cited in several articles.[6] Marx's letters show that he knew of Sieber's reply to Zhukovskii and he mentions Sieber twice in his notes (White, 2001, above). And in 1880–1881, Sieber and his colleagues Ianzhul and Kablukov visited Marx and Engels in their London homes, where they also met Bebel (Koropeckyj, 1990, p. 216; White, 1996, p. 273).

Much of Sieber's work in the decade before his early death in 1888 focused on law (1879–1880, 1883c), poverty (1883a), colonialism (1881a), and, above all, collective property. His texts on the latter subject spanned contemporary as well as historical themes (1878a, 1881b, 1882b, 1882c) and culminated in a big book on primitive economic culture ([1883] 1959) that parallels Marx's own late ethnological writings ([1879–1882] 2002). In addition, Sieber finished his edition of Ricado's writings (1882) and expanded his dissertation (Ziber, 1885).

Personally, a teacher said, Sieber was "a pure idealist, . . . unable to neglect the advice of his conscience" (Romanovich-Slavatinskii, in Scazzieri, 1987, p. 29). This idealism led him, as we will see, to a deep engagement with Marx and *Capital* – an engagement that proved fateful for Russian Marxism (and thus, ultimately, for Russian-influenced Marxism as well).

II. THE INEVITABILITY OF CAPITALISM?

Sieber's reading of Marx was unusual from the start. Most of Marx's early Russian readers turned to *Capital* "to expose the miserable plight of the proletarianized peasant in the West in order to help save the peasant in Russia from a similar plight" (Resis, 1970, p. 227). But Sieber, in contrast to most reactionaries and radicals alike, did not believe that capitalism in Russia could be either halted or bypassed. On the contrary, he quickly became one of the most influential partisans of the conviction that capitalism was destiny, not only for Russia but for the world; and he argued influentially that socialism, too, requires capitalism as an unavoidable prelude. The echoes of this conviction are audible even today.

The roots of Sieber's faith in the inevitability of capitalism can be traced to his Kiev dissertation;[7] but for its full flowering, we have to turn to his texts of the late 1870s and early 1880s. In these later texts, Sieber contends that progress in the coordination of labor is more fundamentally a result of immanent necessity than of class conflict (1879b). Essentially, he says, the complexity of an ever-ramifying division of labor assures cooperation on a growing scale. Capitalism in particular, as a blindly growing system of increasingly specialized and interdependent forms of labor, nurses within itself a cooperative imperative of unprecedented intensity. Ultimately, as he concluded in his ethnological treatise, "no matter how complex and subdivided the participation of social labor may be, the mutual gravitation of industrial groups will overcome this division and each further step of history will lead in reality to a closer interweaving and merging of individual elements of the social-productive process" ([1883] 1959, pp. 467–468; see Koropeckyj, 1990, p. 201).

No necessary stage can be skipped or delayed. Capitalism therefore follows the preceding stage of history the way winter follows autumn; and socialism is imminent as well.

The influence of this argument has often been overlooked. Soviet historians, eager to credit Plekhanov and Axelrod with paternal responsibility for Russian Marxism, seldom say more than a few words about Sieber *en passant*. But it appears, in fact, that Sieber played a large role in winning Russian Marxism for this particular brand of historical determinism. Axelrod, Plekhanov, Blagoyev, Skvortsov, and Fedoseyev – the seminal figures in the first generation of Russian Marxist orthodoxy – were all significantly influenced by Sieber.

Axelrod, who like Plekhanov began as a peasant-oriented populist with Bakuninist leanings, reported later that his turn to Marxism in 1879 sprang from conversations "a year earlier in Bern with Professor Nikolay Ziber . . ." (Ascher, 1972, p. 50). Later Axelrod worked with Sieber and Drahomanov on *Volnoe slovo*. Plekhanov, like Axelrod, was attracted by Sieber's determinism (Walicki, 1979, pp. 436–437; Schapiro, 1967, pp. 130–131), and Sieber's general influence on Plekhanov, his biographer says, was "incontestable" (Baron, 1963, p. 59). Blagoyev, who led one of the first Marxist cells inside Russia (Offord, 1986, pp. 49–76), was also attracted to Marxism by Sieber (Uroeva, 1969, p. 115). The scholar Skvortsov was also lastingly affected by Sieber, and, in turn, influenced not only the activist Fedoseyev (Offord, 1986, p. 146) but also the leading "Legal Marxist" of the 1890s, Struve (Pipes, 1970, pp. 61–63).[8] Many of the other major "Legal Marxists" of the 1890s – including Bulgakov and, less obviously, Frank – also echoed themes from Sieber's writings (Evtuhov, 1997, pp. 31f.; Williams, 1999, pp. 4–5; Evtuhov, 2000, p. 4; Boll, 1970, pp. 17, 36). Bulgakov, in fact, was so indelibly influenced by Sieber that, when he ultimately rejected Marx in favor of the Russian Orthodox church, his principal criticisms of Marx were plainly (albeit not openly) directed against Sieber rather than Marx.[9]

Indeed, Sieber's status as an icon of Russian Marxism was so well established that, in 1892, his name loomed large in a famous debate over the legitimacy of historical determinism. The populist Mikhailovskii, trying to discredit Sieber's inevitabilism as metaphysics, recalled quarreling with him over Sieber's essay (1879c) on Engels' *Anti-Duhring*. Thanks to Plekhanov's scornful reply, it is well known that Mikhailovskii accused Sieber of uncritical Hegelianism.[10] But just as influentially, Mikhailovskii credited Sieber with a maxim which soon entered the folklore of Marxism. "We shall get nowhere," Sieber reportedly argued, "until the peasant is boiled down in the factory cauldron" (Mikhailovskii [1892] 1900, p. 339; cf. White, 1996, p. 338; Resis, 1970, p. 237; Walicki, 1987, p. 437). Just weeks later Danielson reported to Engels himself that Sieber had "been wont to say that 'the Russian peasant must be boiled in the factory cauldron' if we are to reach our economic paradise" (cited by White, 1996, p. 294).

By 1913, when Bulgakov explained his rejection of Marxism, the grim fatalism of this attitude towards the peasantry had achieved such canonical status that Bulgakov could quote this line (without attribution) as the self-evident epitome of the Marxian "illusion" vis-à-vis "the scientifically determined necessity of the development of capitalism in Russia" with which Marx and Engels "blinded themselves and their docile followers" (Bulgakov [1913] 2000, pp. 238, 324).

Lenin, in an early text ([1897/1908] 1970, p. 188), explained his references to Sieber as a means of evading the censors, saying that, "instead of referring to *Capital*, we referred to Sieber's book . . ." Yet Bukharin, writing after the revolution – and hence after the demise of the censorship – felt free to quote Sieber's paraphrase of *Capital* as if it were a direct quote from *Capital* itself (see the translators' note in Bukharin, 1925, p. 70, n. 3).

Sieber, plainly, was a Marxian icon.

III. SIEBER, MARX, AND THE CRITICS

What, then, did Marx value in Sieber's work? As his late writings show, he did not ultimately share Sieber's faith in the inevitability of capitalism. "Nowadays," Vera Zasulich wrote to Marx ([1881] 1983, pp. 98–99), "we often hear it said that the rural commune is an archaic form condemned to perish by history, scientific socialism and, in short, everything above debate. Those who preach such a view call themselves your disciples par excellence: 'Marksists.' Their strongest argument is often: 'Marx said so.' 'But how do you derive that from *Capital*?' others object. 'He does not discuss the agrarian question, and says nothing about Russia.' 'He would have said as much if he had discussed our country,' your disciples retort with perhaps a little too much temerity."

In his draft replies to Zasulich, Marx revealed that he viewed the future of capitalism in Russia as far from predestined. If, in fact, capitalism triumphed, the Russian peasantry would certainly be doomed to proletarianization; but it was conceivable, he argued, that Russia could in fact bypass capitalism by generalizing the collective property relations inherent in the traditional Russian *obshchina*. And, Marx added ([1881] 1983, p. 101), "the Russian 'Marxists' of whom you speak are completely unknown to me."

Sieber, of course, was well known to Marx at this point, both personally and through his writings. But Marx regarded Sieber as an ally with respect to *Capital*, not as an aberrant 'Marxist' philosopher of history. In this connection, Sieber's lucid insight into Marx's most basic categories – value, labor, value-magnitude, the value-forms, and money – proved particularly noteworthy. Consult Sieber, Marx instructed Wagner, if you wish to know how I differ from Ricardo.

Sieber's interpretation of *Capital* was striking, on one level, simply because he saw through the mystifications that ensnared so many economists. "Just how drastically a section of the economists is deceived by the fetishism that clings to the world of commodities," Marx wrote in *Capital*, ". . . is proved . . . by the tediously pointless contention about the role of nature in the formation of exchange value. Since exchange-value is a determinate social form representing the labor that has been applied to a thing, it can no more contain natural matter than, e.g. the rate of exchange."[11]

This contention, as tediously pointless as ever, remained the central item on the agenda of Marx's principal early critics. Marx was faulted for his failure to equate value with use-value by nearly everyone who replied to him. Chicherin was so appalled at Marx's claim that exchange-value contains "not an iota of use-value" that he cited this phrase over and over ([1878] 1998, pp. 324, 325, 341), with mounting incredulity: "No one exchanges objects that are not useful. Thus, when Karl Marx asserts that exchange-value contains not a single iota of use-value, this is not only an unjustified logical leap but also directly contradicts what occurs everyday in the exchange of commodities." Besides, Chicherin added – wrongly – "according to . . . all economists, demand is one of the basic elements in determining value." Hence Marx's thinking contains "not one iota of logic" ([1878] 1998, pp. 324, 341).[12] Similar views were voiced by Knies (1873, p. 119), Roscher (1878a, p. 63), Zhukovskii (White, 1996, p. 235), and Wagner (Marx [1879–1880] 1976, passim), among others.

Wagner, in particular, read *Capital* so carelessly, Marx noted, that he "ranks me among the people according to whom 'use-value' should be 'completely eliminated from science'." And so preoccupied was Wagner with the very first point of Marx's very first chapter that he "has overlooked the fact that even in the analysis of the commodity my work does not simply stop with the dual modality in which it manifests itself [i.e. use-value and exchange-value], but, rather, progresses immediately to the fact that within this duality what is manifested is a twofold character of labor" – that is, Marx's contention that useful labor is not only the source of use-value but, when treated and regarded as "abstract labor," becomes its very opposite as well, the commodity's phantom "value-objectivity." Nor does Wagner grasp that Marx's theory is not, in fact, a "general value theory," but rather an attempt to explain the commodity, which is, he says, the simplest *concretum* in bourgeois daily life ([1879–1880] 1976, pp. 204, 214–217).

On the twofold character of labor – the second of the four central points to which Marx devotes a section in *Capital*, Chapter 1 – Marx's critics have relatively little to say. Roscher simply accuses Marx of parroting Ricardo's value-theory, "without any attempt at demonstration, on the assumption that the Ricardo school is right" (1878a, p. 168, n.) – and without realizing, evidently, that Marx considers his difference from Ricardo on this subject (the distinction between useful and abstract labor) to be the very *Springpunkt* of his original contribution in this field. Chicherin, with comparable acuity, blames Marx, not the market, for "completely disregarding the quality of the labor performed"; "in reality," he announces, "there exist only individual labor-powers" ([1878] 1998, p. 328).[13]

Of livelier interest to Marx's critics is his claim that labor, not capital, is the source of value and thus surplus value. To this they respond with predictable indignation. Roscher taxes Marx for "the most recent relapse into the old error of the unproductiveness of capital" (1878b, p. 127, n. 3) and ripostes that, on the contrary, "capital, if we may so speak, gives tone to everything (1878a, p. 166). For Chicherin, Marx sees profit as "nothing but the illegitimate fruit of another's labor," the latest in a long series "of robberies and extortions." Wagner, too, ascribes to Marx the view that "the surplus value produced *only* by the workers remains in *unconscionable* fashion in the hand of the capitalist entrepreneurs," "a *deduction* or '*robbery*' perpetrated on the worker." In fact, Marx remarks, "I say the direct opposite," noting that the capitalist plays a constructive role in organizing the production of surplus value, and that, in fact, the capitalist normally pays the full value of the workers' labor power (since surplus value springs from the discrepancy between the value of labor-power and the value of the labor *product*). Here, however, in Wagner's eagerness to contend that capitalists deserve profit as a kind of wage, Marx detects "the cloven hoof." Labor, Wagner says, "in the correct *broad* sense," must include "the *intellectual labor* of the director . . ." ([1879–1880] 1976, pp. 227–228, 205). Chicherin, similarly, calls "intellectual capital, or the directing will," the living embodiment of Kantian "practical reason as the motivating force of the enterprise. It is the highest of all factors of production . . ." (1882–1883, Vol. 1, pp. 350, 387).

About the "value-forms," the subject of the third section of Chapter 1, Marx's early critics waxed feebly irate. Only one "tutored in German philosophy," Chicherin complains, would see a "contradiction" in the fact that one commodity "expresses its value in the other; [and that,] therefore, the first plays an active, the second a passive role." Marx's discussion of this point, he sighs, is "long and tiresome" ([1878] 1998, p. 331; cf. Marx [1867] 1976c, p. 139). Roscher, whose insight is as keen as his sense of irony, argues that Marx "personifies things in a manner almost mythological. Thus, according to him, modesty should be ascribed to a coat which exchanges for a piece of linen, and purpose to the linen, etc." (1878a, p. 104, n. 6; cf. Marx [1867a] 1976, p. 24).

Finally, of the intricacies of the concluding section of Chapter 1 (on "the fetishism of the commodity world"), Marx's critics are appropriately silent.

Aside from a few assertions to the effect that Marx is simply self-deluding about the mysteries of the commodity-form – "the contradictions exist only in the author's mind," Chicherin insists ([1878] 1998, p. 330) – the accusing chorus is otherwise mute.

Where Marx's critics are silent, however, Sieber is insightful. In the opening chapters of his thesis he carefully assesses the claims of many economists who say, in one idiom or another, that value and use-value are reciprocally implicated. Bruno Hildebrand's early marginal utility theory (1848) and the supply-and-demand theories of Malthus and Macleod are reviewed and rejected (Scazzieri, 1987, pp. 34–35; Koropeckyj, 1990, p. 197). Others who receive critical attention in this connection include Walras and Rau (Ziber, 1871, Chapters 1–3). When all is said and done, Sieber says at the opening of his Marx chapter, "we . . . have all the grounds for rejecting" such theories: "Neither use-value, nor degree of utility . . . can satisfy us further" (1871] 2001, above).

In the ensuing summary of Marx's early chapters, Sieber could not be clearer about the structure and premises of Marx's theory.[14] He affirms the commodity as the cell-form of bourgeois wealth, explains the dual character of the commodity as use-value and value, and defines the "substance" of value as labor rendered socially "abstract" by exchange: "Labor itself is value . . . In other words, labor is the only *social* creator of those proportions in which acts of exchange take place" ([1871] 2001).[15] Sieber stresses the macro-dynamic merits of Marx's view that value is not only qualitatively abstract, but, at the aggregate level of the social division of labor, can be understood as average socially necessary labor time. "The introduction . . . of this concept once and for all eliminates any possibility of discussing the question of value within those narrow, atomistic confines in which very many economists speak of it: once and for all the ground is cut from under the feet of those [who object] to Ricardo's theory (Walras, Bastiat, Macleod etc.) [by trying] to show its falsity in specific instances . . . No diamond found on the street, no butter, transported twenty times from one place to another [can shake] the truth that the measures of exchange are determined *in general* in accordance with labor . . ." ([1871] 2001).

Like Marx himself, Sieber believed that the locus of Marx's originality lies most profoundly in the discovery of this Faustian duality in the breast of the commodity. "The differences between concrete types of labor serve as a source for that qualitative difference between products without which exchange would be inconceivable. But the same exchange also requires a quantitative similarity and finds [this] in the equality of quantities of labor, abstracted from their concrete properties . . . [The Ricardians] had this kind of labor in mind when they [called it] the regulator of exchange ratios; but they did not go further, did not enter into the distinction between special types of labor, which provide the material for the conception of universal labor and serve as a basis for establishing the formula for value" ([1871] 2001).

Sieber explains, further, that for Marx value "appears" in forms that conceal its ulterior reality. Objectively, value contains "not an atom of matter" (Marx [1867] 1976c, p. 138), and, in fact, exists as a purely social status of labor products "treated and regarded" as units of exchangeability. But in everyday life, value *appears* to inhere in commodities as an intrinsic natural quality. And the "form" this appearance takes, Marx says, is natural as well.

Explaining the latter point is one of the hardest tasks Marx set himself in *Capital*. Part of the difficulty lies in the counter-intuitive quality of Marx's claim that value, in substance, is abstract labor. How, we might ask, can labor be genuinely generic? How, in the real world, can something so tangible and familiar acquire a spectral master status as a "value-objectivity" in which it counts as something entirely social, containing, "as value," not an atom of matter? And what can it mean to say that value has hieroglyphic "forms" in which it "appears" to be the very opposite of its abstract actuality?

Sieber, Marx says, shows an "excellent" grasp of Marx's "purely theoretical stance." Nowhere is this clearer than with respect to these most basic of all questions concerning the premises of value-theory.

IV. SIEBER AND THE WORLD OF COMMODITIES

Unlike Chicherin, Wagner *i tutti quanti*, Sieber fully appreciates the centrality of the part played by use-value in Marx's framework. The commodity, of course, must be useful to be valuable. But value, Marx adds, is not use-value. It is, rather, a special social status which the product acquires as soon as it enters the realm of exchange. Yet because this status is not ordinarily discernible – because "status," however real, is neither tangible nor visible *as such* – the commodity's value must be *represented* to be *perceived*. And in the semiotic reality of daily life in the "commodity world," this representation takes *bodily form*. Value, in short, which is actually the opposite of use-value, nevertheless "takes the form" of use-value.

"Here," Chicherin writes, "the reader stops and asks himself: why is this so?" ([1878] 1998, p. 324). Sieber's answer to this question is a model of clarity. Like Marx – but in contrast to most of his interpreters – Sieber recognizes that Marx's theory rests, in part, on subjective foundations. This is not, of course, the abstract "subjectivity" of marginalism, but rather the lived intentionality of commodity producers, for whom exchange *means* something. Behind the coat's "modesty" and the linen's "purpose" – *obscured* by the "social relations between things" – there lies an actual relationship between producers. The weaver not only *produces* linen as a commodity, but *perceives* linen as a commodity. So, too, the tailor, vis-à-vis coats.

What, then, do these producers see? Specifically, Marx says that producers tend to see the value of their commodities in specific "forms." What, the weaver wonders, is my product worth? The answer, Marx says, is the *form* that value takes – in the *minds* of the producers. "Any objectivity of human labor which is itself abstract (i.e. without any additional quality and content), is necessarily an abstract objectivity – a *thing of thought*. In that way," Marx writes, "a web of flax turns into a chimera. But *commodities* are *objects*. They have to be what they are in an object-like way or else reveal it in their own object-like relationships" (1867a] 1976, pp. 19–20).[16]

This point, in turn, is the key to grasping why Marx places so much stress on the "polarity" and "mutual exclusiveness" of the so-called relative and equivalent value-forms. Simply put, from the standpoint of any given commodity producer, the relative commodity is the commodity *she produces*. The equivalent commodity is produced by *someone else*. "Note carefully!" Marx warns, we find "*two different value-expressions*" in a single exchange because the exchange involves "*two different persons*. As far as A is concerned, *his linen* (we may speak this way, because the initiative [in the exchange] has its origin *in his commodity*, for him) is situated in the relative value-form, and it is *the commodity of the other person* (the coat) on the other hand which is situated in equivalent form. *It is the other way around* from the standpoint of B. *The same* commodity thus *never* – not even in this case – possesses *both forms at the same time in the same value-expression*" ([1867b] 1976, p. 51; italics in the original).[17]

Every exchange, in other words, is a two-way street. And what producers need to know on this street is what their *own* commodities are worth. This is a matter of survival, and hence entirely personal and pragmatic – infinitely far removed, that is, from impersonal or abstract concerns. Altruists or theorists may worry about other producers, but *everyone* worries about his or her own products. For the weaver, thus, the decisive question is *how much* the linen will bring: "*What's my product worth?*"

For Marx, the answer to this question lies in the realm of *value-forms*. Sieber grasps this, and (far more than most expositors, even today) he gives the notion of value-forms a pivotal place in value-theory. If, ultimately, his account of this theory is not "astonishing" for its originality, it is nevertheless remarkably faithful to Marx's reasoning. This is clearest in Sieber's willingness to recognize that the value-forms must be grasped semiotically as core phenomena of structured cognition in a world of value-relations. "Abstract, or universal-human labor," Sieber writes, does not automatically appear as such "in people's minds"; hence it must appear in some other form.[18]

This is the point at which use-value acquires its own second status, Sieber explains. As use-values, commodities now capture the attention of consumers rather than producers; but as values, they play a new role – as *embodiments* of the value of *equivalent* commodities. Echoing Marx, Sieber notes that the value of any given commodity is expressed *in the bodily form of another commodity*. That is, in Marx's most famous example of a simple commodity exchange, when a tailor trades a coat to a weaver in return for 20 yards of linen, the value of the coat appears to be literally and exactly 20 yards of linen. The tailor, who is unlikely to conclude that exchange converts both coat and linen into units of abstract labor, thinks, rather, that her coat is simply worth 20 yards of linen – not 19 yards, not 21, but 20 exactly. And later, when money emerges as the commodity universally equivalent to all others, the coat now expresses its value in a precise quantity of the money commodity – say, $20.00.

Sums of money, then, become the universal language of value; the abstract numeric representation of the time and energy embodied in commodities. Those, like Chicherin, who think that only *Marx* saw the world so abstractly – allegedly *imposing* his view on a world of boundless diversity – misunderstand him at the root. In fact, as Sieber later explained *contra* Chicherin, "Marx presents . . . the whole doctrine of value and its forms not on his own behalf, but as the peculiar way people at a given stage of social development necessarily understand their mutual relations . . ."[19] ([1878b], cited in White, 2001, above).

Value now *appears to be* price. Commodities, that is, appear to have an inherent social relationship with money – while actual producers seem to have no necessary social connections at all, except as "representatives" of their products. Sieber realized that, for Marx, the ultimate truth is the reverse. Value, in actuality, is concrete labor *turned into its opposite by an action that embodies a moment of abstraction* (exchange); and the fact that people see value as price is an expression of fetishism. The actual, ulterior social relations of producers are concealed by "the social relations of things," and the social division of labor – the actual interdependence of producers – is occluded as a result.

Sieber is an exceptionally accurate and faithful reader of *Capital*. Unlike most of Marx's critics, he reads Marx with care. And unlike many of Marx's disciples, he reveals a critical and independent spirit, at times disagreeing with Marx and, often, offering arguments of his own to refine Marx's conclusions. Most pertinently, for present purposes, he argues effectively not only for Marx's view of value as average social labor – the crux of so many interpretations – but also for Marx's oft-neglected corollary thesis, namely, that value "in form" is "a thing of thought." This is a tough proposition to expound or even understand, yet Sieber makes a valiant effort on both levels. Marx was appreciative.

NOTES

1. The translation here, as in several other places below, is slightly emended. Such emendations will not be further noted. And note that Sieber's name is given in two forms. His writings are listed under the name "Ziber," which is the form given in most recent bibliographies. Elsewhere, though, his name is spelled in the Germanic form, which has become standard in the Marxian literature. The pronunciation is the same either way.

2. Scazzieri, who collaborates closely with Alberto Quadrio-Curzio, sees Sieber as a precursor of theorists today who synthesize "circular" accounts of production (derived from Ricardo and Quesnay) with "vertical integration" theories á la Pasinetti. Scazzieri (1987) discusses this parallel vis-à-vis Sieber alone, but Quadrio-Curzio (1986, p. 389) traces its roots to Marx as well.

3. In 1882, as Finance Minister, Bunge created the first inspectorate of labor and imposed restrictions on child labor.

4. In 1880, Drahomanov became one of the earliest proponents of a specifically Jewish socialist party (Rudnytsky [1969] 1987, p. 289). According to David Zaslavsky, Drahomanov's Bolshevik-era biographer: "It would be impossible to formulate more clearly and precisely the tasks which subsequently became the foundation of the first Jewish labor groups, and still later of the Bund, and of the other socialist and communist organizations working among the Jewish proletariat" (1924, pp. 112–113, cited by Rudnytsky, op. cit., p. 291).

5. "Mykola Ziber" is the Ukrainian spelling of the Russo-German "Nikolai Sieber."

6. See Kovalevskii's memoir in the anonymously edited collection *Reminiscences of Marx and Engels*, Foreign Languages Publishing House, Moscow, no date, p. 293.

7. See especially the implications of his quasi-probabilistic argument, derived from Quetelet and discussed by Scazzieri (29–32), about the law-like tendencies of aggregate social phenomena, including the division of labor.

8. Skvortsov sounds remarkably like Sieber in his 1890 book, *The Influence of Steam Transport on Agriculture*, as paraphrased by Richard Pipes (1970, p. 62).

9. See, e.g., Bulgakov's attacks on Marx's "statistical" reasoning, in which Bulgakov focuses not on passages from Marx but, rather, on passages from Quetelet cited by Sieber! (Bulgakov [1913] 2000, pp. 236, 250–252, 322–323, etc.).

10. Sieber, Mikhailovskii claimed, often hid "behind the authority of the immutable and unquestionable tripartite dialectical development" (as cited by Plekhanov [1895] 1974, p. 612). Plekhanov, praising Sieber's "very weighty fund of knowledge," called him "a serious scientist" whose work on primitive economic culture had demonstrated "with the utmost clarity that modes of appropriation are determined by modes of production" (ibid., pp. 801–802, 672).

11. Similarly, in *Zur Kritik der politischen Oekonomie*, Marx had waxed ironic about the "fetishism of German 'thinkers' who assert that 'material' and half a dozen similar irrelevancies are elements of value" ([1859] 1970, p. 35). In this connection Marx singled out Lorenz Stein in particular, who writes, he says, "*con amore about use-values*" ([1859] 1970, p. 28).

12. Even Chicherin's biographers, who generally praise his views, tend to recognize the weakness of this particular foray into political economy. "Of the large corpus of Chicherin's works, this deserves least to be remembered," one concludes, "for Chicherin, a great historian and jurist, always remained a dilettante in economic theory" (Hammer, 1962, p. 242). Eliot Benowitz concurs: "Chicherin's critique of Marx was indeed not very deep . . ." (1966, p. 282).

13. Chicherin, like Roscher, claims that, for Marx, the identity of value and labor is simply "taken as a given." Marx just finds this conclusion "convenient," Chicherin reports: "Let the reader look through all 822 pages of Karl Marx's book; he will find no other reason" ([1878] 1998, p. 325).

14. Sieber opens his discussion of *Capital* with a close paraphrase of Chapter 1 (on the commodity) and of the *Anhang* (on the value-forms) that Marx appended to this chapter in the first edition. He follows this with a digest of Chapters 2 and 3 (on exchange and money). In all, Sieber summarizes Marx's arguments about the dual nature of the commodity (pp. 7–12); the dual nature of commodity-producing labor (pp. 13–18); the "appearance-forms" of value (pp. 49–51, 19, 55–57, 63–70); and commodity fetishism (pp. 35–37; omitting pp. 38–40). He briefly digests Chapter 2 ([1867] 1976c, pp. 182–186) and Chapter 3 as well ([1867] 1976c], pp. 193, 195–197, 200–203, 207–209).

15. So, Sieber adds, "labor is [here] accorded not only the regulating role but also that of determining exchange magnitudes." Hence the error of Koropeckyj's inference (1990, p. 199) that, in contrast to Schumpeter – for whom Marx plainly represented the post-Ricardian view that labor not only regulates commodity exchange but rather is "the essence or substance of their value" – "Ziber seems to lean in the direction of Ricardo in this instance."

16. Others who have glimpsed this point include, besides Sieber and Douai (see below), Yevgenii Pashukanis (who knew Sieber's work – see Pashukanis [1924] 1978, p. 56 n. 18), and a few others. See Smith (1988) for details.

17. Sieber's version of this point is simpler in form, but identical in content. Interestingly, in his digest of Chapter 3, Sieber develops a related point vis-à-vis the weaver's relationship to money (cf. Marx [1867] 1976c, p. 207).

18. Another half-forgotten early expositor of Marxian theory who saw value in this light was Adolf Douai (Douai, 1876). Marx, in 1877, agreed to let Douai translate *Capital* into English, but the translation ultimately fell through – and Douai's connection to *Capital* has subsequently gone unnoticed. More typical, unfortunately, is Lucio Colletti, who was among the few contemporary theorists to see the semiotic implications of value theory. When this became fully clear to him, Colletti broke with Marx, unwilling to accept what he perceived as the dilution of Marx's pure "scientificity" by a subjectivist theory of *mentalités*. See, for details, Jay (1984).

19. It is notable, given the salience of this theme in Sieber's work, that Marx, in his critique of Wagner, specifically praised Sieber's insight into the relationship between value, value-magnitudes, and money.

ACKNOWLEDGMENTS

Librarians who helped track down the various editions of Sieber's 1871 dissertation include Mieke IJzermans of the International Institute for Social History in Amsterdam, Michael C. Stowell and June Pachuta of the University of Illinois at Urbana-Champaign, and Michael Jackson of the University of California-Riverside. Also deserving warm thanks, for translating Chapter 4 of this dissertation ("Marx's Theory of Value and Money," in this volume), are James D. White and Rakhiya Mananova. Other translation help was provided by Lioudmila Abramova and Bill Bennetts.

REFERENCES

Ascher, A. (1972). *Pavel Axelrod and the Development of Menshevism.* Cambridge MA: Harvard.
Baron, S. H. (1963). *Plekhanov: The Father of Russian Marxism.* Stanford CA: Stanford.
Benowitz, E. (1966). B. N. Chicherin. Ph.D thesis, University of Wisconsin.
Benson, S. (1968). Boris Chicherin and the Dilemma of Russian Liberalism. Ph.D thesis, Harvard University.
Billington, J. H. (1958). *Mikhailovsky and Russian Populism.* Oxford: Clarendon.
Boll, M. M. (1970). The Social and Political Philosophy of Semen L. Frank. Ph.D thesis, University of Wisconsin.
Bukharin, N. (1925. *Historical Materialism* (3rd ed.). New York: International.
Bulgakov, S. ([1913] 2000). *Philosophy of Economy.* New Haven and London: Yale.
Chicherin, B. N. ([1878] 1998). Marx. In: G. M. Hamburg (Ed.), *Liberty, Equality, and the Market: Essays by B. N. Chicherin* (pp. 321–350). Originally: Chicherin, B. N. Nemetskie sotsialisty. 2. Karl Marks. In: V. P. Bezobrazov (Ed.), *Sbornik gosudarstvennykh znanii, 6* (pp. 1–39).
Chicherin, B. N. ([1882–1883] 1998). Capitalism and Socialism. In: G. M. Hamburg (Ed.), *Liberty, Equality, and the Market: Essays by B. N. Chicherin* (pp. 406–424).
Chicherin, B. N. (1882–1883). *Sobstvennost' i gosudarstvo,* Vols. 1 & 2. Moscow: Tip. Martynova.
Dan, T. (Fedor Dan) ([1946] 1970). *The Origins of Bolshevism.* New York: Schocken.
Douai, A. (1876). Karl Marx's Capital. In: *The Socialist* (issues 7–17, May 27–August 5).
Drahomanov, M. ([1884] 1996). Draft Constitution for the Ukrainian Society in the Free Union. In: R. Lindheim & G. S. N. Luckyj (Eds), *Towards an Intellectual History of Ukraine* (pp. 171–183). Toronto: University of Toronto Press.
Evtuhov, C. (1997). *The Cross and the Sickle: Sergei Bulgakov and the Fate of Russian Religious Philosophy.* Ithaca and London: Cornell.
Evtuhov, C. (2000). Introduction. In: S. Bulgakov, *Philosophy of Economy* (pp. 1–34). New Haven and London: Yale.
Geierhos, W. (1977). *Vera Zasulic und die russische revolutionäre Bewegung.* Munich and Vienna: R. Oldenbourg.
Hammer, D. P. (1962). Two Russian Liberals. Ph.D thesis, Columbia University.
Hasegawa, N. B. (1972). Russian Liberals at the Crossroads, 1878–1883. Ph.D. thesis, University of Washington.
Hildebrand, B. (1848). *Die Nationalökonomie der Gegenwart und Zukunft,* Vol. 1. Frankfurt: J. Rutten.
Horkina, L. P. (1994). *Narysy z istoriï politychnoï ekonomiï v Ukraïni.* Kiev: Naukova dumka.
Jay, M. (1984). *Marxism and Totality.* Berkeley and Los Angeles: University of California Press.
Kimball, R. A. (1967). The Early Political Career of Peter Lavrovich Lavrov. Ph.D. thesis, University of Washington.
Kleinbort, L. M. (1923). *Nikolai Ivanovich Ziber.* St. Petersburg: Kolos.

Knies, K. (1873). *Geld und Credit*. Berlin: Weidmannsche Buchhandlung.

Koropeckyj, I. S. (1984). Academic Economics in the Nineteenth-Century Ukraine. In: I. S. Koropeckyj (Ed.), *Selected Contributions of Ukrainian Scholars to Economics* (pp. 163–222). Cambridge MA: Harvard Ukrainian Research Institute and Harvard University Press.

Koropeckyj, I. S. (1990). *Development in the Shadow: Studies in Ukrainian Economics*. Edmonton: Canadian Institute of Ukrainian Studies Press and University of Alberta (the 1984 essay is reprinted pp. 163–216).

Lenin, V. I. ([1897/1908] 1960). A Characterization of Economic Romanticism (rev. 2nd ed.). In: V. I. Lenin, *Collected Works*, Vol. 2: *1895–1897* (pp. 129–265). Moscow: Foreign Languages Publishing House.

Lindheim, R., & Luckyj, G. S. N. (Eds) (1996). *Towards an Intellectual History of Ukraine*. Toronto: University of Toronto Press.

Marx, K. ([1859] 1970). *A Contribution to the Critique of Political Economy*. Moscow: Progress.

Marx, K. ([1867] 1976a). The Commodity. In: A. Dragstedt (Ed.), *Value: Studies by Karl Marx* (pp. 7–40). London: New Park.

Marx, K. ([1867] 1976b). The Form of Value. In: A. Dragstedt (Ed.), *Value: Studies by Karl Marx* (pp. 49–70). London: New Park.

Marx, K. ([1867] 1976c). *Capital*, Vol. 1, translated from the fourth German edition, edited by Friedrich Engels. London: Penguin and New Left Review.

Marx, K. ([1873] 1976). Postface to the second German edition of Capital. In: K. Marx, ([1867] 1976c). *Capital*, Vol. 1, translated from the fourth edition, edited by Friedrich Engels. London: Penguin and New Left Review.

Marx, K. ([1879–1880] 1976). Marginal Notes on Wagner. In: A. Dragstedt (Ed.), *Value: Studies by Karl Marx* (pp. 201–229). London: New Park.

Marx, K. ([1879–1882] 2002). *Patriarchy and Property: The Ethnological Notebooks of Karl Marx*, edited by D. N. Smith. New Haven and London: Yale, forthcoming.

Marx, K. ([1881] 1983). Drafts of a Reply. In: T. Shanin (Ed.), *Late Marx and the Russian Road* (pp. 99–123). New York: Monthly Review.

Marx, K. ([1883] 1967). *Capital*, Vol. 1, translated from the third German edition, edited by Friedrich Engels. New York: International.

Meijer, J. M. (1955). *Knowledge and Revolution*. Assen: Van Gorcum.

Mikhailovskii, N. ([1892] 1900). *Literaturnye Vospominaniia i Sovremennaia Smuta*, Vol. 1. St. Petersburg.

Offord, D. (1986). *The Russian Revolutionary Movement in the 1880s*. Cambridge and New York: Cambridge.

Pashukanis, Y. ([1924] 1978). *Law and Marxism*. London: Ink Links.

Pipes, R. (1970). *Struve: Liberal on the Left, 1870–1905*. Cambridge MA: Harvard.

Plekhanov, G. V. ([1895] 1974). The Development of the Monist View of History. In: G. V. Plekhanov, *Selected Philosophical Works* (pp. 542–826). Vol. 1. Moscow: Foreign Languages Publishing House.

Quadrio-Curzio, A. (1986). Technological Scarcity. In: M. Baranzini, R. Scazzieri (Eds), *Foundations of Economics* (pp. 311–338). Oxford: Blackwell.

Resis, A. (1970). *Das Kapital* Comes to Russia. *Slavic Review*, 29(2), 219–237.

Reuel', A. L. (1937). Ziber kak ekonomist. In: N. I. Ziber ([1885] 1937), *David Rikardo i Karl Marks v ikh obshchesstvenno-ekonomicheskikh issledovaniiakh*. Moscow: Sotsekgiz.

Reuel', A. L. (1956). *Russkaia ekonomicheskaia mysl' 60–70-kh godov XIX veka I marksizm*. Moscow: Sotsekgiz.

Roscher, W. (1878a). *Principles of Political Economy*, Vol. 1 (13th ed.). Chicago: Callaghan.

Roscher, W. (1878b). *Principles of Political Economy*, Vol. 2 (13th ed.). Chicago: Callaghan.

Rudnytsky, I. L. ([1952] 1987). Drahomanov as a Political Theorist. In: I. L. Rudnytsky, *Essays in Modern Ukrainian History* (pp. 203–253). Cambridge: Harvard Ukrainian Research Institute.

Rudnytsky, I. L. ([1958] 1987). The Intellectual Origins of Modern Ukraine. In: I. L. Rudnytsky, *Essays in Modern Ukrainian History* (pp. 123–141). Cambridge: Harvard Ukrainian Research Institute.

Rudnytsky, I. L. ([1969] 1987). Mykhailo Drahomanov and the Problem of Ukrainian-Jewish Relations. In: I. L. Rudnytsky, *Essays in Modern Ukrainian History* (pp. 283–297). Cambridge: Harvard Ukrainian Research Institute.

Rusov, A. A., & Volkov, F. (1907). Primechaniia. *Byloe*, *6*(18), June.

Sapitsky, V. (1929). Do istorii ekonomichnoi dumky na Ukraini (Mykola Ziber). *Zapysky Ukrains'koi Hospodarskoi Akademii v Chekhoslovatskii Respublitsi*, Vol. 2.

Scazzieri, R. (1987). Ziber on Ricardo. *Contributions to Political Economy*, *6*, 25–44.

Schapiro, L. (1967). *Rationalism and Nationalism in Russian Nineteenth-Century Political Thought*. New Haven: Yale.

Smith, D. N. (1988). Authorities, Deities, and Commodities: The Problem of Domination in Classical Sociology. Ph.D. thesis, University of Wisconsin.

Uroeva, A. (1969). *For All Men and All Times*. Moscow: Progress.

Walicki, A. (1979). *A History of Russian Thought from the Enlightenment to Marxism*. Stanford, CA: Stanford.

White, J. D. (1996). *Karl Marx and the Intellectual Origins of Dialectical Materialism*. New York: St. Martin's.

White, J. D. (2001). Nikolai Sieber and Karl Marx. In: *Research in Political Economy*, *19* (above).

Williams, R. (1999). General Introduction. In: R. Williams (Ed.), *Sergii Bulgakov: Towards a Russian Political Theology* (pp. 1–20). Edinburgh: T & T Clark.

Zaslavsky, D. (1924). *Mikhail Petrovich Dragomanov: kritiko-biograficheskii ocherk*. Kiev.

Zasulich, V. ([1881] 1983). A Letter to Marx. In: T. Shanin (Ed.), *Late Marx and the Russian Road* (pp. 98–99). New York: Monthly Review.

Zhukovskii, Y. G. (1877). Karl Marks i ego kniga o kapitale. *Vestnik Europy*, *5*.

Ziber, N. I. (Ed.) (1873). Rikardo, D., Nachala politischeskoi ekonomii [Principles of political economy, Part 1]. *Universitetskiia Izviestiia*, *13*, Nos. 1–10 (Kiev Universitet).

Ziber, N. I. (Ed.) (1882). *Sochineniia Davida Rikardo* [David Ricardo's Works, with editorial commentary]. St. Petersburg.

Ziber, N. I. (1869). *Potrebitel'nyia obshchestva* [Cooperative communities]. Kiev.

Ziber, N. I. (1870). K Ucheniiu o rentie [For the study of rent]. *Universitetskiia Izviestiia*, *10*, Nos. 5–6 (Kiev Universitet).

Ziber, N. I. (1871). Teoriia tsennosti i kapitala D. Rikardo, v sviazh s pozdnieishimi dopolneniiami i raz'iasneniiami [D. Ricardo's theory of value and capital, in relation to the latest additions and clarifications]. *Universitetskiia Izviestiia*, *11*, Nos. 1–2, 4–11 (Kiev Universitet).

Ziber, N. I. ([1871] 2001). Marx's Theory of Value and Money. In: *Research in Political Economy*, *19* (above).

Ziber, N. I. (1873b). Zhizn i trudy Davida Rikardo [The life and works of David Ricardo]. *Universitetskiia Izviestiia*, *13*, No. 9 (Kiev Universitet).

Ziber, N. I. (1874). Chto takoe statistika [What is statistics?]. *Znanie*, *8*.

Ziber, N. I. (1875a). Tsiena truda [Cost of labor]. *Universitetskiia Izviestiia*, *15*, No. 2 (Kiev Universitet).

Ziber, N. I. (1875b). *Opyt programmy diia sobiraniia statistike-ekonomicheskich sviedienii* [Towards a program for the collection of statistical-economic data]. Kiev.

Ziber, N. I. (1876–1878). Ekonomicheskaia teoriia Karla Marksa [Karl Marx's economic theory]. *Znanie* (1876, Nos. 10, 12; 1877, No. 2); *Slovo* (1878, Nos. 1, 3, 9, 12).

Ziber, N. I. (1876a). Berlinski griundery ikh moshennichestva [Berlin's entrepreneurs and their deceptions]. *Znanie*, No. 9.

Ziber, N. I. (1876b). Materialy dlia nabliundeniia nad obshchestvenno-ekonomicheskogo zhizniiu russkago goroda [Materials for the observation of the communal-economic life of the Russian people]. *Znanie*, Nos. 3–4.

Ziber, N. I. (1877a). Novieshee fabrichnoe zakonodatel'sto Belikobritani [The latest factory legislation in Great Britain]. *Otechestvennye Zapiski*, Nos. 1, 4, 5.

Ziber, N. I. (1877b). Nieskolko zamiechanii po povodu stat'i Yu. Zhukavskago: 'K. Marksa i ego kniga o kapitale' [Some observations on the publication of Yurii Zhukovskii's article 'Karl Marx and his volume on capital']. *Otechestvennye Zapiski*, No. 11.

Ziber, N. I. (1878a). Obshchinno-pozemel'nyia otnosheniia vladiel'cheskikh krest'ian El'zasa v srednie vieka [Community relationships and land among the peasant proprietors of Alsace in the Middle Ages]. *Otechestvennye Zapiski*, Nos. 1, 4–5.

Ziber, N. I. (1878b). B. Chicherina contra K. Marksa. [B. Chicherin vs. K. Marx]. *Slovo*, No. 2.

Ziber, N. I. (1878c). F. Lassal skvoz ochki g. B. Chicherina [F. Lassalle in B. Chicherin's eyes]. *Slovo*, No. 4.

Ziber, N. I. (1879–1880). Mysli ob otnoshenii meshdy obshch estvennoiu ekonomici i pravom [On the relationship between general economics and law]. *Slovo* (1879, No. 2; 1880, No. 6).

Ziber, N. I. (1879a). Dialektika v eia primienenii k naukie [Dialectics and its application to science]. *Slovo*, No. 11.

Ziber, N. I. (1879a). Fiasko national'nago liberalizma [The fiasco of liberal nationalism]. *Slovo*, No. 9.

Ziber, N. I. (1880). Zemledielie v Soediniennykh Statatakh Siervernoi Ameriki [Agriculture in the United States of Northern America]. *Otechestvennye Zapiski*, No. 11.

Ziber, N. I. (1881a). Obshchinai gosudarstvo v Niderlandskoi Indii [Community and State in the Dutch Indies]. *Otechestvennye Zapiski*, No. 3.

Ziber, N. I. (1881b). Istoriia Shveitsarkoi Al'mendy [History of the Swiss almende]. *Vestnik Europy*, No. 10.

Ziber, N. I. (1882a). Khod vsemirnage khoiziaistva v posliodnee 10-tilietie [The movement of the world economy in the past 10 years]. *Russkaya Mysl*, No. 6.

Ziber, N. I. (1882b). Sud'ba obshchinnago vladieniia v Shveitsarii [The future of communal property in Switzerland]. *Vestnik Europy*, No. 7.

Ziber, N. I. (1882c). Novii trud o pervobitnikh Uchrezhdeniiakh [New work on primitive institutions]. *Otechestvennye Zapiski*, No. 7.

Ziber, N. I. ([1883] 1959). *Ocherki pervobytnoi ekonomicheskoi kult'ury* [Outlines of primitive economic culture]. First published in 1883 by Izd. K. T. Soldatenkova, Moscow, and reprinted as Vol. 2 of Ziber, N. I., *Izbrannye ekonomicheskie proizvedenniia*, Sotsekgiz, Moscow.

Ziber, N. I. (1883a). O vliianii progressa na biednost [The influence of progress on poverty]. *Russkaia Mysl*, No. 6.

Ziber, N. I. (1883b). Raspredielenie pozemed'noi sobstvennosti v Germanii [Property distribution in Germany]. *Russkaia Mysl*, Nos. 1–2.

Ziber, N. I. (1883c). Obshchestvennaia ekonomiia i pravo [General economics and law]. *Yuridicheskii Vestnik*, Nos. 5, 9, 10.

Ziber, N. I. (1885). *David Rikardo i Karl Marks v ikh obshchestvenno-ekonomicheskikh isliedovani-iakh* [David Ricardo and Karl Marx in their socio-economic investigations]. St. Petersburg: Tip. M. M. Stasiulevicha. Reprinted in 1937 in Moscow by Sotsekgiz.

Ziber, N. I. (1900). *Sobranie sochinenii*, Vols. 1 & 2. St. Petersburg: Izdatel.

Ziber, N. I. (1959). *Izbrannye ekonomicheskie proizvedeniia*, Vols. 1 & 2. Moscow: Sotsekgiz.

PART II.

POLITICAL ECONOMY OF CAPITALISM AND OF A SOCIALIST ALTERNATIVE

CAPITAL ACCUMULATION AND THE COMPOSITION OF CAPITAL

Alfredo Saad-Filho

ABSTRACT

This paper reviews the Marxian concept of capital accumulation in the light of Paul Zarembka's (2000) recent contribution, taking into consideration the concepts of competition and composition of capital. It shows that accumulation is best understood through a class analysis. However, the capital relation is influential at different levels and it encompasses a broad range of features of modern society. In this context, this paper proposes a richer and more encompassing analysis of accumulation.

In the latest issue of *Research in Political Economy*, Paul Zarembka (2000) published an important contribution to the analysis of capital accumulation. In his article, Zarembka shows the potential ambiguities in Marx's texts, discusses their implications, and reviews the debates between Lenin, Bukharin, Luxemburg, Grossman and others.[1] The full implications of Zarembka's article cannot be pursued here. In what follows, I offer a modest contribution to his analysis, incorporating a more detailed analysis of the composition of capital and a broader understanding of accumulation.

The composition of capital (including the technical, organic and value compositions, or TCC, OCC and VCC) is highly important for Marx, and it plays an important role at several stages in his analysis. For example, the OCC

Marx's *Capital* and Capitalism; Markets in a Socialist Alternative,
Research in Political Economy, Volume 19, pages 69–85.
Copyright © 2001 by Elsevier Science Ltd.
All rights of reproduction in any form reserved.
ISBN: 0-7623-0838-9

is famously the pivot of the transformation problem and the tendency of the rate of profit to fall,[2] and it plays a critical role in Marx's theory of rent,[3] and in his analysis of technical change and capital accumulation (see below). In spite of the importance of this concept, the composition of capital has often been explained cursorily and understood only superficially and incorrectly in most of the literature.

This article shows that a clearer understanding of the composition of capital can help to substantiate and contextualise some of Zarembka's claims, and contribute to the development of Marx's theory of value, exploitation and capital accumulation. The argument is developed in four sections. The first briefly reviews the Marxian concepts of capital and exploitation. The second explains the meaning and significance of the TCC, OCC and VCC in the simplest (static) case, for heuristic purposes, and in the dynamic context, more relevant for our purposes. The third analyses in more detail the relationship between capital accumulation and changes in the technical, organic and value compositions of capital. The fourth section summarises the argument and draws brief conclusions.

I. CAPITAL AND EXPLOITATION

I.A. Capital and Wage Labour

For Marx, capital is a social relation between two classes, capitalists and workers. This relation is established when the means of production are monopolised by the capitalists, that employ wage workers in production for profit. Once this class relation of production is posited, capital exists in and through things, namely, the means of production, commodities, money and financial assets employed in the process of valorisation:

> Capital is not a *thing*, any more than money is a *thing*. In capital, as in money, certain *specific social relations of production between people* appear as *relations of things to people*, or else certain social relations appear as the *natural properties of things in society* ... Capital and wage-labour ... only express two aspects of the self-same relationship. Money cannot become capital unless it is exchanged for labour-power ... Conversely, work can only be wage-labour when its *own* material conditions confront it as autonomous powers, alien property, value existing for itself and maintaining itself, in short as capital ... Wage-labour is then a necessary condition for the formation of capital and remains the essential prerequisite of capitalist production (*Capital*, *1*, pp. 1005–1006).[4]

There is a relationship of mutual implication between capitalism (the mode of social production), wage labour (the form of social labour), and the commodity (the typical form of the output):

[The] relation between generalised commodity production [GCP] ... wage labor and capitalist production is one of reciprocal implication. First ... when labor becomes wage labor ... commodity production is generalised. On the one hand wage labor implies GCP ... On the other hand, GCP implies wage labor ... Marx shows ... that capitalist production is commodity production as the general form of production while, at the same time, emphasizing that it is only on the basis of the capitalist mode of production that all or even the majority of products of labor assume commodity form ... Finally, the relation of wage labor and capital is also one of reciprocal implication for Marx. Capital is a production relation between the immediate producers and their conditions of production which, separated from them and passing under the control of non (immediate) producers, dominate them as capital ... [T]he rest of the features of capitalism could be seen as the necessary resultants following from any one of these essentially equivalent central categories (Chattopadhyay, 1994, pp. 17–18).

As a totality engaged in self-expansion through the employment of wage labour, capital is primarily *capital in general*. This is the general form of capital.[5] Capital in general can be represented by the circuit of industrial capital, M-C-M', where M and M' are sums of money-capital and C represents the inputs, including labour power and means of production; the difference between M' and M is the surplus value.

The circuit of industrial capital represents the essence of capital, valorisation through the production of commodities by wage labour. However, capital produces not only surplus value; at the social level, the outcome of the circuit is the *expanded reproduction* of capital or, following from the concept of capital, the renewal of the separation between capitalists and wage workers. For this reason, Marx claimed that 'Accumulation of capital is ... multiplication of the proletariat' (*Capital, 1*, p. 764). In other words,

The capitalist process of production ... seen as a total, connected process, i.e. a process of reproduction, produces not only commodities, not only surplus-value, but it also produces and reproduces the capital-relation itself; on the one hand the capitalist, on the other the wage-labourer (*Capital, 1*, p. 724).

I.B. Exploitation

The capital relation implies that the means of production have been monopolised by a relatively small number of people. In contrast, the majority is forced to sell their labour power in order to purchase commodities that, as a class, they have produced previously (see *Theories of Surplus Value, 3*, pp. 490–491). Therefore, capital is a *class relation of exploitation*, which allows capitalists to live off the surplus value extracted from the working class:

Capitalism, and hence capital, requires a lot more by way of the social than private property and the market ... What it does depend upon is wage labour, able and willing to produce a surplus for capital. By implication, the social attached to capital takes the form of class relations ... Capital and labour confront one another as classes with the capitalist class monopolising the means of production or access to livelihood through work. Consequently, workers can only survive by selling their capacity to work for a wage that represents less in terms of labour time than is performed for the capitalist. The surplus labour performed over and above that necessary to provide the wage gives rise to what Marx termed exploitation, and provides for the profits of the capitalists (Fine, 2001, p. 29).

For Marx, the defining feature of capitalism is the exploitation of the class of wage workers by the capitalist class, through the extraction of surplus value.[6] The ratio between the surplus value (surplus labour time) and the value of labour power (necessary labour time) is the rate of exploitation or rate of surplus value. All else constant, the rate of exploitation can increase for at least three reasons: if more hours are worked, if the intensity of labour increases, or if the necessary labour time declines because of productivity growth in the sectors producing necessities (given the real wage). Marx calls the first two cases the production of *absolute surplus value*, while the third produces *relative surplus value* (see *Capital*, *1*, pp. 430–437, 645–646; *Theories of Surplus Value*, *1*, p. 216; Foley, 1986, pp. 50–54; Lapides, 1998, p. 192). Absolute surplus value is generally limited, because it is impossible to increase the working day or the intensity of labour indefinitely, and the workers gradually learn to resist against these forms of exploitation. In contrast, relative surplus value is more flexible and harder to resist, because productivity growth can outstrip wage increases for long periods.

I.C. Competition, Mechanisation, and Class Conflict

Intra-sectoral competition, between firms producing the same use-values, compels each firm to minimise costs in order to maximise its profit rate. This type of competition may be associated with different firm strategies. For example, a longer working day increases the output and may reduce unit costs, because the transfers from fixed capital are spread across larger batches, and there is a reduced risk of technical obsolescence (that Marx called moral depreciation) because the machines depreciate physically more quickly. In contrast, greater labour intensity increases the output, because *more* simple labour is performed in the same period, but this does not affect directly the unit value of the product. Finally, technical progress reduces the simple labour necessary to produce a unit of the product and, consequently, tends to lower its value:

Production for value and surplus-value involves a constantly operating tendency ... to reduce the labour-time needed to produce a commodity, i.e. to reduce the commodity's value, below the existing social average at any given time. The pressure to reduce the cost price to its minimum becomes the strongest lever for raising the social productivity of labour, though this appears here simply as a constant increase in the productivity of capital (*Capital*, *3*, p. 1021).

These technical innovations will be copied or emulated by the rival firms. This process continually erodes the advantage of the innovating firms, while preserving the incentives for further technical progress across the economy. At the level of capital in general, competition and technical change constantly reduce the value of all goods, including those consumed by the workers. All else constant, they permit the extraction of relative surplus value:

Capital therefore has an immanent drive, and a constant tendency, towards increasing the productivity of labour, in order to cheapen commodities and, by cheapening commodities, to cheapen the worker himself (*Capital*, *1*, pp. 436–437).

The most important aspect of intra-sectoral competition is *mechanisation*, or the introduction of new technologies and new machines by the innovating firms. Mechanisation has three principal aspects, two of which were discussed above; it increases the value-productivity of labour and the profit rate of the innovating capitals, facilitates the extraction of relative surplus value and, finally, it is a tool of capitalist control. The Marxian critique of technology has demonstrated that, underneath their seemingly neutral, scientific and productivist (of use value) guise, machines are despotic dictators of the rhythm and content of the labour process.[7] Therefore, in spite of the perception that competition invariably increases physical productivity, reduces commodity values and potentially leads to higher real wages, the relationship between competition and machinery is complicated by two factors. First, firms do not select the technologies that are most productive of use values, but those that are most profitable, and these criteria may lead to distinct outcomes. Second, capitalist attempts to establish control in the production line and in society may introduce further biases in the choice of technology, including the adoption of technologies that are not *prima facie* more profitable, but that facilitate control (see Levidow & Young, 1981, 1985; Slater, 1980). In sum, conflicts between competing capitals, between capital and labour on the shopfloor, and between social groups across society, can influence the choice of technology and the output mix, with consequences that cannot always be anticipated.

II. COMPOSITION OF CAPITAL AND ACCUMULATION

A review of the literature shows very diverse understandings of Marx's concept of composition of capital. Most writers fail to distinguish between the TCC,

OCC and VCC and, when attempting to do so, their views are often distinct from Marx's (for a survey of the understandings of the composition of capital, see Saad-Filho, 1993, 2002, Ch. 6). This section outlines the meaning and significance of the composition of capital; their implications for the study of accumulation are explained in Section III.B.

II.A. Static Case

(i) Productivity of Labour and TCC

The productivity of labour is the mass of means of production that can be processed into final commodities in a given labour time or, alternatively, the output per hour.[8] This notion is captured by the *technical composition of capital* (TCC, which Marx called earlier the physical composition of capital). The TCC is the ratio between the mass of material inputs and the living labour necessary to transform them into the output:

> A certain quantity of labour-power, represented by a certain number of workers, is required to produce a certain volume of products in a day, for example, and this involves putting a certain definite mass of means of production in motion and consuming them productively – machines, raw materials etc ... This proportion constitutes the technical composition of capital, and is the actual basis of its organic composition (*Capital*, 3, p. 244; see also *Theories of Surplus Value*, 2, pp. 455–456).

(ii) The OCC

The TCC is the ratio between a heterogeneous bundle of use values and concrete (even if average) labour; therefore, in most cases it cannot be measured directly, or contrasted across firms with distinct technologies or producing different goods. However, the TCC can be assessed in value terms, which defines the *organic composition of capital* (OCC). The OCC is a 'technological composition' that synthesises, in value terms, the technical relations of production. More specifically, the OCC is the value of the means of production (including fixed and circulating capital) that absorb one hour of living labour (whether paid or unpaid) in a given firm, industry or economy (see *Theories of Surplus Value*, 2, pp. 276, 279; *Theories of Surplus Value*, 3, pp. 382, 387).

There is, however, a severe difficulty with this concept. The value of a bundle of means of production is the product of the values of its components by the quantities used up. Therefore, it is impossible to tell whether differences or changes in the OCC are due to differences or changes in the TCC (i.e. differences or changes in the labour productivity in *this* industry) or from differences or changes in the value of the means of production used up (that reflect the circumstances in *other* industries). However, for Marx there was no ambiguity. As the OCC is a value-reflex of the TCC, it does *not* change if the TCC is constant, whatever may happen to the value of the elements of capital:

> if one assumes that the organic composition of capitals is given and likewise the differences which arise from the differences in their organic composition, then the value ratio can change although the technological composition remains the same . . . The organic changes and those brought about by changes of value can have a similar effect on the rate of profit in certain circumstances. They differ however in the following way. If the latter are not due simply to fluctuations of market prices and are therefore not temporary, they are invariably caused by an organic change in the spheres that provide the elements of constant or of variable capital (*Theories of Surplus Value*, *3*, pp. 383–386, various paragraphs; see also *Theories of Surplus Value*, *1*, pp. 415–416; *Theories of Surplus Value*, *2*, pp. 376–377).

(iii) The VCC

In order to distinguish clearly between different technologies and the use of inputs with distinct values, Marx introduces, in *Capital*, the concept of *value composition of capital* (VCC). The VCC is the ratio between the value of the circulating part of the constant capital (including the depreciation of fixed capital) and the variable capital (paid labour) necessary to produce the output (c/v):

> The composition of capital is to be understood in a two-fold sense. As value, it is determined by the proportion in which it is divided into constant capital . . . and variable capital . . . As material, as it functions in the process of production, all capital is divided into means of production and living labour-power. This latter composition is determined by the relation between the mass of the means of production employed on the one hand, and the mass of labour necessary for their employment on the other. I call the former the value-composition, the latter the technical composition of capital. There is a close correlation between the two. To express this, I call the value-composition of capital, in so far as it is determined by its technical composition and mirrors the changes in the latter, the organic composition of capital (*Capital*, *1*, p. 762.).[9]

(iv) Implications

Marx's contrast between the OCC and VCC in the static case allows him to distinguish clearly between *technical* and *value* differences across distinct production processes. For example, if two firms use the same technology to produce different products using inputs with distinct value (e.g. copper and silver jewellery), their TCCs are obviously identical. This implies that their OCCs are also equal; however, their VCCs are different (in this case, because silver is more valuable than copper; see *Capital*, *3*, pp. 244, 900–901; *Theories of Surplus Value*, *2*, p. 289; *Theories of Surplus Value*, *3*, p. 386–387; this example is inspired by Fine, 1989, pp. 62–63). Similarly, two capitals could have equal VCCs, even if their TCCs and OCCs were different, depending upon the input values. These examples show that differences in the *value* of the

constant and variable capital consumed in distinct industries are captured by
the VCC but not the OCC; in contrast, differences in the *technologies of
production* affect the OCC but they may not be accurately reflected by the
VCC. The concept of OCC is important because it allows the study of *technical*
differences or changes (see below) in production, regardless of the corresponding value differences or changes that affect primarily the circulation of
capital, while the VCC cannot distinguish between them.

II.B. Dynamic Case

(i) TCC, OCC and VCC

It was shown in Section I.C that technical change is usually introduced in individual firms, which raises their TCCs and, consequently, their OCCs and VCCs
(although the three compositions change simultaneously in real time, in logical
terms the TCC changes first, and this shift is reflected by the OCC and, subsequently, the VCC). From the point of view of capital in general, its TCC and
OCC tend to rise in every turnover and, all else constant, commodity values
tend to fall. Because of the conflicting forces of competition, including
mechanisation and declining commodity values, the VCC of capital in general
can either rise or fall through time. The outcome depends upon the sectors
affected by technical change, the speed of the diffusion of innovations, the
structure of the systems of provision of commodities, and other factors that can
be analysed only concretely.

   In general, however, because of technical progress the values at the beginning
of the circuit ('earlier values'), at which the inputs are purchased, are higher
than those at which the output is sold ('later values'). Marx argues that the
OCC reflects the TCC at the *initial* (higher) values of the component parts of
capital, *before* the new technologies affect the value of the output, in which
case the social OCC rises in tandem with the social TCC. In contrast, the VCC
reflects the TCC at the *final* (lower) value of the elements of constant and
variable capital, determined by the modified conditions of production and newly
established in exchange (see Saad-Filho, 1993, 2002, Ch. 6). Therefore, changes
in the social VCC capture the rise in the social TCC *and* the ensuing fall in
commodity values, including those that have been used as inputs:

> This change in the technical composition of capital . . . is reflected in its value-composition
> by the increase of the constant constituent of capital at the expense of its variable constituent
> . . . However . . . this change in the composition of the value of the capital, provides only
> an approximate indication of the change in the composition of its material constituents . . .
> The reason is simple: with the increasing productivity of labour, the mass of the means of
> production consumed by labour increases, but their value in comparison with their mass

diminishes. Their value therefore rises absolutely, but not in proportion to the increase in their mass (*Capital*, *1*, pp. 773–774; see also *Capital*, *3*, pp. 317–323).

(ii) Implications

The OCC is distinguished from the VCC only through the comparison between contrasting situations. If one compares two capitals at the same moment of time, one would contrast the value of the constant capital productively consumed per hour of labour (VCC) with the mass of means of production processed in the same time (TCC and OCC). This case is important theoretically, and it was through the static comparison of capitals with distinct organic compositions that Marx developed, in Part 2 of *Capital*, 3, his transformation of values into prices of production (see Fine, 1983; Saad-Filho, 1997, 2002, Ch. 7).

In a dynamic context, both the OCC and VCC of an individual capital (or capital in general) undergoing technical change can be calculated. These compositions can diverge because the OCC is an *ex ante* evaluation of the (fixed and circulating) constant capital technically required per hour of (paid and unpaid) labour, while the VCC is the ex post ratio between the new value of the (circulating) constant and the variable capital spent in the last phase of production. Thus, the OCC is measured at the time of production, while the VCC is determined in exchange and calculated on the basis of the values newly established by the currently predominant technologies. It was in this context that Marx presented his law of the tendency of the rate of profit to fall, in Part 3 of *Capital* 3 (see Fine, 1989, Ch. 10; 1992).

More importantly, the distinction between TCC, OCC and VCC helps to illuminate the potential implications of capital accumulation. Technical change raises the TCC, the OCC and total input values (because the output increases). However, the VCC, unit output values and future input prices tend to fall. How the actual process of adjustment happens – especially for large blocs of fixed capital – is crucial, because the sudden devaluation of large masses of capital can lead to financial upheaval and crises (see Perelman, 1993, 1999).

III. ACCUMULATION AND THE COMPOSITION OF CAPITAL

III.A. Zarembka's Analysis

Zarembka argues that Marx's definition of accumulation of capital is imprecise and potentially misleading (see p. 185):[10]

Marx first seems to define accumulation to necessarily include an increase in the number of workers under the domination of capital, as both constant capital and variable capital increase. Then, accumulation seems to include a case where the number of workers stays the same or even declines. But then another passage suggests that accumulation could take place even without a change in constant capital. So, what is accumulation of capital? Could accumulation of capital ... be simply $c+v$ increasing with the proportions between c and v unimportant for the definition? ... Most importantly, is it consistent with the very concept of "capital" in Marx? These questions are unresolved in Marx's writing and became an ambiguity embedded in twentieth-century Marxism (pp. 196–197).

The concept of capital, for Zarembka, is that explained in Section I, i.e. the relationship between the capitalist class and the class of wage-laborers (see pp. 184–185). In the light of this (*class*, rather than merely technical, productivist or monetary) concept of capital, Zarembka argues (p. 185) that accumulation has been confused in the Marxian tradition with issues surrounding the organic composition of capital:

> It has been a virtual dogma within Marxism for a century that, as accumulation takes place, the ratio of constant capital to variable capital rises, i.e. the "organic composition of capital" c/v rises ... Yet [for Marx] ... the opposite can occur ... **constant capital may not rise at all – or less than variable capital – as accumulation occurs** (pp. 195–196).

For Zarembka, the debate about the relationship between capital accumulation and the growth in constant capital is misplaced and potentially misleading:

> **the essential factor of accumulation of capital is the increase in wage-labor**, not an increase in constant capital. Note [Marx's] reference to either "more capitalists" or "larger capitalists", but when the issue comes to labor it is simply "more wage-workers" – only the number is important (p. 192).

Given his focus upon the class relation between capitalists and workers, rather than the rising quantity of machines, output or money-capital, Zarembka offers the following definition:

> "accumulation of capital is increase of proletarian labor with its associated constant capital" or, in more modern language, "**accumulation of capital is increase of wage-labor with its associated constant capital**". Accumulation will generally include additional constant capital. If the process of accumulation of capital is related to the production of relative surplus value (i.e. technological improvements), as is typically the case, it should be discussed as such. Whether the organic composition of capital also increases is not directly germane to the issue if and how much capital is accumulating ... if there is no increase in wage-labor, there is no accumulation ... As to increased wage-labor, it can come from:
>
> (1) longer work hours,
> (2) population increase, and
> (3) new proletarianizations concomitant with creation of home markets and markets abroad, including drawing in of new sections of the population such as women and children ...
>
> The definition of accumulation offered here leads to the deepest issues of Marxist thought, the relations and struggles between and among social classes ... It focuses the question to the class issues and away from production or from productivity (pp. 223–224).

III.B. Accumulation, Class, and the Composition of Capital

The class interpretation of capital, explained in section I.A, is the premise of Zarembka's definition of accumulation. This section shows that the analysis of exploitation and competition, in Sections I.B and I.C, and the distinction between TCC, OCC and VCC, explained in Section II, can contribute to a more precise analysis, that enriches our understanding of capital accumulation and contextualises Zarembka's approach. The close relationship between the composition of capital and accumulation is not surprising, for Marx analyses both simultaneously, most clearly in chapter 25 of *Capital, 1*.

It was shown in Section I.A that capital is a class relation that appears through the transformation of goods, services, machines, money, financial assets and labour power into means of valorisation, M-C-M'. The distinction between the essence of capital and its forms of appearance opens the possibility of ambiguity in the definition of accumulation; for example, Zarembka shows that accumulation has been understood in different ways in the Marxian literature, with potentially important consequences.[11] Definitions of accumulation can focus upon the growth of output, money capital advanced, labour productivity or means of production in use (either more or better machines), or upon the growth of labour productivity or employment (Zarembka's own definition). Moreover, these distinct understandings of accumulation can refer to individual capitals or to capital as a whole, depending upon the level of analysis.

Whatever its definition, accumulation is closely related with competition and crisis. Competition forces capitals to maximise profits, which provide the resources for investment and growth; however, competitive pressures give rise to crisis tendencies that can lead to disastrous outcomes, especially bankruptcies, economic depression and high unemployment (see Clarke, 1994). These relations explain Marx's claim that 'the employment of surplus-value as capital, or its reconversion into capital, is called accumulation of capital' (*Capital, 1*, p. 725). Reconversion of surplus value into capital, or expanded reproduction, can occur under two circumstances, extended expanded reproduction, or intensified expanded reproduction (Fine & Harris, 1979, pp. 112–115). The former is associated with the replication of current technologies, or output growth with constant productivity, while the latter explains output growth through productivity increase.

(1) Extended Expanded Reproduction:

(1a) Growth in the quantity of means of production: For the individual capital, increasing the quantity of means of production (machines) replicating the same

technology increases the number of employees, total output and the profit mass, while the TCC, OCC and VCC, the productivity of labour and the rate of profit remain constant. The outcome is identical for capital as a whole, and commodity values remain unchanged.

(1b) Growth in the quantity of simple labour employed: Three possibilities exist:

 (i) Employment growth due to an increase in the quantity of means of production, as in scenario 1a.
 (ii) Employment growth due to an increase in the number of hours worked (absolute surplus value); in this case, for the individual capital, the TCC, OCC and labour productivity remain constant, but the VCC declines and the output and the rate of profit increase because of the decline in average fixed costs. The same is the case for capital as a whole; values may decline due to the lower input values.
(iii) Employment growth due to the substitution of labour for machines: for the individual capital, the TCC, OCC and VCC decline, with uncertain consequences for productivity, output and profit rate. It is the same for capital as a whole, and values may or may not change. The general rate of profit, in principle, rises (more living labour produces more surplus value).

(2) Intensified Expanded Reproduction:

(2a) Rising productivity of labour, given the stock of machines (higher intensity of labour or better training of the workforce): the TCC and OCC remain constant but the VCC declines and labour productivity increase (given the wage rate) because *more* simple labour is condensed in each hour of concrete labour. Therefore, the output and the profit rate of the individual capital increase (absolute surplus value). For capital as a whole, commodity values decline because 'simple' labour becomes more productive.

(2b) Rising efficiency of the means of production (better machines with given employment of labour): in general the TCC, OCC and VCC, labour productivity, output and the profit rate increase, with falling unit costs (unless new machines are introduced because of control rather than profitability, see Section II.C). For capital as a whole, the TCC and OCC increase, with uncertain effects on the VCC and the rate of profit because values tend to decline (relative surplus value).[12] This is the context of Marx's analysis of the tendency of the rate of profit to fall, the counter-tendencies, and the possibility of crisis associated with them (Fine, 1992; see also *Research in Political Economy*, *17*, 1999, *18*, 2000).

Scenarios 1a and 2b are associated with more or better machines, and 1b and 2a with more labour. All scenarios (except, possibly, 1b(iii)) lead to output growth, and all except, possibly, 1b(iii) and 2b, require a greater advance of money capital. These potentially very different scenarios purporting to represent capital accumulation substantiate Zarembka's claim that, for reasons of clarity and comprehensiveness, analysis of accumulation should transcend the appearances and focus upon the essence of capital. He is also right to focus upon the *class relations* underlying capital accumulation.

However, Zarembka's approach is limited in two important ways. First, Zarembka defines accumulation by the quantity of labour employed, with no further qualification, potentially implying that the *number* of workers is the decisive variable. This is insufficient even in its own terms for, as 1b(ii) and 2a show, the same number of workers can perform *more* simple labour through longer hours, greater exertion or better training. More generally, Zarembka's analysis cannot readily distinguish between scenarios 1b and 2a, and it implicitly rejects 1a and 2b as being unrelated to accumulation.

By the same token, it is difficult to accept the claim that the displacement of machines by workers necessarily implies capital accumulation. For example, binding foreign exchange or environmental constraints can force this substitution, potentially leading to a simultaneous reduction in output, the TCC, OCC, VCC and labour productivity, which is hardly conducive to capital accumulation. Conversely, technological unemployment, because cheaper or better machines are available, may lead to higher productivity, TCC and OCC, output growth and lower commodity values (relative surplus value). However, for Zarembka this does not imply capital accumulation unless employment also rises, although the latter plays only a minor role in this form of intensified expanded reproduction.

The potentially conflicting definitions of capital accumulation identified above are symptomatic of three broader difficulties. First, the capitalist use of machines depends upon two related but distinct variables, profitability and control; it does *not* depend directly upon either productivity or the level of employment. Therefore, not only accumulation (however defined) and productivity can move in opposite directions, but the imperatives of competition, profitability and workplace control may come into conflict, leading to uncertain outcomes in terms of mechanisation and accumulation. These conflicting imperatives may have severe consequences for production, profitability and accumulation.

Second, although in most countries (primitive) accumulation generally involves the absorption of increasing numbers of workers into the formal wage labour markets, this is not necessarily the case. Across the world, the expanded reproduction of capital can be based upon the extraction of absolute or relative surplus value, or the abuse of natural resources for consumption or export, in which case the size of the workforce is only one aspect of accumulation. In developed countries, where wage labour prevails, the size of the workforce and the level of wages are not the determining variable; they are determined by the rhythm of accumulation, rather than vice-versa. For example, Marx argues that:

> It is [the] movements of the accumulation of capital which are reflected as relative movements of the mass of exploitable labour-power, and therefore seem produced by the latter's own independent movement. To put it mathematically: the rate of accumulation is the independent, not the dependent variable; the rate of wages is the dependent, not the independent variable (*Capital 1*, p. 770).

Similarly, recent experience across the world shows that sustained growth and the expansion of the economic and political power of capital are compatible with increasing exploitation of the workers and rising unemployment.

Third, accumulation synthesizes the contradictions of capital. Capitalist production is associated with competition, economic growth, sectoral imbalances, and crisis. At this level of analysis, too, the number of employed workers is an important but not decisive variable. As long as wage labour is the form of social labour, and capital rules the reproduction of the labour force, including the state, the legal process, police and the armed forces, the credit system, education, training and immigration rules, the size of the labour force is an important but not binding constraint.

IV. CONCLUSION

This article contributes to the development of Zarembka's (2000) concept of capital accumulation, in the light of a class analysis of capital and the distinction between the technical, organic and value compositions of capital.

Zarembka's definition of accumulation as the development of the relationship between capitalists and wage workers, or the increase in the number of wage working hours performed, offers an important insight into the contradictory world of capital. For example, it shows that capital accumulation is compatible with rising or even falling productivity, the use or withdrawal of machines, and any manner of changes in input and output values.

Development of this approach through the analysis of competition and the composition of capital shows, first, that accumulation synthesizes the contradictions of capital both in production and exchange. Second, there are potential conflicts between the imperatives of profitability and control, which are expressed through competition and mechanisation. Third, shifts in commodity values, due to mechanisation, can lead to crisis. The approach developed in this article implies that economic crises can be due to complex combinations of factors, including technical change, disproportions due to competition and mechanisation, financial upheaval, and class conflict. None of these potential causes of crisis can explain empirical phenomena in isolation but, in the context of a *class analysis*, they can help to illuminate empirical developments more powerfully and insightfully than conventional interpretations.

NOTES

1. For a more detailed analysis of these debates, see Zarembka (2001).
2. See, respectively, *Capital*, *3*, Parts 1–2, Fine (1983) and Saad-Filho (1993, 1997, 2002, Chs. 6–7), and *Capital*, *3*, Part 3 and Fine (1992). The composition of capital is analysed by Fine and Harris (1979, Ch. 4), Fine (1989, Ch. 10; 1990), Meacci (1992) and Weeks (1981, Ch. 8). The tendency of the rate of profit to fall has been the subject of debates in *Research in Political Economy*, *17* (1999) and *18* (2000).
3. See *Capital*, *3*, Part 6, *Theories of Surplus Value*, *2*, Chs. 1–14 and Fine (1989, Ch. 13).
4. Chattopadhyay (1994, p. 18) rightly argues that 'Marx's starting point in the treatment of capital is conceiving capital as a social totality, capital representing a class opposed not so much to the individual laborers as to the wage laborers as a class'.
5. See Grundrisse, pp. 310, 449, 852.
6. 'To Marx . . . the essence of capitalist property is the control of the productive process and therefore the control over laborers. Forced labor rather than low wages, alienation of labor rather than alienation of the product of labor are, according to Marx, the essence of capitalist exploitation' (Medio, 1977, p. 384).
7. See Attewell (1984), Bowles and Gintis (1977), Braverman (1974), Brighton Labour Process Group (1977), Cleaver (1979, 1992), Lebowitz (1992), Levidow and Young (1981, 1985), Marglin (1974), Postone (1993), Slater (1980), Sohn-Rethel (1978) and Spencer (2000).
8. See *Capital*, *1*, pp. 137, 431, 773, 959.
9. Alternatively, 'The organic composition of capital is the name we give to its value composition, in so far as this is determined by its technical composition and reflects it' (*Capital*, *3*, p. 245); see also Harvey (1999, p. 126) and Weeks (1981, pp. 197–201).
10. In this section, page numbers refer to Zarembka (2000) unless stated otherwise.
11. For detailed Marxian analyses of accumulation, see Fine (1989, Ch. 5), Harvey (1999, Ch. 6) and Weeks (1981, Ch. 8).
12. In this case, 'The process of accumulation involves the initiation of the circuit of capital upon the basis of one set of values, and the generation of a new set of values that confronts capitalists at the end of the circuit' (Weeks 1981, p. 194).

ACKNOWLEDGMENTS

I am grateful to Andrew Brown and Alejandro Ramos-Martínez for their helpful comments. I am, however, responsible for the remaining errors and omissions.

REFERENCES

Aglietta, M. (1979). *A Theory of Capitalist Regulation, the U.S. Experience.* London: New Left Books.

Attewell, P. A. (1984). *Radical Political Economy, A Sociology of Knowledge Analysis.* New Brunswick, N.J.: Rutgers University Press.

Bowles, S., & Gintis, H. (1977). The Marxian Theory of Value and Heterogeneous Labour, Critique and Reformulation. *Cambridge Journal of Economics, 1*(2), 173–192.

Braverman, H. (1974). *Labour and Monopoly Capital.* New York: Monthly Review Press.

Brighton Labour Process Group (1977). The Capitalist Labour Process. *Capital & Class, 1,* 3–26.

Chattopadhyay, P. (1994). *The Marxian Concept of Capital and the Soviet Experience: Essay in the Critique of Political Economy.* Westport, Conn.: Praeger.

Clarke, S. (1994). *Marx's Theory of Crisis.* London: Macmillan.

Cleaver, H. (1979). *Reading 'Capital' Politically.* Brighton, The Harvester Press.

Cleaver, H. (1992). The Inversion of Class Perspective in Marxian Theory: From Valorisation to Self-Valorisation. In: W. Bonefeld, R. Gunn & K. Psychopedis (Eds), *Open Marxism.* London: Pluto Press.

Fine, B. (1983). A Dissenting Note on the Transformation Problem. *Economy & Society, 12*(4), 520–525.

Fine, B. (1989). *Marx's Capital* (3rd ed.). Basingstoke, Macmillan.

Fine, B. (1990). On the Composition of Capital, A Comment on Groll and Orzech. *History of Political Economy, 22*(1), 149–155.

Fine, B. (1992). On the Falling Rate of Profit. In: G. A. Caravale (Ed.), *Marx and Modern Economic Analysis.* Aldershot: Edward Elgar.

Fine, B. (2001). *Social Capital versus Social Theory.* London: Routledge.

Fine, B., & Harris, L. (1979). *Rereading Capital.* London: Macmillan.

Foley, D. (1986). *Understanding Capital, Marx's Economic Theory.* Cambridge, Mass.: Harvard University Press.

Harvey, D. (1999). *The Limits to Capital.* London: Verso.

Lapides, K. (1998). *Marx's Wage Theory in Historical Perspective: Its Origins, Development and Interpretation.* Westport, Conn.: Praeger.

Lebowitz, M. (1992). *Beyond Capital, Marx's Political Economy of the Working Class.* London: Macmillan.

Levidow, L., & Young, B. (1981, 1985). *Science, Technology and the Labour Process, Marxist Studies,* 2 Vols. London: Free Association Books.

Marglin, S. (1974). What Do Bosses Do? *Review of Radical Political Economics, 6*(2), 60–112.

Marx, K. (1978a, 1969, 1972). *Theories of Surplus Value,* 3 Vols. London: Lawrence and Wishart.

Marx, K. (1981a). *Grundrisse.* Harmondsworth: Penguin.

Marx, K. (1976, 1978b, 1981b). *Capital,* 3 Vols. Harmondsworth: Penguin.

Meacci, F. (1992). The Organic Composition of Capital and the Falling Rate of Profit. In: G. A. Caravale (Ed.), *Marx and Modern Economic Analysis.* Aldershot: Edward Elgar.

Medio, A. (1977). Neoclassicals, Neo-Ricardians, and Marx. In: J. G. Schwartz (Ed.), *The Subtle Anatomy of Capitalism.* Santa Monica: Goodyear.

Nell, E. J. (1992). *Transformational Growth and Effective Demand.* New York: New York University Press.

Perelman, M. (1993). The Qualitative Side of Marx's Value Theory. *Rethinking Marxism, 6*(1), 82–95.

Perelman, M. (1999). Marx, Devalorisation, and the Theory of Value. *Cambridge Journal of Economics, 23*(6), 719–728.

Postone, M. (1993). *Time, Labour and Social Domination, A Re-examination of Marx's Critical Theory.* Cambridge: Cambridge University Press.

Saad-Filho, A. (1993). A Note on Marx's Analysis of the Composition of Capital. *Capital & Class 50,* 127–146.

Saad-Filho, A. (1997). An Alternative Reading of the Transformation of Values into Prices of Production. *Capital and Class, 63,* 115–136.

Saad-Filho, A. (2002). *The Value of Marx: Political Economy for Contemporary Capitalism.* London: Routledge.

Slater, P. (Ed) (1980). *Outlines of a Critique of Technology.* Atlantic Highlands: Humanities Press.

Sohn-Rethel, A. (1978). *Intellectual and Manual Labour: a Critique of Epistemology.* London: Macmillan.

Spencer, D. (2000). Braverman and the Contribution of Labour Process Analysis to the Critique of Capitalist Production – Twenty Five Years On. *Work, Employment and Society, 14*(2), 223–243.

Weeks, J. (1981). *Capital and Exploitation.* Princeton: Princeton University Press.

Zarembka, P. (2000). Accumulation of Capital, its Definition: A Century after Lenin and Luxemburg. *Value, Capitalist Dynamics and Money, Research in Political Economy, 18,* 183–225.

Zarembka, P. (2001). Rosa Luxemburg's *Accumulation of Capital*: Critics Try to Bury the Message. *Bringing Capitalism Back for Critique by Social Theory, Current Perspectives in Social Theory, 21* (forthcoming).

CRITERIA OF TECHNICAL CHOICE AND EVOLUTION OF TECHNICAL CHANGE

Cheol-Soo Park

ABSTRACT

Dumenil-Levy and Foley (DLF) attempt to show that the falling rate of profit can be induced by applying Okishio's criterion of technical choice to DLF's framework on the evolution of potential technical change. This paper examines what would happen if Shaikh's criterion is applied to DLF's framework on the evolution of potential technical change. The following result is derived: while both criteria induce the K/L (capital-labor ratio) – increasing falling rate of profit at a sufficiently high wage share, only Shaikh's criterion induces the K/L – increasing falling rate of profit under a constant real wage (or a low wage share).

I. INTRODUCTION

In Volume III of *Capital*, Marx presents his proposition on the 'tendency of the falling rate of profit' (TFRP). He considers it one of the general laws of the capital accumulation with apparent paradoxical consequence.

Marx's *Capital* and Capitalism; Markets in a Socialist Alternative,
Research in Political Economy, Volume 19, pages 87–106.
Copyright © 2001 by Elsevier Science Ltd.
All rights of reproduction in any form reserved.
ISBN: 0-7623-0838-9

> The progressive tendency of the general rate of profit to fall is, therefore, just *an expression peculiar to the capitalist mode of production* of the progressive development of the social productivity of labour (Marx, 1984b, p. 213).

There is little doubt that Marx's theory of TFRP is one of the most important subjects in modern debates on Marxian political economy. Broadly speaking, there are two types of the debates on Marx's theory of TFRP.[1]

One is primarily related to macroeconomic issues. The fundamental questions are what kind of macro factor causes the falling rate of profit and whether it can be empirically tested. We may identify three types of explanations for TFRP: increasing organic-composition-of-capital, underconsumption, and profit squeeze. In this debate, Marxian measures of the national product accounts have become an important factor in proving or disproving each theory.

On the other hand, Marx's theory of TFRP is also analyzed from microeconomic perspectives. In this approach, the primary concern is to analyze whether the competitive behavior among individual capitalists can lead to the falling rate of profit. This kind of debate has evolved mainly through Okishio's theorem (Okishio, 1961).[2] Okishio's theorem implies that the rate of profit cannot decrease in the capitalist economy when the real wage rate is constant.[3]

In the debate on Marx's theory of TFRP, Shaikh (1978, 1999) argues that Okishio's theorem depends on a specific criterion of technical choice derived from a specific view of the capitalist competition. Shaikh raises a question as to whether this view represents Marx's concept of competition from which the tendency of the falling rate of profit may or may not be derived. He proposes a criterion of technical choice on the basis of his own interpretation of the Marxian concept of competition, and applies the criterion to explore Marx's theory of TFRP.

While Marx implies that the main culprit for the falling rate of profit consists in the evolution of a specific pattern of technical change (which increases the organic-composition-of-capital), Okishio's theorem does not have direct relation to the evolution of any specific pattern of technical change. Therefore, without regard to the appropriateness of Okishio's theorem itself, it may not provide all the tools adequate to understand Marx's theory of TFRP. Recently, Dumenil and Levy (1995, 1999) and Foley (1999) (DLF), developed a framework on the evolution of potential technical change in which a specific pattern of technical change is not presumed. By applying Okishio's criterion of technical choice to their framework on the evolution of potential technical change, they attempted to show that capitalists would induce a specific pattern of technical change leading to the falling rate of profit.

At this point, we may raise a question as to what would happen if we apply Shaikh's criterion of technical choice (Shaikh, 1978, 1999) to DLF's framework on the evolution of potential technical change. The purpose of this paper is to explore this specific question by using standard analytical and simulation methods. The main result I will derive is as follows: while Okishio's criterion of technical choice induces the K/L (capital-labor ratio) – increasing falling rate of profit under the condition of a high wage share, Shaikh's criterion induces the K/L-increasing falling rate of profit without the condition.

The paper is composed of five sections. In Section II, I discuss Okishio's criterion of technical choice and Shaikh's criterion of technical choice. In Section III, I explain DLF's framework on the evolution of potential technical change. In Section IV, I develop a framework applying Shaikh's criterion of technical choice to DLF's framework on the evolution of potential technical change in reference to DLF's attempt to apply Okishio's criterion to the same framework on the evolution of potential technical change. In Section V, I conclude by summarizing the main results of the paper.

II. THEORIES OF TECHNICAL CHOICE IN MARXIAN POLITICAL ECONOMY

We need to prepare a few definitions and assumptions in order to discuss theories of technical choice in the tradition of Marxian political economy. At given period t, the rate of profit is defined as:

$$r_t \equiv \frac{Q_t - w_t \cdot L_t}{K_t} \tag{1}$$

r_t: Rate of profit at period t

Q_t: Output at period t

w_t: Real wage rate at period t

L_t: Labor at period t

K_t: Capital at period t

Following Dumenil and Levy (1995) and Foley (1999), I assume a simple capitalist production system with one output and two inputs, capital (regarded as a stock of output used in production), and labor. I also assume that the capitalist production process requires only fixed capital and labor. I will ignore depreciation of the fixed capital. Let x_t and ρ_t denote labor productivity and output-capital ratio, respectively. If we express $k_t \equiv K_t/L_t$, then $k_t = (Q_t/L_t)/(Q_t/K_t) = x_t/\rho_t$. I am going to use a pair of x_t and ρ_t, (x_t, ρ_t), in order to represent a technique. If both x_t and ρ_t increase, the new technique saves both labor and capital in producing one unit of output. On the other hand, if $x_t/\rho_t \ (= K_t/L_t)$ increases, the new technique increases the capital-labor ratio, k_t, per unit of output.

In order to understand Okishio's criterion of technical choice, we need to distinguish three measures of the rate of profit. The first measure is *the old rate of profit* established when all individual capitalists adopt a given old technique and the rate of profit is evaluated in terms of old price and old real wage rate. The second measure is *the transient rate of profit* which a capitalist expects from a newly available technique by assuming that all others take the old technique and a given prevalent price system does not change. The rate of profit is still evaluated by old price and old real wage rate. The third measure is *the new rate of profit* established when all individual capitalists utilize a newly available technique. The new rate of profit is evaluated by a new price system and a new real wage rate (if the old real wage rate changes).

Okishio's theorem states that, under a given prevalent price system with a constant real wage rate, if a capitalist chooses a new technique *when* the transient rate of profit is higher than the old rate of profit, the new rate of profit does not decrease.[4] We call the viability condition of choosing a new technique *'Okishio's criterion of technical choice'*.

It is straightforward to prove Okishio's theorem in one-commodity production system assumed in this paper. We may not notice the analytical depth of Okishio's theorem in the system, since the price system does not bring with it any theoretical complexity. Okishio's theorem further asserts that the rate of profit does not decrease under general n-commodities production system.[5] Okishio's theorem plays a very important role in the debate concerning Marx's argument on TFRP. According to the theorem, individual capitalists would not choose any technique leading to the falling rate of profit under a constant real wage rate. Therefore, Okishio's theorem is often used as a means of disproving Marx's theory of TFRP.[6]

Shaikh (1978, 1999) emphasizes that in Okishio's theorem it is assumed that a capitalist who tries to choose a technique does not attempt to cut price.[7] While Shaikh admits that Okishio's theorem is correct under this specific assumption, he argues that the assumption is based on the Neoclassical concept of competition, which is quite distinct from the Marxian concept of competition.

Shaikh argues that in choosing a technique an individual capitalist expects that the price-cutting competition would prevail. He understands the price-cutting competition as one of the most important elements in the Marxian concept of competition. It may mean that in this competitive environment an individual capitalist tries to maximize the expected rate of profit by choosing a technique which can lead to lower unit cost and make room to survive for themselves under the price-cutting competition.[8]

The technique with lower unit cost can be translated into the technique with higher profit margin. We need to distinguish two measures of profit margin in order to present Shaikh's criterion of technical choice properly. The first measure is *the old profit margin* which is calculated with old technique, old price and old real wage rate. The second measure is *the transient profit margin* which is calculated with new technique, old price and old real wage rate.[9]

Under the price-cutting competition, a capitalist takes a new technique when the transient profit margin is higher than the old profit margin. We call the viability condition of choosing a new technique *'Shaikh's criterion of technical choice'*.[10]

III. THEORIES OF THE EVOLUTION OF POTENTIAL TECHNICAL CHANGE

Okishio's theorem, as such, does not indicate what pattern of technical change will actually evolve. It only asserts that if individual capitalists take a given technique the rate of profit would not decrease. It does not explain whether there arises a specific pattern of technical change, which would be an important element in the debate on Marx's TFRP. After we observe a specific pattern of technical change, we may argue that the occurrence of such a specific pattern is compatible with a specific criterion of technical choice. But it seems that the debate on Okishio's theorem does not help us understand whether a specific criterion of technical choice brings with it a specific pattern of technical change.

Recently, Dumenil and Levy (1995, 1999) and Foley (1999) developed a framework on the evolution of potential technical change. The primary purpose of their construction of the evolution of potential technical change is to see whether a specific pattern of technical change would be *induced* when a criterion of technical choice is applied to the framework on the evolution of potential technical change.

In order to analyze the evolution of potential technical change suggested by Dumenil and Levy and Foley (DLF), we need to rewrite the rate of profit in (1) following the framework presented in Foley (1999).

$$r_t \equiv \frac{Q_t - w_t \cdot L_t}{K_t} = \frac{x_t - w_t}{k_t} \tag{2}$$

As defined before, x_t ($\equiv Q_t/L_t$) is the index of the labor productivity and k_t ($\equiv K_t/L_t$) is the index of the capital intensity and ρ_t ($\equiv Q_t/K_t$) is the output-capital ratio. Let us define the growth rates of x_t and ρ_t as:[11]

$$\gamma_t \equiv \frac{x_t - x_{t-1}}{x_{t-1}} \tag{3}$$

$$\chi_t \equiv \frac{p_t - p_{t-1}}{p_{t-1}} \tag{4}$$

Accordingly, if individual capitalists adopt a new technique, the rate of profit can be expressed as in (5).

$$r_t = \frac{Q_t - w_t \cdot L_t}{K_t} = \frac{x_t - w_t}{k_t} = \frac{x_{t-1} \cdot (1 + \gamma_t) - w_t}{\left(\dfrac{x_{t-1} \cdot (1 + \gamma_t)}{p_{t-1} \cdot (1 + \chi_t)} \right)} \tag{5}$$

The evolution of potential technical change may be characterized in terms of the growth rate of the labor productivity, γ_t, and the growth rate of the output-capital ratio, χ_t. Dumenil and Levy (1995, p. 216) suggest that the evolution of potential technical change has three properties: (i) it is a random process since the result of innovation cannot be predicted; (ii) technology is only modified locally from the previously existing technology; and (iii) the innovation is neutral in the sense that the probabilities of saving either input are a priori equal.

Figure 1 shows some possible forms of the evolution of potential technical change.[12] A point within the circles and ellipse indicates an available technique and it is randomly drawn from a uniform distribution.

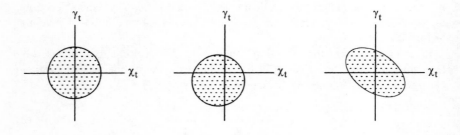

(a) circular/zero center   (b) circular/negative center   (c) elliptic

Fig. 1.   Form of the Evolution of Potential Technical Change.

In Fig. 1, a technique located in the first quadrant has a capital-saving/labor-saving innovation. On the other hand, a technique located in the second quadrant is characterized by a capital-using/labor-saving innovation, while a technique located in the fourth quadrant is characterized by a capital-saving/labor-using innovation.

Figure 1(a) shows that there is an equal probability of innovating each type of technique illustrated above. It does not appear realistic since the type of innovation in the first quadrant (saving both capital and labor) is less likely to occur than the type of innovation in the second or the fourth quadrants. On the contrary, Fig. 1(b) and Fig. 1(c) presume that there is some tradeoff between capital-saving innovation and labor-saving innovation. Dumenil and Levy (1995, 1999) analyze the properties of the evolution of potential technical change represented by Fig. 1(b). Foley (1999) pursues the properties of the evolution of potential technical change represented by Fig. 1(c).

We may note that Figs 1(b) and 1(c) do not favor a priori the evolution of the technical change increasing the technical composition of capital, K/L. If we draw a 45-degree line passing the origin, we can see that either side of the area has the same probability. As we will see later, the line distinguishes K/L-increasing technical change from K/L-decreasing technical change. Therefore, the figures presume that the evolution of potential technical change is a priori neutral in terms of the movement of K/L. The main task of this paper is to explore how the rate of profit and K/L would evolve over the long run path of the capital accumulation when a specific criterion of technical choice is applied to a specific form of the evolution of potentially neutral technical change. In the following, I continue our discussion on basis of the two types of the evolution of potential technical change.

IV. TECHNICAL CHOICE AND TECHNICAL CHANGE[13]

We are now prepared to analyze what features of technical change would evolve when a specific criterion of technical choice is applied to a specific form of the evolution of potential technical change. Since Dumenil and Levy (1995, 1999) and Foley (1999) pursue the theoretical analysis of applying Okishio's criterion of technical choice to the evolution of potential technical change, I will only briefly replicate it. Instead, I analyze in more detail what would happen when Shaikh's criterion of technical choice is applied to the evolution of potential technical change. Following the theoretical analysis, I provide simulations showing what features of technical change would evolve under different criterion of technical choice.

IV.1. Okishio's Criterion of Technical Choice and the Evolution of Technical Change

In order to understand DLF's approach, we first need to identify the *viability set* in which an individual capitalist takes a new technique in terms of Okishio's criterion of technical choice. Dumenil and Levy (1995, p. 218) and Foley (1999, p. 11) show that the viability set from Okishio's criterion of technical choice may be expressed in the linear relation between γ_t and χ_t, whose slope depends on the level of wage share.[14] Figure 2 shows the viability set from Okishio's criterion of technical choice; the p-p line is the viability frontier. The area enclosed by p-p line and circle (or ellipse) is the viability set. A and B indicate the viability techniques. When the wage share increases, the viability frontier turns counterclockwise.

Second, let us identify the capital-labor ratio increasing set. The condition of increasing the capital-labor ratio is $\gamma_t > \chi_t$.[15] Figure 3 shows the capital-labor ratio increasing set; the q-q line indicates the capital-labor ratio increasing frontier. The area enclosed by p-p line, q-q line and circle (or ellipse) is the capital-labor ratio increasing set under the viability set from Okishio's criterion of technical choice. A and B indicate the capital-labor ratio increasing techniques under the viability set from Okishio's criterion of technical choice.

For the analysis of the movement of the rate of profit and K/L, it is necessary to obtain both the mean value of the growth rate of the labor productivity, $\bar{\gamma}$, and the mean value of the growth rate of the output-capital ratio, $\bar{\chi}$. Dumenil and Levy (1995, pp. 235–236) and Foley (1999, p. 11–13) theorize that, as the wage share increases, the mean value of γ_t increases and the mean value of χ_t decreases.[16]

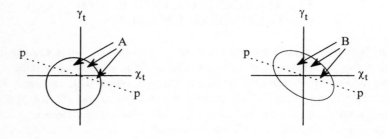

(a) circular/negative center   (b) elliptic

Fig. 2. Viability Set from Okishio's Criterion of Technical Choice.

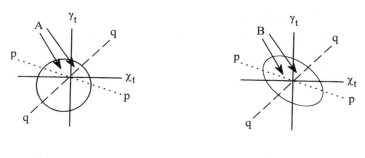

(a) circular/negative center   (b) elliptic

Fig. 3. Capital-Labor Ratio Increasing Set from Okishio's Criterion of Technical Choice.

Now, we move to the analysis of how the capital-labor ratio and the rate of profit would evolve when Okishio's criterion of technical choice is applied to DLF's framework on the evolution of potential technical change. First of all, let us examine how the capital-labor ratio would evolve over periods. The mean value of the capital-labor ratio at period t is:

$$\left(\frac{\bar{K}_t}{L_t}\right) = \frac{x_{t-1} \cdot (1+\bar{\gamma})}{\rho_{t-1} \cdot (1+\bar{\chi})} = \left(\frac{K_{t-1}}{L_{t-1}}\right) \cdot \left(\frac{1+\bar{\gamma}}{1+\bar{\chi}}\right) \tag{6}$$

The capital-labor ratio would increase at a high wage share, in which the mean value of the growth rate of the labor productivity, $\bar{\gamma}$, is high and the mean value of the growth rate of the output-capital ratio, $\bar{\chi}$, is low.

For the analysis of the movement of the rate of profit, first, let us assume that the real wage rate is constant. In this case, Okishio's criterion of technical choice does not induce the (K/L-increasing) falling rate of profit. This is exactly a conclusion of Okishio's theorem. Under a constant real wage rate, when the transient rate of profit is higher than the old rate of profit, the new rate of profit does not fall in comparison to the old rate of profit. Therefore, when Okishio's criterion of technical choice is applied to DLF's framework on the evolution of potential technical change, the (K/L-increasing) falling rate of profit is not induced.

Next, let us examine more in detail the case of a high level of constant wage share which Dumenil and Levy (1995, 1999) and Foley (1999a) focus on. First of all, we need to express a constant wage share in terms of $w_t = \theta \cdot x_t = \theta \cdot (x_{t-1} \cdot (1+\gamma_t))$, where $0 < \theta < 1$. In reference to (5), the mean value of the rate of profit at period t can be expressed in terms of the mean values of γ_t and χ_t:

$$\bar{r}_t = \frac{x_{t-1} \cdot (1+\bar{\gamma}) - \theta \cdot x_{t-1} \cdot (1+\bar{\gamma})}{\left(\dfrac{x_{t-1} \cdot (1+\bar{\gamma})}{\rho_{t-1} \cdot (1+\bar{\chi})}\right)} = (1-\theta) \cdot (\rho_{t-1} \cdot (1+\bar{\chi})) \tag{7}$$

At a high wage share, the mean value of the growth rate of the output-capital ratio, $\bar{\chi}$, will become negative. This signifies that the rate of profit would decrease over periods.

Dumenil and Levy and Foley conclude that when wage share is set at a high level and Okishio's criterion of technical choice is applied to their framework on the evolution of potential technical change, the capitalist economy generally tends to evolve on the path of an K/L-increasing falling rate of profit. The result may not be trivial because it explicitly shows that the K/L-increasing falling rate of profit is *induced* in the capitalist economy.

IV.2. Shaikh's Criterion of Technical Choice and the Evolution of Technical Change

Let us examine what would happen if we apply Shaikh's criterion of technical choice to DLF's framework on the evolution of potential technical change. In parallel with DLF's attempt, I first analyze the movement of the capital-labor ratio and the rate of profit by assuming a constant real wage rate. Afterwards, I pursue the case of a constant wage share.

First of all, let us identify *the viability set* in which an individual capitalist takes a new technique under Shaikh's criterion of technical choice. For this purpose, we need to explicitly express the old profit margin, p_{t-1}, and the transient profit margin, p_t.

$$\pi_{t-1} = \frac{P_{t-1} \cdot Q_{t-1} - P_{t-1} \cdot w_{t-1} \cdot L_{t-1}}{Q_{t-1}} = P_{t-1} - P_{t-1} \cdot w_{t-1} \cdot \left(\frac{1}{x_{t-1}}\right) \tag{8}$$

$$\pi_t = \frac{P_{t-1} \cdot Q_t - P_{t-1} \cdot w_{t-1} \cdot L_t}{Q_t} = P_{t-1} - P_{t-1} \cdot w_{t-1} \cdot \left(\frac{1}{x_t}\right) \tag{9}$$

It is important to notice that profit margin is characterized by the labor productivity in this simple framework. If a transient profit margin with a new technique is higher than the profit margin with the old technique, that is, $\pi_t > \pi_{t-1}$, then,

$$P_{t-1}{}^-P_{t-1} \cdot W_{t-1} \cdot \left(\frac{1}{X_t}\right) > P_{t-1}{}^-P_{t-1} \cdot W_{t-1} \cdot \left(\frac{1}{X_{t-1}}\right) \Leftrightarrow \frac{-1}{X_{t-1} \cdot (1+\gamma_t)} > \frac{-1}{X_{t-1}}$$

$$\Leftrightarrow \gamma_t > 0$$

Under Shaikh's criterion of technical choice, an individual capitalist utilizes a new technique if $\gamma_t > 0$. Figure 4 shows the viability set from Shaikh's criterion of technical choice corresponding to the two forms of the evolution of potential technical change.[17] The p-p line is the viability frontier. The area enclosed by p-p line and circle (or ellipse) is the viability set. A and B indicate the viability techniques.

Again, it is necessary to examine the mean values of γ_t and χ_t in order to trace the movement of the capital-labor ratio and the rate of profit. Let us attempt to get the mean values of γ_t and χ_t in reference to the viability set from Shaikh's criterion of technical choice.[18]

When the evolution of potential technical change takes the form of *uniform circular distribution with negative center*, we may observe that the mean value of γ_t is *positive* and the mean value of χ_t is *negative*. We may expect the result from Fig. 4(a). The circle is symmetry from γ-axis at negative χ_t. Therefore, the mean value of χ_t for an arbitrary given γ_t (> 0) within the circle is a negative number. Accordingly, if we get sum of this number over $0 < \gamma_t \leq a-\delta$ (a: radius of circle, δ: center of circle), we can understand the mean value of χ_t will be negative. On the contrary, we can recognize that as far as $\delta < a$ (and so the

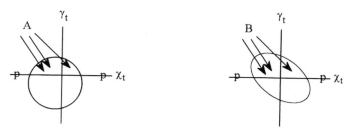

(a) circular/negative center   (b) elliptic

Fig. 4.   Viability Set from Shaikh's Criterion of Technical Choice.

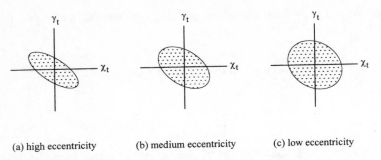

(a) high eccentricity   (b) medium eccentricity   (c) low eccentricity

Fig. 5.   Form of Uniform Elliptic Distribution with Different Eccentricity

circle is not completely located within the third quadrant), the mean value of γ_t should be positive.[19]

In the case of *uniform elliptic distribution*, it is difficult to get the mean values since it involves elliptic integrals. Therefore, I take an indirect route to trace the mean values of γ_t and χ_t: I draw samples from uniform elliptic distribution with different eccentricity and then calculate the mean values of γ_t and χ_t. Figure 5 shows the form of the uniform elliptic distribution classified by the relative level of eccentricity which I use in calculating the mean values of γ_t and χ_t. The eccentricity is measured by how far its shape is different from circle.[20] Through the repeated experiments, I observe that the mean value of γ_t is positive and that of χ_t is negative. Again, we may conjecture from Fig. 4(b) that the mean value of γ_t is positive and that of χ_t is negative.

Therefore, we may conclude that the mean value of γ_t is positive and the mean value of χ_t is negative under Shaikh's criterion of technical choice when the evolution of potential technical change is characterized by *either* uniform circular distribution with negative center *or* uniform elliptic distribution.

Next, let us look at the capital-labor ratio increasing set within the viability set from Shaikh's criterion of technical choice. Since x_t is Q_t/L_t and ρ_t is Q_t/K_t, the capital-labor ratio increasing set can be deduced as follows:

$$\frac{K_t}{L_t} > \frac{K_{t-1}}{L_{t-1}} \Leftrightarrow \frac{x_{t-1} \cdot (1 + \gamma_t)}{\rho_{t-1} \cdot (1 + \chi_t)} > \frac{x_{t-1}}{\rho_{t-1}} \Leftrightarrow \gamma_t > \chi_t$$

Figure 6 shows the capital-labor ratio increasing set within the viability set from Shaikh's criterion of technical choice.[21] The q-q line indicates the capital-labor ratio increasing frontier. The area enclosed by p-p line, q-q line and circle (or

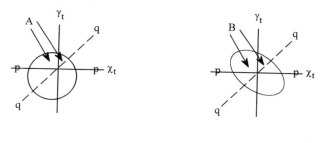

(a) circular/negative center   (b) elliptic

Fig. 6. Capital-Labor Ratio Increasing Set from Shaikh's Criterion of Technical Choice.

ellipse) is the capital-labor ratio increasing set within the viability set from Shaikh's criterion of technical choice. A and B indicate the capital-labor ratio increasing techniques within the viability set from Shaikh's criterion of technical choice.

In Fig. 6, the capital-labor ratio increasing set within the viability set appears to be larger than the capital-labor decreasing set within the viability set. This implies that when the transient profit margin is higher than the old profit margin, there is a higher probability that the adopted technique increases the capital-labor ratio. However, in order to trace the movement of the capital-labor ratio more precisely, we need to calculate the mean value of the capital-labor ratio at period t, which is determined by the mean values of γ_t and χ_t.

$$\left(\frac{\overline{K}_t}{L_t}\right) = \frac{x_{t-1} \cdot (1 + \bar{\gamma})}{\rho_{t-1} \cdot (1 + \bar{\chi})} = \left(\frac{K_{t-1}}{L_{t-1}}\right) \cdot \left(\frac{1 + \bar{\gamma}}{1 + \bar{\chi}}\right) \tag{10}$$

Since the mean value of γ_t is positive and the mean value of χ_t is negative for both circular/negative center and elliptic cases, we can expect that the capital-labor ratio will increase for both forms of the evolution of potential technical change.

Finally, let us examine how the rate of profit would move depending on the evolution of the real wage rate when Shaikh's criterion of technical choice is applied to DLF's framework of potential technical change.

First of all, it is important to examine what would happen when real wage rate, w_t (> 0), is fixed at 'w.' For the purpose, we need to write the equation for the mean value of the rate of profit at period t, in reference to (5).

$$\bar{r}_t = \frac{x_{t-1} \cdot (1+\bar{\gamma})-w}{\left(\dfrac{x_{t-1} \cdot (1+\bar{\gamma})}{\rho_{t-1} \cdot (1+\bar{\chi})}\right)} \tag{11}$$

The part of the numerator, $x_{t-1} \cdot (1+\bar{\gamma})$, will increase over time since $\bar{\gamma} > 0$. Also, the denominator, $(x_{t-1} \cdot (1+\bar{\gamma}))/(\rho_{t-1} \cdot (1+\bar{\chi}))$ will increase since $\bar{\gamma} > 0$ and $\bar{\chi} < 0$. It means that the rate of profit will be determined primarily by the two parts *without* regard to 'w,' as time goes by. That is, the mean value of the rate of profit at period t will be:

$$\bar{r}_t = \frac{x_{t-1} \cdot (1+\bar{\gamma})-w}{\left(\dfrac{x_{t-1} \cdot (1+\bar{\gamma})}{\rho_{t-1} \cdot (1+\bar{\chi})}\right)} \cong \rho_{t-1} \cdot (1+\bar{\chi}) \tag{12}$$

In this case, the rate of profit will be also determined by the mean value of χ_t. It will decrease for both the uniform circular distribution with negative center and the uniform elliptic distribution since the mean value of χ_t tends to become negative.

Next, let us examine a constant wage share case. As before, I utilize the following formula for a constant wage share:

$$w_t = \theta \cdot x_t = \theta \cdot (x_{t-1} \cdot (1+\gamma_t)) \qquad (0 < \theta < 1) \tag{13}$$

By using w_t in (13) and the mean values of γ_t and χ_t, we can rewrite the rate of profit in (5) as:

$$\bar{r}_t = \frac{x_{t-1} \cdot (1+\bar{\gamma})-\theta \cdot x_{t-1} \cdot (1+\bar{\gamma})}{\left(\dfrac{x_{t-1} \cdot (1+\bar{\gamma})}{\rho_{t-1} \cdot (1+\bar{\chi})}\right)} = (1-\theta) \cdot (\rho_{t-1} \cdot (1+\bar{\chi})) \tag{14}$$

We can see that the movement of the rate of profit is determined by the mean value of χ_t. We concluded the mean value of χ_t would be negative for both the uniform circular distribution with negative center and the uniform elliptic distribution. Therefore, the rate of profit will decrease for both the uniform circular distribution with negative center and the uniform elliptic distribution.

IV.3 Simulation

We now proceed to do some simulations which apply each criterion of technical choice to DLF's framework of the evolution of potential technical change.[22] On the basis of the theoretical analysis we performed in Sections IV.1 and IV.2, let me pursue the simulation with the condition of a constant real wage rate followed by the simulation with the condition of a high level of constant wage share.

It is straightforward to implement the simulation process. First, we need to draw random values of γ_t and χ_t, from a uniform circular distribution with negative center and a uniform elliptic distribution. Second, for each distribution, we need to *compare* the old rate of profit (the old profit margin) *with* the transient rate of profit (the transient profit margin) if we accept Okishio's (Shaikh's) criterion of technical choice. If the transient rate of profit (the transient profit margin) is not higher than the old rate of profit (the old profit margin), an individual capitalist takes the old technique. Otherwise, an individual capitalist takes the new technique. Finally, we need to trace how the capitalist economy evolves over periods of time.[23]

Figures 7(a) and 7(c) show the simulation results derived from applying Okishio's criterion of technical choice to a uniform elliptic distribution of potential technical change. Figure 7(a) assumes a constant real wage rate. In this case, we are unable to find the (K/L-increasing) falling rate of profit. On the contrary, Fig. 7(c) assumes a high level of constant wage share.[24] The rate of profit tends to decrease and the capital-labor ratio tends to increase over periods. Therefore, the results do not seem to contradict what we would expect from the theoretical analysis.

Figures 7(b) and 7(d) show the simulation results derived from applying Shaikh's criterion of technical choice to a uniform elliptic distribution of potential technical change. Figure 7(b) assumes a constant real wage rate. The rate of profit tends to decrease[25] and the capital-labor ratio tends to increase over the periods. Figure 7(d) assumes a high level of constant wage share. Again, the rate of profit tends to decrease and the capital-labor ratio tends to increase over the periods. Therefore, the results do not seem to contradict what we may expect from the theoretical analysis.

V. CONCLUSION

In this paper, I have dealt with a current issue which evolved from the debate concerning Marx's argument on the tendency of the falling rate of profit in the capitalist economy: Does the rate of profit tend to fall when a specific criterion

(a) Okishio's criterion of technical choice and a constant real wage rate

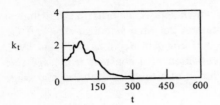 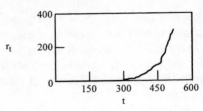

(b) Shaikh's criterion of technical choice and a constant real wage rate

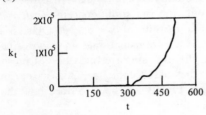 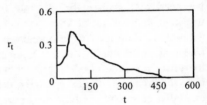

(c) Okishio's criterion of technical choice and a high wage share

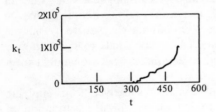 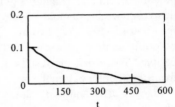

(d) Shaikh's criterion of technical choice and a high wage share

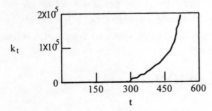 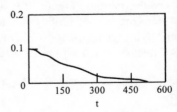

Fig. 7. Uniform Elliptic Distribution of Potential Technical Change.

of individual capitalist's technical choice is applied to an unpredetermined evolution of potential technical change?

The main results derived are: (i) when a constant real wage rate (or a low wage share) is assumed, Okishio's criterion does not induce the (K/L-increasing) falling rate of profit, while Shaikh's criterion induces the K/L-increasing falling rate of profit; and (ii) when a high wage share is assumed, both criteria of technical choice induce the K/L-increasing falling rate of profit.[26]

In Okishio's criterion of technical choice, the level of wage share directly affects the viability set; this is not the case in Shaikh's criterion. Each viability set leads to the different mean values of the labor productivity and the output-capital ratio. Again, the different mean values can lead to the different movements of the rate of profit and K/L. Therefore, we may conclude that the different criterion of technical choice leads to the different explanation of the movement of the rate of profit and K/L. As Shaikh argues, a different concept of capitalist competition may be critical in understanding the conclusion.

ACKNOWLEDGMENTS

I would like to thank Duncan Foley, Anwar Shaikh, Paul Zarembka, and the referees for their helpful suggestions and comments on previous versions of this paper. The usual disclaimer applies.

NOTES

1. The classification is quite mechanical; both are closely related.
2. Cullenberg (1994, pp. 3–12) gives a chronological review of the debate on Marx's theory of TFRP in which he emphasizes the importance of Okishio's theorem.
3. Okishio's theorem has been discussed in several contexts. First, it is examined in the history of economic thought. Groll and Orzech (1989) attempt to trace the origin of Okishio's theorem as far back as to Marx himself. Second, there are several attempts to examine whether Okishio's theorem can be applied to more general production systems. Warskett (1991) shows that, within joint production systems, there are some cases where the viability condition alone can not prove Okishio's theorem. Third, there is an attempt to see the condition of the falling rate of profit within Okishio's theorem. Roemer (1981, pp. 134–145) shows that, under the assumption of cost-reducing, capital-using, and labor-saving technical change, the rate of profit will fall in general if the relative share of labor remains constant. Sweezy (1942) might be the original source in this direction. Fourth, there are a few attempts to see whether the presumptions of Okishio's theorem reflect Marx's idea on TFRP. For an example, we may refer to Foley (1986, pp. 125–140) focusing on the concept of labor-power or Shaikh (1978, 1999) focusing on the Marxian concept of competition. Fifth, Kliman (1997) claims to refute Okishio's theorem on the ground that its conclusion does not follow from its own premises.

4. In one-commodity production system, each measure of the rate of profit can be expressed in physical unit of output.

5. Okishio (1961) uses Hawkins-Simon condition for the proof and Roemer (1981, pp. 97–98) shows it by applying Frobenius-Perron theorem.

6. Parijs (1980) criticizes the falling rate of profit theory of crisis on the basis of Okishio's theorem.

7. According to Shaikh, an individual capitalist in Okishio's theorem is a price-taker.

8. Shaikh (1999, pp. 11–20) gives a detailed explanation on how the technique with a lower unit cost can result in a comparatively higher (expected) rate of profit under the price-cutting competition.

9. Both measures are explicitly defined in Section IV.2. In the explicit forms, we may note that if the transient profit margin is higher than the old profit margin, the profit margin from the new technique is higher than the profit margin from the old technique *when* outputs from both techniques are evaluated at any price (which is usually expected to be lower than the old price under the price-cutting competition). Therefore, instead of the profit margins defined in this paper, we may use the old and the transient profit margins whose outputs are evaluated at a new (expected) price in order to express the price-cutting competition more clearly. Nevertheless, this does not affect the results of my analysis since it leads to the same condition for transient profit margin › old profit margin.

10. This paper does not aim at dealing with which criterion is more appropriate in explaining the capitalist technical choice. It mainly focuses on comparing them in terms of induced technical change.

11. Since labor productivity and output-capital ratio are generally positive, γ_t and χ_t should be greater than -1.

12. Dumenil and Levy (1999, pp. 5–8) discuss more about several forms of potential technical change.

13. Before discussing the relationship between technical choice and technical change, I would like to mention a little bit about my paper from a methodological point of view. In this paper, I assume a one-commodity production system and I present my argument under the traditional equilibrium concept embedded in Okishio's theorem. The framework allows me to simplify my analysis. For example, I can easily trace the rate of profit since it is derived from the ratio of the quantity of the same commodity. On the other hand, we can not rule out the possibility that this paper has a few limitations directly derived from the framework. First of all, my analysis may not be easily applied to n-commodities system. For example, the results of my analysis may not be stated as such under n-commodities system due to the potential problems (e.g. capital controversy) caused by the difference between one-commodity system and n-commodities system. Second, it does not deal with any disequilibrium states involved in technical change. Many authors take interest in the dynamic/disequilibrium process accompanied with technical change from various points of view. My paper does not explicitly deal with this issue.

14. Let us express $r_t' \equiv dr_t/dt$. I assume r_t' measures the change in the rate of profit from the previous period to the present period. Since $r_{t-1} = (x_{t-1} - w_{t-1})/k_{t-1}$, $r_{t-1} = \rho_{t-1} \cdot \phi_{t-1}$ if we put $\phi_{t-1} \equiv (x_{t-1} - w_{t-1})/x_{t-1}$, which can be easily transformed into an expression for wage share. Let us denote r_t^e as expected profit from adopting a new technique. It is assumed that, in deciding whether or not to adopt a new technique, an individual capitalist expects the real wage rate not to change. That is, $w_t' = 0$. Then, $r_t^{e'} = [(x_t' - w_t') \cdot k_{t-1} - (x_{t-1} - w_{t-1}) \cdot k_t']/(k_{t-1})^2 = \rho_{t-1} \cdot (x_t'/x_{t-1}) - \rho_{t-1} \cdot \phi_{t-1} \cdot (k_t'/k_{t-1}) = \rho_{t-1} \cdot (\gamma_t - \phi_{t-1} \cdot (\gamma_t - \chi_t)) = \rho_{t-1} \cdot ((1 - \phi_{t-1}) \cdot \gamma_t + \phi_{t-1} \cdot \chi_t)$. Therefore, $\gamma_t = (\phi_{t-1}/(\phi_{t-1} - 1)) \cdot \chi_t$, which is the

viability frontier from Okishio's criterion of technical choice. We may notice that $-\phi_{t-1}/(\phi_{t-1}-1)$ represents the ratio of profit over wage. It should also be noted the exact linear relation is derived in the continuous time framework. If we want to derive it in the discrete time framework, we need to make an approximation.

15. See Section IV.2.

16. For the uniform circular distribution with negative center, we may have manageable formulas for the mean values of γ_t and χ_t. For the uniform elliptic distribution, it is hard to have manageable formulas for the mean values of γ_t and χ_t since it involves elliptic integrals. Foley (1999, pp. 12–13) attempts to calculate the mean values of an ellipse by approximating it with a lozenge.

17. It may be compared with Fig. 2.

18. When γ_t of a newly available technique is outside of the viability set, γ_t and χ_t of the technique become zero because individual capitalists maintain old technique.

19. It is possible to get the same result more analytically since we can have manageable formulas for the mean values in this case.

20. If there is no eccentricity, ellipse is transformed into circle with zero center. As explained in Section III, we disregard the case of circle with zero center.

21. It may be compared with Fig. 3.

22. The main purpose of the simulations is to understand the theoretical analysis pursued in Sections IV.1 and IV.2 by means of numerical examples and visualization. Since the structure of the economy assumed in this paper is simple, we can easily take advantage of simulation method. In addition, the simulations contribute to the understanding of some propositions (e.g. those involved in elliptic integrals) which can not be completely proven by analytical method.

23. For the simulations, I assumed x_0 (labor productivity) = 1, k_0 (capital-labor ratio) = 1 and w_0 (real wage rate) = 0.9. Therefore, it is assumed that the initial rate of profit is 0.1. If we apply each criterion of technical choice to a potential technical change with uniform circular distribution with negative center, we get similar results.

24. The critical level of wage share, beyond which the rate of profit and the capital-labor ratio show a specific movement, is determined by the concrete shape of the distribution of potential technical change.

25. In this case, as we see from Fig. 7(b), the rate of profit is increasing during some initial periods. In general, the rate of profit is affected by x_t/k_t and w_t/k_t. If w_t is proportional to x_t as in Figs 7(c) and 7(d), the rate of profit is affected only by x_t/k_t from the beginning. On the contrary, if w_t is constant as in Figs 7(a) and 7(b), the rate of profit is affected by both x_t/k_t and w_t/k_t. The rate of profit increases if the level of the decrease in w_t/k_t is greater than the level of the decrease in x_t/k_t. The initial periods of Fig. 7(b) correspond to this case. In Fig. 7(b), the tendency is eventually subdued and the rate of profit is dominantly affected by x_t/k_t, as w_t/k_t rapidly converges to zero.

26. We can easily analyze the case of a low wage share by applying the same analytical and simulation methods.

REFERENCES

Ahmad, S. (1991). *Capital in Economic Theory: Neo-classical, Cambridge and Chaos.* Hants: Edward Elgar.

Baldani, J., & Michl, T. R. (2000). Technical Change and Profits: The Prisoner's Dilemma. *Review of Radical Political Economics, 32*(1), 104–118.
Bowles, S. (1981). Technical Change and the Profit Rate: A Simple Proof of the Okishio. *Cambridge Journal of Economics, 5*(2), 183–186.
Cullenberg, S. E. (1994). *The falling Rate of profit: Recasting the Marxian Debate*. London: Pluto Press.
Dumenil, G., & Levy, D. (1993). *The Economics of the Profit Rate*. Vermont: Edward Elgar.
Dumenil, G., & Levy, D. (1995). A Stochastic Model of Technical Change: An Application to the U.S. Economy. *Metroeconomica, 46*(3), 213–245.
Dumenil, G., & Levy, D. (1999). The Classical-Marxian Evolutionary Model of Technical Change. Paper presented in the *URPE* Session of the ASSA meetings.
Foley, D. (1986). *Understanding Capital*. Cambridge: Harvard University Press.
Foley, D. (1999). Simulating Long-Run Technical Change. *Mimeo*. New York: New School University.
Foley, D., & Michl, T. R. (1999). *Growth and Distribution*. Cambridge: Harvard University Press.
Freeman, C. (1994). The Economics of Technical Change. *Cambridge Journal of Economics, 18*(5), 463–514.
Groll, S., & Orzech, Z. B. (1989). From Marx to the Okishio Theorem: A Genealogy. *History of Political Economy, 21*(2), 253–272.
Kliman, A. J. (1997). The Okishio Theorem: An Obituary. *Review of Radical Political Economics, 29*(3), 42–50.
Laibman, D. (1992). *Value, Technical Change and Crisis: Explorations in Marxist Economic Theory*. New York: M. E. Sharpe, Inc.
Marx, K. (1987). *Capital*, Vol. I. New York: International Publishers.
Marx, K. (1984a). *Capital*, Vol. II. New York: International Publishers.
Marx, K. (1984b). *Capital*, Vol. III. New York: International Publishers.
Michl, T. R. (1992). Capital and Labor Productivity. *Review of Radical Political Economics, 24*(2), 45–50.
Nakatani, T. (1980). The law of falling rate of profit and the competitive battle: comment on Shaikh. *Cambridge Journal of Economics, 4*, 65–68.
Okisho, N. (1961). Technical Changes and The Rate of Profit. *Kobe Univ. Economic Review, 7*, 85–99.
Parijs, P. Van (1980). The Falling-Rate-of-Profit Theory of Crisis: A Rational Reconstruction by way of Obituary. *Review of Radical Political Economics, 12*(1), 1–16.
Roemer, J. E. (1981). *Analytical Foundations of Marxian Economic Theory*. Cambridge: Cambridge University Press.
Shaikh, A. (1978). Political economy and capitalism: Notes on Dobb's theory of crisis. *Cambridge Journal of Economics, 2*, 233–251.
Shaikh, A. (1980). Marxian Competition versus Perfect Competition: Further Comments on the So-Called Choice of Technique. *Cambridge Journal of Economics, 4*(1), 75–83.
Shaikh, A. (1999). Explaining the Global Economic Crisis. *Mimeo*. New York: New School University.
Sweezy, P. M. (1942). *The Theory of Capitalist Development*. New York: Monthly Review Press.
Warskett, G. (1991). Choice of Techniques and Theorem of Okishio. *Metroeconomica, 42*(2), 125–136.

ON THE POLITICAL ECONOMY
OF SOCIALISM: AGAINST
THE REGULATION OF SOCIAL
RELATIONS BY MARKETS

Martijn Konings

ABSTRACT

This paper offers a critique of the theory of market socialism and then proceeds to develop the central point of the argument – that socialism is inherently antithetical to the regulation of social relations by markets – in a more constructive manner. After a brief introduction, a summary of the contemporary market socialist case (second section) and an examination of the conceptual status of the market (third section), it is shown that the institutional arrangements proposed by market socialists are consistently subject to the totalizing rationality of market regulation (fourth section). A critique of market regulation is presented in the subsequent (fifth) section, and some implications for the theorization of the political economy of socialism are drawn out through a discussion of several transformative projects (sixth section). The conclusion outlines a perspective for further enquiry.

Marx's *Capital* and Capitalism; Markets in a Socialist Alternative,
Research in Political Economy, Volume 19, pages 107–153.
Copyright © 2001 by Elsevier Science Ltd.
All rights of reproduction in any form reserved.
ISBN: 0-7623-0838-9

I. INTRODUCTION

It is by now commonplace to state that recent years have witnessed an adjustment of the traditional assumptions, means and aims of socialism. Phrases such
as this often serve to conceal the drastic downward adaptation of the aspirations
entertained by the Left. Both the demise of Eastern European communism and
the problems that have beset Western welfare states have undermined the notion
that socialism of whatever kind might offer a viable or desirable alternative
to the marketization of society. Socialism is now widely equated with the
overweening power of the state and the suffocation if not plain oppression of
individual rights.

Ironically, much of the established account of socialist politics is shared by
the Left itself. The failure to look beyond what liberal apologists define as
socialism has resulted in a virtually complete neglect of elements in the socialist
tradition that escape the statist legacy, and in an attendant inability to counter
the arguments of the neoliberal Right. The institutionalized Left has lost the
capacity to conceive of emancipatory strategies in terms other than states and
markets, in this way corroborating the rule of capital.

Far from contributing to its resolution, the fashionable theory of market
socialism epitomizes the crisis of socialist politics. Market socialism is most
accurately designated as an attempt to sketch the contours of a revitalized
socialism capable of coping with what are perceived to be the demands posed
by modern times and its processes of social heterogeneization and globalization.
Market socialists' attempts to construct a 'feasible socialism' have come to
occupy such a central position that in a recent collection of articles it is claimed
that 'market socialism is now one of the main topics of debate on the Left
world-wide' (Ollman, 1998a, p. 2).

This paper will first present a critique of the market socialist perspective,
after which I will proceed to develop the central point of my argument – that
socialism is inherently antithetical to the regulation of social affairs by markets
– in a more constructive manner. This point should not of course be taken
to mean that socialist endeavors and transformative efforts are meaningless as
long as markets are around; what it does mean is that these endeavors and
efforts will have to work against and challenge the operation of market forces.
Rather than adopting the neoliberal discourse of states and markets, socialism
should seize upon this forced self-reflection to dig up ideas, strategies and
organizational alternatives that fell from grace when statist socialism took center
stage.

II. THE CONTEMPORARY MARKET SOCIALIST CASE[1]

It is the legacy of statism that advocates of market socialism are keen to break with. According to them, the statist traditions of socialism have done much to discredit the very set of ideas underlying Left politics and that is why new ways should be sought to express and realize what have always been the core values of socialism. What socialists should learn from liberalism is that a constitutionally limited state and the concomitant delimitation of a private sphere of non-interference are essential preconditions of attempts to give a practical content to the ideal of human autonomy. From this it is concluded that private property and decentralized market institutions should be accepted as a proper way of regulating the day-to-day affairs of society. These cannot, of course, be the same sorts of private property and markets as found in capitalist societies. Therefore, we need to distinguish between capitalist markets and socialist markets.

Under market socialism, markets would be employed as instruments society has at its disposal to regulate its own affairs. Market regulation would not be valued because it is ordained by the unalienable and natural rights of the individual, but for its ability to direct and coordinate human activity in a manner both rational and respectful of individuals' desire for autonomy. Much more than under capitalism, therefore, markets would be embedded in an institutional framework that is to ensure their working for the common good. Common to all market socialist proposals is the notion that full private ownership of the means of production is unjustified and that society (or its representative) should be able to exercise property rights over capital. As a consequence, the basic idea of market socialism is that combining market regulation with some kind of socialization of capital will make for a feasible socialism. Put simply: '[t]he key idea is that the market mechanism is retained as a means of providing most goods and services, while the ownership of capital is socialized' (Miller 1989, p. 10). A strategy built around these two core elements will be able to redeem the promises of emancipation always held out by the socialist tradition, without however falling foul of the demands posed by modern times.

Markets are said to be endowed with many valuable qualities which a socialist society cannot afford to dispense with. According to market socialists, Eastern European communism as well as social democracy have severely overestimated the rationality of government regulation, intervention and ownership. The capacity of states and their bureaucratic regulatory instruments to gather knowledge of, give expression to, and implement conceptions of the social good, has turned out to be very much more limited than classical socialism could ever be bothered to contemplate. Unlike state bureaucracies, markets do possess an inbuilt respect for individual preferences, thus allowing individuals to pursue their own personal projects and engage in transactions of their own choice. In this way allocative efficiency will be ensured and the popular association of socialism with waste of resources dispelled. Market competition provides agents with the requisite incentives and this makes intricate principal-agent problems considerably more tractable (for example, when society is the principal). Competition also generates dynamics of technological innovation and economic growth. Furthermore, price mechanisms are capable of handling the large information flows daily transmitted in modern societies; there is no need for a central authority to gather the knowledge which is of real concern to only a few people or simply incapable of being consciously communicated by nature. Thus, liberty as the absence of visible constraints happily coincides, through the mechanism of the invisible hand, with the furtherance of the interests of society at large.

The institutional arrangements proposed for the social ownership of capital come in many sorts and sizes. Obviously, comprehensive state ownership and control of enterprises are ruled out. On the other hand, all market socialist models feature the abolition of large private holdings of capital. In most proposals the bulk of society's productive activities is to be conducted in largely autonomous enterprises linked by markets, while society as a whole, usually represented by the state, retains some substantial rights in regard to the productive resources employed. So although capital is operated by enterprises participating in market competition much as they would under capitalism, they do not come to exercise full ownership rights. Society remains the ultimate owner of the stock of social capital and enterprises lease their capital from the state as society's representative. Ordinarily enterprises must at least maintain the value of the leased capital and pay a capital charge. It turns out that much of the market socialist case rests on the possibility of separating ownership rights and control rights[2] as this has been brought about under corporate capitalism. On this account, classical socialism has erred in conflating ownership regimes and coordination mechanisms. The distinction between social ownership and private ownership is by no means coterminous with the distinction between *ex ante* coordination by planning and *ex post* coordination by markets. Markets and capitalism are not equivalent. Similarly, there is no need for a central authority to coordinate the whole of society *ex ante* to give content to the idea of socialism for it is perfectly feasible to combine forms of social ownership with coordination by markets.

The central question to be answered is the following: does market socialist theory succeed in outlining the elements of an adequate re-embedding of markets? Although the claim that socialist markets are compatible with the values and goals of socialist politics is frequently put forward as a substantive argument, it is by itself not much more than a tautology and rather begs the question as to what exactly a socialist re-embedding of markets would consist of. It is imperative, therefore, that we obtain a clearer picture of the conceptual status of markets.

III. THE CAPITALIST REGULATION OF SOCIAL RELATIONS BY MARKETS

Markets pre-date capitalism. This fact is often adduced in support of the market socialist disarticulation of markets and capitalism. That markets have existed in non-capitalist societies does no doubt demonstrate that there is no simple equivalence between markets and capitalism. However, it does not warrant the conclusion that capitalism and markets are only contingently related. Perhaps we should focus on the role played by markets instead of their presence or absence. For the role played by markets in pre-capitalist societies is qualitatively different from the role and functions of markets under capitalism (and also, as will become clear later, from those assigned to markets in a market socialist society).

It is not, then, that the existence of markets as such is the defining feature of capitalism; it is the *regulation* of human affairs and relations by markets that endows capitalism with its distinctive features. Tautologically, markets take on regulatory functions when people lose their capacities to control and steer the development of society. This, in turn, occurs when people are separated from each other as well as the means of producing their livelihood. Essential to the development of capitalism has been the creation of markets for labor, land and capital, alienating the worker from his own labor-power, the means of production and ultimately society at large. Market competition becomes a mode of regulation as a result of this extension of markets; market exchanges are transformed into market forces (according to Devine's (1988) distinction, to be discussed below).

Coterminous with the divorce of the producers from the means of production and the universalization of markets is the institutional separation of state and society, the abstraction of people's common interest from the social relations in which they participate. The exercise of class rule by means of seemingly independent acts of exchange (sale of labor-power for money-wage) requires and presupposes the abstraction of a political authority serving as a repository of coercive power. The capitalist state is in a very real sense both the creation and creator of capitalist social relations of production; it has played a major role divesting workers of their residual rights of access to communal productive resources and has retained an essential role in the reproduction of prevailing production relations throughout the history of capitalism.

Market regulation, then, is not a natural structure reflecting the timeless logic of economic choice; its imposition through the separation of the bulk of the population from the means of production is a historically contingent outcome of social struggle. Markets are politically created through the institution of private property, and the economy as a separate realm of society comes into existence only as a result of this. It is of particular importance to emphasize the political origins and nature of free market economies: 'the differentiation of the economic and the political in capitalism is, more precisely, a differentiation of political functions themselves and their separate allocation to the private economic sphere and the public sphere of the state. This allocation separates political functions immediately concerned with the extraction and appropriation of surplus labour from those with a more general, communal purpose' (Wood, 1995, p. 31). The failure to enquire behind, question and criticize this differentiation of functions severely limits the range of 'feasible' emancipatory, transformative efforts: 'assuming the separation of politics and economics as a starting point (. . .) is not a theoretically innocent starting assumption. It is to assume the automatic reproduction of the particular human social relations which bring about and sustain this institutional separation' (Rosenberg, 1994, p. 132). To assert that market forces are economic entities that may be impelled forward, countered or adjusted by political intervention, is precisely to theoretically reproduce the mystifying institutional arrangements of capitalist society, as well as to foreclose the possibility of uncovering the ways in which they are related. Market forces are as much political as economic constructions.

Consequently, the economic and the political are best conceptualized as different forms assumed by capitalist social relations; their separation is not absolute, but formal. In the structuralist tradition, the dividing line between state and society was reified and absolutized only to assert an ultimate functional unity under the determination of the economic level. Theoretical attempts to accord due weight to agency and political struggle have all too often resulted in the dissolution of the structuralist categories rather than an increased purchase on reality. The crucial yet oft-neglected contribution of the state derivation debate (see Holloway & Picciotto, 1978) was to point out that any desire to retain the base-superstructure metaphor, however modified, is problematic, and that politics and economics are to be understood as the historical forms assumed by the class struggle under capitalism. It is only after social relations have taken on a particular form that their function can be theorized – a function they can either perform, or fail to perform. The abstraction of the state from society is a historical, non-necessary outcome of protracted and recurrent social struggles which is not accomplished once-and-for-all: the institutional separation of politics is not only the outcome, but also the context and object of class struggle. The dividing line is, therefore, continuously contested and subject to change and re-form. In other words: contestation occurs within, against and over the differentiation of political and economic functions. 'The separation of the economic and the political is not an objective feature of a structure imposed by the logic of capital, it is an institutional framework which is only imposed on capitalist relations of production through a permanent class struggle, a framework which is accordingly a constant object of class struggle, which is only reproduced and transformed through that struggle' (Clarke, 1991, p. 46).

What we normally refer to by 'free market economy', then, is a set of social forms. These forms, through which people are dissociated and constituted as individual property-owners, are potentially in contradiction with the 'human condition', mundanely understood as the necessity for people to work together in order to produce their livelihood. The fundamental contradiction of market regulation is the contradiction between the (trans-historically) social character of production and the separation of people from each other and the means of production through the imposition of the commodity-form. It must be stressed that this contradiction should not merely or primarily be understood as the social-ization of labor within the confines of privately-owned enterprises, but rather as the society-wide conflict between the functional requirements of production and its organization around private appropriation. It is a contradiction between social form (free markets) and function (the continuation of production, at the same time reproduction of the ensemble of social relations organizing production).

Now, for (re)production to occur, some sort of association must take place. The working classes find themselves compelled to offer their labor-power for sale on the labor market. The labor-power is bought by a capital-owner and subsequently labor and capital are combined in a temporary association, allowing production to take place. The association occurs on terms set by the owner of the means of production whose sole motive for temporarily disposing of her capital is the anticipation of its augmentation. She will therefore be bent on retaining control (which may be exercised on her behalf by an appointed manager) over the production process and for this reason the capitalist enterprise will generally be of an hierarchic nature. Hierarchic planning under capitalism is contingent on the dissociation of society: the latter is prior to the former.

From this it must be concluded that the notion that 'the social relations constituting capitalism involve a *duality* of fundamental conflicts' – i.e. class antagonism and competitive antagonism – and that 'it is the *combination* of these two social antagonisms which provides capitalism with its characteristic 'laws of motion'' (Barker, 1997, pp. 51–52) is mistaken. Competition and class struggle are not two different dimensions along which contemporary society is structured; competition is the very means by which capital conducts the class struggle, it is 'merely a particular way of organizing the class struggle' (Cleaver, 1996, p. 91). Understanding free market economies as historical forms of class struggle should not lead us to locate that struggle primarily in the place where it is often most visible, namely in the enterprise. Alienation of people from each other and the means of producing their livelihood, hereby setting them up against each other in rivalry, is the very mode in which the 'laws' (regularities of the class struggle) of capitalism are executed.

These remarks should also serve to undermine the idea that the ubiquitous presence of hierarchies in contemporary societies in itself points to the gradual supersession of capitalist production relations and the transformation of capitalism into an organized society; although enterprises may grow to command vast resources and gain considerably leeway with regard to the employment of these resources, their activities remain ultimately directed to exchange competition. Both government and enterprise hierarchies find their broad, long-term goals set for them. There is nothing intrinsically anti-capitalist (let alone socialist) about planning; as long as market regulation prevails and mechanisms for direct allocation derive their purpose from the rivalry of society's fragments (as expressed in prices), markets and hierarchies are complementary.

The state's role is initially perhaps most obvious in the definition and protection of property rights. However, given the contradictory development of a free market society, it is inconceivable that the interlocking of state and society could resemble the liberal image of a minimal state. The development of modern capitalism has witnessed a multiplication and intensification of the functions performed by the state in response to the obstacles to capital accumulation. The institutions of the state are therefore in a very material way directly implicated in the inner workings of capitalism.[3] It follows that the equation of capitalism to private ownership is an oversimplification. The dependence of the masses on capital is reproduced (and challenged) in many ways; the universalization of the commodity-form is not a once-and-for-all act, but must constantly be renewed. The resilience capitalism has displayed over the last century cannot be explained without theorizing the many different roles states can and must play, both by means of direct intervention and by channeling popular emanci-patory pressures. The circuit of capital reproduction consists of many moments which are, at the same time, possibilities for supersession and transformation.[4]

Nevertheless, it is the differentiation of social relations into political and economic forms, the both social and dissociating construction of market regulation, that endows capitalism with its historical specificity. What is distinctive about capitalism is that it is not a system of naked oppression and unconstrained exercise of power, but that power, government and authority are institutionally separated (always tendentially) from material production based on generalized exchange. Domination under capitalism is achieved by a subtle intertwining, or rather, disengagement, of self-movement and coercive power. This means that the rationality (i.e. the way actors are made and enabled to behave in a manner functional to reproduction) imposed through market regulation should be central to the analysis of capitalist society. For the very concept of capitalism to have some meaning, the economic sphere must 'stand on its own' to a certain extent. As it is just a matter of observation that reproduction does occur and that social production organized around private appropriation repeatedly succeeds in 'delivering the goods', there has to be some coherence to the idea of coordination by an 'invisible hand'. The fact, then, that crisis tendencies are endemic to capitalist social formations cannot be deduced from a knowledge of their form only; for they stem from the contradiction between this form and what it is imposed upon (its content).[5] Market regulation is not internally inconsistent or incoherent in a purely logical sense; it is its contradictory relation to what it is supposed to regulate that sparks the crisis tendencies characteristic of capitalist development and necessitates the continuous reorganization of production relations by the state. The imposition of an alienating market rationality and the resistance of this imposition is what class struggle is about.

The self-absorbed rationality of market regulation will be investigated in the fourth section, while its contradictory nature will be the object of attention in the fifth section. Without pretending to offer anything remotely resembling an exhaustive analysis of market regulation and the conflict between the functional requirements of social reproduction and its organization through markets, in the remainder of this paper I will concentrate the discussion on the issues of motivation and information. For coordination of economic activities to occur, at least two functions must be fulfilled: the information- and the motivation-function. Under any mode of coordination, within any set of social forms, actors must be properly motivated to perform the actions consistent with social reproduction and they must possess the information to be able to do this. Singling out for discussion the issues of information and motivation will allow me to examine the case for market socialism (which rests to a large extent on the alleged superiority of markets with regard to motivation- and information-functions), as well as to shed light on problems and questions of socialist political-economic organization that have remained undertheorized in the socialist (and particularly the Marxist) tradition (as is often rightly noted by market socialists).

IV. MARKET SOCIALISM AND THE TOTALIZING LOGIC OF MARKET REGULATION

The first market socialist model was presented by Lange (1970) [1939], who took up the challenge laid down by Von Mises (1935).[6] The latter had argued that the common ownership of the means of production would not allow for economic calculation and a rational organization of economic activity. Given the impossibility of valuation in kind by a central authority in a complex economy, and in the absence of a market for capital goods, there would be no way of learning the value of production goods. Calculation and rational allocation require the universal presence of a mechanism to reduce the qualitatively diverse range of goods to a common denominator, i.e. free competitive markets which produce prices.

Lange's model of market socialism allowed for markets for both consumer goods and labor-power, but not for capital goods. He argued that Von Mises had conflated two meanings of the concept 'price', namely the exchange-ratio of two goods on the one hand, and 'the terms on which alternatives are offered' (Lange, 1970, p. 61) on the other, and that this distinction rendered the calculation problem soluble. For it is only in the latter sense, i.e. in their parametric function, that prices are indispensable for rational calculation and allocation; and these indices of alternatives could be derived without recourse to competitive market processes. Given the fact that consumers' preferences are expressed in demand prices on the consumer goods' market and the amount of resources available is also known, the index of alternatives is determined by the production functions. And since the central planning authority would have 'exactly the same knowledge, or lack of knowledge, of the production functions as the capitalist entrepreneurs have' (1970, p. 61), it would be perfectly capable, by means of a trial-and-error procedure, of imputing prices in the more fundamental sense to capital goods. Accounting prices, then, perform the same parametric function as market prices under capitalism. With rational prices and the possibility of cost calculation being established, managers of publicly owned enterprises are instructed not to maximize profits, but to choose those production methods that will minimize average costs and then to set prices at the level where they equal marginal costs.

Although Lange took Von Mises's challenge as a technical problem to be resolved with the instruments of neoclassical theory, the argument was precisely that the formation of exchange-ratios in and through market competition is the only feasible way of acquiring knowledge of 'the terms on which alternatives are offered' in a world too complex and too dynamic to be understood by a single mind in one instance. What underlay the debate, then, were two rather different views of market processes. As we will see, the differences between these two approaches are substantial and the adoption of one or the other will be seen to lead to radically opposed conclusions on the (in)compatibility of markets and socialism. Much revolves around the social *meaning* of market competition, which was much better grasped by Von Mises than by Lange. I will argue that a more adequate conception of market regulation than the one put forward by neoclassical economics will invalidate the fundamental idea of market socialism and set it on a slippery slope of marketization. Once the regulation of social interaction by markets is accepted, the Austrian arguments for full-blown capitalism are much more coherent than the arguments for market socialism. Nevertheless, we should not allow the differences between neo-classical and Austrian theory to blind us to the common ground on which these theories are built: both rest on a variant of naive individualism. The rejection of this common ground will re-open the door to an advocacy of socialist strategies. The Austrian assertion of the impossibility of a socialist organization of production is itself founded on an inadequate view of how actors do and conceivably could interact, i.e. of the social conditions of agency. This short-coming is linked up with its excessively narrow definition of the social and political framework necessary to sustain a free market economy.

The assumptions adopted by neoclassical theory regarding motivation and information are profoundly problematic. First, actors are assumed to be utility-maximizers. It will suffice here to point to the obvious fact that people often act on emotional, normative and affective grounds that are, except by definition, not rational. By sticking to the tenet of rationality, the neoclassical conception of motivation and choice leaves no room for real, meaningful choice. Individuals are slaves to their own preferences which they mechanistically optimize. The outcome of market processes is therefore implied in the assumptions made. The first assumption is in a way based on the second, because individuals can only be said to be truly rational when they are fully informed. Information, therefore, is assumed to be freely available; genuine, irreducible uncertainty does not exist. It is fair to regard this as an expression of naive positivism. Ironically, if actors were in possession of perfect information, they would not need to engage in market exchange: if every market participant is a Walrasian auctioneer as well, then the mediating function of prices becomes entirely redundant. When individual choices are reduced to picking the maximum point on a pre-given and knowable preference-scale under conditions and constraints fully known, the market process is entirely determined. The economy is simply viewed as 'a quantitative balance of things' (Lavoie, 1985, p. 85) from which meaningful, purposeful agency is expunged. This makes the market a black box: a certain input automatically yields a certain output.

Hayek followed through the points made by Von Mises, elaborating what has come to be known as the Austrian theory of market processes. The core of Hayek's attack was his stress on the economic problem as the problem of the dispersal of relevant knowledge. The neoclassical theory on which the market socialist case was built, rested on an untenably positivist conception of the nature of knowledge and information. Market socialists erred in identifying 'the economic problem' as the problem of determining the optimal structure of production under the assumption of full and objective information on opportunity costs (the 'terms'). The information that would be required can never be given as such to 'a single mind' but exists 'solely as the dispersed bits of incomplete and frequently contradictory knowledge which all the separate individuals possess' (1949, p. 77). For most practical purposes, knowledge exists only as subjective, tacit, and unorganized knowledge. The real economic problem, then, is not a problem of optimization under conditions of full information, but instead of the very mobilization and utilization of this information. Lange could only rest his case upon the formal similarity of economic choice under capitalism and socialism by glossing over the prior problem of data-acquisition, i.e. by conflating subjective and objective knowledge, the information available to cognitively limited individual actors and to the Walrasian auctioneer.

Insofar as a 'logic' of economic choice does exist, it does not refer to the mechanistic selection of the best means to further a given end on the basis of objectively known opportunity costs, but must take into account the conditions of imperfect information and irreducible uncertainty, i.e. it pertains to 'the subjective alternatives perceived but forgone by the decision maker at the instant of his choice' (Lavoie, 1985, p. 101). Information on production functions is not only not 'in the air', to be collected by market participants or planning authorities, but often not even known as such by the producer ('entrepreneur') until she discovers it in the course of her rivalry with other producers. Prices, meanwhile, do not perform a parametric function, pre-existing competition and balancing quantities of things, but are variables constantly transmitting the new information mobilized by entrepreneurs who use price cuts as an instrument of competition. Costs and prices are in continuous movement and influence each other through entrepreneurial mediation. Similarly, profits are found, not mechanistically maximized. Competition, then, is not a 'perfect' matter of marginally adjusting quantities at given prices; it is a pluriform process the results of which cannot be known until after it has actually taken place.

The ways in which Austrian theory recasts the concepts of economic theory, has far-reaching consequences for the case for market socialism. The point made explicit by Hayek is that the partial reintroduction of competition, along market socialist lines, does not do very much to immunize socialism primarily conceived as central hierarchic planning from its irrationalities. '[I]f competition is to function satisfactorily, it will be necessary to go all the way and not to stop at a partial reintroduction of competition' (1935b, p. 220). Markets would be unable to perform the regulatory functions assigned to them by the market socialists, precisely because of the restrictions imposed on market competition. As a result, confining public ownership to the means of production hardly reduces the intractability of the tasks facing the planning authority: it still needs to know about as much as when it would be planning and administering all of society's economic affairs.

Hayek advances several specific arguments pointing to the need for genuine capital markets. Here I will highlight only one. The market socialist proposal for the replacement of profit maximization with a set of rules issued by the central authority to the production managers ignores the fact that, even for the managers, cost phenomena are much more elusive and less definite than supposed by Lange and neoclassical theory. Production managers will simply be unable to discover their lowest possible costs if they are not allowed the entrepreneurial freedom to engage in competitive processes. When, in addition, motivational aspects are taken into account, the broader issue of the (financial) responsibility of the managers arises. If the central authority has less relevant information than the production managers, then the latter enjoy a decision making discretion which may be incompatible with the general interest. Only by somehow obtaining the same information as the managers themselves possess, can the planning authority ascertain that the managers are acting according to its rules. This would defeat the purpose of instituting market socialism. Thus, market competition fulfils many more functions than recognized by neoclassical theory, and all these would fall on the shoulders of the central authority. Competition conceived as a discovery process in which entrepreneurs' own interests are at stake cannot be replaced by a simple set of rules.

By linking problems of motivation and information in this way, Hayek already furnished the ingredients for a theorization of the principal-agent problem.[7] An agent is supposed to represent her principal's interests in return for a reward. If the principal does not have the same information as her agent, a monitoring problem arises; the principal's inability to ascertain whether the agent is adequately pursuing her interests, opens up a decision making discretion within which the agent may further her own interests. How, then, does the principal ensure that her agent acts in accordance with the principal's interests without acquiring the same information as is available to the agent? Three relevant types of principal-agent relations may be distinguished: those between society and state, state and production managers, and managers and workers. In the remainder of this paper, I will leave aside the relation between managers and workers nor will I consider the possibility of active malfeasance of state personnel (the claim that states cannot properly represent society does not hinge on this supposition).

Now, summarizing the Austrian case against socialism and for capitalism, it is claimed that problems such as the principal-agent one can be satisfactorily resolved only in a free market society where pervasive and continuous rivalry ensures that individuals are motivated to utilize the knowledge available to them in a manner conducive to the coordination of an irreducible variety of individual plans. The presence of a price mechanism serves to elicit and convey the information relevant to other people's individual projects, and enforces responsible behavior by firmly linking decision making powers to accountability. Dispersed and tacit knowledge is mobilized and translated into market prices by the rivalrous activities of the entrepreneur who has a personal stake in the conduct of her business.

Market socialist models of more recent origin are, much more than Lange's, in full appreciation of the virtues of real market forces. What Bardhan and Roemer (1993) call the fifth generation debates do not anymore attempt to simulate any markets but to employ market forces in a social scheme (not necessarily a plan). The ambition to centrally fix the prices of production goods has been relinquished along with the idea that firms should be publicly owned in the sense that the state is the principal holder of both income rights and control rights (Bardhan & Roemer, 1993, p. 7). By and large, market socialists have abandoned their indignation with the anarchic character of market competition in order to concentrate their efforts on rescuing socialist principles of equality by showing that market forces can work for the common good by themselves quite well. Much has happened, both theoretically and in the real world, since Hayek passed judgment on Lange's scheme, and therefore it would be useful to examine the rationale behind the retreat from Lange to the contemporary market socialist models.

Brus's work (1972, 1973, 1975, Brus & Laski, 1989) represents a gradual retreat from socialist ambitions in favor of a model with few non-capitalist features named 'market socialism proper' and is for this reason very instructive for the argument made here. Writing from an 'actually existing socialism'-perspective, he considers the problems and incongruities of centralized command systems and attempts to outline the possibilities for and conditions of decentralization.

In the centralized model the state sector comprises the 'relations between the economic administrative organs and enterprises and between enterprises themselves' (1972, p. 71). This model contains money and commodity forms which are introduced in order to prevent the problems associated with an excessively bureaucratized command system based on the in-kind allocation of productive resources. In the latter system, enterprises would always enjoy some scope for autonomous activity because the state is unable to monitor every individual action. This scope would often be exploited in the knowledge that the state as the director of society will assume responsibility for the results of enterprises' behavior. Here the problem of the soft budget constraint makes itself felt (see Kornai, 1993): the limited possibilities for making firms regard centrally determined planning targets as effective budgetary constraints on their own behavior. However, the money and commodity forms introduced within the centralized framework in order to cope with this problem are only allowed to play a passive role. They do not steer the movement of resources but merely serve as administrative recording devices. Their main purpose is to enable the derivation of profit and loss accounts containing meaningful information that allows the center to hold individual production units accountable. Enterprises are not allowed to make their own investment decisions and planning is still central, direct and imperative.

However, the informational function of profits is premised upon the firm's ability to respond with a minimum degree of flexibility to changing circumstances. Therefore, hardening the budget constraint requires a decentralization of investment decisions in order to establish a link between decision making power and accountability. Genuine decentralization through markets is the hallmark of the decentralized model. This does not mean that the aspirations to planning have been relinquished, but rather that the overall social plan and the units of social production are linked through the (indirectly) regulated market mechanism instead of through administrative directives. Brus argues that an active (instead of passive) market mechanism (i.e. market regulation) may be used as part of a central plan. This would amount to the state's role being reduced to directly determining the way income is to be divided and the main investment trends. Enterprises, still state-owned, operate autonomously and make decisions on the basis of their profit and loss accounts (profitability principle). They obtain investment rights, can expand and go into bankruptcy. They may not, however, set up new enterprises, nor are (horizontal) capital flows between branches and firms permitted. This increased market regulation of current economic decisions allows the central planners to concentrate their finite efforts and capacities on long-term planning. The decisions taken centrally are 'filled out' by decentralized modes of decision making.

However, competitive market relations do not by themselves work to realize plan targets: the center's attempts to devolve the tasks it is not equipped to deal with provides enterprises with the opportunity to wield these newly acquired decision making powers in a manner inconsistent with the social interest. For the 'filling out' to be achieved, the market institutions need to be (indirectly) regulated. The state's ability to influence the decisions of autonomously operating enterprises rests on the parametric function of prices (their independence from private interests). Prices can be manipulated (e.g. by means of taxation) so as to affect the profit and loss accounts of enterprises in a manner consistent with social priorities, i.e. so as to translate centrally determined priorities into effective (budget) constraints.

But the functioning of manipulated market prices as parameters, as 'strings pulled by the center, to which firms will react like puppets' (Kornai, 1993, p. 45), is precisely what cannot be presupposed. The impetus to economic dynamics provided by the introduction of market relations call for the horizontal reallocation of capital, and regulation of this by the state would defeat the purpose of decentralizing reforms. A notable hardening of the budget constraint will remain a vain hope as long as the considerable scope for initiative is combined with the imposition of restrictions incompatible with decentralization as marketization. Decentralization of current investment decisions necessitates the introduction of capital markets.

The persistence, even after considerable decentralization, of the soft budget constraint bears out the inherent tension between the state's role as society's impartial representative ('agent') and its practical role as one (albeit an extraordinarily large, well-resourced and powerful one) of the parties interacting in economic life. The differentiation of these two roles arises from the limitations to the state's universality, meaning that it is not a perfectly informed Walrasian auctioneer overseeing the whole of society made up of easily regulated mechanistic individuals. The result is a discrepancy between function and the limited availability of capacities and resources. The idea that it is easier to regulate activities already subsumed under a mode of regulation than to regulate these directly cannot but be predicated upon a conception of this mode (the market mechanism) as a black box yielding a certain output for any given input. To couch the argument in terms of the principal-agent problem: because the state as principal does not possess the motivational and informational capacities to monitor its agents (enterprises) in the manner and with the intensity required, it is incapable of being a good agent of society, the ultimate principal. In a sense, proposals to decentralize investment decisions and retain public ownership combine the worst of both worlds: firms are free to engage in irresponsible behavior and the pursuit of private gain in the knowledge that the state probably will ultimately assume that responsibility and come to their rescue.

From these considerations the rationale behind Brus's and Laski's (1989) advocacy of 'market socialism proper', 'a truly monetarized economy in which all goods are supplied as commodities' (1989, p. 110), is clear. The only difference between market socialism proper and capitalism is that under the former the means of production are not privately owned; however many crucial rights are exercised by enterprises, the state retains the status of principal. The public ownership element consists in the levying of a general capital charge. However, it does not demand a lot of imagination to envisage much the same scheme as a tax levied on capital under capitalism. By reducing socialism to a reformed kind of capitalism, Brus and Laski seem to ignore the very nature of the problems that have so often been encountered by Left strategies.

Not all market socialists feel forced to concede quite so much to the case for capitalism. Some recent models, such as Roemer's (1994) and Yunker's (1992), make more explicit use of an argument that has been implicit in the above discussion to a certain extent, to wit, the opportunities opened up by the separation of ownership and control (entrepreneurship) as it exists under contemporary capitalism. If capitalist firms can be made to work for their share-holders, why could not the share-holders be replaced by society as represented by the state?

However, this proposal rests on a flawed conception of the precise nature of this separation. It overlooks the fact that the separation of ownership and control does not apply as such generally or absolutely: owners (principals) still need to be able to control the controllers (corporate managers, agents) to a certain extent, even if the aim is reduced to the derivation of capital income; and this was precisely the problem discussed earlier. In this respect, the owners of large holdings of capital fulfill a crucial function monitoring corporate managers and eliciting information concerning performance and conduct of business; in response to disappointing figures share prices will fall and this will make it more difficult for the firm to raise capital. The solution of the principal-agent problem under capitalism is to an important extent due to the concentration of ownership rights and the concomitant presence of strong private interests. Dispersed share-holders would have insufficient incentives to monitor managers' performance. However, interests strong enough to function as an effective principal are nowhere to be found in the state structure. Share-holders under capitalism have at their disposal means to control the controllers that the socialist state would have to do without.

To this argument it might, in turn, be replied that it is perfectly feasible to mimic capitalist financial arrangements by setting up intermediary institutions acting as principal of managers and as agent of the state. This is only a sensible argument if we rely on the one-sided neoclassical conceptualization of the principal-agent problem, focusing on incentives rather than the interrelation between motivational and informational factors as outlined in the above (cf.

Adaman & Devine, 1996, pp. 525–526; 1997, pp. 65–69). On that account, it is indeed possible to hold on to market socialism by 'lining up' the actors in such a way that all of them are under the appropriate incentives to which they will respond in mechanistic fashion. Otherwise, the introduction of intermediary institutions would merely amount to a displacement of the problem, and would probably again represent one of more steps towards dissolution of the market socialist organizational structure. Wherever one might wish to locate the point of a sustainable balance, the direction is towards the expansion of market regulation and market forces.[8]

The point that emerges from the above discussion is that the market socialists' acceptance of markets as the proper regulators of human interaction forces them to accept the rationality that this imposes upon actors; this foils their attempts to re-introduce a substantial social rationality because these will sooner appear as truncations of market forces than as beneficial interventions. '[T]he market cannot regulate an economy in the absence of private ownership of the means of production, competition, market-determined monetary prices and profit maximization' (McNally, 1993, p. 173). The question that market socialists fail to address is that of the social meaning of market rationality, regulation and competition. Von Mises and Hayek pursued the fetishized view of markets to its logical end: as soon as markets come to regulate social interaction, they will impose their own asocial and expansive rationality. Accordingly, there is little point in trying to interfere with or even plan a process when we are dispossessed of, *and* persistently refuse to struggle to regain, the basic means and levers to control it. This refusal is the market socialist contribution to socialist theory.

Market socialist models only acquire a semblance of viability on a neo-classical account of market processes, which in effect denies the existence of actual competition between actual persons and actual regulation of human affairs by anarchic markets. The advocacy of market competition and regulation as elements of a socialist society relies heavily on stripping these of their essential attributes. Consequently, anything is possible as long as the actors are 'lined up' or 'drawn up' properly, each under the incentives to which she will respond so as to mechanistically maximize her pre-given preferences. Markets come to function as black boxes that may be employed as technical instruments to realize social goals. What neoclassical theory hides from view is that market relations are forms of the social capital relation and tend to shed their institutional character once the conditions of their subjection to social control have disappeared ('disembedding', 'absolutization'). Put differently: the market socialists failed to realize that the markets they regarded as balances of things and tried to put at the service of mankind's common interest, already were expressions of social relations.

Austrian theory, rather than emptying categories of agency and competition so as to be able to fit these into any social scheme, considered agency in a situation where agents are connected by relations of buying and selling. For the purpose of socialist theory, it is instructive to read Hayek as giving an account of alienation as a social process rather than as an anodyne condition devoid of agency and rivalry. If competition and alienation were conditions involving no real antagonism, then we would just have to wait for the Walrasian auctioneer in the guise of the market socialist theorist to define a social good and a scheme to realize it. The extreme subjectivism of Austrian theory foreclosed this option of bringing objectivism back in. What market socialists want, is to reclaim autonomy and self-determination long after they have given up its basic preconditions. Re-embedding markets asks for wholly different measures than the ones proposed by market socialists. If it is assumed that human interaction needs to be regulated by markets as the exclusive alternative to hierarchic planning, an inexorable logic of marketization is encountered.

V. AGAINST MARKET REGULATION

All this is *not* to suggest that Hayek provided an adequate account of what markets actually do and do not do. As forceful as the Austrian case against market socialism is on the assumption that social relations need to be regulated by markets, so problematic is this very idea. 'The Mises-Hayek critique of socialism according to the criterion of calculation is inseparable from an underlying theory of economic life – one that rests on the most thoroughgoing methodological individualism – and lacks coherence outside the framework of that theory' (McNally, 1993, p. 197). This coincides with my earlier observation that market regulation is not incoherent or inconsistent in a logical sense; it is its incompatibility with the nature of what it is supposed to regulate that sets up contradictions and sparks the crisis tendencies typical of market societies. Given its extreme subjectivism, in Austrian theory there is no consideration of a possible conflict between the (trans-historical) social functional requirements of reproduction on the one hand and the separation of individuals from each other and the means of production through markets on the other. In fact, markets *solve* the central problem of dispersed knowledge. Real competition between individuals (human agents, not utility-maximizers) is a natural condition, not itself the outcome of social struggle. As a consequence, Hayek's account of agency in a market society is wrong. The institutional framework for a free market economy as specified by Austrians is seriously underdeveloped. Although the Austrian school explicitly devotes attention to the functions fulfilled by the market economy's legal and monetary framework, this does not even add up to a remotely adequate account of what the institutional pre-conditions of a market economy look like. What is lacking is the realization that the free market is originally itself an 'instituted process' (Polanyi, 1985) – albeit one that is in contradiction with its own social nature and consequently constantly expanding to sweep away its institutional preconditions.

To put it plainly: the extreme subjectivism on which the edifice of Austrian theory is erected, should be rejected. This is again best considered under the two headings of motivation and information. First, self-interested competitive behavior directed at individual gain is, rather than a natural inclination, itself a mode of socialization which will never be found in pure or unmitigated form. The utilitarian calculus is inapt for arriving at a description of actors' exchange behavior on markets not only because actors are not calculating and maximizing all the time, but also because the day-to-day functioning of a market society is crucially dependent on the presence of a significant measure of 'trust' and moral inputs.

Second, the rejection of a naive positivist and objectivist epistemology does not necessitate an endorsement of an extreme subjectivism and should not lead us to regard free markets as a feasible method of dealing with problems of information. As Hodgson (1988) convincingly argues, cognitively limited actors are necessarily reliant on social institutions for the formation of a conceptual framework allowing them to process raw sense data and subsequently employ the information obtained to engage in meaningful action; this holds regardless of the exact nature of the information. Then there is the simple observation that a great deal of possibly important information is not by nature tacit or inarticulate; this is not to suggest that it is readily available, but rather that it might be capable of being codified and transferred given the appropriate social arrangements. Furthermore, knowledge that cannot be discursively communicated is often referred to as a skill; it might not be possible to transfer the skill by mere verbal communication, but that leaves open the possibility of communication of the method of skill acquisition. Considerations such as these should serve to direct our attention to the fact that knowledge is not primarily an attribute of individuals but a social product (Wainwright, 1994). Having brought back knowledge and information from the autonomous realm of exchanging individuals to the level of society, i.e. having 'resocialized' and 'repoliticized' it, we are again in a position to examine the intricate relation between knowledge, coordination and power. People's motivational and cognitive capacities, it has to be concluded, are socially constructed, and are inextricably bound up with and vary with the social context they find themselves in.

These elementary observations would ground an exploration of the contra-diction between the functional requirements of production and the form in which production is organized. For the benefits and coherence imputed to market regulation are largely contingent upon the notion of people being naturally isolated competitors. It should be concluded that the private character of knowledge and information is to a very important extent a consequence of, rather than a rationale behind, the organization of social production through markets. This insight was, as recently argued by Adaman and Devine (1996, 1997), the core of Dobb's neglected contribution to the socialist calculation debate. Exploring the economic problem from a dynamic perspective too, Dobb (1955) arrived at a different conclusion than Hayek. Against the Austrian claim that the price mechanism elicits and conveys all the relevant information, he argued that the failure of markets to take into account (and of prices to reflect) dynamic interdependencies, make them most unsuitable for achieving rational allocation. Dobb, in other words, stressed uncertainty arising from the atomistic uncoordinated decision making constitutive of market forces instead of the uncertainty stemming 'from the objective nature of things' (1995, p. 77). Uncertainty is less a consequence of individuals' innate cognitive limitations than of capitalist forms of social organization. Because prices do not contain all the relevant information, price mechanisms are poor coordination mechanisms. From this Dobb deduced, in particular with respect to investment allocation, the need to replace *ex post* coordination with *ex ante* coordination by means of central planning. Unfortunately, this plea for central planning as the proper alternative to the price mechanism's incapability to register 'the shadows cast by coming events that still have to be realised' (1955, p. 77), signals a relapse into the assumption of the objective availability of information and a failure to appreciate the Austrian critique of this assumption.

In a similar vein, O'Neill (1988) most instructively restates classical Marxist objections to market regulation in terms of information, coordination and communication. According to him, the market mechanism fails to communicate all the relevant information to the relevant individuals because these individuals are in competition and in many cases have an interest in withholding relevant information on their own projects from each other. The market blocks rather than enables the communication of information. In addition, by allowing only for individual action to further individual interests, market regulation paralyzes attempts at collective coordination when all participants do possess the relevant information. Furthermore, Hayek's conception of 'relevant knowledge' is extraordinarily narrow. For one thing, it includes only quantitative information – prices can only differ along a quantitative dimension. That consumers of tin often do not need to know why and how tin has become more scarce cannot legitimately be generalized into the claim that all information other than that embodied in market prices is redundant to everyone. Whatever

'relevant knowledge' might include, it certainly excludes information needed
to pursue projects the benefits of which are not easily couched in terms of
private gain. Market prices tell us little, if anything, about the environmental
effects of production, nor does moral indignation get translated into market
signals. And, although this takes us far beyond the functional transmission of
information, markets certainly prevent and distort the communication of the
practical theories serving to denaturalize established identities and routine
agencies that are basic to any type of transformative effort. Market economies,
in a very real and consequential way, mystify the oppressive character of their
underlying social relations (Ollman, 1998b). All in all, the one thing that markets
are eminently suitable for is the transmission of information concerning matters
of individual consumption without any social ramifications.

While the Austrian critique of market socialism spelt out the meaning and
implications of the expansive rationality that market regulation imposes, it failed
to consider how this dissociating rationality is in permanent conflict with its
social and political origins and how the reproduction of an economy of generalized market exchange (perpetuation of class rule) is dependent upon a range
of flanking institutions contravening the multifarious manifestations of this
contradiction. This failure is evinced by Hayek's exaggeration of the extent to
which any government measure not designed to promote competition and to
strengthen the framework of a free market order, would necessarily be irrational
and spark off chains of perversities. The virtues of catallaxy have always proven
much more tangible and less elusive than Hayek would have us believe. But
on the other hand certainly not as malleable as much of the socialist tradition,
notably social democracy, for a long time supposed. The point we should take
from Hayek is, I believe, that if market forces are to be regarded and to function
as the mainspring of social welfare, they cannot be curtailed at will without
adversely affecting their supposed beneficial results. What the Von Mises-Hayek
position amounts to, is the claim that if one of the foundations of capitalism
(the capital market) is taken away, then capitalism will stop functioning. The
Austrian critique of market socialism merely tells us, first, how capitalism would
work if it were a coherent system of regulation, that is, if the dissociation of
human beings did not set up a set of contradictions, and, second, why if it is
made to stand on one leg (market socialism's proposal), it will function much
less than half as 'well'. But this is only problematic if it is taken for granted
that human beings are such limited and incompetent creatures (in terms of both
motivational and cognitive capacities) that they would never be able to sensibly
manage their own common affairs.

My argument against *both* market socialism *and* capitalism, then, is premised
on the simultaneous appraisal *both* of the totalizing logic of market forces, *and*

of market regulation as setting up a fundamental contradiction between the social and political conditions of production and its (dissociating) organization, i.e. on an integral understanding of market competition and regulation as outcome, context and object of class struggle. The critique of market socialism grasps the first element, market socialism grasps neither of these properly. Market forces are constituted through differentiated economic and political forms, but the rationality of these forces results in an incessant destruction of their non-economic institutional preconditions. All this may sound as if I am trying to reconcile irreconcilable points of view. A likely retort would be that *either* markets are social institutions and can as such be regulated and employed to advance the social good, *or* individuals are natural isolated competitors and collective control is illusory on principle; one cannot have it both ways. But the problem from a socialist perspective is precisely the *loss* of self-determination and control. Alienation and loss of self-determination are social processes and relations of struggle, not given conditions.

Market socialism shares the mistaken conception of social and political dimensions as external to (not implicated in the constitution of) and somehow grafted onto the forces of the market economy with social democracy. An understanding of the double-faced, contradictory nature of market regulation is essential to an adequate assessment of the predicament of Western welfare states and social democratic politics. The debate about the crisis of the welfare state seems to balance between perceptions of fundamental unsustainability and frontal assault, and marginal gradual attrition in the face of its firm entrenchment. And indeed, on the one hand advanced capitalism could not possibly exist without an elaborate state apparatus fulfilling the many functions that it does; the sort of free market order envisaged by neoliberalism would immediately collapse under the weight of its own contradictions. On the other hand, however, it would be a severe mistake to maintain that the difficulties experienced by national economic management and the institutions of the Keynesian welfare state are the result of temporary or 'external' disturbances and are not rooted in the generic deficiencies of the conceptions of governance and steering capacity that underlie these institutions. Offe (1984), for example, captures this ambivalence in the phrase 'crisis of crisis management'. In a very material sense, advanced capitalism cannot live with or without a welfare state.

Social democracy deluded itself into thinking that the political domain was an open, unbiased field that could be captured and wielded to rein in the dynamics of capitalism. The conviction that the state is by its nature an opportune instrument for realizing socialist ambitions against the workings of the market economy ('politics against markets'), has always had a very strong (and debilitating) hold on social democratic thought. The faith in the coordinating capacities of hierarchic state institutions have fuelled its 'constructivism'. We search in vain for an awareness of the constraints imposed upon social democratic transformative efforts by declining to challenge and reconstitute the relation between political and economic forms. Again, there is no reason to deny the significant gains made by parliamentary social democratic parties in the 'democratic class struggle'. But the definite limitations of a strategy relying on the capitalist state to realize its emancipatory program, i.e. the limits of the 'social-engineering state', have come forcefully to the fore in the last decades. This, to be sure, is the 'crisis of socialism'. Contemporary proponents of market socialism, keen to break with social democratic statism, seek to mimic the structure of neoliberal discourse by 'circumventing the state' (Pierson, 1995). As an alternative to the technocratic steering institutions of the welfare state we are offered a largely depoliticized economy with a 'built-in' socialist element. As shown in the above, market socialist theory thus gets entangled in a never-ending search for solving principal-agent problems and hardening budget constraints. What is consistently lacking is the realization that the market economy *is* political and constantly repoliticized and therefore always rife with these very phenomena. Challenging the nostrums of neoliberalism on its own mystifying terms by circumventing the state is simply not a viable option. Reasoning with the dichotomies of liberal theory amounts to a refusal to engage in a reconstitution of the relations between the political and the economic and this can only hinder and abort genuine emancipatory and transformative efforts.

Market socialism, it becomes clear, is a variant of social democracy, a mixed economy of markets and hierarchies (Panitch, 1986). As Pierson (1993, 1995) very convincingly argues, the most we might get out of pursuing the market socialist project, is a kind of welfare capitalism. At the same time, this is the only sense in which market socialism might come to represent a 'feasible socialism'. 'There is an irony here. The market socialist model is very much one for 'socialism in one nation-state'. Yet interest in market socialism was largely fuelled by the seeming impossibility of pursuing a national-based socialist or social democratic strategy (. . .) It is precisely because incomes policies, full employment and a national consensus on citizenship (. . .) were so difficult to sustain that socialists found themselves having 'to learn to love the market' (Pierson, 1993, p. 194). Market socialism remains firmly ensnared in the false dichotomies of liberal theory.

Therefore, the major question facing socialism is *how* to avoid the liberal pitfalls outlined in the above and *how* to transcend its false dichotomies. To begin with,[9] how do we answer Nove's challenge: 'there are horizontal links (markets), there are vertical links (hierarchy). What other dimension is there?' (1983, p. 226). Phrased differently, in a way that contains the answer: which kinds of associations may people enter into that do not conform to the rationality of a prior dissociation? Which forms of non-hierarchic association would effectively challenge and defy market regulation? Now, beyond markets and hierarchic planning, we find democratic self-governing associations. Socialization should not be conceived as an association of dissociated and alienated individuals but as the supersession of an imposed market rationality by social individuals appropriating the manifold preconditions of their self-government.

In the above it has been shown how market socialist theory has tried to accommodate pressures for decentralization of decision making competencies through a depoliticization of the economy, by introducing ever more market mechanisms. A more promising manner of coming to terms with the inherent limitations to the coordinating and controlling capacities of centralized state structures, that is, with the state's incapacity to be an adequate agent of society, would be to strive to realize a transfer of state power to democratic groups in civil society. Before his surrender to liberalism, in two books Brus (1973, 1975) provided tentative clues as to the opportunities for decentralization as democratization instead of marketization. What this might have resulted in, is a notion of a plurality of interests directly involved in the democratic determination of the employment of society's key resources. In these writings Brus propounds a conception of the socialization of the means of production as a *process*: this, one would presume, implies that whatever the starting-point, society must at all times reinforce and/or renew its grip on the allocation of productive resources because there simply are no agents or mechanisms capable of acting or functioning on society's behalf: delegation of agency will result in its relegation. The social interest does not pre-exist its expression and construction in a meaningful way, neither in anonymous state structures nor in invisible hand mechanisms allegedly ensuring the harmony of partial and universal interests. To whichever tendentially separated sphere power and oppression may have been displaced, in the end self-government must take place in civil society precisely because relegating emancipatory efforts to one or another sphere would already mean to isolate particular areas of social life from the reach of these efforts. (Great care must be taken here: civil society must once again not be understood as the famous realm of post-Marxism where anything can happen because determinations have been removed (where to?, impinging upon what?) and agency is unconstrained (but purposeless). I am here stating a condition, the *locus* of self-government.) 'Civil society, not the state and not the economic enterprise, is where self-government takes place' (Devine, 1991, p. 208). However, because of his inability to imagine democracy as something other than as essentially a narrowly political phenomenon, Brus's perspective remained too clouded to rid himself of spurious recipes for making parts of society work for the benefit of the whole.

As hinted at by Blackburn (1991, p. 37), who does not follow through his own point either, in between the 'single mind' and the isolated mind we find a meeting of minds. This observation should allow us to overcome the drawbacks of socialist theories offering different state-market configurations in response to the weaknesses they find with each other. Elson (1988) has taken up this point against market socialism: recognizing that coordination often takes place by a 'third hand' of informal networks and relations as a real alternative to both markets (invisible hand) and bureaucracies (visible hand), she proposes a 'socialization of the market' instead of 'market socialism'. Unfortunately, Elson seems to 'recoil from the full implications of her own analysis' (McNally, 1993, p. 213). Her main motivation for holding on to market regulation is that the informational and coordinating functions of market prices cannot be dispensed with. Prices enable us to make choices and the information they provide may be insufficient and in need of supplementation, but is at the same time indispensable. There is no urgent need to strive to abolish markets, as they can be socialized. To this end, amongst other things Elson proposes to publicize processes of price formation through the institution of public bodies disclosing all kinds of relevant information and the free provision of access to information networks. Social control is a matter of transparency, not of *a priori* planning based on centralized knowledge.

A similar stress on the socialization of information and knowledge is found with Wainwright (1994) whose book is devoted to the development of an emancipatory politics of knowledge, that is, to finding 'ways of socializing knowledge of the market' (1994, p. 173). Contesting on the one hand the positivist conception of knowledge of the post-war social engineering state, and on the other hand Hayek's assumption that practical, unorganized knowledge is an individual attribute and his claim that market-generated prices communicate all the relevant knowledge, she outlines a view of knowledge as a social product and opens up a perspective of social transformation. Wainwright's 'third hand' are the 'social relations that are neither market nor plan, neither the haphazard outcome of individual activity nor the design of an all-knowing central authority' (1994, p. 148). Accordingly, socialization and democratization mean the forging of an 'alliance between public institutions and independent associations' (*Ibid.*).

Notwithstanding the fact that both of these positions are substantially different from the market socialist one, there remains a sense of confusion with respect to the actual (pre)conditions of self-government. For it is far from clear that these positions do away with precisely those defining features of market societies that are responsible for the individualization and privatization of knowledge and coordination. The conditions of subordination of markets to the proposed social-ized coordination are supposed to be present rather than made the object of enquiry. The important recognition of the social character of market regulation (absent in market socialist thought) may lead us onto the road towards the theorization of a socialist alternative; unfortunately, it does not by itself do much to define this. Market regulation is always 'impure' (Hodgson 1988) and a 'third way' in that it is in constant need of fresh social inputs not generated by market forces themselves. However, the problem was that their expansive tendencies make an enduring encroachment on market forces distinctly infeasible. Relying too much on heavily underdetermined conceptions such as 'socialization' always carries the danger of ending up protecting capitalism from itself. Butler, reasoning from a perspective similar to Wainwright's, puts it as follows: '[a] sense of community is itself a causal outcome (. . .) socialists conjure up an alluring vision and assert it against a world which lacks the basic practical conditions for its viability' (1995, pp. 135–136). Socialization, therefore, should not be understood as the democratization of market regulation and coordination (leaving intact its rationality), but as democratization as itself a mode of regulation and coordination. For in the end, 'there is an irreducible contradiction between the regulatory functions of the market and its capacity for 'socialization'' (Wood, 1995, p. 289).

These last remarks are not in any way meant to downplay the vital importance of socializing information and knowledge; it is merely to insist that this should be indissolubly conceived as part of the establishment of a 'transformative framework' (Butler, 1995) connecting both popular and specialist knowledge, understandings and grievances to social capacities for agency. There is little point in privileging impotent agency over unguided agency. Knowing things is not enough to transform them: actors must possess the means, be in the position to act upon this knowledge. A democratic transformation of the coordination and regulation of social interaction can only be effected by agents associated in such a way as to be able to exercise a whole range of capacities and to overcome the very real obstacles in their way. Generation and communication of knowledge is essential to these efforts, but theory cannot substitute for practice.

VI. ASSOCIATIONS AGAINST CAPITALISM

I do not want to claim any originality for the insight that the search for socialist alternatives should prompt us to consider the merits of forms of democratic association going beyond the familiar dichotomies of markets and hierarchies.

However, the progression of capitalist hegemony up to the point of the wide-spread acceptance of hierarchies (hierarchic associations) as the exclusive alternative to markets warrants a restatement. The theme of association is, in fact, already present in Marx's (and Engels's) work (see Schlechte 1982). Marx's understanding of socialist transformation is familiar enough not to require a lengthy treatment. As capitalism progressed and the contradiction between the oppressive relations of production and the development of the productive forces intensified, the working classes would reach a degree of class awareness allowing them to unite in a party and replace the existing organization of production with an association of the direct producers. Production would not anymore be ruled by (the anarchy of) the market as the only social bond, but would be organized democratically by the producers themselves, according to the principle of need. Two things should be noted here. First, as already indicated, one of the recurring themes in the socialist tradition has always been a certain frustration with the paucity of Marx's comments on what the socialist organization of production would look like on a more institutionally concrete level. Most importantly, Marx seemed little aware of any potential conflict between democratic self-government and central planning. Second, more than a century of capitalist development has done a lot to dent many socialists' faith in the centrality of the working class as the agent of transformation. Although it would be rather silly to reproach Marx for all the topics he did not address in any detail, his relative silence on the first point does seem to be at least partly bound up with a confidence in both the imminent numerical majority and the self-organizing capacities of the proletariat, neither of which can be taken for granted anymore. This section will review a number of emancipatory projects that seek to address these problems. While Marx's vision of socialism retains all of its salience, it is of crucial importance for socialist theory to spell out its institutional implications (without, of course, engaging in the design of blue-prints). And while it is precisely the absence of any guarantees of history that makes it necessary to complexify and concretize our understanding of association and transformative agency, a conception of the working class as composed of those who share interests deriving from their subordinate position in the social organization of production remains nonetheless as indispensable for the socialist project as it ever was.

The theme of association has recently been taken up by the project of associative democracy,[10] which attempts to sketch a number of positive principles for the reorganization of social relations while aiming to unseat class from the privileged position it has always occupied in the Marxist tradition. The theory of associative democracy harks back to the ideas of guild socialism and the English pluralists (see Hirst, 1989) although it departs in a number of ways from these. Cole's guild socialism was concerned to rescue social pluralism from Marxist class reductionism and to this end it stressed the value of functional representation, meaning that 'there must be (. . .) as many separately elected groups of representatives as there are distinct essential groups of functions to be performed' (Cole, 1920, p. 33). Democratic association necessarily involves a certain measure of representation, but this is only legitimate if interests (given with function) rather than persons are represented. This explains Cole's aversion of the representative institutions of liberal-democratic politics.

In the advocacy of functional representation as the basis for association lies a difficulty which runs through much of both guild socialism and associative democracy and which mars many of their very useful insights concerning the organization of socialist democracy. For functions can only be determined in relation to a given, historically specific social organization of reproduction. I do not think it is possible to construe the notion of 'function' in a way that is unrelated to the maintenance of a set of social forms. This, obviously, precludes a genuinely transformative perspective and sets quite stark limits to the emancipatory potential of guild socialist proposals. And to preempt a possible, if rather awkward, reply: the difficulty is not resolved by suggesting that association should be based on the anticipated structures of the future socialist society and that functional representation should be conceived in a prefigurative manner. Ignoring the constraints imposed by the present does not bring the future socialist society any nearer; the mere vision of a future society (an isolated utopia, not grounded in an analysis of social development) cannot form the basis of a challenge to existing society. Individuals simply do not possess interests that can be functionally represented; neither under capitalism nor under socialism.

To be sure, associative democracy prudently avoids frequent use of the term 'function'. Indeed, Hirst explicitly criticizes the doctrine of functional representation for its failure to see that there is no such thing as 'real representation'; representation is inherently imperfect because it always entails a certain degree of substitution and reconstruction. In his own words, the danger of functional-democratic thinking is 'that it tends to regard certain social interests and certain social groups as fixed. The functional 'interests' to be represented are taken as givens, with the assumption that the basic order of society is unchanging' (1990, p. 14). Only the active, voluntary involvement of citizens (exercise of voice) in associations organized around the representation of common interests can prevent oligarchies and assure accountability. But even under the most propitious of circumstances some individuals will be disinclined to participate some of the time. Therefore it is imperative that they have the option of exit. Consequently, associative reform schemes will have to supplement, not supplant, the existing representative institutions of liberal democracy.

The supplementation of liberal-democratic institutions with associative-democratic institutions would rest on two pillars. The first is the origination in civil society of a plurality of voluntary associative initiatives. Individual interests are best pursued in alliance with other citizens sharing those interests. The individual's capacities for self-determination are best developed when she is actively participating in the very social processes which shape her life and affect her interests. The market and the ballot-box are poor substitutes for this. The second pillar is the publicization of civil society through the devolution of public authority and the pluralization of the state. This transfer of state sovereignty enables the associations to be truly self-governing. Together these two elements would bring about the politicization of civil society, and they would thereby open up the possibility of making accountable those interests and actors who are ordinarily protected by the fictive liberal distinction between public and private. Politics, on this account, is not the government of citizens by distant and anonymous state structures, but the continuous management of citizens' affairs by those citizens themselves through institutionalized processes of negotiation and communication. Liberal parliamentary democracy is supplemented by democracy as deliberation and this makes possible the construction of overlapping notions of common good.

In other words, the coordination of citizens' activities is socialized: information is purposefully communicated and citizens' aims and motivations are consistent with social interests for the very reason that they themselves have been involved in their discursive construction. The fostering of a cooperative mutualism will supersede the inefficiencies and inequities endemic to competition and uncoordinated decision making. Associative coordination rests on the 'pluralist social negotiation of social priorities' (Martell, 1992, p. 169). Principal-agent problems and soft budget constraints are not solved by relegating them to an allegedly autonomous mechanism setting up chains of distrust, but by directly involving the affected interests in the decision making, monitoring and enforcement procedures. Depoliticizing civil society is self-defeating because late capitalism is already politicized through and through; late capitalism is an organizational society where market regulation has been replaced by the hierarchies of enterprises and government and mainly serves to link organizations. Depoliticization through the introduction of market relations in practice comes down to surrendering society to corporate capital. Associative political economy purports to come to terms with current realities instead of fighting an outdated image of free market capitalism. The acknowledgement of an irreducible diversity of interests and identities is combined with institutions encouraging the discursive coordination and negotiation of these into substantial common interests: liberalism and socialism reconciled. The salient question thus becomes whether associative democracy effectively safeguards itself from the problematic tendencies inherent in the aim 'to rescue the complexity of Civil Society from economic reductionism by stressing the equally important interests people have as consumers, patients, students, members of communities, etc.' (Schecter, 1994, p. 122) that it shares with guild socialism.

The theory of associative democracy, just like the theory of guild socialism, certainly offers many useful insights into the possible structures of collective action and the mechanisms and instruments of socialization strategies. And, importantly, it would be unfair to criticize associative democracy for failing to reconsider the demarcations of state and civil society. This is precisely what it proclaims to be doing: it explicitly distinguishes itself from social democracy, market socialism as well as the fashionable current of civic republicanism. The latter is faulted for extolling political participation and civic virtue in the absence of a realization that the institutions of contemporary capitalism do not neatly conform to the liberal distinction between public and private and are already deeply implicated in the 'private' economic sphere. However, it is far from clear that the theory of associative democracy satisfactorily conceptualizes the constitutive forms of capitalist society and the opportunities for their transformation. It might go beyond those socialist theories that accept the need for market regulation by stressing the central importance of reconstituting the relationships between market economy, civil society and the state, but the very fact that this conventional triad is still employed as such – that is, that the market economy is not primarily analyzed as itself a set of social forms, that the state cannot be adequately theorized as an abstraction from society itself, and that 'civil society' still features as the privileged interposed realm of relatively unconstrained voluntary agency and interaction – indicates that it is incapable of grasping *how* the compartmentalization of society constrains associative efforts and poses problems to the realization of a genuinely democratic and self-governing society. In other words, it fails to offer a convincing account of how democratic self-government would differ from liberal democracy.

Associative democracy is still oblivious to the oppressions of civil society. Given the concentrated (non-complex) inequalities in the distribution of a range of resources (money, power, knowledge and information, contacts, communicative capacities, organizational capacities, etc.) characteristic of actually existing civil societies, there is a clear danger that the organization of civil society through voluntary associations and the pluralization of state sovereignty may come down to the handing over of public power to the strongest partial or private interests – the result may be 'a democracy of and for the powerful in the context of a residual state' (Amin, 1996, p. 310). For civil society is 'an arena of social contestation' (1996, p. 328) and the inequalities between the contesting parties will be reflected in the opportunities for and the outcomes of associative initiatives.

The possibility of 'regionalizing' capital is essential to the associative-democratic program but is hard to envisage without reforms much more radical than those proposed, designed to foreclose capital's exit options. Streeck (perhaps unexpectedly) wonders whether associative democracy can 'restore a functionally complete political community with a boundary around it, which could stop the exodus from democratic politics and collective social obligations' (1995, p. 191). Whatever, then, the status of the concept of late capitalism, the changes it is supposed to capture certainly cannot include the *supersession* of market competition by organizational structures. The highly visible presence of organizations and political institutions does not represent a qualitative break in/with capitalist development. Capitalism did not get politicized when it entered its current, 'late' phase; it has never corresponded to the model of liberal theory and has been political from its very inception. Consequently, proposals for pluralizing state sovereignty stem from a problematic idea of the form and role of the state. The state cannot be a sponsor of transformative projects; it is a field on which these projects must operate, as well as an object of these ('in and against the state'). Not a 'lean' state, but a democratization of the state, or, rather, a democratic reconstitution of the relations between state and society is what is called for. Similarly, Amin suggests that what we are in need of is a 'broader tide of democracy' (1996, p. 322) with as its main elements a fundamental recasting of liberal constitutional and legal safeguards, a thorough democratization of the state, a socialization of the ownership and control of capital, and the fostering of participation in decision making processes through associations.

Associative democracy fails to understand the demarcations between state and society as the outcome, context and object of social contestation, i.e. class struggle. This makes its task much lighter than it would otherwise be: it can be 'soft on capitalism' (Levine, 1995) without reneging on its transformative and emancipatory promises. For any of the range of social interests and identities may freely participate in the discursive construction of social goals and these will in turn reflect the former more or less equally. In a sense, the associative-democratic theorist simply demands more of the citizen (namely, to become self-governing) than the civic republican or communitarian theorist does (namely, to be a virtuous, participating citizen/subject), but does not provide her with better tools. Lacking a genuinely transformative element, associative democracy is essentially a 'politics of identity', the fundamental problem of which consists in its naturalization of directly observed identities. Any emancipatory project should certainly celebrate and promote the value of pluralism, but it is questionable whether pluralism is best advanced by lumping all observed identities and interests together as equally foundational and constitutive of capitalist society. Exerting itself to avoid the pitfalls of functionalist essentialism, associative democracy commits the error of the 'exaggeration of agency'. 'Subordinates have, after all, a lack of agency. That's what makes them subordinates' (Heftler, 1997, p. 79). To deny that there are fundamental axes of conflict running through the infinity of differences we observe is to define away the entire problem of the systemic logic of market forces. Then, indeed, can emancipatory politics be about giving each interest its due weight instead of challenging the prevalence of one interest over another. Capitalism is deprived of its historical *differentia specifica* and the social organization may be altered at (the theorist's) will.

In other words, the supposition of a continuity between liberal democracy and socialist democracy is dependent upon the theoretical isolation of spheres of society and ascribing them autonomy. Understanding emancipatory politics as a more or less straightforward extension of democracy presupposes the possibility of disarticulating the democratic element of liberal democracy from its capitalist element and transposing it onto the rest of society. But, as Wood (1986, 1995) argues, this is precisely what cannot be done; democracy under capitalism is certainly a conquest of popular resistance but at the same time it represents a limitation of democracy and it is deeply implicated in the reproduction of capitalist social relations through its mystification of the privatization and de-politicization of power. The pitfalls of functionalism can only be avoided by stressing the constitution of society through open-ended class struggle (labor's presence 'in and against' capital), not by assigning politics an autonomous logic which might then serve to challenge the underlying structure, that is, by superimposing unstructured indeterminacy (radical democracy) on reified structures (the economy). Taking the latter route will result in unsatisfactory accounts of how socialist democracy would differ from capitalist democracy. 'Democracy' is a highly indeterminate/underdetermined concept and therefore the specificity of socialist democracy will have to be spelt out. The focus of enquiry should be the *conditions* of democratic self-government by associations. As stated in the title of Wood's book 'Democracy against capitalism', democracy and capitalism are antithetical; the struggle for a truly democratic society must be a struggle against capitalism, not an attempt to supplement the institutions of liberal democracy. Socialism is not simply 'more democratic' than capitalism endowed with parliamentary democracy; it must be democracy of a different quality that has very limited use for the institutions characteristic of liberal democracy.[11]

In an important sense, the entire socialist tradition can be seen as made up of attempts to understand the distinctiveness of socialist democracy. And even though so far I have been mainly concerned with showing the shortcomings of some of these, it would certainly be imprudent to simply dismiss them as deficient and inadequate and proceed to develop our understanding of the specific nature of socialist politics on the basis of a purely theoretical conception of capitalism, i.e. one that abstracts from the way in which its development has been shaped by these different forms of resistance. For ultimately, the question of capitalism's integrative and co-opting capacities and the transformative potential of particular types of agency is a historical question. Our theorization of socialism, then, needs to be developed by conceptualizing the differential transformative capacity of socialist forms of organization. Since it is, within the scope of this paper, obviously impossible to discuss a variety of organizational forms even in only a superficial way, I will here concentrate on some insights drawn from council communist theory[12] – insights which, I believe, have been unduly neglected and are not adequately represented in many other parts of the socialist tradition.[13]

In so far as council communist theories discard the obsession with 'smashing' and anti-gradualism, they suggest valuable correctives to the strategies discussed in the above by focusing attention on the conditions of social transformation and democratic self-government by associations. The 'obsession' is to a certain extent found in the work of Mattick (1978) who at times seems to hold that any emancipatory activity not corresponding to particular council forms and not consciously aiming to effect a radical overhaul of the social order, must necessarily get caught up into the structures of the capitalist system. The extraordinary and counter-intuitive implication of this would be that subversive agencies can only be said to have any significance and to be consequential if they result in an overthrow of the capitalist system. But capitalism is not and cannot be a closed system: market forces possess a systemic logic but their constitution through contestation endows them with both an inherent vulnerability and the openness required for subsuming new social inputs under these expansive tendencies. Socialization is a process (as well as relation of struggle) and to suppose that this process sets in only after some meta-theoretically defined starting-point, is not very instructive. There is no point in consigning transformative agency to the day of the revolution.

What I understand to be the valuable contribution of council communism is its outline of the prefigurative organization of class interests into associations (re)appropriating control over the functional preconditions of production and thereby arrogating themselves functions previously the preserve of the political community. Associative democracy, if one wants, but now on more fertile soil. Since capitalism is not an 'economic system', transforming capitalism is equally about transforming politics as the (historical and conceptual) other side of a competitive market economy separating people from each other and the means of production. Politics in the sense of organized (institutionalized), public adjudication between incompatible interests will never wither away. But when these incompatibilities and differences do not anymore (or progressively less) directly concern the distribution of individuals' life chances and do not result in the fundamental opposition of interests as encountered in capitalist society, a genuine pluralism as well as the possibility of adjudication and coordination through means other than (the threat of) coercion and competition comes into view. Therefore, the fostering of a counter-culture of solidarity and cooperation, inimical to the competitiveness and antagonism of capitalist society, is indissolubly tied to the program of council democracy.[14] Against Second International dogmatic materialism, council communists were concerned to re-unite theory and practice by according non-material ('spiritual', 'conscious') aspects their due weight. Communication of the range of possibly relevant kinds of knowledge is conditional upon the presence of non-competitive and non-hierarchic modes of interaction. What we find is that a considerable number of the elements of what has been termed a transformative framework are now systematically related.

Some of these considerations are also reflected in the theorization of socialist democracy propounded by Devine (1988, 1991; see also Adaman & Devine, 1996, 1997).[15] Taking issue with market socialism, he answers Nove's challenge as follows: 'there is no other dimension – but vertical links do not have to be hierarchical, in any authoritarian sense, and horizontal links do not have to be market based, in the sense of being coordinated *ex post* by the invisible hand of market forces. Both can be based on negotiated coordination' (1988, pp. 109–110). Devine proceeds to set out a model of democratic, participatory planning that addresses the critique of market socialism and thus avoids a relapse into the advocacy of central planning. The basic principle of self-government is that 'decisions and their implementation are the responsibility of and should be undertaken by those affected by them' (1988, p. 141). Consequently, social ownership should be constructed as 'ownership by those affected by the use of the assets in question' (Adaman & Devine, 1997, p. 76). The only way out of the crisis of agency (i.e. the painful awareness of the impossibility of permanently delegating agency) by which socialism has been afflicted, is the association of individuals sharing interests into self-governing associations. All the affected interests participate in institutionalized processes of negotiated coordination ('negotiated coordination bodies') through which decisions concerning the allocation of society's productive resources are taken in a cooperative manner. Investment decisions should be taken at the most decentralized level as is consistent with the principle of inclusion of all affected interests.

This 'pyramidical' discursive construction of social interests does not preclude the employment of market mechanisms. The disaggregation of the concept of the market into market exchanges and market forces points the way towards a precise understanding of how and under which conditions the effects generated by exchange-interactions between individuals tend to get beyond the control of those individuals (i.e. the historical *differentia specifica* of capitalism, its systemic logic). In Devine's theory, 'market exchanges' refer to transactions between producers and users of goods and services on the basis of a given production structure, whereas 'market forces' denote the absence of *ex ante* coordination of decisions concerning changes in productive capacity, i.e. the extension of market coordination to investment decisions. Market exchanges become uncontrollable and unpredictable market forces once market coordination is extended to investment decisions. 'Thus, market exchange coordinates the use of existing productive capacity, but changes in the structure of productive capacity are negotiated and coordinated ex ante by those affected by them' (Adaman & Devine, 1997, p. 76). Production units compete amongst each other for custom in the absence of any attempt at *ex ante* coordination. They set prices equal to long-run average cost, comprising labor costs, a centrally determined capital charge and the costs of bought-in inputs. These market exchanges do not spawn market forces: deciding changes in the allocation of productive assets is the privilege of the affected interests participating in the negotiated coordination bodies. To perform this task, the latter have a variety of sources of quantitative and qualitative information at their disposal. Three sorts of quantitative information are available: 'first, accounting data on the performance of each enterprise, generated by the use of their existing capacity (i.e. by market exchange); second, estimates of expected changes in demand or costs in relation to existing activities; third, estimates of expected demand and costs in relation to potential product or process innovations' (Adaman & Devine, 1996, p. 534). In addition, two sorts of qualitative information are furnished by the interests participating in the processes of negotiated coordination: 'first, judgements about the reasons underlying differential performance by enterprises; second, the views of those affected about the economic and social situation prevailing in the communities and regions in which disinvestment might occur, the priorities for regional distribution agreed through the democratic political process, and the concerns of other interests represented' (*ibid.*).

This outline of participatory planning takes into account both sources of imperfections of knowledge that have been identified in the above. While it is in full appreciation of Dobb's insights into the inefficiency of atomistic social organization and concomitant privatization of information, it does not rely upon unwarranted assumptions of objectively available knowledge to advocate bureaucratic central planning as an alternative, but incorporates a range of institutions for the social generation, discovery, articulation and communication of knowledge. The broad participation in cooperative negotiation processes ensures a generalization of the discovery function from the Austrian entrepreneur to all affected interests. Coordination is made into an explicitly social undertaking and it is therefore capable of solving many of the informational and motivational problems that have been seen to be insoluble under other institutional arrangements.

There remain, however, some problems and ambiguities with Devine's proposal. Among these is not in any case the objection raised by Blackburn that '[w]hile the multimillion-product complexity of a modern economy can be monitored, requiring it to be positively 'negotiated' is asking a very great deal' (1991, p. 48, n.72). As is noted by Devine and Adaman themselves (1996, p. 77, n.74; 1997, p. 534, n.1), this comment can only stem from a failure to appreciate the fundamental distinction between market forces (that can be replaced with participatory planning) and market exchanges. Furthermore, what Devine shows with particular clarity is that if we do not wish to be ruled by market forces, the only option is to constantly renew the grip on society's development through democratic participation in the planning of the allocation and use of its key resources. And indeed, this demands time, effort and resources (but, for one thing, not necessarily more than are spent on the solution of transaction problems in advanced capitalism).

Another point raised by Blackburn seems to have more validity: how are irresolvable differences decided? Also: how and by whom are the rules of negotiated coordination to be determined? Which interests are legitimate? These matters cannot of course themselves be the outcome of negotiated coordination processes. In Devine's model this does not really emerge as a problem because he envisages the institutional arrangements for consultation and negotiation as existing alongside representative institutions based on majority decision making. However, this coexistence may very well give rise to significant incongruities and an explicit theorization of these issues is absent. The underestimation of these difficulties might be bound up with an underestimation of the constitutive role of the political sphere. There seems to be a lingering notion that in some way transforming the economy is a more urgent and fundamental task than transforming political institutions. It is as if the post-Marxist dissolution of economic categories is resisted by to a certain extent clinging to a base-superstructure model of economics and politics. Hence, '[t]here is perhaps a contradiction between the radical imagination Devine shows about the possibilities of economic transformation and the timid political strategy in which he seeks to contain it' (Callinicos, 1993, p. 208). For example, a certain tension exists between the assertion that '[c]ivil society, not the state and not the economic enterprise, is where self-government takes place' (Devine, 1991, p. 208) and the claim that participatory democracy should be envisaged 'as a process of interaction and negotiation based on a three-way relationship between elected representative bodies, the administrative structures of the state, and self-governing groups within civil society' (*ibid.*).

In other words, it is not clear that Devine offers a fully convincing account of which elements enter into the formation of market forces. The consequence of this might be an underestimation of the areas and moments of socialization and transformation. The relative neglect of the *form* of politics and the state is matched by the absence of an explicit conceptualization of market regulation and market forces as the context, object and regularized outcome of social contestation. It is hard to see how the continued existence of a labor market could be prevented from giving rise to a competitive antagonism that would jeopardize the high degree of consensualism required for the satisfactory functioning of the negotiated coordination institutions. The proposed introduction of a basic income is an important step in the right direction but here, still and again, the contradiction between the market's regulatory functions and its capacity for socialization surfaces.[16] A basic income accomplishes at best a part of one half of the task faced: it makes the allocation of income partially independent from the performance of wage-labor (decommodification) but this does not render any more tractable (and perhaps even less so) the problem of how labor could be allocated in accordance with socially defined criteria without sacrificing the autonomy of the individual.

I have no substantial answers to this extraordinarily intricate problem, but two connected points deserve some attention. The basic problem is that freeing people from the pressures of the labor market while at the same time ensuring the continuation of social production requires a high degree of trust and willingness to cooperate in procedures of communication and negotiation. This immediately brings us back to the problem of the ultimate political authority supervising processes of negotiation and it might seem that sooner or later we would have to revert to liberal constitutionalism in order to avoid despotic practices. However, the option of a basic income already demonstrated that constitutionally codified rights need not take a liberal form. In addition, socialization could be critically extended by means of the free provision of life's primary necessities.

The idea of natural economy and calculation in kind may not be very useful for most purposes, but I think that it could fruitfully be applied to the provision of this vitally important set of goods (see Dobb, 1955, Mandel, 1986, McNally, 1993). Even the most ardent subjectivists cannot deny that humans have an hierarchy of needs and that the arrangements appropriate to the supply of goods satisfying basic needs, common to everyone, can be determined in a reasonably precise and uncontentious way. In turn, the satisfaction of basic human needs being guaranteed, it is hoped that the sharpest edges of the explication of social interdependencies through negotiated coordination will have been blunted and that it will prove an effective procedure even for dealing with contentious issues. The intention of these remarks is less to suggest a set of institutional arrangements than to emphasize that the emancipation of the individual and the socialization (de-privatization) of interdependencies are mutually sustaining and that these should be pursued as two sides of the same process: '[t]he goal of socialism is not so much the socialization of the individual as the personalization of society' (Mandel, 1986, p. 26).

The shortcomings found also account for the lack of a clear perspective on how the transformation from capitalism to socialist democracy would come about. Devine repeatedly stresses the transformative element contained in his model, but at the same time he distinguishes 'between the transformatory dynamic contained within the model and the process of transition from existing capitalist and statist societies to a society based on the model' (Devine, 1988, p. 189). This distinction in effect amounts to a severance of the link between reform and revolution, between strategy and end-state that has done so much to frustrate the realization of socialist ambitions. For all its similarities to Devine's model, this severance is notably absent in council communist thought.[17] Perhaps reasoning in terms of models while consigning the issue of their institution to a later moment, is not very conducive to an elaboration of the 'recasting of the politics of working class struggle' as a 'politics of alliance for the replacement of capitalism by a diversity of social projects' (Cleaver, 1996, p. 94). Furthermore, I am inclined to think that the tentative remarks laid down in the previous paragraph could provide some clues as to the progressive transcendence of class interests in favor of a genuine pluralism and the realization of an 'irreducible multiplicity of alternative ways of being' (Cleaver, 1996, p. 89). Although Devine's insights should set many of the terms for future debate, it seems that much is to be gained from an attempt to draw out the implications for transformative strategies of a detailed understanding of capital as a complexly constituted dynamic relation between capital and labor, that is, a historically specific process-relation assuming and constituted through different forms.

VII. CONCLUSION

These critical comments are admittedly very imprecise and unsystematic. Let me concisely state a few points delineating a perspective from which these questions should be approached and investigated further. Many market socialists would view this perspective as unrealistic, overly ambitious, and immodest. But it is precisely the 'modest' confinement of political ambitions to capitalism's interstices (that can only be conceived of) as the imperfections of an otherwise impenetrable bulwark that occludes from view its totalizing logic continuously reproduced through regularized social contestation. A socialism whose ambitions go beyond contenting itself with the crumbs capital wipes off the table, will have to build on the understanding of capitalist social formations as outcome, context and object of class struggle. This means investigating the specific relations obtaining between politics and economics as shaped by the course of the class struggle. All too often socialist theory is mesmerized by the 'automatic' economic development of capitalism. As an antidote to the relegation of agency to a superimposed political domain, attention should be shifted to the many ways in which the working classes have challenged the rule of capital and thereby shaped the development of capitalism.

Clear and useful insights into the obstacles to be overcome, the constraints imposed upon transformative agencies by the complex institutional fields into which previous chains of agency have rigidified, and the conditions of strengthening emancipatory agencies by association and combination – these can only be gained by digging up and studying a variety of socialist strategies, ideas and experiments. While the temptations of reformism and social democracy's current deadlock as well as the problem-ridden development of 'actually existing socialism' should certainly be carefully scrutinized, of more importance than ever is the analysis of the organizational alternatives and forms of resistance which have fallen into oblivion in the course of the twentieth century and may offer more or less coherent sets of ideas currently lying beyond the stretch of our collective imagination. Under which circumstances did these movements and initiatives arise, what did they look like, and what were the obstacles on which they eventually foundered? What was their differential transformative potential, how have they shaped capitalist development, and how was the threat they posed defused? What insights or even guidelines for action under contemporary capitalism do they offer? It is only by looking for answers to these kinds of questions that we can come to understand which kinds of agency and which organizational forms are characterized by a logic of cumulative re-form rather than subject to a progressive integration into the rationality of capitalism. And only in this way can we make some progress towards specifying underdetermined catch-all concept such as socialization and democratization, and gain insight into the preconditions of effective association and self-government. What socialism, therefore, is in desperate need of is a political economy of labor (see Cleaver, 1979, Krätke, 1996).

And for the very reason that the development of class struggle is open-ended, there is a point to these endeavors. Not because the newly acquired comprehension could somehow be directly 'applied'; nor is there much point to the (often perfunctory – after all, it is a matter of secondary importance) mustering of agents who might be willing to bring the theorist's ideas onto the political agenda – perhaps it is here that greater modesty should be exercised. Rather, socialist theory only acquires its meaning within transformative frameworks serving to relate potential agents to the institutional settings in which they find themselves, i.e. to clarify and make intelligible actors' relations to their social contexts (see Butler, 1995). Ultimately, all forms of collective action flow from shared appraisals of social reality. The unity of theory and practice should mean the construction of social frameworks facilitating the communication of knowledge and the development of common understandings. An essential requirement for this is to practice what has been termed 'institutional concreteness' (a requirement this paper falls foul of). This does not imply direction of research efforts to irrelevant details or merely entertaining anecdotes; what it does imply is the need to devote plenty of energies to the proper specification of indeterminate concepts. It is simply the case that effective agency is conditional upon a properly detailed understanding of one's position in relation to one's surroundings. Since actors lack the capacity to gain knowledge of the state of the entire world, or to be motivated by abstract considerations without any apparent purchase on their own lives, social science purporting to advance the cause of socialist transformation must be able to contribute to the generation of these understandings. People's struggles are not guided by a desire to abolish the anarchy of the market or the inversion of object and subject; they struggle against the concrete manifestations of the social relations designated by these concepts. Most of the time actors' concerns are concrete, regional and tangible. It follows that socialist theory will have to be able to inform highly particular strategies, struggles against local injustices and emancipatory efforts not undertaken under the banner of class struggle.

To phrase this slightly differently, socialist theory should understand and posit itself as what it is: social science, that is, knowledge of society that is itself social.[18] This would entail dispensing with both the invention of new agents willing to implement the theorist's schemes to replace discredited or incapacitated ones, and the reliance on automatic developments to bring about a once-and-for-all overhaul of the social order. Only a down-to-earth social science, inspiring because sober, committed to analyzing structured relational processes of human agency and interaction, can avoid having recourse either to the arbitrary introduction of objective structures beyond the grasp of human actors, or to unconstrained, discursively constructed agencies, and only such a social science will therefore be in a position to further the cause of socialist transformation.

NOTES

1. The following section does not pretend to give anything close to an exhaustive overview of market socialist models and theories. It is merely intended to reflect what I understand as the core ideas of market socialism. The relevant specific arguments will be presented later, integrated with my critique of them. For reasons that will become clear, I omit a discussion of what is often perceived as a distinctive characteristic of market socialist theory, namely the issue of labor management and cooperatives. For contemporary advocacies of market socialism, see Blackburn, 1991; Brus & Laski, 1989; Miller, 1989; Nove, 1983; Roemer, 1994; Weisskopf, 1993; Fleurbaey, 1993; the contributions to Le Grand & Estrin, 1989; Schweickart, 1995, 1998; Lawler, 1998; Yunker, 1992. I do not consider Elson's (1988) model a kind of market socialism.

2. A spurious conceptual distinction in that ownership is always a bundle of rights one of which is the right of control. The separation of ownership and control then amounts, in loose terms, to a bifurcation of the 'mythical' liberal conception of ownership into use rights and income rights. I shall stick to common usage. See further Christman, 1994.

3. The state defines and enforces laws, provides public goods, conducts monetary and fiscal policy (which includes the arduous task of revenue collection (taxation)), is immediately involved in the construction of money and credit-markets, contravenes monopolistic practices by means of competition policies, regulates labor markets, de- and re-commodifies labor-power, imposes regulations on the production process in the enterprise, sets up arrangements for welfare provision, owns public companies, channels popular demands through parliamentary-democratic and corporatist institutions, etc.

4. A first and very tentative objection to market socialism in this context could be formulated as follows: socialization of capital ownership reduces to quite a meaningless project if it is pursued in isolation, in abstraction from the variety of other elements entering into the formation of market forces. In capitalist society private ownership of the means of production becomes capital by virtue of its articulation with the other moments of the capital process-relation. The thrust of Marx's critique of utopian socialism lies, in my view, not so much in its alleged opposition to thinking about what socialist society might look like, but in the argument that it is not an option to arbitrarily retain those features of capitalist society that seem to have valuable qualities and discard those elements which seem less praiseworthy.

5. As Altvater puts it, '[f]ull 'marketization' (. . .) sets up contradictions which stem from the nature of the commodities traded on markets' (1993, p. 66).

6. My interpretation of the calculation debate follows the historical account offered by Lavoie (1985). Kirzner's (1988) claim that the distinctiveness of the Austrian approach

was only developed in the course of the debate is an interesting and important one, but cannot be explored within the scope of this paper. It may be thought that the extent of my concern with the Austrian critique of market socialism is somewhat excessive for a Marxist attempt to criticize market socialism and ground the theorization of the political economy of socialism. However, the problem is precisely that Marxists' inclinations to criticize market socialism in terms of the categories of *Capital* do not generally put us on very fertile ground for addressing the obstacles and problems faced by socialist strategies. As will become clear, the Austrian critique of market socialism, purporting as it does to be at the same time a critique of socialism tout court, explicates crucial points that remain rather underdeveloped in such Marxist critiques (and in the Marxist tradition more generally). For otherwise excellent Marxist critiques of market socialism, see McNally, 1993 and Chattopadhyay, 1998.

7. As such this problem is largely a preoccupation of neoclassical theory, but for the purpose of this essay it is helpfully stated by explicitly focusing on Austrian themes of discovery and genuine uncertainty. Problems that seem soluble under conditions of 'risk', are likely to look less tractable when genuine uncertainty enters the scene. See Adaman & Devine, 1997, pp. 57–59, for an account of how the principal-agent problem is solved when it is stated in neoclassical terms.

8. A slightly different way of phrasing this would be that the critique of market socialism does not depend on the validity of the liberal conception of private property ('consolidated property rights') but rather relies, given the private character of information, on the necessity of connecting accountability to private interests.

9. Many authors tend to regard insights like the following as the end rather than the beginning of a search for answers. But the critique of capitalism does not render the theorization of socialism redundant; attempts to reduce the latter to the former are doomed to failure. Nor is it at all fruitful to theorize socialism in isolation from what it is supposed to be a negation of. Divorcing the two results, quite simply, both from and in intellectual poverty.

10. See, most prominently, Hirst, 1994 and Cohen & Rogers, 1995.

11. Levine (1995, p. 166) offers a sloganesque reminder for this: 'socialism is the soil, democracy the seed, liberty the flower.'

12. See, for instance, Korsch, 1969, Rachleff, 1976, Mattick, 1978, Barker, 1987.

13. Amongst the theoretical and historical varieties of association that would need to feature in such an overview are, other than the ones already discussed in the text, producer and consumer cooperatives, anarcho-syndicalism, Austro-Marxism, trade unionism, economic democracy, local exchange systems. See Schecter, 1994 for some interesting discussions, and Bock, 1978 for an investigation into German Left radicalism. See Boggs, 1995 for an overview of the mainstream socialist tradition from a perspective sympathetic to radical currents.

14. This was, of course, a distinctly proletarian culture. A likely counter-argument would be that the working class has been subject to disintegration for almost a century and that ideas to revive proletarian cultures are worthless. They are. What is argued here, is that there are groups in society that have common interests deriving from their subordinate position in social reproduction and that these interests are sufficiently strong to warrant associative initiatives. These interests are by no means either monolithic or self-evident. Hence the paramount importance of organization through association around real matters and of the construction of transformative frameworks.

15. It is indicative of the crisis of socialist theory that one of the very few elaborate theorizations of socialism has received relatively little attention and discussion (at least when compared to some of the 'feasible' theories of market socialism).

16. This applies a fortiori to the real libertarian case for basic income as set out by Van Parijs, 1995.

17. Austro-Marxism (see Bottomore & Goode, 1978), renowned for its efforts to contravene the split in the international socialist movement, also offers interesting thoughts on the severance of, and the conditions of linking, reform and revolution.

18. See Krätke's (1996, especially pp. 110–119) discussion of Marxism as social science.

ACKNOWLEGMENTS

Many thanks are due to Leo Panitch and Michael Krätke for their help and comments. I would also like to thank Veit Bader, Marcel van der Linden, Paul Zarembka and three anonymous referees for their comments.

REFERENCES

Adaman, F., & Devine, P. (1996). The economic calculation debate: lessons for socialists. *Cambridge Journal of Economics*, *20*, 523–537.

Adaman, F., & Devine, P. (1997). On the economic theory of socialism. *New Left Review*, *221*, 54–80.

Altvater, E. (1993). *The future of the market. An essay on the regulation of money and nature after the collapse of 'actually existing socialism'*. London/New York: Verso.

Amin, A. (1996). Beyond associative democracy. *New Political Economy*, *1*(3), 309–333.

Bardhan, P. K., & Roemer, J. E. (1993). Introduction. In: P. K. Bardhan & J. E. Roemer (Eds), *Market Socialism. The Current Debate* (pp. 3–17). Oxford: Oxford University Press.

Barker, C. (1987). Perspectives. In: C. Barker (Ed.), *Revolutionary Rehearsals* (pp. 217–245). London/Chicago/Melbourne: Bookmarks.

Barker, C. (1997). Some reflections on two books by Ellen Wood. *Historical Materialism*, *1*, 22–65.

Blackburn, R. (1991). Fin de siècle: socialism after the crash. *New Left Review*, *185*, 5–66.

Bock, H. M. (1976). *Geschichte des 'linken Radikalismus' in Deutschland. Ein Versuch*. Frankfurt am Main: Suhrkamp Verlag.

Boggs, C. (1995). *The socialist tradition. From crisis to decline*. New York/London: Routledge.

Bottomore, T., & Goode, P. (Eds) (1978). *Austro-Marxism*. Oxford: Clarendon Press.

Brus, W. (1972). *The market in a socialist economy*. London/Boston: Routledge & Kegan Paul.

Brus, W. (1973). *The economics and politics of socialism*. London/Boston: Routledge & Kegan Paul.

Brus, W. (1975). *Socialist ownership and political systems*. London/Boston: Routledge & Kegan Paul.

Brus, W., & Laski, K. (1989). *From Marx to the market: socialism in search of an economic system*. Oxford: Clarendon Press.

Butler, A. (1995). *Transformative politics. The future of socialism in Western Europe*. New York: St. Martin's Press.

Callinicos, A. (1993). Socialism and democracy. In: D. Held (Ed.), *Prospects for Democracy* (pp. 200–212). Cambridge: Polity Press.

Chattopadhyay, P. (1998). Capitalism as socialism. Defence of socialism in the socialist calculation debate revisited. A Marxian approach. Available at http://www.gre.ac.uk/~fa03/iwgvt2/files/98sat1brcha.rtf

Christman, J. (1994). *The myth of property. Toward an egalitarian theory of ownership.* New York/Oxford: Oxford University Press.

Clarke, S. (1991). The state debate. In: S. Clarke (Ed.), *The State Debate* (pp. 1–69). London: MacMillan.

Cleaver, H. (1979). *Reading* Capital *politically.* Brighton: Harvester Press.

Cleaver, H. (1996). Theses on secular crisis in capitalism. In: C. Polychroniou & H. R. Targ (Eds), *Marxism Today. Essays on Capitalism, Socialism, and Strategies for Social Change* (pp. 87–97). Westport/London: Praeger.

Cohen, J., & Rogers, J. (1995). Secondary associations and democratic governance. In: E. O. Wright (Ed.), *Associations and Democracy. The Real Utopias Project.* Vol. 1 (pp. 7–98). London/New York: Verso.

Cole, G. D. H. (1920). *Guild socialism re-stated.* London: Leonard Parsons.

Devine, P. (1988). *Democracy and economic planning. The political economy of a self-governing society.* Cambridge: Polity Press.

Devine, P. (1991). Economy, state and civil society. *Economy and Society, 20*(2), 205–216.

Dobb, M. (1955). *On economic theory and socialism.* London/Boston: Routledge & Kegan Paul.

Elson, D. (1988). Market socialism or socialization of the market? *New Left Review, 172,* 3–44.

Fleurbaey, M. (1993). Economic democracy and equality: a proposal. In: P. K. Bardhan & J. E. Roemer (Eds), *Market Socialism. The Current Debate* (pp. 266–278). Oxford: Oxford University Press.

Hayek, F. A. (1935a). The nature and history of the problem' In: F. A. Hayek (Ed.), *Collectivist Economic Planning* (pp. 1–40). London: Routledge & Kegan Paul.

Hayek, F. A. (1935b). The present state of the debate. In: F. A. Hayek (Ed.), *Collectivist Economic Planning* (pp. 201–243). London: Routledge & Kegan Paul.

Hayek, F. A. (1949). *Individualism and economic order.* London/Henley: Routledge & Kegan Paul.

Heftler, V. (1997). The future of the subaltern past: toward a cosmopolitan 'history from below'. *Left History, 5*(1), 65–83.

Hirst, P. (1989). Introduction. In: P. Hirst (Ed.), *The Pluralist Theory of the State. Selected Writings of G. D. H. Cole, J. N. Figgis, and H. J. Laski* (pp. 1–47). London/New York: Routledge.

Hirst, P. (1990). *Representative democracy and its limits.* Cambridge: Polity Press.

Hirst, P. (1994). *Associative democracy. New forms of economic and social governance.* Cambridge: Polity Press.

Hodgson, G. (1988). *Economics and institutions. A manifesto for a modern institutional economics.* Cambridge: Polity Press.

Holloway, J., & Picciotto, S. (Eds) (1978). *State and capital. A Marxist debate.* London: Edward Arnold.

Kirzner, I. M. (1988). The economic calculation debate: lessons for Austrians. *Review of Austrian Economics, 2*(1), 1–18.

Kornai, J. (1993). Market socialism revisited. In: P. K. Bardhan & J. E. Roemer (Eds), *Market Socialism. The Current Debate* (pp. 42–68). Oxford: Oxford University Press.

Korsch, K. (1969). *Schriften zur Sozialisierung.* Frankfurt am Main: Europäische Verlagsanstalt.

Krätke, M. R. (1996). Marxismus als Sozialwissenschaft. In: F. Haug & M. R. Krätke (Hg.), *Materialien zum Historisch-Kritischen Wörterbuch des Marxismus* (pp. 69–122). Hamburg.

Lange, O. ([1939] 1970) On the economic theory of socialism. In: B. E. Lippincott (Ed.), *On The Economic Theory of Socialism* (pp. 57–142). New York: August M. Kelley Publishers.

Lavoie, D. (1985). *Rivalry and central planning. The socialist calculation debate reconsidered.* Cambridge/New York: Cambridge University Press.

Lawler, J. (1998). Marx as market socialist. In: B. Ollman (Ed.), *Market Socialism. The Debate Among Socialists* (pp. 23–52). New York/London: Routledge.

Le Grand, J., & Estrin, S. (Eds) (1989). *Market socialism.* Oxford: Clarendon Press.

Levine, A. (1995). Democratic corporatism and/versus socialism. In: E. O. Wright (Ed.), *Associations and Democracy. The Real Utopias Project.* Vol. 1 (pp. 157–166). London/New York: Verso.

McNally, D. (1993). *Against the market. Political economy, market socialism and the Marxist critique.* London/New York: Verso.

Mandel, E. (1986). In defense of socialist planning. *New Left Review, 159,* 5–37.

Martell, L. (1992). New ideas of socialism. *Economy and Society, 21*(2), 152–172.

Mattick, P. (1978). *Anti-bolshevik communism.* New York: M. E. Sharpe, Inc.

Miller, D. (1989). *Market, state and community. Theoretical foundations of market socialism.* Oxford: Clarendon Press.

Nove, A. (1983). *The economics of feasible socialism.* London: Allen and Unwin.

Offe, C. (1984). *Contradictions of the welfare state.* London: Hutchinson.

Ollman, B. (1998a). Introduction. In: B. Ollman (Ed.), *Market Socialism. The Debate Among Socialists* (pp. 1–3). New York/London: Routledge.

Ollman, B. (1998b). Market mystification in capitalist and market socialist societies. In. B. Ollman (Ed.), *Market Socialism. The Debate Among Socialists* (pp. 81–121). New York/London: Routledge.

O'Neill, J. (1988). Markets, socialism, and information: a reformulation of a Marxian objection to the market. *Social Philosophy & Policy, 6*(2), 200–210.

Panitch, L. (1986). The impasse of social democratic politics. In: R. Miliband & L. Panitch (Eds), *The Socialist Register* (pp. 50–97). London: Merlin Press.

Pierson, C. (1993). Democracy, markets and capital: are there necessary economic limits to democracy? In: D. Held (Ed.), *Prospects for Democracy* (pp. 179–199). Cambridge: Polity Press.

Pierson, C. (1995). *Socialism after communism. The new market socialism.* Cambridge: Polity Press.

Polanyi, K. (1992). The economy as instituted process. In: M. Granovetter & R. Swedberg, *The Sociology of Economic Life* (pp. 29–51). Boulder/ Oxford: Westview Press.

Rachleff, P. J. (1976). *Marxism and council communism. The foundation for revolutionary theory for modern society.* New York: Revisionist Press.

Roemer, J. E. (1994). *A future for socialism.* London: Verso.

Rosenberg, J. (1994). *The empire of civil society. A critique of the realist theory of international relations.* London/New York: Verso.

Schecter, D. (1994). *Radical theories. Paths beyond Marxism and social democracy.* Manchester/ New York: Manchester University Press.

Schlechte, H. (1982). Der Assoziationsgedanke bei Karl Marx und in den Anfängen der elementaren Arbeiterbewegung. In: *Jahrbuch für Geschichte, 25* (pp. 111–138). Berlin: Akademie-Verlag.

Schweickart, D. (1995). *Against capitalism.* Cambridge/Paris: Cambridge University Press & Editions de la Maison des Sciences de l'Homme.

Schweickart, D. (1998). Market socialism: a defence. In: B. Ollman (Ed.), *Market Socialism. The Debate Among Socialists* (pp. 7–22). New York/London: Routledge.

Streeck, W. (1995). Inclusion and secession: questions on the boundaries of associative democracy. In: E. O. Wright (Ed.), *Associations and Democracy. The Real Utopias Project. Volume 1* (pp. 184–192). London/New York: Verso.

Van Parijs, Ph. (1995). *Real freedom for all. What (if anything) can justify capitalism?* Oxford: Clarendon Press.

Von Mises, L. (1935). Economic calculation in the socialist commonwealth. In: F. A. Hayek (Ed.), *Collectivist Economic Planning* (pp. 87–130). London: Routledge & Kegan Paul.

Wainwright, H. (1994). *Arguments for a New Left. Answering the free-market Right.* Oxford U.K./Cambridge USA: Blackwell.

Weisskopf, T. E. (1993). A democratic enterprise-based market socialism. In: P. K. Bardhan & J. E. Roemer (Eds), *Market Socialism. The Current Debate* (pp. 120–141). Oxford: Oxford University Press.

Wood, E. M. (1986). *The retreat from class. A new 'true' socialism.* London/New York: Verso.

Wood, E. M. (1995). *Democracy against capitalism. Renewing historical materialism.* Cambridge: Cambridge University Press.

Yunker, J. A. (1992). *Socialism revised and modernized. The case for pragmatic market socialism.* New York: Praeger.

PART III.

IDEOLOGY

ALIENATION, IDEOLOGY AND FETISHISM

Thierry Suchère

ABSTRACT

Marx acknowledges the importance of the symbolic dimension in human activities. It is a veil that must be lifted to enable scientific study. Critical theory is defined as the operation of deconstructing the world of appearances. It is shown that there is an evolution in the ideas and subjects that Marx investigates. Changes in his use of terminology are examined: firstly from the perspective of alienation, then via the concept of ideology, and finally with reference to commodity fetishism. Capital *(1867) marks a break in the evolution of Marx's thought. Initially, Marx saw the logic of appearances within a market economy as a distorted reflection of the material world, but then came to the paradoxical view that the symbolic dimension was a constituent of economic activity.*

INTRODUCTION

Using the chronology of his writings and his use of language over time, we examine here, the different aspects of Marx's thought on the question of representations in their relation to human activity. We will show that his ideas are internally consistent, symbolic dimension is a locus of unknowing that we need to be able to set aside in order to perform the act of knowing. Marx

Marx's *Capital* and Capitalism; Markets in a Socialist Alternative,
Research in Political Economy, Volume 19, pages 157–172.
© 2001 Published by Elsevier Science Ltd.
ISBN: 0-7623-0838-9

consistently strove to reveal the reality behind the symbolic dimension; it is the role of critical theory to do this. According to Goux (1978) this conception originates with the iconoclasts (the interdictions against representations of the Divinity from the beginnings of Judaism) and was developed by Freud (the dream in its relationship to the unconscious). In this area of Marx's investigation, there are constant shifts in his vocabulary and his use of terms. Marx examined this question firstly from the perspective of alienation (the order of the religious), then with reference to the concept of ideology (the political sphere), arriving finally at the themes of fetishism and reification (the market sphere). These modifications in vocabulary became irreversible. For example, the concept of ideology was central to Marx's preoccupations in *The German Ideology* (1845), but has totally disappeared in *Capital* (1867). Thus Marx's thinking on this theme does contain clear breaks: for example, while examining the logic of appearances in a market economy, Marx paradoxically, came to think of the symbolic as one of the constituent dimensions of economic activity, whereas before he treated it as only a distorted reflection of the material world.

I. MATERIALISM?

Consider what Marx means by materialism. We find here, expressed at the highest level of generality, the origin of the well-known thesis relating to the nature of the symbol and its importance in human activity. Materialism emphasizes the primacy of the material over the conceptual. As a product of the brain, thought itself depends on the material. The function of thought is to appropriate external reality so as to facilitate the interpretation of it and the mastering of it in action. The individuals' representations are either a faithful or a distorted reflection of a reality that exists independently of how people think. The symbolic dimension is then considered as a secondary phenomenon. For example, there is no history of ideas since they find their explanatory principle outside of themselves – in the history of the material and concrete changes that people experience.

Originating in philosophy, the materialist thesis is applied to the social sciences. In *A Contribution to the Critique of Political Economy* (1859), Marx writes that human activity takes the form of a relationship with Nature (the productive forces) and of a relationship with other people (relations of production). The articulation of the productive forces and the relations of production form the base upon which the intellectual, political, spiritual and artistic experiences of an era are built. Forms of consciousness are therefore derived precisely from material life and are analyzed in terms of it. Traditional materialism goes further by defining itself in opposition to the symbolic dimension. In *The German Ideology* (1845), the symbolic dimension appears as a place of ignorance that we need to be able to set aside in order to carry out acts of knowledge. At best, the representations constructed by individuals are a faithful reflection of a material reality (the ideal); at worst, they are a distorted image of reality, as in the allegory of the cave (ideology). Given the objective, knowable nature of reality, there is no reasonable excuse for our ignorance of it. The base has as much objectivity as Nature. It therefore obeys the laws that science can reveal by going beyond the fantasmagorical representations that man produces from it. So the base can be theorized but we can't say anything from a pure logical point of view as to the content of ideology.

From this perspective, Marx definitively settled the question of symbolism in his analysis of ideology in *The German Ideology* (1845) so as to concentrate better on his study of the laws of motion of capital, as exemplified in *Capital* (1867).

In contrast, there might be another Marx who acknowledges the importance of the symbolic dimension in human activities. In *Capital*, Marx employs the metaphor of the bee and the architect to show that human activity has its own specific nature, using not only a material underpinning, but also symbolic representations. The product of the worker pre-exists in his mind. Man makes sense of things in contrast to animals that follow their instinct. Man's relationship with reality is at the same time knowledge of it. Representations appear then as a necessary mediation, or as a constituent of the object. For Lukacs, "the category of mediation as a methodological lever to overcome the simple immediacy of experience is therefore not something to be introduced from the outside (subjectively) in objects, nor a value judgment or an obligation that should be imposed on their existence. It is the demonstration of their own objective structure" (Lukacs, 1923, p. 203). For Gramsci (1930–1935), the world thus described is humanly objective. Therefore, we do not have reality on the one hand and representation on the other, but an interrelation between the two elements within a complex totality.

In *The German Ideology* (1845), Marx also indicates that language intervenes in our social relationship with nature. A purely material relationship can only be conceived of as a form of fiction: that of an asocial and direct relationship between man and nature that has never existed. Our relationship with nature is social in that it involves a certain knowledge of reality that is shared by the community to which we belong. According to Gramsci (1930–1935), the world we have access to is historically subjective (situated in time) and universally subjective (shared by others). In other words, it is because the structure is always invested with the symbolism of a social group that it ceases to be absolute or purely natural (something which has never been), to become concrete or historical-social.

Finally, in the foreword of *A Contribution to the Critique of Political Economy* (1859) Marx notes that fundamental changes took place firstly on the base, in the form of an opposition between the development of the productive forces and the relations of production. It is also necessary according to Marx, for people to become aware of this conflict, so that they may push it to its logical conclusions. If this consciousness doesn't emerge or is not total, it necessarily leads to historical contradictions (For example, French peasant support for Napoleon III as Marx describes in *The Eighteenth Brumaire of Louis Napoleon Bonaparte* (1852) or the development of Nazism and Fascism in Europe).

II. ALIENATION: PROJECTION IN THE IMAGINATION

Chronologically, Marx's initial thesis on the symbolic dimension led to his analysis of alienation. In *Theses on Feuerbach* (1844), Marx considers alienation as a mechanism of projection of the essential qualities of man into a fantasmagorical image, namely that of God. It is a multidimensional concept. Marx uses two terms: *"Entfremdung"* (or the idea of a divorce, understood with a negative meaning) and *"Entausserung"* (the notion of exteriorization, of objectification as a projection in the object). These terms he employs almost in an undifferentiated way, which implies that these ideas refer back to one another. Alienation begins with individual's loss of the attributes of the real self (*"Entfremdung"*) and continues with the compensatory projection of these same attributes in the figure of God (*"Entausserung"*), a pure form that ultimately dominates man, though produced by man. Separation therefore precedes exteriorization, or objectification.

Alienation presupposes the cognitive capacity to represent something other than what it appears to be. The imaginary is not thought of as being without the possibility of distinguishing between the signifier and the signified, only man can do this. For Castoriadis (1984), alienation means the particular form taken by the relationship between the individual and this imagination under the conditions of a class society. What prevails under alienation is the heteronomy, which is decoded in the figure of the other. In a real sense, alienation refers to the mechanism which, during an exchange, leads to the transfer of a property right of what belongs to me to the profit of another. In a psychoanalytical sense, alienation is defined as the substitution of the discourse of others for one's will. Freud made the distinction between the conscious, under the control of the ego, and the unconscious escaping all control, and manifesting in the imagination, which, under certain circumstances, imposes its law on the subject. In many ways, the other is the entity that dominates me, which speaks in and for me, though produced by me. Under alienation, forms of a collective amnesia also appear, related to the origin of the problem. One is thus referred back to the biblical scene of the golden calf: it cannot be adored as God unless the community forgets its animal and human origin.

For Marx, the desire to try to tear away the veil of religious illusion, to proclaim its insignificance to the world, is sterile if one does not in fact question its conditions of production, which are themselves located at another level. Freud will say something very similar in his theories about psychoanalytical therapy (the patient's returning to the source of the neurosis). For Marx the religious illusion finds its origin in human misery, and therefore in the real world. It is his impotence to realize himself fully in society that man projects towards Heaven. Behind the question of alienation lies the impossibility for man of completely satisfying his aspirations for a collective life, or to become reconciled with the community in a world dominated by bourgeois egoism and private property (the schizophrenic pair 'bourgeois/citizen' in Hegel's work). But Marx goes beyond a philosophy that would remain purely within the conscious level. The full realization of man's essence can only come from a practical questioning of these same material conditions, and it will be the work of a class, the proletariat, which does not defend any particular interest since it owns nothing in its own right.

The mechanism of man's symbolic projection will be considered in the context of *Capital* (1867), in relation to the developments on ideas of commodity fetishism. In a psychoanalytical sense, the fetish designates the imaginary substitute constructed by an individual from one thing that comes to replace the desired person and in the absence of which no orgasm is possible. For Marx, fetishism reflects the individual's perceptions of social relations (relationship between men), in the guise of a relationship between things (the exchange relationship between commodities), or by projecting the properties of this social relationship (exploitation and surplus value) into the body of a commodity with magical properties – gold. However, the projection of the value in the body of the commodity is an objectification. In the workshop, only a subjective form of work is undertaken: one which expresses itself in a specific content (as an act of a weaver or a baker and as the observable differences of productivity between one individual and another). But the market only recognizes the work in an abstract form, which relate to a pure expense of physical force, whose intensity is measured by reference to the norm of the socially necessary working time. Thus the transformation of private work into a social form only occurs with the sale of the commodity. The properties of work become objective and face the worker as an alien reality: one that is embodied in the commodity. The value produced by work, appears as an inherent characteristic of the commodity, like its weight or its color. However, merely questioning the conditions of existence can lead to a break with illusion, and one knows from Lenin (or even Marcel Duchamps) that urinals will be made of gold in Communist society. Ironically, we also know that Freud assimilates gold to excrement because the desire for accumulation can be traced directly to the phenomenon of retention at the anal stage.

III. IDEOLOGY: A THEORY OF POLITICS

We pass from alienation to ideology in Marx, as his intellectual progress led him to substitute the problem of the subject with that of the structure of social relations. *The German Ideology* can be thought of as an answer to Stirner's *The Unique and its Property*. For Stirner, all reference to the universal (the State, the national interest) is an appeal to a fiction that denies and dominates the only existing reality: the individual. For Marx, in a rebuke to the young Hegelian left, merely denouncing ideology is not enough to fight it effectively. Here again, we have to go back to the conditions that produce it. The world of ideas has no autonomy. The origin of the ideas man produces lies at the level of a lived reality, in a direct relationship with nature and with other people.

The representation an individual makes of his own conditions of existence may be objective or illusory. Ideology is a false belief that individuals develop about the form of social ties. Marx implicitly assumes that, in primitive societies, people could have lived under conditions of complete transparency as to their conditions of existence. But this representation becomes falsified when the division of labour intervenes and is consolidated under the conditions of class society.[1] The characteristic of class societies is that it is based on the relations of domination that appear when the differentiation of roles is seen as hierarchical. Domination is conceived via a relationship of complementarity that unites hegemony and coercion (Gramsci, 1930–1935), violence and ideology (Althusser, 1970), force and consensus (Godelier, 1984). Material domination is founded in and is reinforced by spiritual domination. No society can in the long term depend on purely physical coercion. At the very least, one must guarantee the loyalty of the forces of repression. Thus all societies operate on a basis of opacity; they do not need to have perfect self-knowledge. Ideology thus appears as an erroneous belief of individuals in the legitimacy of the power of the ruling class. It is ideology that creates the confusion between problems of individuals and social problems in the sense that "individual repression is the dreamed instrument (in both senses of the term) of social repression" (Auge, 1974, p. 70). It produces individuals who, according to Althusser, walk alone.

For Marx, ideology appears as a form of discourse about reality, produced by specialists – intellectuals such as teachers, economists and civil servants. It is made possible by the distinction between manual and intellectual work.[2] The failure to situate one's activities in their true material conditions leads one to imagine that things are different from what they actually are. Rendering this discourse autonomous in relation to reality permits the fantasies of ideologists. It is clear that ideology belongs to the political order: the content of ideologists fantasmagorical discourse operates as a denial of the unequal and contradictory nature of class societies, and substitutes the fictional notion of a community of interests as appeared in the neutrality of the state. For example, in ideology the inequalities of wealth are necessarily explained by the differences between the talents created by nature. Inequality is always compensated for by the formal equality promoted by the existing social order (Paradise, universal suffrage, equality in market exchanges). During periods of extreme tension, politics may drift towards using scapegoats such as Jews or immigrants. The point is to bind the masses to the ruling class in an alliance, by reference to shared values or the idea of a fictional community (the national interest, morality, religion, the homeland). Power can never be clearly exercised solely in the interests of the ruling class. It needs to present itself, at least in its discourse, as representing the public interest, that goes beyond individual particularities. Thus ideology, in its form and content, is presented as being itself the locus of unreality, and as an instrument of power, based on ignorance.

History in Marxism, has its basis in reality. It exists as the contradiction between the development of productive forces and the nature of the relations of production. In other words, the potential of technical progress, of growth can only emerge at a certain moment of history by questioning the organizational forms that emerge around the operations of production, distribution and the sphere of consumption. Here, the superstructure is of secondary importance. In the sphere of ideas, people become aware of a conflict that they may push to its logical conclusion. In a period of uncertainty and of loss of stability, ideological discourse appears to offer a range of solutions. But the solution exists in reality before it exists in thought. In *A Contribution to the Critique of Political Economy* (1859), Marx writes: "Mankind thus inevitably sets itself only such tasks as it can solve, since closer examination will always show that the task itself arises only when the material conditions for its solutions are already present or are at least in process of formation." (Marx, 1859, p. 273). In other words, to work effectively, ideological discourse must be compatible with the problems encountered in the real world and must also be held by a class possessing a realistic project for achieving dominance.

The End of History can be represented as leaving behind the era of ideology, as a moment when the conditions of a clear relationship between humanity and its conditions of existence are finally in place. This break with the discourse of ideology comes less from denunciation than from practical action, by the effective questioning of the alienating conditions of existence. The revolution would be the work of a mass who have suffered supreme injustice and who, therefore, are the bearers of universal forces – the proletariat. It is seen as a non-class (in the sense that it does not defend any particular interest because it has nothing) which will abolish social classes, and thus abolish basis of domination and ideology. The proletariat is immunized against ideological discourse because it is rooted in practical activity and distanced from theoretical questions. It lives daily in the reality of exploitation that no discourse can mask. The solution to the proletariat's practical problem lies in practical action.

Marx's analysis of the relationship between the proletariat and ideology is nevertheless ambiguous for two reasons. Firstly, if rhetoric has no effect on the masses, we need to rethink who the ideological language is addressing – necessarily one of the two protagonists of history, the dominant or the dominated. Labica (1987) notes clearly that the ruling class does not need internal ideological discourse. It merely needs to be where it is, to enjoy its place in the social structure and to defend it.[3] Ideological discourse is addressed to the other class, the dominated, who may themselves not be fooled because they are able to see the difference between discourse and practice. But in any case, real history (Fascism, the degeneration of the Communist bloc) challenges the Marxist conception of an omniscient and clear-sighted proletariat. In *The Eighteenth Brumaire of Louis Napoleon Bonaparte* (1852), Marx provides the elements of another line of thought, in which he refers to the notion of class consciousness and the distinction between a "class in itself", defined by its objective material situation, and a "class for itself", defined by its collective consciousness of shared interests. Class-consciousness is the self-knowledge people would possess if they could perceive their situation clearly. Lukacs (1923), who consecrated a major work to this matter, says: "the adequate rational reaction must in this way be seen as part of a typical situation determined in the process of production. This awareness is neither the sum nor the average of what the individuals who form a class, taken one by one, think and feel. However, the decisive historical action of the class as a whole is determined by this consciousness and not by the thoughts of the individual" (Lukacs, 1923, p. 73). The position of the proletariat at the heart of the social structure therefore gives it the possibility of reaching a true awareness about real relationships, but this awareness is not dictated by the situation. In other words, the meaning of History cannot be read off from messianic proletarianism. It is always susceptible to oscillations between progress and barbarism.

Secondly, how should we theorize the links between Marxist theory and the practical actions of the proletariat or between the intellectual Marx and the working class outside the ideological framework? The idea of the proletariat as the bearer of a specific ideological language is a nonsense for Marx. The proletariat is the very negation of power, and thus of ideology. Possible answers to this are provided by those who classify Marxism as a "science" in contrast to the forms of utopian socialism that preceded it, and which themselves are part of ideology. Gramsci theorizes the relationship between thought and revolutionary practice differently by introducing the idea of the organic intellectual. The mass only becomes a class within the logic of organization, and thus by an awareness of shared interests in opposing the existing oligarchies (class consciousness!). There is no organization without an intellectual whose role it is to propose an alternative view of the world that could provide a substitute for common sense (understood as view which, at given eras, is incoherent, disintegrated). Mass organizations therefore need to provide themselves with a group of independent intellectuals who contribute to the education of the people in the sense of defeating the cultural hegemony. From this perspective, Marxism or the philosophy of praxis as given by Gramsci (1930–1935) is certainly ideology. The philosophy of praxis is a view of the world the proletariat acquires and which will come to form a substitute for the historically outdated ideologies used by the bourgeoisie.

For Gramsci (1930–1935), all history is the history of class struggle or of confrontation between two hegemonic forms. So there is not the dominant ideology on one hand and the submission of the exploited on the other, but competing ideologies. Political subversion goes through phases of symbolic struggle that aim to modify people's perception of the world. What is at stake in this symbolic struggle is the redefinition of the conditions of collective action. Where a mass existed a class must emerge (the expression of a collective with full awareness of its own interests) which always presents itself as the instrument of progress and the public interest. The bourgeoisie triumphed over feudalism, within the framework of an alliance with the proletariat, and in the name of freedom, equality and brotherhood. With his metaphor of passing from mobile warfare to trench warfare, Gramsci shows that ideology presents itself symmetrically as an element of resistance by the dominant order in the face of disaster (collapse of the stock-exchange, the crisis) These theses of Gramsci mark a break with orthodox Marxism because they endow ideology with full effectiveness.

Ideology is a product of the reflection of intellectuals located outside practical action. Its essence can only be a distorted image of the real world. It is the nature of ideology to be a form of ignorance. Maybe the mature Marx goes further. He questions the specific ideology of the economists and then the foundations of economic activity, as *Theories on Surplus Value* attests. The phenomenon studied is then much more complex since it is relationships between people which present themselves in their own appearances, under the form of relations between things. Ideology is then not the distorted reflection of the conditions of existence, but the reflection of an already imaginary relationship with these same conditions of existence (Althusser, 1970). In other words, it is no longer located within the logic of a discourse about the real, but within a discourse whose basis is the representations people have of their own conditions of existence (a sort of meta-discourse). The relationship with reality is not conceived of outside the category of mediation, and it is the mediation which is immediately problematic because it is located within the domain of the imagination (meaning the ability to represent something as other than it is). A well-understood reflection on ideology therefore only finds its extension in Marx's work on the logic of appearances in a market economy – the theme of commodity fetishism at the heart of *Capital* (1867).

IV. FETISHISM AND REIFICATION: A THEORY OF MARKET

The opening lines of *Capital* (1867) state that capitalism presents itself as an immense accumulation of commodities. From the analysis of a simple commodity society, one can deduce the tools and concepts necessary to understand capitalism. Firstly a product becomes a commodity if it appears in the form of an object that has utility for at least a part of the demand. If a product finds a buyer in the market, it is for society to recognize that the work done has not been furnished at a pure loss. Market mechanisms therefore work as a posteriori acceptance procedures for the positions freely adopted by individuals within the division of labour. Secondly, we know that the rate at which two commodities are exchanged is dictated by the law of socially necessary working time, according to Marx. The market also functions as a validation procedure for the effectiveness of each producer in his respective work, a procedure that establishes the amount of working time a society wishes to allocate to the different branches of industry. In other words, behind the impersonal market mechanism lies a social division of labour, whose laws are understood as a demonstration of the existence of an organic solidarity or of a social relationship (in the sense of a necessary or non-contingent relationship between individuals belonging to the same society). A glance at other forms of social organization allows us to see more clearly the nature of the relationship that is woven every day in commodity exchange. For example, in an authentically Communist society, the social division of labour would have a far more transparent form because it would not be veiled by the blind laws of the market. Autonomous and united individuals would democratically and explicitly define the order of priorities for the needs to be satisfied and how working time and the means of production should be distributed among the various branches of industry.

Marx sees fetishism as a phenomenon inherent in commodity society. It is an assimilation of the previously described relationship between people to a relationship between things, because under capitalism relationships between individuals must take the deceptive form of commodity exchange. A commodity is the object upon which the properties of a social relation are projected. Value appears as if it is written in the very material of the commodity as one of its natural properties, thus ignoring the law of socially necessary working time. In its very appearance this exchange appears to be regulated by the behaviour of the intrinsic properties of the commodity. The reference to gold which, in Marx's terms, is merely a particular commodity leads to an extra degree of embeddedness in the imagination, for example, in the mechanism of interest on a loan through which the magical ability of money to produce money is seen. Within the logic of interest, any connection with production is lost, and its very appearance functions to mask a deeper reality – that of exploitation. For Marx, the deconstruction of the symbolic dimension is seen as one of the possible dimensions of the act of understanding.

For Lukacs (1923), the theme of reification is seen as an extension of the problem of commodity fetishism, sketched out by Marx. Fetishism as a symbolic projection of the relationship between things on a social relation is extended into the reification that assimilates people to things. At the origin of capitalism lies what, for the individual subject, makes him perceive an object as exchange value where previously he only saw use value. Economic logic begins when the primacy of exchange value over use value is clearly affirmed. All social relations are then perceived by actors through the prism of a quantifiable and calculable form (its exchange value), and of a commodity form (as a manipulable object). In capitalism, reification completely permeates all dimensions of human life, up to and including the individual's capacity for work (his/her labour power), which is assimilated to a commodity in the exchange, and which is treated as such in the murky laboratory of production. It is within a dehumanised proletariat, reduced to the rank of an object at the heart of the process of production that reification appears with the greatest violence. In the scientific organization of work, human activity is seen as a simple object, analyzed, decomposed and recomposed after rationalizing its elementary gestures. All forms of subjectivity are denied as sources of error to leave room for the norm, calculated by the control office (operating times). In the process of production itself, the proletariat adopts the attitude of an automaton, of the object submitted to laws over which it has no control.

Reification, therefore, intervenes because the commodity and its exchange value appear as norms of an objectivity true to the spirit of capitalism. The economic categories form part of the framework of capitalism, the tools used by agents within a figurative relationship to their daily reality. Capitalism is registered in an imagination that reflects the way objects are treated (as commodities, exchange value), how subjects think of themselves and are constituted (as a labour force), and how relationships between agents are treated (under the form of a reified relationship between commodities, quantifiable via the mediating categories of price and quantity). Anything that cannot be expressed in a quantifiable and manipulable way (price, salary, productivity) is not objectified and is analyzed as sound deprived of meaning. The very essence of economic activity thus has no tangible existence outside the imagination that contains it. The economy is primarily made up of representations. Looking at a commodity, for example, the material dimension of the object lies in the uses it permits (use value as a natural form), and in concrete work (shown first as the specific action of a weaver or shoemaker and secondly as the differences in ability or intensity in the same work between one individual and another).[4] In contrast, the value form appears, according to Marx's terms, as a pure creation of thought, a chimera, a quality. "The reality of value of commodities differs in this respect from Dame Quickly, that we don't know where to have it. The value of commodities is the very opposite of the coarse materiality of their substance, not an atom of matter enters into its composition. Turn and examine a simple commodity by itself, as we will, yet in so far as it remains an object of value, it seems impossible to grasp it" (Marx, 1867, p. 16). The value form is only seen by making an equivalence between pieces of concrete work (as the exchange of the shoemaker's shoe with the sheet of the weaver) under an abstract form that is a pure representation. In commodity exchange, the negation of subjectivity proper to the concrete form, works by substituting a fictional norm, the socially necessary working time for the production of the commodity.

The logic of appearances then becomes one of the constituent dimensions of the structure in which this is embodied. It is here that there is a major break with the traditional manner of conceptualizing the relationship between superstructure and base. Representation is present in the productive forces as the way men acquire means in the face of external nature, in order to be able to think about it and to organize it. It is also present in the relations of production where it contributes to the organization of men in relation to one another, in their relationship with nature. The distinction between base and superstructure is therefore of a functional order. Consider the example of primitive societies. They are anti-economic because they refuse to work any more than what is necessary for simple reproduction. In primitive societies, demographic regulation (controlling group size to fit the possibilities offered by nature) plays the same role that economic activity plays in capitalist societies. The distinction between base and superstructure is therefore in a primary sense, functional. As Godelier (1984) says, this does not prejudge the type of social relation to which the role of base is devolved. In primitive societies, family relationships and the link with nature function as the two constituent elements of an imaginary construct from which objects are learned about and on which the life of the group is organized (from the taxonomy of plants to the deification of nature whose prodigality conditions the group's survival via the ideology of the gift/counter-gift as an expression of collective solidarity). The distinction between base and superstructure is therefore in a secondary sense, of a functional order. "Indeed the superstructural and ideological level forms part of the structure and the social being. It nevertheless forms part of conscience or ideology with a specific function relative to the other parts of the structure. A work of art or of science, the human comedy of Balzac for example, is not the French railway system. On the contrary, it is exactly and solely in virtue of that – society realizes through it a specific function that it could not realize any other way (by producing bolts for example) that it is a part of society. That which makes it a part is thus precisely what differentiates it from the whole to which it belongs" (Colleti, 1972, p. 62).

VI. ACTION IN POLITICS

In Marx's intellectual legacy, there is conflict between two conceptions exclusive one to another. These conceptions generally focus on only one aspect of the thought of the great philosopher. The traditional materialism as systematized by Lenin (1908) (incidentally placing himself squarely in the line of Engels' thinking) who considers the symbolic dimension as a secondary order phenomenon. In contrast, there exists a heterodox Marxism (Gramsci, Lukacs, Korsh . . .), that is often forced to self-criticism, for which we could not conceive economy without society or society without economy. For these authors, the structure must necessarily be embodied in a specific symbolism.

Traditional materialism leads us to think of the relation between individuals and their imagination as a veil that only has to be lifted to achieve understanding.

The structure would be objectifiable, knowable in its very trajectory, because it obeys laws. The superstructure would be the non-essential or the epiphenomenon that escapes all logic. With traditional materialism, critical theory is constructed on the model of empirical-analytical science (physics, biology). It tells the truth, beyond the illusory representations that individuals construct on reality. Under these conditions, Marxism becomes a dogma or is seen as a scientism that registers the totalitarian drift seen in the labour movement. There is no effective place for a debate when the truth is confounded with the official line of the Party. The very essence of politics is denied to the benefit of a bureaucracy that manages problems that have become technical.

Contrary to this idea, there are those who think that the structure as a whole is imprinted with a historical-social or subjective dimension. "History is precisely the history of the uninterrupted upheaval of forms of objectivity that shape the existence of men" (underlined by Lukacs, 1923, p. 230). History remains open and is composed of struggles between competing hegemonic forms, supported by antagonistic social classes. Political subversion therefore begins in cognitive subversion, which aims to promote other visions of the world, or other classification schemes. In defending this idea, critical theory is neither neutral nor relativistic. It is constructed by assuming a point of view: that of the construction of a just social order. Starting from this position, it leads to a particular way of dividing up the existing order according to a classification scheme that belongs to critical theory, to produce a view of specific forms: class struggle, exploitation. . . . There is nevertheless no truth that critical theory could claim or which could be contradicted in the manner one observes in the empirico-analytical sciences. One cannot say anything true when the reality that concerns us is merely emerging. Critical theory is a complete projection from action into utopia. The only thing that counts is the weight of its contribution to the emancipation of individuals.

NOTES

1. Marx's implicit position on the transparency of reality in primitive societies is highly questionable, according to the discoveries of modern anthropology. We know that primitive societies are charged with imagination, meaning the capacity of representing something differently from what is. Economic activity, for example, is at the same time a religious activity, a family relationship and other things besides. The exchange of goods is related to the exchanges in alliances, to the game of prestige, and even constitutes a reminder of the dependence of the individual on the community. The birth of modern society presupposes that human activity loses symbolic significance in order, according to Goux (1978), that one is only presented with a pure system of quantitative, calculable and rationalisable relationships. For Castoriadis (1975),

representing the individual as a manipulable and calculable object is no more and above all no less imaginary than to see in him an owl or the reincarnation of the sun God. Marx's position seems stronger on the question of the existing link between the emergence of class society and the State. Primitive societies are anti-economic because they function equally against all forms of power. The struggle against production and against the appropriation by one group of the surplus value, is struggle against the constitution of the minority power.

2. The question of the relationship between the emergence of power and the confiscation of knowledge, seems to be an interesting line of thought. Godelier (1984) suggests the hypothesis of a primitive division of labour under which a caste of priest-warriors would emerge, who would benefit from this knowledge. Privileged access to the God for some would correspond symmetrically to the forced work for nearly all. The function of the dominant group would be the more valued for being rooted in the imagination and that of the dominated just as devalued by being practical. Tort (1988) suggests a confiscation of real and common knowledge to the benefit of this same caste under the effect of its transformation into an esoteric language (hieroglyphs in Egypt). In modern times, the discourse of a group of intellectuals serves the dominant, (the guard dogs of the French writer Paul Nizan), but still it does not emerge from the dominant class, nor is it in a relationship of strict economic dependence on it. The complementary relationship between ideological language and the problem of power depends on two conditions: (i) the ideologue sees his function and his personality recognized and valorized by the system (a system that recognizes him as "the only real man, the one that thinks" cannot be, to his eyes, fundamentally bad): (ii) the ideological devices (the school, the press . . .) in which the ideologue registered his activities, reproduce themselves. The relative autonomy of the ideological is an alibi of neutrality in favor of the institutions. This is why ideology is not lived as such, but as innocence itself (see Bourdieu & Passeron, 1970).

3. The dominant class probably does not need internal ideological discourse. In contrast, it needs at least to recognize itself in values of the discourse that it addresses to the other: the proletariat. P. Bourdieu [1979] demonstrates that the ideological discourse will be all the more believable when it is produced naturally and is all the more natural when it objectively serves the interests of the one that pronounces it. Sincerity then becomes one of the conditions of efficiency. "A good editor of Le Figaro, the famous French conservative daily, whose own choice it was to become editor and has been chosen according to the same mechanisms, knows how to recognize a good journalist of Le Figaro, to the fact that he has the tone suited to address the readers of this newspaper, that, without doing it on purpose, he speaks the language of Le Figaro naturally and that he could be the model reader of the paper" (Bourdieu, 1979, p. 267). As for Mao, he considered that "The fish always rots from the head", implying then that a dominant class that did not recognize itself anymore in the values of its own discourse would be in a state of advanced decomposition.

4. Marx theorizes that use value is linked to the material dimension of the commodity. He develops a purely functional approach to the object. Veblen goes further by introducing the notion of conspicuous consumption. He shows that the commodity is also (or firstly?) the bearer of meaning. It is a sign with which the phenomenon of group identification and the game of differentiation between social groups is played out. Consumption operates as a transformation of the economic value (money) into sign of prestige (the concept of distinction for Bourdieu, 1979). Use value then finds its

foundation in a value sign, in the sense that the symbolic difference is what is looked for in the act of consumption. Use value is no longer a natural form as Marx claimed, but a social form. For Marx, exchange value presupposes use value. Baudrillard, on the contrary, thinks that use value finds its justification in exchange value. If each of us could freely dispose of everything he/she wanted, he would not know how to begin. So the neutralization of exchange value kills use value." Outside of this logic, humanity needs nothing. What one does need, it is what is bought and sold, what is calculated and chosen" (Baudrillard, 1972, p. 260).

REFERENCES

Althusser, L. (1970). *Essays on Ideology*. London: Verso.
Auge, M. (1974). *La construction du monde: religion, representation, ideologie*. Paris: Maspero.
Badiou, A., & Balmes, F. (1976). *De l'ideologie*. Paris: Maspero.
Balibar, E. (1993). *The Philosophy of Marx*. London: Verso.
Baudrillard, J. (1972). *For a Critique of the Political Economy of the Sign*. Saint Louis: Telos Press.
Bourdieu P., & Passeron, J. C. (1970). *Reproduction in Education, Society and Culture*. Beverly Hills: Sage Publications.
Bourdieu, P. (1979). *Distinction: a Social Critique of the Judgement of Taste*. Cambridge Mass: Harvard University Press.
Castoriadis, C. (1975). *The Imaginary Institution of Society*. Cambridge U.K.: Polity Press.
Colleti, L. (1969). *From Rousseau to Lenin*. London: New Left Books.
Duprat, G. (1980). *Analyse de l'ideologie tome 1: problematiques*. Paris: Galilee.
Duprat, G. (1982). *Analyse de l'ideologie tome 2: thematiques*. Paris: Galilee.
Godelier, M. (1984). *The Mental and the Material:Thought, Economy and Society*. London: Verso.
Goux, J. J. (1978). *Symbolic Economies: after Marx and Freud*. Ithaca NY: Cornell University Press.
Gramsci, A. (1930–1935). *Prison Notebooks*. New York: Columbia University Press.
Labica, G., & Bensusan, G. (1982). *Dictionnaire critique du marxisme*. Paris: PUF.
Labica, G. (1987). *Le paradigme du Grand-Hornu: essai sur l'ideologie*. Paris: PEC-la Breche.
Lenine, V. I. (1908). *Materialisme et empiriocriticisme*. Moscow: Editions du Progres.
Lukacs, G. (1923). *History and Class Consciousness: Studies in Marxist Dialects*. London: Merlin Press.
Marx, K. (1845). Theses on Feuerbach. In: *Oeuvres philosophie*. Bibliotheque de la Pleiade, Paris: Gallimard.
Marx, K., & Engels, F. (1845). *The German Ideology*. London: Lawrence and Wishart.
Marx, K., & Engels, F. (1852). *The Eighteenth Brumaire of Louis Napoleon Bonaparte*. Paris: Editions Sociales.
Marx, K. (1859). *A Contribution to the Critique of Political Economy*. New York: International Publishers.
Marx, K. (1867). *Capital*. Chicago: Encyclopaedia Britanica.
Tort, P. (1988). *Marx et le probleme de l'ideologie: le modele egyptien*. Paris: PUF.
Vincent J. M. (1973). *Fetichisme et societe*. Paris: Editions Anthropos.

THE WORLD AS A GAME IN SRAFFA
AND WITTGENSTEIN: A CASE STUDY
IN MODERN BOURGEOIS IDEOLOGY

Jørgen Sandemose

ABSTRACT

This article makes a comparative analysis of works of Ludwig Wittgenstein and Piero Sraffa, notably Philosophical Investigations and Production of Commodities by Means of Commodities respectively. In the process, the authors' method and its underlying philosophical assumptions are criticised. While Sraffa's text is taken to represent a view of society that fits in nicely with Wittgenstein's conception of the structure of language games, it is also implied that Sraffa's thinking about economic relations might very well have inspired the development of Wittgenstein's philosophy. The article argues that their common methodological effort must be considered distinctively bourgeois.

INTRODUCTION

Since at least the First World War, one of the most important features of ideology in capitalist society has been that the ruling class has lost the force to develop independent theory. To a continually increasing extent it has

Marx's *Capital* and Capitalism; Markets in a Socialist Alternative,
Research in Political Economy, Volume 19, pages 173–231.
ISBN: 0-7623-0838-9

depended on theoretical frameworks with a provenience from different shades of purported socialist thinking.

There is a tendency among all ruling classes to represent their own specific interests as a collectivist and universal virtue. During the last eighty to hundred years, elements of socialist thought has been actively used in that representation on part of the bourgeoisie. This tendency has been fortified by the growth of distinct bourgeois lines of thought inside socialist currents. All in all, there has evolved alleged socialist movements, often state-supporting, "Social Democrat", "National Socialist" and so on, that have helped to transform an original socialist collectivism into some kind of bourgeois universality, thus stabilising a wavering class rule.

Glaring instances of such a movement, endowed with state power, are the so-called communist regimes in Eastern Europe after the Second World War, and in Soviet Russia even from the beginning of the Thirties. The collapse of these regimes a dozen years ago was taken by many to represent the end of "communism" proper. This rather premature conclusion is worth mentioning here, because it is in an indirect consequence of the effectiveness of a propaganda that for more than half a century had spread the illusion that communist aims were compatible with class rule directed against workers' interests.

That effective propaganda lent considerable momentum to ongoing efforts to interpret any revolutionary socialism, especially the Marxian one, with categories belonging to traditional bourgeois philosophy and social science. The result is, as could be expected, a watering-down of "Marxism".

As regards economic theory, by far the most important single contribution is the one made by Piero Sraffa (1898–1983). That his results are accepted without question by a large body of students and scholars with an original affinity for revolutionary solutions, shows the importance of calling them to a thoroughgoing account. Further, it seems clear that bringing them to account has to take into consideration Sraffa's close affinity with the ideology of the "communist" movement in the Twenties and Thirties. It has to be asked, again, whether that ideology did represent anything more than a trade-unionistic, blind alley in the struggle of the working class.

It is one of the aims of this essay to underline the importance of Sraffa's contribution by showing that the structure of his theory corresponds fairly well to a form of reasoning developed by Ludwig Wittgenstein (1889–1951). As Wittgenstein's work can reasonably be regarded as both the most influential and the most characteristic of modern bourgeois ideological efforts, a study of such a coalescing of structures should be of great importance for the development of essential Marxist arguments against contemporary bourgeois thought in general.

The concept of "language games" was introduced by the later Wittgenstein to denote the social origin of language, rules and logic. While it is true that traditional philosophy up to that point largely had neglected the study of such an origin, it is by no means clear that Wittgenstein's contribution offers any starting-point for a radical analysis of rules and language. He takes the social reality of humans to be explicable in terms of categories that do rather seem to condemn them to an existence in a realm of coercion.

Nevertheless, Wittgenstein's theory is, as mentioned in the first section below, now and then taken to present a critical theory of alienation related to Marx'. That is still another fact making it convenient – for a critic – to analyse the internal relation between Sraffa and Wittgenstein through a "Marxian" idiom. My implicit conclusion in this respect is that their theories complement each other in a fairly distinctive way. However, the primary aim of the essay is to lay a basis for investigation of the political significance of their common methodical approach.

Sraffa's *Production of Commodities by Means of Commodities*, published in 1960, soon became one of the cornerstones of the critique of official bourgeois academic theories that made itself felt in the wake of the Western "students' revolt" from 1968 on. The widespread circulation of anthologies like those edited by Sen, by Hunt & Schwartz, and by Harcourt & Laing are among the chief indications of this fact. Sraffa's book has in this way come to exercise a profound influence on a whole generation of university teachers.

In the longer run, it became fairly evident that the main stream of the "students' revolt" – contrary to widespread beliefs inside the otherwise hetero-geneous "movement" itself – in no way formed an alternative to bourgeois thinking, only a refreshment of it. It paved the way for paradigms that seemingly took into account the new forms of political articulation on part of the working class, not least the growing importance of trade unions for state structure and governmental decision making. And while upholders of such paradigms did not realise that the said forms reflected just a development of corporative traits of bourgeois society, they held their own theories to be expressions of a Marxian approach to the analysis of that society. Such views never met with serious opposition, and are still among the most influential sources of misinterpretation of Marxism, constituting an important reformist force.

In fact, the "Sraffian" paradigm is rather a Ricardian one, in a distinctly Keynesian guise. The working class is presented not as a potentially revolu-tionary subject, but rather as a mass of individuals whose existence is *a priori* bound up with the productive sphere, and whose political expression is limited to "trade union consciousness". Working class politics, then, is in principle reduced to a wage bargaining whose most important paradigmatic function is to turn an undetermined set of equations into a determined one. As will be shown below, this last operation is, on Sraffa's premises, equivalent to the formation of his very *concept* of capital.

The corollary is that there is in fact no "capital" given prior to the production process (even prior to a Böhm-Bawerkian 'period of production'). Which, in its turn, means that the working class cannot be seen as subjugated or as – to use Marx' expression – "subsumed" under capital at all. The Marxian theory implies that the worker is "freed" from ownership of means of production and is allowed to work only on condition that he may uphold production in a time span exceeding the one that would suffice to produce equivalents to goods required for his own physical reproduction. Such coercion – determining the entire form of existence of the class of wage labourers – is completely ignored in the "neo-Ricardian" models inspired by Sraffa. Indeed, the provenience of a distinct class of "workers" would seem to be enigmatic under such circumstances.

As a result, the alleged study of social relations takes on a wholly performative content: These relations are seen as moves in a kind of game, where, as is by definition the case in a game, the parties are considered to stand on equal footing from the outset. (Just the kind of abstraction that is often conveniently made by the parties in negotiations on a work-place!) Any reasonable conception of the genesis of the relation between capital and wage labor is thereby precluded.

I try to show that such thinking is not confined to a certain kind of class-dominated social "science" (*in casu* economics), but that it rather originates in that kind of bourgeois thinking that we – tentatively – might call "philosophical". It is at this point that the relation between Sraffa and Wittgenstein gets its real importance. That can be seen not only from a comparison between the "game"-related thinking embedded in the Sraffian model on the one hand and the Wittgensteinian "language games" on the other. It can also be seen to emerge from an analysis of a proximate consequence of Wittgenstein's theory: The necessary downgrading of working humans (and, for that matter, of humans in general) which results from any "game"-ridden theory is as striking in Sraffa's case as it is in Wittgenstein's.

Given this frame, I divide the essay into three main sections. The first one concentrates on Wittgenstein's later philosophy, as presented in his writings after about 1930. Through the four subsections I also make some critical comments on the foundations and corollaries of Wittgenstein's vital concept of "language-games", hopefully showing both its shortcomings and its relatedness to the method implicit in Sraffa's economic model. In the second section I make (through four subsections) some remarks on the status of Sraffa's work, and undertake a critical summary of the most important traits of his model, a system of "simultaneous" production equations. (Sraffa's analyses of joint production, fixed capital and land are omitted.) In the third section, I present some conclusions concerning the relation between Sraffa and Wittgenstein, with a view to the ideological function of their thought. Thus, in a first subsection, I venture to make an interpretation of "language-games" which might fit the social theory implicit in Sraffas model, while also possibly indicating a way to understand the relation between the two authors. I conclude the essay with a subsection on the "analyticism" coming to the fore in the works of Sraffa and Wittgenstein, thereby knitting together some loose threads from my own casual remarks on the history of philosophy.

I. FUNDAMENTALS OF WITTGENSTEIN'S LATER PHILOSOPHY

I.1. The Philosophical Investigations and Marx' Fourth Thesis on Feuerbach

Some academic intellectuals have been tempted to assimilate the thought of Ludwig Wittgenstein (especially, of course, the *Spätphilosophie*) into the Marxian analysis of ideological phenomena of bourgeois society. Such attempts seem to have their chief *movens* in Wittgenstein's theory of logical form developed after the *Tractatus logico-philosophicus*. In the *Philosophical Investigations*, a seemingly new theory on the relationship between meaning and inference was put forward. Instead of simply regarding a valid conclusion as a consequence of certain premises, the *form* of the premises in question was taken to be a consequence of (or, better, perhaps: a part of, or implicit in) a certain mode of being on the part on the judging subject, a mode that anticipates the content of the conclusion.

The point may be illustrated by an example formulated by Mounce (1981, p. 113) in one of the most enlightening of introductions to the main lines of Wittgenstein's thought:

> In other words, we should be prepared to say of someone that he understands 'Everything on the table is red' only if, in asserting it, he were prepared to assert of any given thing on the table (this apple, for example) that it is red. Asserting the latter is a condition for asserting the former.

A fortiori, if I posit a hypothetical judgement or proposition, shortening it to the form of *modus ponens*, "if *p*, then *q*", then I am saying that the presence of *p* compels me to admit the presence of *q*. We are apt to call this the necessary result of the form of the sentence, and to regard it as a consequence of the meaning *of the premises*. Per contra, Wittgenstein holds that the premises themselves get their "meaning" from the fact that I am disposed to accept that *q* is, in the moment I mean to recognize *p*. If I say that the existence of wolves in a given area necessarily implies the existence of the canine species in the same area, I am in fact saying that such a proposition is something that follows from my *foregoing and simultaneous* willingness to accept the canine species if I accept the wolves. And similarly, since the disjunctive form of judgement has the hypothetical form embedded in itself, the proposition "*a* is either *F* or *G*", or "the canine exemplar is either wolf or fox", refers to a simultaneous disposition to exclude the one at the inclusion of the other. And such a disposition, Wittgenstein implies, has to be regarded as a fact produced in a given social environment. It represents a social reality and is a social result. The things I want to do, the things I accept as being possible to do, the whole specific range of options that do present themselves to me, are conditions excisting by virtue of and through a social environment in which I am an active participant.

According to Wittgenstein, what is determined and developed in such environments is, most importantly, a set of *rules*. In the above mentioned "language game" expressing itself in what we call "logic", the proposition "this exemplar is not a wolf, and consequently it is a fox" has got a *form* that is understood as a *rule* for the use of sentences of the form "*a* is either *F* or *G*". They are consciously present as determining the *meaning* of any specific general sentence. However, as it is pointedly said by Mounce (1981, p. 114),

> these rules are not the reflection of some deeper lying logical structure. The propositions of logic do not reflect what underlies the rules but are a crystallization of the rules themselves, these rules deriving their point from what surrounds them, the social life into which they enter.

That is, we cannot say (as was upheld in the *Tractatus*), that the meaning of a proposition is derived from a given *system* of intelligible statements. Its meaning is so to speak dependent on its own intelligible "consequences", that is, on inferences being made in the specific social context of conscious human beings.

Since this kind of analysis implies that the meaning-reference-relation has a form that definitely runs counter to a general and quite dominating way of thinking, Wittgenstein's contribution is often understood as a discovery of alienation in the present human condition. It allegedly shows the existence of a real movement which is mystified and hidden from those whose very action it is. And by Western scholars one sometimes sees the assertion made, with varying emphasis and in a more or less authoritative tone, that this constitutes a parallel between Wittgenstein and Marx. Mounce's following comment (1981, p. 119) on Wittgenstein's argument may be taken as representative of such thinking:

> The reason why these points are overlooked is that our sense of what is relevant or appropriate, not simply in mathematics and music but in social life generally, is often influenced by factors we have forgotten or of which we are hardly even aware, and, then, when we philosophize we are inclined to suppose that the factors that influenced it exist independently of human activity altogether, . . .

He goes on to draw a comparison with Marx, who is said to have

> noted a tendency to attribute, as it were, to the nature of things what is really the product of people's own actions. For example, people sometimes believe, or act as if they believed, that the workings of the state are something more than the activities of those who comprise the state or carry on economic affairs;

In fact, all this brings to light a misunderstanding of the Marxian theory of the commodity and of the form of value. Marx' criticism of "commodity fetishism" is a constructive one: It aims not simply at the discovery of a kind of alienation, but also at a description of the means necessary for its abolition; and in so doing, it describes the social circumstances which are bringing forth both the alienation and its abolition.

To see how far this is removed from Wittgenstein's theory of logic as it is presented in the *Investigations*, let us go back to the kind of argument Marx used against the philosophy of Ludwig Feuerbach, more than twenty years before the publication of the first volume of *Capital;* more specifically, to his so-called "Theses on Feuerbach", written in 1845, as a kind of prelude to the critique of Feuerbach in the *German Ideology.*

The main theme of this polemics against Feuerbach is the latter's critique of religion, a critique that, according to Marx, is a halfway house. The important Fourth thesis runs as follows (Marx, 1969, p. 6):

> Feuerbach starts out from the fact of religious self-alienation, of the duplication of the world in a religious world and a secular one. His work consists in resolving the religious world into its secular basis. But the fact that the secular basis detaches itself from itself and establishes for itself an independent realm in the clouds, is something which can only be explained by the self-cleaving and self-contradictory nature of this secular basis. The latter, then, has to be understood in its contradiction as well as revolutionised in practice. Thus, for instance, when the earthly family has been discovered as the secret of the holy family, the former must itself be annihilated in theory and in practice.

Now, Wittgenstein in the *Investigations* can scarcely (regardless of what he in fact wanted or not wanted to do) be said to make serious efforts to explain *the reason why* logical inference presents itself in an alienated form. That is to say that from a Marxian point of view he might be understood to adhere to a Feuerbachian stage of development: He points to the fact of alienation, but he makes no attempt to explain it in any serious sense, let alone attempt to revolutionise its basis. This is all the more conspicuous since according to Wittgenstein a proposition is something that arises in human "language-games", that is, as we have seen, in determined social circumstances. However, a scrutiny of this category will show, I believe, that it is scarcely lends itself to any critical investigation of bourgeois society: Rather, it has serious apologetic traits as regards the functioning of capitalist social relations.

I.2. Wittgenstein's Concept of "Family Likenesses" Contra Dialectical Concept Theory.

The later Wittgenstein's theory of concept formation is as crucial for an understanding of his thought as is his concept of games (let alone language-games). And in fact, in the *Philosophical Investigations* the two are tentatively explained in terms of each other.

In §65 of the *Investigations*, Wittgenstein discusses the concept of *language*, which he immediately makes equivalent to *language-games* (in the plural, that is). He refuses to point out a mark common to all entities that could be reckoned as candidates of being subsumed under such a concept. Rather, he tells us that *"Erscheinungen"* like these games, taken in their numerical totality, do not have anything at all in common (although common marks may be found in a great many of them). When we give them the common name of "game", it is not because of such a mark, but because they are *"related* [verwandt] to one another in many different ways" (Wittgenstein, 1953, p. 31).[1] Wittgenstein's way of thinking implicitly but quite distinctively presupposes a nominalist approach. The reflecting subject is external to the actual objects, a relation made explicit by formulations in §66 (cf. Wittgenstein, 1953, p. 31):

> Betrachte z. B. einmal die Vorgänge, die wir "Spiele" nennen. Ich meine Brettspiele, Kartenspiele, Ballspiel, Kampfspiele, usw. Was ist allen diesen gemeinsam? – Sag nicht: "Es muss ihnen etwas gemeinsam sein, sonst hiessen sie nicht 'Spiele'" – sondern *schau*, ob ihnen allen etwas gemeinsam ist. – Denn wenn du sie anschaust, wirst du zwar nicht etwas sehen, was *allen* gemeinsam wäre, aber du wirst Ähnlichkeiten, Verwandtschaften, sehen, und zwar eine ganze Reihe.[2]

These types of relations, called "family likenesses" (§67) by Wittgenstein, are what characterise his theory of concept formation.

The theory has been hailed as a breakthrough of historical importance.[3] And it has been criticised, but most often in too overbearing a way. Its weaknesses are obvious, so that its relative popularity has to be explained by way of historical reasons, as we shall see.

Actually, Wittgenstein's contention that it will be impossible to find one common distinguishing mark among a given set of entities (like "die Vorgänge, die wir "Spiele" nennen") separated from the activity of the reflecting and judging subject, looks suspiciously like a truism. For naturally, if such a "mark" could be found, we would still have to explain why it is of a kind that successfully excludes facts or activities other than "games", thus giving us an adequate limit for the *definiendum*. But then, a theory of concept formation like the one criticised by Wittgenstein, never played an important role in the history of philosophy; or if it did, it was just as a passing *Gestalt*.

Further, a serious difficulty immediately arises concerning the determination of "relatedness" ("Verwandtschaft"). In §65, Wittgenstein states that it is by reason of a relatedness (or of a plurality of such relations) that we give a set of entities a common name. But if no single likeness can be counted as common to all individuals of a type X, and to them alone, it would seem reasonable that there might exist some likenesses between the Xs which were also likenesses between what we would call members (individuals) of other types, like Y or Z and so on. Consequently, we would have to search for criteria excluding the Ys and the Zs. And obviously, such criteria could not be of the same kind as those that were hitherto taken to generate our understanding of "likenesses". The concept of the existence of such criteria would, in any case, incorporate the concept of the existence of the general concept ('Game', for instance), since without it no measure for the form or content of the criteria would be available. The concept would then be presupposed. Such difficulties might throw a Wittgensteinian back onto the road of distinguishing marks. For others, it might help to confirm the unsatisfactory character of both modes of thinking.

At this point an historical overview, however brief, is necessary. It would at the very least be worthwhile reviewing the difference between forms of essentialism and traditional nominalism.

The essentialism of Platonic (*universalia ante res*) as well as of Aristotelian (*universalia in rebus*) fabric lost their fundamental *raison d'être* together with the onset of modern relations of production. The possibility of free labour and of exploitation initiated through a buying of commodities (especially of labour power) marked an era of outer, mechanical relations between men and between men and nature – this last term being taken as the *Inbegriff* of all possible means of production. The time of nominalism had come: It was no longer an alien thought that the naming of objects depended on a free subject – a subject no longer tied to nature through slavery, serfdom or filial forms of property. Similarly, it could now stand to reason that men were not required on divine or natural grounds to presuppose that given characteristics made individuals into members of kinds. From now on, men were thought to make subsumptions out of their own thought and will.

However, such views were in their turn seriously shaken by Kant. For one thing, he radically limited the possibility-range for (realistic) subjective concept formation. These new limits, posited through concepts of the forms of Space and Time and of Categories of the intellect tied to these forms, enabled him to define human serfdom in a revolutionary way: Through that definition, he was, ipso facto, able to give a definition of human freedom which also had revolutionary implications. The Kantian theory of practical freedom is a most important milestone in the development of the theory of human freedom. And when the core of Kant's theory was developed further by Hegel, the starting point was precisely the former's practical philosophy.

Later, the *"linke Hegelianer"* Karl Marx came to a conclusion that in effect could be summed up as follows: The image of universal freedom of Kant and Hegel could be realised only if it was accepted as a result of revolutionary, political action on the part of the working class. True universality had to move in stages, initially brought forward by a given, particular class interest.

The main body of the bourgeois reaction after Hegel, from the 1830s on, had in fact, however unconsciously, come to the same conclusion. And the fear of the possible revolutionary consequences of its own thought led it to interpret "the modern proletariat" of Marx and Engels as a rude mass of paupers, to whom real culture is inaccessible.

Thus there evolved a contempt of the "masses" that became prominent in the thinking of Kierkegaard and his followers, and also popular in crucial forms of bourgeois science – dominated as they have been by so many a variant of Malthusianism – be it Darwinism, explicit eugenic theories or an aloof "welfare" ideology.

Now, in Hegel's philosophy an abolition of nominalism, implied already in Kant, acquired prominence. In the bourgeois reaction against Hegelianism, it came to be a widespread opinion that Hegel's attitude marked the development of a new realism of concepts – that is, to an essentialism. Consequently, parts of its philosophical thinking again took up nominalism, while parts of it preferred the return to an essentialism thought to be relatively untouched by modernity. Wittgenstein's concept theory is a late but typical example of the first tendency. The explicit Platonism of Bertrand Russell, which was soon to be a welcome target for Wittgenstein, is typical of the second.

The form of dialectic that Hegel initiated implied an abolition of nominalist as well as essentialist procedure. Nevertheless, it held on to elementary rules of limitation in definitions, developed from the time of Socrates and Plato. In the case of the concept of 'Game', this would recquire positing the question: What is *not* 'Game'? Evidently, when we use this term it is meant to delimit an activity of some kind from activities which are *serious*; that is the *intention*, and further analysis is required if one wants to explore the problem of whether such an intention is itself serious, or could be brought to a satisfying end. This has nothing to do with the kind of realism that is evidently the target of Wittgenstein's critique. It means that concepts are developed in the subject's active relation to its world.

The thinking activity trying to determine a not-serious entity or a concept thereof, is itself, then, an instance of that which its object is not. It is working seriously to determine entities that demonstrate seriousness only *via negativa*. When we discover seriousness and hard work inside a game, that is not a token that all serious activity could be regarded as placed inside rules of the same kind. On the contrary, it means that the game has been really and effectively limited from the serious world, so that there are no other solutions outside the game itself. This is a consciousness often provoking desperation, for breaking the rules would lead the subjects right into the world of seriousness!

In his work *Homo ludens*, Jan Huizinga pointed out that a game "is no action in the common meaning of the word", since its description tends to be of such a kind that the concept employed in the noun is usually repeated in the verb: As for instance in the German, "*ein Spiel spielen*".[4] It forms a closed kind of activity, and as such it is also in evidence in Wittgenstein – partly in his aversion against explanations, partly in his most emphatic argument for such a view in the *Investigations*:

> Our mistake is to look for an explanation where we ought to look at what happens as a "proto-phenomenon". That is, where we ought to have said: *this language-game is played* [. . . *dieses Sprachspiel wird gespielt*] (§654).

Consequently, one might think that Wittgenstein's empiricist way of approaching the problem of general concepts is superdetermined by a bias favouring precisely the game-relation. At no cost is he going to be taken as a *Spielverderber*! If he had met the problem with a will to define via limitations, he would ipso facto have had to concede that he was placed outside the world of games, or, rather, outside *any* single game.

It is not unusual to place Wittgenstein's philosophy in the Kantian tradition. The best argument for doing so would seem to be that the Kantian way of looking at the world of the subject and its objects of knowledge, "*Erscheinungen*", has about it the same kind of aura as has a game: What the subject meets there, are phenomena whose form it has itself constituted.

Likewise, in a game, the objects one meets are seen through the idiom of a determined set of rules constituted throughout by subjects.

If that is an adequate comparison, Wittgenstein's thinking can be taken to be some kind of *Transzendentalphilosophie*: We are moving inside language-games, and since language is the limit of this world, we cannot say anything decisive about it. It is turned into a *Grenzbegriff*.

Against this way of thinking, which, contrary to Kant's, does not tell us anything about the road to freedom, the Hegelian tradition is apt to argue, as it does against Kant, that the limit cannot be known as such unless it is abolished as limit; knowing the limit means being at both sides of it. It can be only something already overcome.

Therefore, the argument will include a claim of self-reference, asking how it is possible for a thinker to adhere to such a theory without explaining how it is possible to know a game to be a game at all. Which in its turn includes the question about the nature of a possible alienation forcing us to misunderstand language. How is it that the

> general notion of the meaning of a word surrounds the working of language with a haze which makes clear vision impossible (§5),

as it is said in the *Investigations*? We are not given any answer, but are just told that it is possible to see through the fog if we investigate language as it is functioning in its more primitive kinds, that is, in simple language-games, easy to overview.

I.3. The Concept of Language-Games: Critical Remarks

At the beginning of the *Philosophical Investigations*, in §2, Wittgenstein gives an example of what he calls "language" or "language-game". It is a primitive and simple one, presumably meant to facilitate a basic understanding of the concept. And, also to provide a simple structure which might serve as a foundation on which a more complicated building can be erected step by step.

"A is building with building-stones",[5] and in this he has an assistant, B. Given such a situation, Wittgenstein thinks it possible, with the help of the use of just a few words, to construct a language or a "language-game", which, although it might be primitive, is *complete*. It consists in A shouting out names of the elements he needs: "block", "pillar", "slab", "beam", and in B bringing to him these elements based on what he has been taught their "names" are.

There are many conceivable objections to calling this "a language", but Wittgenstein simply instructs us, as a master builder would instruct an assistant: "Conceive this as a complete primitive language." In §1 the author demonstrates the same unwillingness to discuss presuppositions: In exposing a related case of language use, he precludes questions about the background of the actions of *a persona dramatis*, simply presupposing that he is acting as described: "-Well, I assume that he acts as I have described. Explanations come to an end somewhere."

Such abruptness may be defended in many ways. For one thing, it is always reasonable first to let the philosophical exposition start somewhere, and then accept that this starting point is being criticised hand in hand with the progress of exposition. Also, it is conceivable that the problems that are scrutinised, themselves justify the practice in question.

Indeed, this last kind of justification might seem sympathetic to Wittgenstein. In the instances he has given he specifies by saying that they represent "primitive forms of language" of the same kind which a "child uses . . . when it learns to talk". And "[h]ere the teaching of language is not explanation, but training" (§5). According to Wittgenstein, it is conceivable that the "complete, primitive language" from the building site has its definition extended:

> We could imagine that the language of §2 was the *whole* language of A and B; and even the whole language of a tribe. The children are brought up to perform *these* actions, to use *these* words as they do so, and to react in *this* way to the words of others (§6).

Of all the considerations of the nature of "language-games" which we find in the *Philosophical Investigations*, few, if any, are more penetrating or detailed than these remarks from the beginning of the work. There is, however, a marked absence of didactical introduction to the concept. The *Investigations*, whose aim is to rehabilitate the *description* of phenomena as opposed to their *explanation*, clearly implies being in possession of an idea of an adequate description technique. Consequently, it might be expected that in Wittgenstein's later work the concept of language-games tend to mechanically replace the 'elementary propositions' of the *Tractatus*. These were, in an all-too well known analytical style, introduced dogmatically as untouchables; they were to be reckoned as mutually detached elements, though perhaps not as elements in a logical atomism, which in its turn might have been incompatible with the early Wittgenstein's contention that there existed a unity of language, presupposed in every conceivable proposition.

Still, in the *Investigations*, a critical front against positions of the *Tractatus* comes to the fore which might have the power of devastating all such dogmatism. For in fact, the language-games are not understood as entities purely given. Language, that is, the language-game, says Wittgenstein, is, e.g. (in "language 2", as he calls it), "meant to serve for communication between" (§2) builder and assistant.[6] The game has, so to speak, taken hold outside itself, by virtue of a determinate purpose. Without a purpose, no game. Further, the "communication" *("Verständnis")* in such a case is no purely final purpose, but a purpose which is itself a means, namely, to get a building constructed.

Nevertheless, it seems to represent a major problem that Wittgenstein apparently finds that a description of a language-game is adequate as soon as the game has been connected to a single, described purpose. He wants to understand language as a game in a social context, and then, as we can understand as the work progresses, to interpret such a context as the origin of each and every logical rule. Consequently, Wittgenstein is often taken to be aiming at effecting a liberation of philosophy and formal logic from notions of lawlikeness or adherence to rules directing thought independently of human practice.

I will try to show that this approach fails to capture an adequate concept of what actually constitutes human practice, not to mention human freedom.

To begin with, due attention should be paid to Wittgenstein's use of the word 'game' in these connections. In fact, it amounts to the use of a *concept* of 'game' *('Spiel')*, since it is never without reason that we insist on using specific words for specific purposes. Wittgenstein's use of the term makes an implicit contrast between the "world" that is the immediate object of his description, and a "world" of seriousness, a "world" of objectivity seemingly stripped of the kind of reciprocity which we are apt to combine with "games". In fact, such a contrast may be found and identified in the difference between the mass of human "language-games" on the one hand, and on the other the conception of a general human "form of life" which Wittgenstein clearly takes to be their basis. "This complicated form of life"[7] is the resultant of human natural history, taken in a very general sense. It is opposed not by any other human form of life, but of the "forms of life" typical of different species of animals, perhaps also of plants. It is simply the most complicated *Lebensform*, incorporating language use and giving rise to language-games.

Now, for Wittgenstein, the term "language-game" covers not only certain words and sentences, or certain ways of handling those entities, but also the activity that is typically tied to these ways and modes. In the case of the builders, the whole of the building activity, the whole range of its physical actions evidently included, is called a "game", or a "language-game", a term indicating Wittgenstein's assumption of the priority of language in all social contexts (§7).

Taken as such a fairly general description of specifically human behaviour, the concept of 'language-games' has got its obvious difficulties. The human form of life has traditionally been regarded as something that can be adequately described through what we might call the subject – object model. And ultimately, it is based on labour and working activities that belong in quite another genus than do game and playing activities. Regardless of the form of its organisation, labour goes on for the purpose of constructing objects outside itself. Through a game on the other hand, nothing seems to be constructed but performative confirmations of its own rules and structures.[8]

For Wittgenstein, that was not the case. Through "language-games" we are rather, he thinks, constituting a "world". The threatening contradiction in the theory calls for remedies working against some of the otherwise necessary conditions making a game into a game – against, then, its own closed character.

Hence Wittgenstein is apt not only to concentrate on the game as a bundle of rules, not only on immediate rule-governed actions, but also to point out activities that go along with the game without being vital or necessary parts of it. Such actions or activities are not rule-governed through the game in question and not (at least not necessarily) rule-constituting. The following remarks from the *Investigations* seem to make his point (Wittgenstein, 1953, p. 39):

> Doesn't the analogy between language and games throw light here? We can easily imagine people amusing themselves in a field by playing with a ball so as to start various existing games, but playing many without finishing them and in between throwing the ball aimlessly into the air, chasing one another with the ball and bombarding one another for a joke and so on. And now someone says: The whole time they are playing a ball-game and following definite rules at every throw.

> And is there not also the case where we play and – make up the rules as we go along? And there is even one where we alter them – as we go along (§83).

In this text, Wittgenstein seems to find instances of activities starting with indifference to any aim, producing idioms in which *new* games might be initiated. It is reminiscent of his reflections, published in the *Remarks on the Foundations of Mathematics*, on a graphic illustration of a machine component (Wittgenstein 1956, p. 236):

> Our having learned a technique brings it about that we now alter it in such and such a way after seeing this picture.

> 'We decide on a new language-game'.
> 'We decide *spontaneously*' (I should like to say) 'on a new language-game.'

Now, the fact that such changes occur "spontaneously"[9] or take place in an aimless context is just what one would have to expect. Wittgenstein's language-games are, as we shall see, usually presented as being dependent on long-term training and practice; paradoxically, "new" language-games have to be generated through some sort of negation of that structure. They are created "spontaneously", like maggots in Aristotle's *physis*. Here, the consequence of not considering a definition by limitation from the outset, indeed makes itself painfully felt.

If it were acceptable to regard Wittgenstein as a thinker in the Kantian tradition – language-games taking the role of categories – then the structure referred to above would serve as something like a perfect illustration of the use of classical philosophical principles in creating the new irrationalism. In fact, it seems related to the kind of irrational choices that are fundamentals of Kierkegaard's theory of man passing from one kind of "existence" to another. The determining force is no longer reason or intellect, but the will, which here is seen as a factor taking over control in the necessary interludes between periods of categorical reasoning.

H.-G. Gadamer has argued that in playing, it is the game itself that takes over the subject-role, while the players experience the consequences of a subjugation they themselves have chosen (Gadamer, 1972, pp. 101–102). That, seen in isolation, is a way of thinking that Wittgenstein presumably would have taken as relevant: A game represents a structure that superdetermines the participants. In classical philosophy, however, as it developed in the Hegelian stream, such an entity ('game') is understood in a wider context, a context which determines as the regular (rule-determined) actions of the game, as well as "aimless" ones. Any "spontaneous" action, even before it could be turned into a new game, finds its place in that context. To this extent, it is senseless to make distinctions between rule-governed activities on the one hand, and "aimless" ones on the other.

That would represent a forceful argument against any assumption to the effect that the theoretical priority of the game-structure might be upheld in spite of spontaneous action. There obviously do not exist structures that compel us to regard such actions as connected with the creation of *games*. Their spontaneous form makes them completely contingent in relation to such a possibility.

In no way, then, can a game-structure be explained through itself. On the other hand, arguments of these kinds evidently result from the fact that dialectical philosophy thinks it possible to transcend any subjective subjugation – be it to a Kantian *"Erscheinungswelt"* or to game-structures.

I.4. *"Linguistic Idealism": Performative Analysis*

In the literature on Wittgenstein there is a conspicuous absence of critical discussions on the role of the concept of 'game'. Largely, the term seems to be accepted in a way which itself is quite as self-justifying as is a factual game.[10] However, as is soundly implied by Rhees (1958, p. xiii), it is vital to the whole context of Wittgenstein's thinking that he finds that

> [t]here is something about the way in which we use language, and in the connection of
> language and thinking – the force of an argument, and the force of expressions generally

– which makes it seem as though recognizing it as a language were very different even from recognizing it as a move in a game. (As though understanding were something outside the signs; and as though to be a language it needs something that does not appear in the system of signs themselves.)

Here, the importance of being able to analyse language, and a fortiori language-games, in the same manner as one studies a *game* proper, is rightly stressed.

So one is apt to take a positive view of possible constructive deviations from the main trend, as we meet them in works by Anscombe (1981) and Bloor (1996) where the importance of the 'metaphor' (as it is called by Bloor) of "game" is being consciously stressed and elaborated. In these cases, however, the authors' aim is to justify the concept of 'game' as a key to a paradigm of a "new" kind of idealism. Bloor understands the Wittgensteinian effort as "breaking down the distinction between the subject and the object of knowledge." Alluding explicitly to the objective idealist's concept of *right*, he states that "[t]he resonance is with those aspects of the idealist tradition associated with Hegel, not Berkeley." To illustrate this point, he remarks that "[w]e refer to our "rights", but ultimately [*sic*] our rights *are*, or *reside in* those very acts of reference – and so also with the other items amenable to this analysis."[11]

In point of fact, there is no distinct idealist flavour about such truths (as we shall see, it is a question of what one takes to be the content of those "acts of reference"). They are, e.g. consistently used by Marx, as when he illustrates a relation between two commodities, whereof the one (via its owner) is expressing and measuring its value in the other, with an overt relation between men:

> There is something special with such determinations of reflection. This man, for instance, is king only because other men relate themselves to him as subjects. Contrariwise, they think they are subjects because he is king.[12]

Such "determinations of reflection" are propositions of quite a special kind: They presuppose the accomplished establishment of the institutions in question. In the example just mentioned, one commodity is taken to be an equivalent because of certain traits in its very material nature, while it really could not serve as an equivalent at all, had it not been for the social institution of "exchange". If my statement "I have to make a bow to the king" has a performative setting, it is only because the kingship is already established, and obviously this cannot be explained by the performative actions in question. Or better, it cannot be explained by *any* performative act whatsoever. A state of local chieftainship may be upheld through rituals expressed by performatives; and while the same holds true for kingship, the transition from the one state to the other needs quite another type of explanation.

In calling the form of thinking in question a "determination of reflection", Marx is making use of the critical vocabulary developed by Hegel. In the latter's "Lehre vom Wesen"[13] the term is used to indicate a certain kind of appearance (*Schein*), where the thinking subject is forced to take its own thought-constructions to represent an alien, given reality. Small wonder, then, that Marx's use of the kingship example appears as a note to his elaboration of the theory of "commodity fetishism", where he is making the point that a commodity-owner, when expressing the value of his own product in the material of another's, unconsciously is creating the appearance that the social category of "value" is a natural, sempiternian one – belonging, so to speak, to the "natural history" of humans.

We shall meet the form of this commodity fetishism below, in the course of a critique of Sraffian production equations. Meanwhile, let us proceed to the cardinal instance in Bloor's exposition, where the starting point is taken not in an alleged, traditional idealist way of definition, but in a problem which is being formulated by Wittgenstein himself (1956, p. 401) during his reflections on mathematics, though being clearly connected with the theme of commodity production:

> What sort of certainty is it that is based on the fact that in general there won't actually be a run on the banks by all their customers; though they would break if it did happen?!

Wittgenstein is here touching on themes related to the field of interest of Cambridge acquaintances and colleagues such as Sraffa and Keynes.[14] His words are taken by Bloor to be "a request to analyze our confidence in the "soundness" of a bank." Bloor goes on (1996, p. 367):

> Clearly it consists in part, but crucially, in the beliefs of its depositors. These beliefs are beliefs about other people's beliefs, and in particular about their beliefs in the bank's soundness. No matter how "fundamentally" sound we think the bank is, if nobody else believes in its soundness we had better get our savings out quickly. Others' beliefs in the bank's unsoundness make it *true* that it isn't sound. The soundness or otherwise of the bank is ultimately [*sic*] *constituted* by beliefs about its soundness or unsoundness.

Taken as a description of a certain theoretical position, this would seem to be a quite satisfying reflection of the views involved in Wittgenstein's conception of "language-games". The theory of "linguistic idealism", as expressed in examples like these, apparently shatters much of the spell that still surrounds it in the eyes of commentators. As a consequence, the vulnerability of the said theory comes strongly to the fore.

Let us formulate a couple of theses in connection with the banking example: (1) In spite of the unlimited mass of possible cases in the history of the last five hundred years, there certainly never was a bank going bankrupt without there being effective reasons other than the one mentioned by Bloor. (2) A bank cannot possibly go bankrupt for the reason mentioned by Bloor.

Firstly, let us concentrate not on the question concerning the truth (of which, by the way, I am convinced) of (1) and (2), but rather on the question about standards for determining such an issue. The serious point is that as long as the argument relies completely or "ultimately"[15] on performative phenomena, that is to say, on phenomena internal to a "game", it is a priori impossible to open the argument to other forms of explanation. Now, this is not in itself a devastating critique. At first glance it might simply look like an example of the Popperian claim that a theory is to be taken seriously only when it can be falsified – a claim that has too obvious self-referential flaws. However, the argument turns the tables (I would suggest) when we proceed precisely to this last-mentioned claim of self-referential consistency. For as was seen above, the *existence* of the game cannot – without bad circularity – be explained through itself or through other games. That is to say, the historical development behind the existence of a banking system, and the necessary conditions for the system involved in that development, cannot legitimately enter the structure of the Bloorian argument.

Secondly, let us look at the possibly most important consequence of such a limitation, namely that there then is no way in which elements embedded in the genesis of the phenomenon, in casu the banking system (as we may call it), can be *understood as* upholding the system, be it in a transformed shape or otherwise. No such conditioning can be expressed by the theory, albeit the theorist may be all the more inclined to believe in one. This would mean that there is no theoretical way in which to reconstruct the connection between the existing "game" and its historical basis.

Even to those who might think that a bank could collapse because of beliefs in its unsoundness, it would certainly seem weird to concede that its existence could legitimately be monocausally explained through beliefs in its soundness. The reason is that its existence evidently has to be explained by constructive acts, including an investment, which presuppose its not already being there. It is explained through a relation that cannot possibly involve any such belief. Bloor's argument is presupposing that from a certain point in time after its foundation, the original motivation, say a will to gain money on lending out capital, is no longer there. Instead, we now have just a belief in the bank's soundness. But naturally, belief in such soundness is dependent upon a belief in the bank's power to make money. Such a belief involves considerations of the same kind as those that led to the founding of the bank, considerations that reflect socioeconomic circumstances which are not in any way limited by rules in a "language-game of banking". And naturally, it is this dependence upon this general connection between a bank and its social surroundings that explains the rather important fact that banks never collapse for Bloorian reasons. The beliefs of bourgeois economic participants are shaped by their overall social background, albeit reflected in irrational forms in their "animal spirits". In fact, explaining a phenomenon inside this economic system by way of "distrust" makes it equally susceptible to explanation by way of "trust", which is what we in fact tend to do when a wave of confident speculation leads to major collapses. The welter of different moods and feelings, all seemingly capable of explaining vital actions while they in fact do nothing more than to keep each other in a barren balance, is itself a reflection of an economic mode based on exploitative mysteries in production.

This can be seen in the fact that Bloor's argument rests on a *petitio principii*. For it is not meaningful to talk about belief in the beliefs of others without adding the reflection that such beliefs are themselves incorporate beliefs about others' beliefs. Bloor's own belief, a belief which, in the present example is to be taken as a belief in the soundness of the bank, may itself count as such an incorporate belief. Here, one has to take seriously Bloor's formulation of the condition "if nobody else ...", which in fact makes his argument self-destructive. With Bloor, there is a "we", or an "I", in short *a subject* among other subjects, who may believe the bank to be sound indeed, or has got no clear opinion on the matter.[16] Consequently, none of its customers is in a position to take it as a given fact that nobody else believes the bank to be sound. And, consequently, they may think the bank to be sound, on the same basis that made Bloor think they held it to be unsound. One should note that Bloor's way of arguing plainly relies on the presence of a subject not sharing the conviction of "others". But then, his point has already abolished (*aufgehoben*) itself, to use an Hegelian term. There is no means present to help us, or to help any depositor, to decide how many depositors simply feel uncertain, how many that are persuaded in one direction or other, etc. The collective consciousness described by Bloor is not the state of mind present in a host of depositors a microsecond prior to their starting a bank run. On the contrary, it simply describes the general feeling of instability present ever and everywhere in the capitalist system. So in fact, it points to the necessity of explaining bank runs by way of reactions to fundamental structures independent of performative ones.

The rather obvious relation that our beliefs involve belief in others' belief in our beliefs, in fact points to a common background of experience which gives real weight to our decisions concerning which things to believe and which not to believe. That is the reason why no bank ever has gone bankrupt on

Bloorian grounds. For his "grounds" are real grounds only in the moment they are considered as reflections of a deeper structure.

This is not to deny that a bank may go bankrupt after a run of depositors, while another, financial conditions being identical, may experience no trouble of that kind. But the point is that the bankruptcy cannot be *explained* in Bloor's way. For it is clear from the above that *in principle* no one can have an overview that guarantees him a relative numerical overweight of a particular view of the bank's position among the mass of depositors. Consequently, it is without meaning to say that others' beliefs make it "true" that a bank is sound or unsound. For in that case, it is equally "true" that it is sound when unsound, and vice versa.

However, what is surely certain, is that every depositor knows that there will be a gap between the amount of cash at the bank's disposal at a given point in time and the total money amount deposited. This is presupposed by Bloor himself, and rightly so. But then, what is presupposed by the depositors, is nothing less than a consciousness of the very concept of a bank, or rather, its *definition*. Which, in its turn, means that the bank is created and upheld by precisely the structure of beliefs that Bloor thinks he can use to describe its dissolution.

Now, should one wish to adhere to the line of reasoning proposed by Bloor, one would have to turn the argument: Since it cannot be *beliefs* among depositors that create the downfall, it is the run that creates the belief in an insolvency. While a belief has the standing of formal subjectivity and can explain no event, the factual run is an *event* that can be apprehended and explain other events. However, as such it is just an outer, mechanical cause, and can explain at most other outer causes, *qua* events of the same order. However, what is essential for all that takes place inside that order, is that human beings act according to what they take to be *definitions* by limitation. They are not living inside games.

While theories of the Bloorian kind can scarcely be upheld, their existence as an influential ideological stance is in itself an important historical fact. We might suggest that Wittgensteinian thinking is an uncritical reflection upon the fact that the capitalist development tends to create a social formation where its specific mode of production takes the form of an apparent self-reproducing substance. From a certain historical point in time, the production system looks like a self-subsisting game in itself. Further, we might argue that the possibility of bankrupts is showing us the real limits of the system. Bankrupting points to basic facts that set the performative social theory out of play, and consequently it cannot be explained by such a theory either.

II. PIERO SRAFFA AND THE CORE OF HIS MODEL

II.1. On Theory and Criticism

In his Preface to the *Investigations*, Wittgenstein mentions two men as having had decisive influence on the development of his own ideas – Frank Ramsey and Piero Sraffa. It might be worth noting that both made important contributions to bourgeois economic theory – Sraffa most eminently so, being a trained economist. But further, Wittgenstein (1953, p. viii) declared a special debt to Sraffa, who "for many years unceasingly practised [a criticism] on my thoughts": "I am indebted to *this* stimulus for the most consequential ideas of this book."

Sraffa (1898–1983) did publish rather little.[17] However, his four perhaps best-known works, the articles "Sulle relazioni fra costo e quantità prodotta" (1925) and "The Laws of Returns under Competitive Conditions" (1926), his "Introduction" to the *Works and Correspondence of David Ricardo* (1951), and the book *Production of Commodities by Means of Commodities*, which was published in 1960, are all evaluated as classics of their *genre*. His theoretically most important ideas are put forward in the work of 1960, which may be read as an attack upon neoclassical capital theory and in effect upon all kinds of marginalism. In the present article, it is adopted as the key text for a study of his possible influence on Wittgenstein. In fact, the manuscript grew into a synoptic form precisely during the period when relations between Sraffa and Wittgenstein were at the closest.[18]

Some words of warning are pertinent at this juncture. When searching out structural likenesses between the works of these protagonists, it cannot be a question of pointing at specific themes elaborated by the one and then taken over by the other, even if done in indirect and disguised ways. Certainly it might be more to the point to talk about reciprocal influences, but the existence of such relations frequently goes without saying, and elaborations of them most often turn into banalities. Rather, possible structural parallels should be taken not as starting-points, but as products of class-based ways of gaining consciousness of the world. They should be understood as results of a given ideological coercion, presenting themselves as tempting ways of appropriating a reality whose basic structures might otherwise stand forth in a form all too true and all too base.

It is not in the least surprising that men of the same kind of (academic) profession and bourgeois background, both otherwise reacting against rather primitive ways of thinking dominating their respective disciplines, should develop a particular mode of thought that superdetermines the method they are using, however different those disciplines may be thought to be. To a Sraffa reacting against an all too obvious lack of reflection in the marginalist camp, there corresponds a Wittgenstein arguing against primitive Anglo-Saxon empiricism. They both seek remedies in some kind of reflection upon human activities. Taking the activity aspect of human beings as the essential one, in contradistinction to theories that seemingly focus on substantial and unchanging factors, is a tempting alternative. In fact, such an escape route was easy to combine with a political stance in seeming favour of working class associations, trade unions, even "communist" parties – especially since these (at the latest in the beginning of the Thirties) had replaced Marxist activity with reformist and trade-unionistic practice. The aloof, romantic bow to working men, an "active" part of humanity, so evidently present in the aristocratic and authoritarian Wittgenstein, thus nicely fits together with his opposition to mainstream philosophy. On the whole, it should be taken as quite a general trait of radical intellectuals in the Thirties (precisely as in the Seventies) that they are seeking some kind of alliance with working class interests in their own struggle against outlived modes of bourgeois thought.[19] To the extent that such academic intellectuals are unable to see the liberation of the working class as a movement *sui generis*, as the own work of the said class, they are in fact *not* interested in any liberating activity; what interests them, might then in fact very well be an activity *per se*. That is precisely the traditional outcome by reformist political movements, their slogans crowned by Eduard Bernstein's *dictum* "the aim is nothing, the movement everything".[20]

As one can infer from what is pointed out above concerning the structure of "language games", such an activity *per se* is just what gives us the very concept and definition of a "game". In the following pages, I will try to show that in the techniques and distributive coercion of Sraffian production equations, human beings are necessarily left to function precisely as relata inside the game-relation. Such a constellation is scarcely consciously chosen by Sraffa, who, as we know, was rather critical to Wittgenstein's formulated theoretical positions. The heart of the matter lies much deeper, perhaps even deeper than anything Wittgenstein had in mind when he referred to Sraffa in his Preface. What is happening, is that a certain class-determined social position demands that its victims conceive of the world as a joking relationship.

It might well be, as is suggested by Roncaglia (1978, p. 122)[21] that Sraffa's relation to Wittgenstein, as it comes to the fore in *Production of Commodities by Means of Commodities*, implies that the book describes merely one of a number of language games in the economic sphere. Such possible options, be they presented consciously by the author or not, would change nothing as regards the factual, unapprehended ways of looking at social relations which make themselves felt in the texts.

Further, as is the case with so many a debate on Wittgenstein's later work, a discussion of Sraffa's book is apt to raise the issue as to what extent one is dealing with a positive theory, or whether the position discussed should be understood as a "pure" critical stance of some sort. In discussions relating to the *Philosophical Investigations* and the strong relativistic position upheld in that work, the very same relativism is frequently being argumentatively used to defend the Wittgensteinian position. Thus, Wittgenstein's unexplicated introduction of "language-games" often seems to be excused by arguments to the effect that one's fundamental frame of reference cannot be properly explained anyway, since it is presupposed in every explanation. It is precisely such fallacious reasoning that has led to a situation where virtually no attempt is made to expose the conceptual content of 'game'. Also, there is reason to believe that the fact that the relation between Wittgenstein and Sraffa has been subject to little investigation is one of the reasons why the same relativistic idiom is applied also to the study of the latter's work.

The apologetic tendency in such thinking makes itself felt in its positing of a dichotomy between critical activity and positive theory construction. In fact, undue separation of these activities is all too easy. Even criticism confined to showing internal inconsistencies in a theory has its own presuppositions. There is no good reason to go on concealing them. And anyway, it is always useful to discuss a criticism in view of its implications – be they implicit or explicit.

Sraffa's book has the subtitle *Prelude to a Critique of Economic Theory*. The last two words are commonly taken to refer to neo-classical theory. From this one might be tempted to conclude that the book has a purely critical, not constructive purpose. But taken *per se*, that would be a fallacy. Rather, Sraffa is ambiguous in this matter. In his Preface (Sraffa, 1960, p. vi) he informs the reader of his "set of propositions"

> that, although they do not enter into any discussion of the marginal theory of value and distribution, they have nevertheless been designed to serve as the basis for a critique of that theory. If the foundation holds, the critique may be attempted later, either by the writer or by someone younger and better equipped for the task.

Sraffa, then, regards his book as a "foundation", and not as an actual critique. If we take his words literally, and if we are after his own view of the matter, it would not seem unreasonable to conclude that we have before us the construction of a positive theory. That theory might be seen as developed through critical activity – just as when Marx (who subtitled his *magnum opus* "Critique of Political Economy") said that in his work there was to be found an exposition of (economic) categories which were criticised precisely through that exposition. The Sraffian "theory" in question should, however, not be called a positive *system*, since Sraffa's notes on the book of 1960 (kept in the Trinity Library, Cambridge) make it clear that he was adverse to any such notion.

Anyway, in practice, a point is sooner or later reached where the criticism of a would-be scientific text can no longer take account of whether its author meant it to function in one way or another. For, given the plurality of possible and actual positive theories, no critical effort can avoid making critical formulations that cannot be reconciled with some or other "positive theory". Rather, it would seem that only a belief in the possibility of reciprocally isolated "language games" could appear as a justification for seriously thinking that in principle alleged critical efforts may be isolated from alleged constructive theory.

If we take the Marxian corpus to include a "positive theory" of economics, it will be seen below that Sraffa's book, perhaps unwittingly on part of the author, presents important conclusions that decisively are incompatible with it. That goes, evidently, also for marginalist theory. From the standpoint of these theories, it is, in spite of any generous interpretation of Sraffa's Preface, impossible not to regard his "set of propositions" as a construct based on presuppositions which necessarily must be criticised in their own right.

II.2. Sraffa's Model of "Production for Subsistence": Exposition and Critique

Strangely enough, very few efforts have been made to clarify what bearing Wittgenstein's remarks in the Preface might have on the development of method in the *Investigations*.[22] It is difficult to find other than only relatively *ad hoc*, yet maybe fruitful comparisons.[23] A good example is one made in a work by Viggo Rossvær (1971, p. 254) where a possible connection between Wittgenstein's examples of elementary language-games and Sraffa's model construction of a primitive society and its production system is hinted at. Quite to the point, Rossvær quotes the following four first sentences of Sraffa's *Production of Commodities by Means of Commodities*:

> Let us consider an extremely simple society which produces just enough to maintain itself. Commodities are produced by separate industries and are exchanged for one another at a market held after the harvest.
>
> Suppose at first that only two commodities are produced, wheat and iron. Both are used, in part as sustenance for those who work, and for the rest as means of production – wheat as seed, and iron in the form of tools (Sraffa, 1960, p. 3).[24]

The society in question is described as a an entity producing on the basis of its own natural resources (labour power included), without any historical *specifica* being emphasised. Since Sraffa nevertheless talks about "commodities" as well as of "exchange" of them, he leaves open the possibility that these categories be interpreted as economic realities covering all kinds of human material production. *Ex hypothesi*, the existence of two kinds of products leads to a picture of a two-industry economy. The economic activity through one year might, as in Sraffa's own example, look like this:

280 qr. wheat +12 t. iron → 400 qr.wheat

120 qr. wheat + 8 t. iron → 20 t. iron

It is a token of what one might call Sraffa's "naturalist" view of commodity relations that the term "exchange value" comes to the fore already at this point, even as relations baked into the material process of society: "such values spring directly from the methods of production", and they here take the form of the ratio "10 qr. of wheat for 1 t. of iron" (§1).

The point is important for other reasons too. The theme of the first three paragraphs of Sraffa's book is what he calls production "for subsistence", not for surplus. Subsistence production may also take place with more than two sectors of production, but in such a case one necessary consequence disappears. Sraffa uses the following example for a three-industry system:

240 qr. wheat + 12 t. iron + 18 pigs → 450 qr. wheat

90 qr. wheat + 6 t. iron + 12 pigs → 21 t. iron

120 qr. wheat + 3 t. iron + 30 pigs → 60 pigs

"The exchange-values", Sraffa tells us, "which ensure replacement all round are 10 qr. wheat = 1 t. iron = 2 pigs" (§2). It follows:

> It may be noticed that, while in the two-industry system the amount of iron in wheat-growing was necessarily of the same value as the amount of wheat used in iron-making, this, when there are three or more products, is no longer necessarily true of any pair of them. Thus in the last example there is no such equality and replacement can only be effected through triangular trade (§2).

Actually, a reader might have supposed that the two-industry system, because of the fixity of the quantities of mutual interchange, could have been generally labelled a "system of redistribution", or the like. "Exchange value" could well have been interpreted as a concept viable only under the explicit trading relations of the three-or-more-industry system. Sraffa, however, de facto leaves open the possibility to describe even the "depth structure" of human production by way of that category.

This gives rise to a problem as regards the realism of the model. In the two-industry system, we get a defined set of "exchange values", while commodities "are exchanged for one another at a market held after the harvest". This seems to exclude the existence of money or of a money-commodity. It further seems to mean that "those who work" are directly represented in the production through a quantity of wheat. They are (since there is no mention of 'classes') supposed to consume all the food of the society in the process of producing the same quantity. This means that what is in fact their individual consumption, is being interpreted as a productive one.[25] The possible difference from a (schematic view of a) system of production based on slave labour is blurred – apart, of course, from the fact that there is no food left for slave-owners. Sraffa himself summarises the point at a later stage in the exposition saying that it means regarding

> wages as consisting of the necessary subsistence of the workers and thus entering the system on the same footing as the fuel for the engines or the feed for the cattle (§8).

As we shall see, this indicates the coming of some serious analytical problems as soon as relations of 'production for subsistence' turn out to be interpreted as conditions underlying 'production with a surplus'. However, there still remain difficulties to be coped with in the first chapter of the book.

Firstly, let us, for reasons of exposition, reproduce Sraffa's notation of the "general case" of a multiple-industry system. The prices or 'values' are – for reasons already mentioned – to be treated as unknowns in the system of production equations. They figure with the letter p, and they are taken to be quantities "which if adopted restore the initial position" (of subsistence production) (§3). The commodities to be produced are called $a, b, c, \ldots, k$, and their relative prices $p_a, p_b, \ldots p_k$. The annual quantity produced of a commodity is referred to by capital letters; A is the said quantity of a, B the corresponding quantity of b, etc.

The "general case" appears as follows:

$$A_a p_a \; + \; B_a p_b \; + \; \ldots \; + \; K_a p_k \; = \; A p_a$$

$$A_b p_a \; + \; B_b p_b \; + \; \ldots \; + \; K_b p_k \; = \; B p_b$$

$$\ldots \ldots \ldots \ldots \ldots \ldots \ldots \ldots \ldots \ldots \ldots \ldots$$

$$A_k p_a \; + \; B_k p_b \; + \; \ldots \; + \; K_k p_k \; = \; K p_k$$

The presupposition of pure subsistence production implies that "the sum of the first column is equal to [the sum of] the first line, that of the second column to [that of] the second line, and so on" (§3).

Now to the remaining difficulty:

The (only) unknowns in the system are the relative prices or "values", as Sraffa is apt to call them. One might suppose that the number of unknowns should then be taken to be k. However, for Sraffa it goes without saying that the accounting has to be effected through a commodity internal to the system. He consequently has one commodity (at random, for the time being) taken "as standard of value and its price made equal to unity", an operation which leaves us with $k - 1$ unknowns. And consequently the system can be regarded as determined:

> Since in the aggregate of the equations the same quantities occur on both sides, any one of the equations can be inferred from the sum of the others . . . This leaves $k - 1$ independent linear equations which uniquely determine the $k - 1$ prices (§3).

The fact that the determination of the system is dependent upon such a choice of a "standard of value", is of some consequence. Surely, no one equipped with a formal education in economics would find anything strange in Sraffa's procedure on this occasion. However, a critical look will reveal that the operation is meaningless, strictly speaking.

An economic system can be furnished with a "standard of value" (a money-commodity, or something like it) only as a result of the interaction between its members, and then, naturally, in their capacity of being commodity-owners. Such a situation of interaction has been observed by Sraffa himself; as we have seen, he describes the expression

"10 qr. wheat = 1 t. iron = 2 pigs"

as "exchange values". And rightly so; however, the expression is one-sided, in that it takes into account only the simple, uncomplicated community of commodity-owners, leaving aside their mutual disjunction, their reciprocal exclusion of each other, as *private* owners of property.

By Marx (whose method Sraffa actually believed he followed in some respects) this negative interaction is described as a disjunctive judgement, which we reproduce here in Sraffian guise:

"10 qr. wheat = 1 t. iron *or* = 2 pigs".[26]

Naturally, since this commodity-world consists of just three exemplars, we are left with only two other expressions to the same effect, namely e.g. "1 t. iron = 10 qr. wheat = *or* 2 pigs", alternatively e.g. "2 pigs=10 qr. wheat *or* 1 t. iron".

The genuine disjunctive expression, which is based not simply on the *or*, but on the *either-or*, is in fact clearly being employed by Marx, as can be seen from the fact that he is describing each and every *equivalent* as excluding every other in this *"entfaltete"* form of value (Marx, 1966, p. 234).[27] The correct "notation" therefore strictly speaking is

"10 qr. wheat = *either* 1 t. iron *or* = 2 pigs",

whereby it is expressed that a commodity can be exchanged against not more than one at a time, as long as the magnitude of exchange-value is supposed to be identical for all exemplars.

Obviously, such judgement-forms are chosen by Marx in his analysis of the commodity because they are immediately showing how the process starts out from the standpoint of an active subject, having its range and possibility of expression constructed and limited in the very act of exchange (or of potential exchange).

Now, what a subject expresses in this way is the *value* of his product. Since the products are physically heterogenous in relation to each other (in any contrary case there would not have been any need for exchange), this value has to be a substance which is common to them in some abstract fashion. The fact that the product "10 qr. wheat" has got a value, is not to be seen from its isolated being, but only from a value-expression, whose simplest form corresponds to any equation of the form "10 qr. wheat = 1 t. iron."

Two notable consequences follow.

Firstly, it gives no sense analytically to *choose* a commodity with the object of using it in measuring or as a *numéraire*. If such a commodity has come to exist, like, e.g. gold in the modern capitalist (world) economy, it is because it has been steered into its role as a result of (inter)subjective, but alienated action on part of the world of commodity-owners. *That* is the process in need of exposition.

Secondly, since the value of a commodity perforce is expressed only in another one, it is of no use to concentrate on the "value" or "price" of this other commodity, if a standard of prices is desired. The fact that the value *expresses* itself in another commodity, can only mean that it is expressed *not* in the value of this other commodity (for no entity can be expressed by itself), but (as it then follows) in the physical aspect of it.

Let us elaborate this second point. The commodity *iron* may function as *numéraire* for the commodity *wheat* only in so far as the iron, as a material substance, may be divided into parts: Since 10 qr. wheat is equal in value to 1 t. iron, a portion of 100 kg iron equals the value of 1 qr. wheat, etc. The commodity "wheat" gets its value expressed in a material measure (iron), and the value gets the form of *price* as soon as the measuring process takes the form of counting on the *numéraire* as on a measuring rod.[28]

Under such circumstances, the commodity that serves as a measure *and* as a *numéraire*, be it iron or gold or some other product, can strictly speaking

have no "price" at all. In bourgeois society, the "prices" of commodities are
their expressions in gold,[29] and gold consequently has got no "price", but rather
a virtually endless chain of value-expressions, with other commodities
functioning as "form of equivalent" (as Marx puts it). An expression like "two
ounces of gold are worth $200" is just a way of saying that each and every
such equivalent has the price of $200, or rather, of 2 ounces of gold.

II.3. Sraffa's Model of "Production with a Surplus"

When Sraffa introduces the more realistic model with the emergence of an
annual surplus product, he does so on the basis of the subsistence model. Now,
a surplus calculated in *values* or prices, indifferently to how and where it is
produced, will have to be distributed to every individual industry according to
its value size, irrespective of the composition between its means of production
and its employed labour force – be it measured in values, through a regular
physical measuring rod, or through "pure" artihmetics. In no other case will
the rate of the surplus be a rate *of profits* in any ordinary sense. Such a
distribution, however, cannot, according to Sraffa, be effected before it is
possible to know the prices of the goods that make up the physical composition
of capital, since the prices of these aggregates determine the mass of profits
their respective owners are to receive. Those prices cannot, on the other hand,
be determined without reference to the rate of profit, since the quantity of profits
must form an increment in them. Consequently:

> The result is that the distribution of the surplus must be determined through the same mech-
> anism and at the same time as are the prices of commodities.
>
> Accordingly we add the rate of profits (which must be uniform for all industries) as an
> unknown which we call r (§4).

The system then is

$$A_a p_a \quad + \quad B_a p_b \quad + \quad \ldots \quad + \quad K_a p_k \quad (1+r) \quad = \quad A p_a$$

$$A_b p_a \quad + \quad B_b p_b \quad + \quad \ldots \quad + \quad K_b p_k \quad (1+r) \quad = \quad B p_b$$

$$\cdots \cdots \quad \cdots \quad \cdots \cdots \quad \cdots \quad \cdots \quad \cdots \quad \cdots \cdots \quad \cdots \quad \cdots \cdots$$

$$A_k p_a \quad + \quad B_k p_b \quad + \quad \ldots \quad + \quad K_k p_k \quad (1+r) \quad = \quad K p_k$$

Sraffa's reasoning on this point reflects traditional bourgeois economic thinking
dominant since at least Walras. However (or, rather: precisely for such reasons),
caution is appropriate. In fact, if the rate of profits has to be thought of as

simultaneous with the prices of the goods and other expenses in relation to which it is to be calculated, how can it be supposed to be secondary or derived in relation to the said expenses? That is, how can it properly be called a rate of profits at all? Might we not just as well say that a money sum equal to what we call the sum of "profits" has got a priority over a sum equal to those expenses? In fact, it is as if we are situated inside a kind of game, in a neutral reciprocity where each factor is as important as the other, and without possibility to catch sight of the genesis and the fundamental forces in play. This is not a constellation of Hegelian brand, as Bloor would have us believe: Rather, we are like puppets being subjugated to a *"Spiel der Abstraktionen":* Playing the parts that Hegel localised in his analysis of the immediate and naïve consciousness of nature as an object of science.

If that description is right, Sraffa's option for the relations of "production of subsistence" as the basis for the structure of surplus production, is rather high-handed. He *assures* us that it is a basis, it might *seem probable* that it is, but that is all. Meanwhile, the whole further development of the model is in danger of losing some of its sense. Let us now return to that development.

A crucial difference between production for subsistence and production with a surplus in a system employing assumptions such as Sraffa's, is that while in the first all commodities, directly or indirectly, enter into the production of all others, in the second there will arise a production of luxuries. These by definition cannot be employed as means of production. Likewise, they do not enter the basket of subsistence consumption goods. The consequence (on Sraffian premises) is that there comes into being products which "have no part in the determination of the system" (§6).[30] This gives rise to the following important definition-like propositions:

> The criterion is whether a commodity enters (no matter whether directly or indirectly) into the production of *all* commodities. Those that do we shall call *basic*, and those that do not, *non-basic* products.

> We shall assume throughout that any system contains at least one basic product (§6).

It is important to note that the introduction of the rate of profits in the special way described above also means the dissolving of what Sraffa thinks is a *contradiction*: It means the addition of *one unknown* to the system, which otherwise would have become permanently "self-contradictory" (cf. §4), by the introduction of another independent production equation.

This way of thinking significantly coincides with a general, reformist ideological strain. "Contradictions" are seen as something entering the scene together with a distribution problem,[31] thus ruling out the theoretical possibility that the base of the mode of production itself is contradictory. The vital political issue is here thought to be the distribution of *produced* goods, not of the original conditions of production itself.

This is anticipated in Sraffa's treatment of wages: they take on new aspects, since now, "besides the ever-present element of subsistence, they may include a share of the surplus product" (§8). As a consequence, Sraffa chooses to treat the whole of the wage as a variable quantity, departing from the practice followed in earlier paragraphs. Also, he from now on assumes "that the wage is paid *post factum* as a share of the annual product" (§9). Instead of wages being represented by production equations for subsistence products, they consequently appear as definite quantities, called w, paid in each industry for its annual quantity of labour, called L. The annual quantity of L employed in the aggregate economy is taken as unity. The system of equations now appears in the following form (§11):

$$A_a p_a \;+\; B_a p_b \;+\; \ldots \;+\; K_a p_k \;(1+r) \;+\; L_a w \;=\; A p_a$$

$$A_b p_a \;+\; B_b p_b \;+\; \ldots \;+\; K_b p_k \;(1+r) \;+\; L_b w \;=\; B p_b$$

$$\ldots\ldots\ldots\ldots\ldots\ldots\ldots\ldots\ldots\ldots\ldots\ldots\ldots\ldots\ldots\ldots\ldots\ldots\ldots\ldots$$

$$A_k p_a \;+\; B_k p_b \;+\; \ldots \;+\; K_k p_k \;(1+r) \;+\; L_k w \;=\; K p_k$$

It is a token of the vital position now occupied by the distribution problem, that Sraffa at this point disposes of "the arbitrarily chosen single commodity" (§12) which up to this point has served as a unit of account. Instead, he turns the value of the commodities that make up the whole net product, or "national income", equal to unity (again §12). This gives us one new equation, but still leaves us with a "surplus" of one variable (the wage w, the rate of profits r, and the k product prices).

In his Chapter III, "Proportions of labour to means of production", Sraffa introduces a procedure which amounts to turning the wage into an independent variable, thus determining the system mathematically. The distribution problem forms the context:

> We proceed to give the wage (w) successive values ranging from 1 to 0: these now represent fractions of the national income (. . .). The object is to observe the effect of changes in the wage on the rate of profits and on the prices of individual commodities, on the assumption that the methods of production remain unchanged (§13).

Peculiarities in the different branches of production lead to divergent ratios between value of means of production and the wage. A steady reduction in the wage (which naturally is taken to reflect homogeneous labour in all branches) will then lead to a steeper growth of profits in the labour-extensive industries than in others – provided prices did not change along with the reduction (which they of course do).

In his treatment of the problems of measurement which follow, Sraffa points out that there will exist a specific or 'critical' proportion between labour and means of production which, if actually employed, would provide "an even balance" for the industry in question: "the proceeds of the wage-reduction would provide exactly what was required for the payment of profits at the *general* rate" (§17).[32] But naturally, since this same industry may employ as means of production commodities bought from any other industry, whose products will change their values or prices as a result of the wage reduction under consideration, such a 'critical' proportion is hard to discover. Sraffa finds that it has to be actually employed by an industry, *and* that "one and the same proportion recurs in all the successive layers of the industry's aggregate means of production without limit" (§21).

Sraffa now introduces a concept of a *value-ratio*, namely between the national net product and the means of production.[33] This ratio is a refined version of the "proportion" of labour to means of production. It is, of course, like the last one, "in general different for each industry and mainly depends on its particular circumstances of production" (§22). Sraffa continues:

> There is however an exception to this. When we make the wage equal to zero and the whole of the net product goes to profits, in each industry the value-ratio of net product to means of production necessarily comes to coincide with the general rate of profits. However different from one another they may have been at other wage levels, at this level the 'value-ratios' of all industries are equal.
>
> It follows that the only 'value-ratio' which can be invariant to changes in the wage, and therefore is capable of being 'recurrent' in the sense defined in §21, is the one that is equal to the rate of profits which corresponds to zero wage. And *that* is the 'balancing' ratio (§22).

With this manoeuvre, Sraffa *ipso facto* has introduced his concept of the "Maximum rate of profits", R, which, he says, "has been suggested by Marx, directly through an incidental allusion to the possibility of a fall in the rate of profits 'even if the workers could live on air'" (Sraffa, 1960, p. 94).[34]

Of course, as a tool, R is purely analytical. It may be used without any industries being without direct labour power. It is an abstraction which takes the form of an actual ratio, by Sraffa called R', in a given system of production. It is scarcely to be expected, though, that it is present as a value-ratio in a factual, given industry; and consequently, it is not probable that one could identify a given commodity which reflects the structure of production in such a 'critical' industry. Sraffa finds it necessary, then, to construct it as a "composite commodity", a product imagined as a *concretum* put together by elements from different commodities existing in the actual system. The conditions of such a "composite standard commodity" are given through R', which in turn is conditioned through successive layers of industries producing means of production. Consequently, not only the Standard commodity, but also the average rate of profits r, which is potentially an R', are conditioned solely by relations proper to basic commodities.

Sraffa now goes on to show that it is possible to derive from "any actual economic system" the proportions between basic products which would satisfy the requirements of an imagined composition of materials making up a "standard composite commodity". He also shows (Ch. V, §§36–44) that the set of multipliers which have to be used for such a task, is always unique under the conditions described so far. Consequently, a "standard commodity", making up "a standard capable of isolating the price-movements of any other product so that they could be observed as in a vacuum" (§23), is a possibility.[35]

Since the analysis of distribution is of such a vital importance in the issue, Sraffa points out that

> [w]e shall as a rule find it convenient to take as unit of the Standard commodity the quantity of it that would form the net product of a Standard system employing the whole annual labour of the actual system (§26).

Measuring relative price movements through the medium of the Standard commodity consequently implies a continuous "straight-line"-relation between wages and the rate of profits: Every decrease in the wage will imply an equivalent increase in the rate of profits, and vice versa. The immediate necessary condition is that the wage is expressed through the Standard commodity, and that condition is *ipso facto* fulfilled here.

That, conversely, also means, as Sraffa puts it, that "if we make it a condition of the economic system that w and r should obey the proportionality rule in question, the wage and the commodity-prices are then *ipso facto* expressed in Standard net product, without need of defining its composition, since with no other unit can the proportionality rule be fulfilled." We are then in fact, as he says, "enabled to use a standard without knowing what it consists of."

However, Sraffa goes on to point out that further reasoning about the "straight-line"-relation leads to the discovery of another "measure for prices of commodities", namely "the quantity of labour that can be purchased by the Standard net product". The reasoning, which tacitly posits r as the independent variable (a technique we shall return to in a moment) is as follows:

> In effect, as soon as we have fixed the rate of profits, and without need of knowing the prices of commodities, a parity is established between the Standard net product and a quantity

of labour which depends only on the rate of profits; and the resulting prices of commodities can be indifferently regarded as being expressed either in the Standard net product or in the quantity of labour which at the given level of the rate of profits is known to be equivalent to it. This quantity of labour will vary inversely with the Standard wage (w) and directly with the rate of profits.

Thus if $r = 0$ and $w = 1$, the said quantity will be equal to the quantity of labour which has been used in production, which is just another way of saying that the workers dispose of their entire net product as long as no capitalist is present. If $r > 0$, and is presumed to increase steadily towards R ', then the said quantity of labour will have to increase, because the corresponding change in distribution (the appropriation by the capitalists of an ever increasing part of the net product) simply denotes that the labour that is annually employed in creating the net product gets *relatively* cheaper (as expressed in the Standard net product), and consequently can be appropriated in an ever increasing quantity.[36]

The alternative measure of value introduced by Sraffa can be regarded as a way of vindicating a kind of labour theory of value. Sraffa holds it to be "more tangible" than the idea of a standard of which we do not know the content. But in fact, it scarcely is. For what is the content of a "quantity of labour"? Sraffa describes it as something that can be "purchased". But really, what might be "purchased" or bought is something that has got a value. In any variant of the labour theory of value, material commodities have a value, because of the labour bestowed on them. That is, labour (under specific social circumstances) is value-producing. And that naturally means, as Marx was eager to point out, that it cannot itself have a value. So it cannot (in any real and conceptual sense) be purchased at all.[37] It is just a precondition of any "sale" and any "purchase".

It is easy to see that potentially, such misconceived use of language may be connected with a confusion of the concepts of "labour", respectively of "labour power". Labour power is not actual labour, but potential labour. It may, further, have what "labour" does not have, namely "value". It is expressible as a material entity, consisting of physical elements making intentional activity possible.

Thus, when Sraffa writes about the "variable quantity of labour" in question, he is in fact writing of the commodity labour power, *not* of direct labour or living labour. He can write as if the purchase of labour power equals a purchase of a "quantity of labour" precisely because he has already been operating with "homogeneous labour" (§10)[38] inside a *de facto* given rate of surplus value.[39] For then it is clear from the outset to which quantitative degree the whole of the net product will exceed the part made up by equivalents to wages.

Consequently, one might say that an important step towards getting rid of the confusion between labour power and labour on Sraffian premises would consist in accepting the Marxian position: Namely, that under the conditions prescribed by capital, a worker is not allowed inside the factory gates unless he has already accepted a more or less given ratio of surplus value, that is, to work for a longer time span than what would be necessary for the production of equivalents to the wage goods.

Should Sraffa have wanted to deny that he was in fact using the purchase of labour *power* as a gateway to his alternative *numéraire,* he would have had to argue that he was in fact thinking of the Marxian category of abstract labour, that is, labour perceived in precisely the social determination in which it is creator of value. But in that case, aside from the fact that living labour cannot be purchased even if it is taken *in abstracto*, he would have had to explain the contradistinction between abstract and concrete labour; and naturally, no such theme is even hinted at in his book.

And then still another difficulty would emerge, namely that an adaptation of this Marxian category of concrete labour *versus* abstract labour would remind one of the problem of how to explain the transference of produced value onto the finished product. This problem, which Marx resolved through the theory of the dual character of labour, is not even seen by neoclassical or "neo-Ricardian" economics. The retention in the product of a quantity of value existing in the means of production consumed in the process of creating a new commodity is just taken for granted. It seems odd that would-be Marxists have set focus on discussing the distribution problem in such contexts, totally ignoring the deeper problem of the character of labour.

Sraffa says about his alternative "measure of value" that "all the properties of an 'invariable standard of value' ... are found in a variable quantity of labour" (§43). However, his two measures are not conceptually interchangeable, since the Standard wage (w), as we have seen, is a precondition of establishing them. Consequently, a *material* composite commodity still makes up the foundation of the system.[40] And the economic system remains overtly dependent on a way of thinking that in principle must accept choosing any *numéraire* at random – reflecting a mode of thought whose basic contingency in the applied method is also seen in the fact that labour, which actually includes in itself the true key to all measures of value, is here tentatively taken as standard in an incorrect and random fashion.

As we have foreshadowed, the construction of a measuring rod that guarantees a simple connection between distributive elements (it is often said to represent a solution of "Ricardo's riddle") now gives occasion to a significant theoretical development on part of Sraffa: He changes the independent variable. The following extract would seem to be of great importance for an understanding of his relation to "Wittgensteinian" thinking:

The choice of the wage as the independent variable in the preliminary stages was due to its being there regarded as consisting of specified necessaries determined by physiological or social conditions which are independent of prices or the rate of profits. But as soon as the possibility of variations in the division of the product is admitted, this consideration loses much of its force. And when the wage is to be regarded as 'given' in terms of a more or less abstract standard, and does not acquire a definite meaning until the prices of commodities are determined, the position is reversed. The rate of profits, as a ratio, has a significance which is independent of any prices, and can well be 'given' before the prices are fixed. It is accordingly susceptible of being determined from outside the system of production, in particular by the level of the money rates of interest (§44).

The deeper background for such an operation might well be the fact that in Sraffa's system of simultaneous equations it is by definition impossible to present a theory of the causes of the factual level of the rate of profits. Rightly and paradoxically, Sraffa gives it an independent significance. In his book, no more is said about the issue. However, if its introduction is to have any sense at all on part of the author, it is reasonable to suppose that the allusion to the interest rate is meant as a preparatory device for introducing the "banking system", as a systematic, "performative" background of explanation – along Bloorian lines, in fact.

II.4. Reduction to "Dated" Quantities of Labour

The change of independent variable gives Sraffa the adequate starting position[41] for a final thoroughgoing criticism of some traditional concepts of "capital". In the chapter "Reduction to dated quantities of labour" (§§45–49) he examines relative prices by resolving them into wages and profits, these being regarded as constituent elements. The procedure implies that the production equation symbols for *produced* commodities are replaced by the labour symbol (L): The prices of means of production used in successive years are resolved into labour terms, and the production equation for commodity 'a', which, as we have seen, was presented as

$$A_a p_a \ + \ B_a p_b \ + \ \ldots \ + \ K_a p_k \ (1+r) \ + \ L_a w \ = \ A p_a,$$

may now take the form

$$L_a w \ + \ L_{al} w \ (1+r) \ + \ \ldots \ + \ L_{an} w \ (1+r)^n \ + \ \ldots \ = \ A p_a.$$

Each of the elements of "indirect labour" (as we may call it) is here combined with the present rate of profit, "projected" backwards in time to cover the time span it (the labour) has been embodied in the means of production. The commodities that make up the means of production of A are then replaced "with *their own* means of production and quantities of labour". This replacement presupposes that the last-mentioned elements "be multiplied by a profit factor at a compound rate for the appropriate period, namely the means of production by $(1 + r)^2$ and the labour by $(1 + r)$" (§46).[42] Next, the prices of the factors which enter these latter, produced still a year earlier, are in their turn multiplied, the means of production by $(1 + r)^3$ and the labour by $(1 + r)^2$. The symbol n above indicates that the calculation can be pushed on indefinitely. Still, a total resolution into quantities of dated labour is impossible: "Beside the labour terms there will always be a 'commodity residue' consisting of minute fractions of every basic product" (§46). However, for all practical purposes, the residue may be ignored.

Now, imagine two commodities, produced by different owners. The physical structure of the two production processes is the same, but their history of construction differs in some respects. One of them, for instance, applied X more units of labour onto its machinery Y years ago than did the other, which added a corresponding amount at another point in time.

There are only two possible cases in which the two commodity prices would be identical here. Firstly, if $r = 0$ in our year of observation, since the labour units in the production equation would then have to be multiplied by zero, and consequently "the value of a labour term depends exclusively on its size, irrespective of date" (§47). Secondly if $r = R$. In that case, the labour terms vanish together with the workers, the latter possibly living "on air". The commodity residue then "becomes all-important as the sole determinant of the price of the product" (§46).

In all other cases, any change in the existent r would provoke relative changes in the prices, changes which, as Sraffa shows, could even amount to "*reversals in the direction of the movement of relative prices, in the face of unchanged methods of production*" (§48, italics added). That "is due to the compounding effect on the labour terms of the rate of profits exponent in processes with different time distributions of inputs."[43]

Now, one might say that this alternative way of showing the production equation of a commodity seemingly results in a definite proof against the methodical tenability of the neo-classical "production function". Sraffa's own conclusion, supported by most of his academic readers, goes even farther: The above-mentioned reversals "cannot be reconciled with *any* notion of capital as a measurable quantity independent of distribution and prices" (§48).

In practice, the proof has never been contested, and theoretically it stands as strong today as it did forty years ago. There has been a tendency actively to ignore it, on the ground that some of the Sraffian presuppositions in constructing the Standard commodity are captious. While there may be some truth in this last point, such a way of reasoning is fallacious. The fact that it has been possible to construct such a standard on a basis that has to be accepted by both parties in the debate gives it a *raison d'être* good enough.

Besides the fact that it is being built on the Standard commodity, the proof is dependent on the idea of a Maximum rate of profits. No such presupposition is alien to the basics of the theories that are the primary targets of Sraffa's polemics. In particular, his way of reasoning about the genesis and structure of the *numéraire*, however contrary to Marxian dialectics, is scarcely rejected by more than just a handful of academic economists today. The same can be said of the principle behind the "Reduction to dated labour" and its importance, since the "production function" of neo-classical economics as a matter of course works with a symbol for labour as well as for "capital".

What Sraffa is showing is that the basic concept of that capital theory is redundant. The "production function" presupposes that analysis of prices and distribution follow *a posteriori* in relation to the stipulation of a given magnitude of working "capital" (and, likewise, of "labour"). Sraffa shows that it really cannot be done, on the basis of generally accepted measuring theory. And consequently one is apt, though Sraffa says nothing about it, to conclude that *no* true concept of "capital", even as a preliminary to the quantifying process, is possible here. How were one to think about a concept of "capital" which did not in itself contain the conditions of being quantified or expressible in numbers? Given the overall importance of the said concept in economics, one might say that this critique on part of Sraffa corresponds to Wittgenstein's critique of the "general notion of the meaning of a word" (*"der allgemeine Begriff der Bedeutung der Worte"*) in the *Investigations* (§5).[44] That notion was upheld in the *Tractatus*. Just as a general proposition like the disjunctive expression "*a* is either *F* or *G*" according to the later Wittgenstein obtains its meaning through rules incorporated in the general active human form of life, by Sraffa the general notion of capital is possible only through simultaneous, rule-governed actions.

Now, such a view of the notion of 'capital' is untenable on Marxian premises. As can be seen from his explication of the genesis of prices of production[45] Marx considers the size of the invested capital (constant and variable, "c" and "v") as given in values directly expressing social necessary labour time inside specific industries. And naturally, no difficulty can arise from such a procedure as soon as it is understood that all commodities directly making up "c", like all those indirectly[46] making up "v", get their values measured prior to their circulation.

Since this follows from Marx' way of investigating capital as a magnitude of *value*, the point can be seen also in the elementary stages of his theory, to wit, in the analysis of the commodity: The disjunctive form of the relative value expression, be it formulated as in Marx, "20 yards of linen = 1 coat *or* 10 lbs.

tea, *or* etc.", or as we have presented it above, "10 qr. wheat = *either* 1 t. iron *or* = 2 pigs", shares a basic presupposition with all other expressions of value: It reflects the existence of a common denominator. According to Marx, the denominator is, further, human labour in the abstract. Since that entity is immediately *measurable*, as labour time, the function of the eventual measuring rod cannot be influenced by pecularities belonging to commodities whose condition for being posited inside the equation is precisely the existence of this denominator. Consequently, Sraffa's "Wittgensteinian" view of the measuring process, where components of the commodity exchange are being intertwined and reciprocallly modified to construct a measuring rod, cannot be reconciled with the logical structure of commodity exchange (and *a fortiori* of circulation). And it might well be, though of course it cannot be explored here, that the later Wittgenstein's view of logical form suffers from a corresponding defect – despite its possible advantages over the *Tractatus* view.

Sraffa's treatment of the concept of capital, alongside his view of the determination of the rate of profits, consequently represents a point in his argument which definitely is incompatible with both the Marxian and the marginalist theory. It shows the impossibility of treating his "set of propositions" as if they were not elements (actual or potential) in another, alternative positive theory.

On the other hand, Sraffa's conclusion could be said to follow a Wittgensteinian scheme: "Capital" *may* be an acceptable general concept, but only when adapted to the very process of price formation. That means that the concept is a function of the combined individual actions of a large group of owners of goods, that is, "capitalists", each acting in a particular pragmatic way to uphold a specified technology, so to speak a given "technique", like a "language-game", yielding a surplus. And as long as the wage is treated as a dependent variable, the workers can be regarded as active "subjects" on equal footing with the owners.[47] Their political action leads to changes in the division of the net product, that is in distribution, and *a fortiori* in relative prices; consequently, no general concept of "capital" can emerge without the combined activity of all[48] the members of the two classes.

If this is an admissible point of view, built as it is on considerations about the Sraffa-Wittgenstein relation, it still is quite clear that the concept of the involved "subjects", be they workers or capitalists, has got its nature considerably changed since the introduction of a "production for subsistence".

It is quite unclear how we should envisage this transformation taking place. In fact, in the "extremely simple society" of subsistence production, which one may compare with Wittgenstein's examples of primitive language-games, "values spring directly from the methods of production" (§1). It is difficult to know how, if ever, one would be able to separate natural categories from social ones. And in that case, inside which kind of idiom, "socially" or "naturally", are we to understand the change to higher forms of production?

This problem or dilemma is in fact to be found in Wittgenstein's work. We may now relevantly return to the question concerning primitive kinds of language-games, looking for a possible theoretical motive force which might connect them with Sraffa's implications of social and economic activities equally primitive or basic.

III. SOME CONCLUSIONS ON THE SRAFFA–WITTGENSTEIN RELATION

III.1. Language-Games as Bordering Cases

In the *Philosophical Investigations*, the concept of language-games from the first paragraphs onwards is a concept of primitive forms. The contention that the builders' activity should be viewed as a "complete primitive language" seems absurd. How can a language serve communication between people in relation to a certain goal, when that goal is not expressible in the language itself? How is it possible to know the difference between "round" and "square" objects without it being possible to use these words in the game?

In fact, the primitiveness of suppositions is underlined in Wittgenstein's first tentative definitions of his object. In §7 he says that the use of his builders' language may be thought of

> as one of those games by means of which children learn their native language. I will call these games "language-games" and will sometimes [*manchmal*] speak of a primitive language as a language-game.

> And the processes of naming the stones and of repeating words after someone might also be called language-games. Think of much of the use of words in games like ring-a-ring-a-roses.

> I shall also call the whole, consisting of language and the actions into which it is woven, the "language-game".

The key concept of the *Investigations* is, then, introduced as a naming of a limited activity that we might call 'imitating language in general'. At the face of it, this limitation is soon given up. "Language-game" becomes a common name for a host of activities, and such naming goes on seemingly without discrimination or clear-cut method. However, the element of primitiveness returns again and again where crucial matters, like definitions, are at stake:

> It is easy to imagine a language consisting only of orders and reports in battle. – Or a language consisting only of questions and expressions for answering yes and no. And innumerable others. – And to imagine a language means to imagine a form of life (§19).

Garver (1994, p. 254) finds this example "indefensible" (perhaps together with the one in §2), and rightly so, one may say. However, there are a good many similar instances. In *Zettel*, with its close relation to themes of the *Investigations*, we hear (Wittgenstein, 1967, pp. 92–93) of a tribe of "automata", potential slaves for humans, being learnt what is required to understand us when we "want to give them orders and to get reports from them" (§529). This -discussion, also, leads over to imagining "a tribe of men, unacquainted with dreams" getting to understand the word "dream" (§530). We read that "[t]here could also be a language in whose use the impression made on us by signs played no part" (§145), and we are asked to "[i]magine that the people of a tribe were brought up from early youth to give no expression of feeling *of any kind*" (§383). It also fair to mention §§206–207 in the *Investigations*, where the author tries to imagine a people speaking a "language" without structural regularity.

We also have several instances of "societies" or "tribes" which can be regarded as socially fairly well developed (in fact, at least one of the instances just referred to might also be understood as such a one), but which are primitive in their relation to certain language-games which count as "developed" in our own society (e.g. measuring practices). A celebrated instance refers to wood-sellers who "piled the timber in heaps of arbitrary, varying height and then sold it at a price proportionate to the area covered by the piles", or made calculations according to even stranger standards (Wittgenstein, 1956, p. 94). According to Garver, this latter occurrence seems to refer to creatures whose "form of life would differ from ours as much as that of dogs and lions". And on the example of the builders he remarks, leaning on Rhees, that "on the one hand they seem to be human, since they are said to be builders and are said to be speaking a language; on the other hand they seem not to be human, since their "language" is crude and confined to just one rather narrow activity" (Garver, 1994, p. 244).

However, this may be exactly the *punctum saliens*. It might seem that what Wittgenstein really tries to do here, is to approach a border-line between the "complicated" human form of life and other forms. Such an approach can be conceived as a means to help to understand the concept of 'language-game', distinctively human as it is. *That* may be the meaning of Wittgenstein's rather obscure remark in §19 of the *Investigations*, that "to imagine a language is to imagine a form of life": As long as as it is possible to *imagine* a language-game, however primitive, one has to do with humans. The host of weird examples, of which some are referred to above, should then be interpreted as vague references to a borderline. They scarcely could be taken as attempts to *determine* such a line; as Wittgenstein well knew, such a concept determination would have to be understood as underlying the structure of a language-game, which would mean that it could not be used to draw a line outside all such games. However, there is a passage in *On Certainty* (§358 sq.) which seems to demonstrate a pressing need to make headway with the matter: The certainty we feel in regarding some kinds of conviction as *truths*, is here on the one hand conceived as a "form of life", which on the other hand is said to mean precisely "that I want to conceive it as something that lies beyond being justified or unjustified; as it were, as something animal" (Wittgenstein, 1969, p. 46e).[49]

Hence we perceive the shadow of a second possibility: While it is hard to draw a line between on the one hand a form of life (namely, the human) which consists of language-games, and on the other a mass of non-human forms, it at least could be said that the form which comprises the language-games is something given from nature. While the human form is a different one from the lion's, it too has got an – presumably – animal foundation.

Such reflections can do little more than to lend an ideological superstructure to attempts of the Sraffian kind: Categories that we all recognize as social – "value", "price" and so on, are counted as *also* natural, albeit exclusively for the human species. However, there would seem to be a parallel here to the kind of enigma we meet in Sraffa concerning the relation between a subsistence economy and the game-like structure typical of "production with a surplus". All of which may point out to us the true meaning of Wittgenstein's contention that Sraffa's mode of reasoning had conveyed to him the importance of an anthropological stance (cf. Monk, 1994, p. 261).

On the other hand, the *Philosophical Investigations* would scarcely seem to be of great help in developing a theory of value worthy of the name. As regards Sraffa's equations, we have seen how any commodity in his system is tentatively regarded independently of its relation to other commodities. Its value is not seen as expressed in another product, and there is no notion of any one process whereby commodities (through their owners) consign certain other commodities via reciprocal action to function as a *numéraire*. Such action, which by Marx led to a separation between the concepts of measure of value and of *numéraire* respectively,[50] reflects the social relations between commodity-owners, first and foremost their *need* for the property of others. This need is not only of a material kind, but also reflects the idea that no one can establish a concept of a thing – be it in commodity-form or else – without connecting the substrate of the said thing with that of another one. The existence of such a theory in Marx underlines the economic aspect of his theme: It is a portrait of a relation between people and desired objects. By Sraffa, it does not seem to be so; questions concerning measurement are "solved" from the outside, the author arbitrarily "choosing" the standard and/or the principle for its construction. Such a method corresponds to a philosophy that abstracts from the material relations between men and objects, and concentrates on the relations between men, in language, and then to return to the objects only via the medium of that language. Such a philosophy concentrates on analysing processes of naming and reference. In Wittgenstein's *Tractatus*, for instance, objects are treated exclusively as names. The lack of living, social connections between the entities of the world that this fact seemed to disclose, led the author to adopt a theory of language-games, where the naming of the objects would seem to contain an important social aspect.

However, the crucial instances of such "games" observed in this section seem, as one might have expected, to show the impossibility of their leading to conceptions of objects that are able to meet obvious requirements for serious economic theory. On the contrary, the very idea that it should be appropriate to treat the words and meanings of, for instance, the "builders' game" as a language, let alone a "complete" language, is at odds with such a claim. For in the language-games we meet a self-centered, performative sector of the world. Words, or objects, like "slab" and "block" are meant to have a meaning in spite of the fact that they cannot even be uttered in a relation to a "house" that might be the (unknown) aim of the building process. Since they are words that perforce cannot be understood as dependent on words for objects outside the game, they evidently cannot depend on each other inside the game either. The same goes without saying for all the respective objects, since they are "objects" only through existence in a game.

In fact, to posit words and objects in such performative settings must have seemed to be a necessity to Wittgenstein. Had he not placed them so, he would have had no means to tie them down to a level that corresponding to something other than the "totality of language" that one meets in the *Tractatus*. Had those "games" portrayed, say, technical processes, including man's effort to transcend himself in the act of steering them, the road to totality would seem to lay open. Wittgenstein would have none of it. That is the main point about language-*games*.

While consequently such a concept theory (for so it obviously may be called) is contrary to the content of economic theories proper, it might be regarded as very well adapted to a theory of the Sraffian kind. When Sraffa, or for that matter academic economists in general, chooses material measuring rods at random, he evidently (if implicitly) presupposes that each and every commodity may be treated in that same manner. That is, a "commodity" in theory is an isolated entity: The "economic" model is unreal. The road is open, not to any totality, but to a closed field, which includes a tacit consensus about the conviction that serious matters, such as the cause of the level of the rate of profits, are not to be explained.

As long as the commodity is seen as isolated, it of course also loses all of its man-made ability to duplicate itself, as it happens when one recognises that its value is so to speak projected onto the commodity it may be exchanged against. This duplication in its turn is a function of the duality of intentions laid down in the production of commodities. They are produced in order to be sold *and* to serve a material need. That means that we may perfectly well experience the production process, say, the building of a house, merely as subordinated to the goal of earning money. In that case, the corresponding language-game might be expected to include a wide range of expressions and signs belonging not strictly to the technical process. These might represent reactions against the capitalist control of the enterprise, against the work routines imposed, and so on. *Mutatis mutandis*, a similar modification of a technical game would occur on a building site in imperial Rome, in classical Athens or in contemporary Highland Burma. In short: "Pure" cases of techniques in Wittgenstein's sense do not exist. Every intention will complicate his issue and demonstrate the inadequacy of the theory.

Of course, Wittgenstein knew as much. In the *Investigations*, he is as sceptical against the explanatory value of "intentions", as he is against suppositions of essences:

> An intention is embedded in its situation, in human customs and institutions. If the technique of the game of chess did not exist, I could not intend to play a game of chess. In so far as I do intend the construction of a sentence in advance, that is made possible by the fact that I can speak the language in question (§337).

In the *Remarks* (as in the *Investigations*), he emphasises the point along with a defense of the view that the meaning of a word is its use:

> It becomes queer when we are led to think that the future development must in some way already be present in the act of grasping the use and yet isn't present. – For we say that there isn't any doubt that we understand the word . . ., and on the other hand its meaning lies in its use. There is no doubt that I now want to play *chess*, but chess is the game it is in virtue of *all its rules* (and so on). Don't I know, then, which game I wanted to play until I *have* played it? Or are all the rules contained in my act of intending? Is it experience that tells me that this sort of play usually follows this act of intention? So is it impossible for me to be certain what I am intending to do? And if that is nonsense, what kind of super-strong connexion exists between the act of intending and the thing intended? – Where is the connexion effected between the sense of the expression "Let's play a game of chess" and all the rules of the game? – Well, in the list of rules of the game, in the teaching of it, in the day-to-day practice of playing (I, §130 = Wittgenstein, 1956, p. 89).

Such thinking may be met with arguments of the same kind as those we employed against Bloor. The game of chess, together with all its existing rules, is a kind of invention. It has been created. These acts of creation are in no case explicable through Wittgenstein's theory. Rather, they contradict it. Further, it stands to reason that the human ability to make original creations is not something set aside in ordinary, everyday thinking. It represents the never tranquil force of human reason and its ability to make intentions on a background of totality.

The Sraffian production equations may seem to represent a basket of techniques of an ahistorical character. Exchange relations are presented as resultants of technical coefficients, so that, as soon as the surplus is there, it produces social classes that do not transcend a given technical game, but, rather, are "playing" the said transmitted game. As soon as one realises that techniques are human products, however, such ideas are open to the severest criticism.

The very weakness of the theory explains its more bizarre features. The force of human reason is not an easy thing to conceal. In formulating his view on the monopoly significance of teaching, training and everyday practice, Wittgenstein is bound to have felt the argumentative gap consisting of an intentional theory *manqué*. The want of explication of the creative force produces a conspicuous vacuum. In spite of all, it has to be let into the theory. And, truly, there we find it: in his search for antropoids. For such beings, once we allow them a human character of sorts, in their very existence presuppose human beings of a higher carat. The mode of thinking legitimises, and promotes, a view of common humans as a species of inferiors.

In fact, it would surprise if a theory like Wittgenstein's, characterised also by its lack of reflection on the history of philosophy and contemporary culture, should not easily fall victim to the darker trends of the surrounding political world. W. T. Jones has rightly remarked (1975, Ch. 11) that the philosophy of the later Wittgenstein, developed as it was by a prestigious logician, presented itself as an attractive alternative to people who despised the philosophy of Sartre and Heidegger for only superficial reasons. In effect, Wittgenstein's tribes of slaves and automata represent (like those integrated in the Sraffian equations) the same world-picture that does Nietzsche's views of "man and superman", or Kierkegaard's imagery of the relation between the Religious One (the bearer of consciousness of sin), the bulk of Christendom and, at the bottom of the barrel, the residue of the human race.

Such thinking corresponds nicely to Wittgenstein's authoritarian political views and style, connected with the socially conditioned aloofness of colleagues like Keynes and Sraffa or of the whole "Cambridge Circus". However, the root of the trouble lies deeper.

III.2. The Misery of Analyticism

As Hegel made manifest the latent, anti-nominalist theory of concept formation inherent in Kantianism, he elaborated Kant's manner of thinking about
serfdom as an entity whose abolition might be shown through the construction
of the concept of Reason. His deservedly famous analysis of the apperception's
"Herrschaft und Knechtschaft" was the most radical attempt to understand
Reason as an entity made possible through, and necessarily through, the understanding of the abolition of servitude, that is of the basis of the "Dependence
of Self-Consciousness" (cf. Hegel, 1970, Ch. IV, A).

As we have seen, Western philosophy after Hegel had its reasons for giving
up this thought. But since the historical realities which Hegel hoped to get
abolished were – and are! – still there, the problems immediately generated
by servitude made themselves felt all the same. But now, since true philosophical thought is conceived as compatible with a situation that leaves
the problem of servitude unsolved in theory, one naturally gets the problem
of slavery presented so to speak from the outside, with a vengeance, as an
analytical question.

Of course, the members of this whole ideological stem, from Schopenhauer
and Kierkegaard to bourgeois ideologists of the 21st century, may excuse themselves by pointing out that Hegel's theory of freedom was otherwise unrealistic.
While this is true, it does not absolve them from the corollary of their inability
to grasp the main idea as well as to elaborate it in adequate directions.

In the Marxian way of doing those things, the lack of freedom is basically
interpreted as alienation from the possession of the means of production. It
is a hardened version of the commodity fetishism, that "determination of
reflection" which follows from the relation of commodities. If it is the case, as
Marx will have it, that the exchange process makes the equivalent for each and
every commodity, that is, its own predicative form, stand forth as something
created by nature, then the whole scenario toughens when the subject finds itself
divorced from the mass of such commodities, which constitute the means of
production of an entire society.

We have seen how and why it is not possible for the Sraffian theory of the
commodity, nor for its possible Wittgensteinian follow-ups, to come anywhere
close to capturing these points. On the contrary, there is good reason to believe
that such theorists are themselves spectacular victims of the said fetishism.[51]
From Sraffa's equations arise the spectacle of a set of values and prices
belonging to material techniques taken *per se*. That neatly corresponds to
Wittgenstein's thought that there is nothing socially or mentally important

outside the going-on of techniques, the continual updating and renewal of certain production processes.[52]

While such views may give us new insights into the theoretical basis of the Keynesian concept of "full employment", it also points to a clear-cut misunderstanding of concept theories of Marxian-Hegelian brand.

This is well borne out in the quoted passage from Rhees,[53] where the troubled situation of philosophy is related to ignorance of an alleged parallell between expressions and moves in games. If words corresponded to objects in an un-problematic way, such as we have seen must be the case with a game-internal "slab", then the good sense of Rhees' (and Wittgenstein's) way of putting the question follows as a matter of course. For then an object corresponding to an expression could not be thought of as an entity co-formed by "intentions" or "essences"; it must be one-dimensionally determined through our factual use of its expression in a language-game.

Rhees' contention is, I take it, that traditional concept theory acts as if "understanding were something outside the signs". But, allowance made for differences in terminology, this clearly is a misunderstanding. Thinkers like Kant, Hegel and Marx all presented theories to the effect that understanding is *not* outside the "signs", nor outside the "objects". Their reaction against mechanistic thinking, be it in its rationalist or empiricist (sensualist) form, implied precisely as much. Also, their theories plausibly explained how everyday experience could evolve on a corresponding basis.

The corresponding theory of the twofold character of "things" made it possible for Marx to show how the value of a commodity, and thereby the commodity itself, is expressed in the use-value (or, rather, in the material substrate) of another one. This enabled him to explain the so-called commodity fetishism through the same mechanism that allowed him to demonstrate that the bare fact of measuring economic quantities presupposes a splitting of the objects. Just as important were the consequences: Firstly, he was able to construct (or, better: to reconstruct) a concept of capital that implied that its corresponding magnitude might consistently be measured independently of any knowledge of the prices of its products.[54] That in its turn was due to two factors: on the one hand, that capital as a physical mass of objects was to be regarded precisely as a developed form of the material substrate of the value-expression (exchange value); on the other, that these objects, as equivalents to quantities of the money-commodity, were conceived also as *qualitatively* identical with it, insofar as they all were regarded as quantities of one common substance, namely, (abstract) labour.[55] Simultaneously, it was made clear that those objects, the physical face of capital, were presupposed by the subject to be alienated property, a fact which made Marx *define* 'capital' as a kind of "transsubstansiation".[56] No Sraffian critique of general notions can ever approach such a concept, based as it is on a theory of objectivity alien to Ricardian thinking.

As we have seen, the structure of the Sraffian "production with a surplus" takes the self-presupposing form of a game, as soon as the surplus is distributed with reference to the existence of r. It is not clear how any basic, determining factor is to be identified. In the Marxian frame, on the other hand, the means of production as well as the wage are reducible to an amount of "abstract labour time", which necessarily forms the denominator for the total amount of surplus value or profit. Living labour in the widest (exploitative) setting forms the background: Labour and seriousness form reality.

When one points to such an alternative kind of thinking, protests arise. All kinds of critics of the Marxian way of "transforming"[57] values to prices tend to agree that the procedure followed by Sraffa (which itself, of course, involves no "transformation", since "value" and "price" are identical entities for him) is the correct one. Usually, their argument for this rather strange view is that the capital advanced is treated as a price quantity by the capitalists. While this argument abstracts from the task of science, which is to investigate objective structures independently of subjective prejudices, it has also got a purely derived form. The fact is that the critics could not possibly, even if they wanted to, argue that there existed an objective level of values, different from a level of prices. For from the onset they have treated the object, the commodity, in a one-dimensional way, making impossible any cleavage of the kind that made it possible for Marx to develop a theory of a *numéraire* distinct from quantities of value.

To say it as pointedly as possible: It is a question of definitions of the "object". Hegel as well as Wittgenstein would have accepted Frege's *dictum* that it is "a law about what men take for true" that "[i]t is impossible for human beings . . . to recognize an object as different from itself".[58] But naturally, Hegel's position is that in spite of that impossibility, an entity cannot be apprehended as an object unless it is being split by consciousness. That differentiation guarantees its unity, that is, our apprehension of it as one substance. This is caused by the *presence* of consciousness in the "object", in the "sign", not by it being somewhere outside it. But look now at Wittgenstein's (1956, p. 89) comments on Frege's sentence:

> When I think of this as impossible for me, then I think of *trying* to do it. So I look at my lamp and say: "This lamp is different from itself". (But nothing stirs.) It is not that I see it is false, I can't do anything with it at all. (Except when the lamp shimmers in sunlight; then I can quite well use the sentence to express that.)[59]

Hopefully, there are not many who are unwilling to accept that this is argumentative nonsense. It does not even pretend to be concerned with the constitution of the object. Nevertheless, it has been taken seriously by many a follower of Wittgenstein, whose picture of classical philosophy has to be as dubious as his own.

Marx said (1968 (a): Vol. 3, 491) of classical political economy that it practiced an "analytic method", with a progressive function in the historical context:

> It hasn't got an interest in developing the different forms genetically, but on the contrary to lead them back to their unity through analysis, because it starts from them as from given presuppositions. But analysis [is] the necessary presupposition of the genetical exposition, of the conception of the real formative process in its different phases.

What Wittgenstein's method and Sraffa's Ricardianism have in common, is a species of analytic approach. To a certain extent, they mirror the method of what is generally called analytical philosophy. However, there is scarcely anything left over of any progressive political content. They accept the surface appearance of phenomena, basically through their bowing to the ideologically produced homogeneous form of the object. There is nothing present to lead them on to the simple reflection that the closed character of each and every language-game, as well as of each and every production equation, might be an ideological image derived from the isolated form of private ownership of each and every sector of the mass of heterogeneous means of production.

To keep it apart from the constructive analysis of classical bourgeois method, such thinking may deservedly be called "analyticism" – alluding to its tendency to practice analysis for the explicit reason of blocking any genetic approach.[60] Its diagnosis is perhaps as critical as is the judgement to the effect that *Philosophical Investigations* represents "the misery of Ludwig Wittgenstein".[61] From beginning to end of the work, investigation of the source of alienation is being postponed. To ascribe it to a possibility of language going on holiday gives no sense outside the fairy-tales, as long no explanation is given as to what might coerce us to such uses of language.

So it seems that one has to admit the possibility that the reaction against classical philosophy (and political economy) is explicable along apologetic lines in a degree too high for comfort. In addition, there may be raised serious doubts about it deserving the name of philosophy at all. Plato's proposal of giving the name "philodoxy" – love of opinion – to ideological currents fond of calling themselves philosophical, still stands. And, as regards the number of candidates for reference, it possibly stands even stronger than it did in the midst of ancient Greek sophistry.

However, Wittgenstein's ideology cannot easily be pushed aside; it is a product of hard realities, as is its present magnetism. That it appears to reactualise the story of the emperor's new clothes – as the author himself generously allows for (1953, p. 125) in his search for the grounds of alienation – is altogether another matter:

> You think that after all you must be weaving a piece of cloth: because you are sitting at a loom – even if it is empty – and going through the motions of weaving.[62]

NOTES

1. I am quoting Wittgenstein's Philosophische Untersuchungen for the most part (here, as noted, §65) in the translation of G. E. M. Anscombe, *Philosophical Investigations*, Oxford 1953 sqq. In certain cases I make use of the German original as published in the Suhrkamp edition, Frankfurt am Main 1971.

2. I am making use of the German original because of the divergence in Anscombe's translation, which runs as follows: "Consider for example the proceedings that we call "games". I mean board-games, card-games, ball-games, Olympic games, and so on. What is common to them all? – Don't say: "There *must* be something common, or they would not be called 'games'" – but *look* and *see* whether there is anything common to all. For if you look at them you will not see something that is common to *all*, but similarities, relationships, and a whole series of them at that."

3. See, for instance, Bambrough (1960–1961) and W. K. C. Guthrie (1971, p. 120).

4. Quoted by H. G. Gadamer (1972, p. 99).

5. *Philosophical Investigations*, §2. Hereafter referred to by paragraphs in the text only, unless otherwise noted.

6. The German original has *"Verständnis"*, for which "communication", however customary, might be a dubious translation.

7. One often finds expressed the opinion that Wittgenstein's plurality of language-games is matched by a plurality of "forms of life" – perhaps even to the extent that each language-game is connected with a specific "form of life". This view does not seem fit to survive the scrutiny of Newton Garver, whose results (Garver, 1994) I take to be definitive in this respect. The term "form of life", whenever referred to in this article, should be taken to have the content for which Garver argues. (It might be noted that Rossvær, (1971, p. 281 sq.), taking Wittgenstein to operate with a plurality of forms of life corresponding to language-games, uses this view to make a distinction between on the one hand language-games as primitive languages, and on the other language-games as "parts of language" (Rossvær, 1971, pp. 281–282). On the background sketched above, I clearly cannot share his belief in this distinction as an important one by Wittgenstein. (See especially III.1, below.)

8. I have touched upon these subjects in Sandemose: 1980, where I also tried to point out the relation between Wittgenstein's theory and the aloof, utopian socialism of Saint-Simon as well as the latter-day "Technocracy" of Howard Scott.

9. For a similar use of the word, see Wittgenstein 1967, p. 73.

10. Also, one comes across blatant one-sidedness, as with Garver, who opens an introductory survey with the following: "What Wittgenstein takes for granted is patterns of human behavior which he calls 'language-games'. As the name implies, these activities, which are "countless", are ones in which the use of language plays [sic!] an

important role" (Garver, 1994, p. 14). He goes on at length, without ever commenting on the fact that the name also implies something about the whole structure of the activities.

11. Quotations from Bloor, 1996, p. 358. It will, hopefully, be shown later on that Bloor's understanding of Hegel's position is not entirely adequate.

12. Marx, 1966, pp. 231, 274. My own translation from the German, from the first (and best elaborated) edition (1867) of the first chapter of *Capital*.

13. That is, the second part of the *Science of Logic*, or *Wissenschaft der Logik*, 1815–1816.

14. Wittgenstein's relation to *inter alia* these two men are discussed in Skidelsky, 1994, passim, and in Monk, 1990, esp. 392–394. Both works are highly to be recommended.

15. The reader will have noted that Bloor is employing this fairly strong term in both instances. When he also says (see above) that the "soundness" [only?] *in part* consists of depositor-beliefs, he simply seems to confuse the issue. In fact, he really argues to the effect that it *wholly* consists of such beliefs.

16. As it appears from the quotation above, Bloor is even illegitimately identifying a belief in the bank's unsoundness with an absence of belief in its soundness.

17. A bibliography, comprising some 28 works, mostly shorter articles, is to be found at pp. 104–105 in Potier, 1991, 104–105.

18. According to Robert Skidelsky (1994, p. 291), the manuscript was really finished by 1928. This is disharmonious with Sraffa's detailed account of the genesis of the book (cf. Sraffa, 1960, vi).

19. A delightful example is Keynes' suggestion (1936, p. 267) that trade unions may function as a kind of surrogate banking system, to the extent that their joint action might steer working class demand in a way that would lead to investments, through its influence on the rate of interest. One may also point at Joan Robinson's view (1971, p. 94) of trade union activity as compensating for lack of competition in a pseudo-monopolistic economy.

20. The all too obvious links between this way of thinking and an activistic "socialism" á la Sorel and Mussolini ought to serve as a reminder of the political dangers inherent even in seemingly refined theoretical positions.

21. However, Roncaglia's exposition is doubtless open to serious objections. His thesis (ibid.) that "the marginal theory of value and distribution" de facto "has been constructed, one might say, on the basis of a philosophical position (. . .) similar to that of the early Wittgenstein" (*Tractatus*), is really not substantiated in any way whatsoever. Further, the very thought that the field of economic theory should be composed of spheres so heterogeneous in relation to each other as to make possible viable solutions without studying the totality, is so awkward that one might have expected the author to attempt to justify it explicitly. Still, no such attempt is being made, not even in the corresponding discussion in his second book on Sraffa (Roncaglia, 2000, 55–60). (Here, Roncaglia's argument to the effect that there exist a methodical parallel between marginalism and Wittgenstein's *Tractatus* is even weakened by the postulate that the *Tractatus* stand for logical "atomism".) From any position related to Marxism, it should go without saying that a justification for a procedure of reciprocal isolation of theoretical fields would have to be taken from an analysis of the economy and its exploitative setting itself.

22. This is all the more remarkable in face of the fact that Sraffa was rated very highly by Wittgenstein when it came to acknowledging his own debts in the theoretical

field. The following remark stems from 1931: "Boltzmann, Hertz, Schopenhauer, Frege, Russell, Kraus, Loos, Weininger, Spengler, Sraffa have influenced me" (Wittgenstein, 1980, p. 19). And initially, the listing was simply "Frege, Russell, Spengler, Sraffa". As noted by David G. Stern (1996, p. 473), "it is very likely that the authors are arranged in chronological sequence." For those interested in Wittgenstein's estimation of the relative importance of Sraffa's ideas for the way of thinking of the *Philosophical Investigations*, it may be worth noting that Ramsey's name is absent from both lists.

23. Clearly, Roncaglia's work, referred to above, represents no exception. Terry Eagleton (1982, pp. 64–90) makes comments on "Wittgenstein's friends", mentioning Sraffa virtually without any references to his works, wrongly supposing that he stands in line with Gramsci. On this latter relation, see below, note 61.

24. The work is hereafter referred to by paragraphs, and in the main text only, unless otherwise noted.

25. These terms are not employed by Sraffa. They are of Marxian origin.

26. Cf. Marx, 1966, p. 232.

27. This disjunctive form is preceded by a "[f]irst, or simple form of relative value", a form which has two aspects, corresponding to the categorical as well as the hypothetical form of the judgement. In this form, just two commodities are contrasted to each other. (For these matters, see Sandemose, 1982, the essence of which I first presented in the dissertation Sandemose, 1973. The disjunctivity of the form is noted also by Leo Apostel (1979), in the first and translated edition of his article "Logique et dialectique" (1978). It might be noted that according to Aristotle, the only thing or relation that cannot be a taken as a predicate for a single substance, is another single substance. It can be said that Marx makes a break with that rule. But as he wrote: "Es ist kaum verwunderlich, dass die Oekonomen, ganz unter dem Einfluss stofflicher Interessen, den Formgehalt des relativen Wertausdrucks übersehen haben, wenn vor Hegel die Logiker von Profession sogar den Forminhalt der Urteils- und Sclussparadigmen übersahen" (1966, p. 274). Marx is scrutinising the *form* of the expression, so one should forgive him that he is unduly downgrading the work of 18th-century logicians.

28. These conceptual determinations are developed by Marx, who as we shall see, made an important distinction between the function of a commodity as *a measure of value* and its function as a *numéraire*. (In the German: *Maß der Werte*, respectively *Maßstab der Preise*.).

29. A fact which means that values of commodities are being measured in gold, or rather, in representations of gold, as a prerequisite for their circulation. That is why the (in Marxian terms) "organic composition" of the capital producing the physical substance of the numéraire-commodity can have no influence upon relative prices. Likewise, it means that all industries enter into the construction of the rate of profits. See Sandemose, 1976, especially Ch. 4. See, further, for a keen sense of the way commodity-values are expressed (while the author nonetheless, *mirabile dictu*, accepts Bortkiewicz' "correction"), Salama, 1984, p. 169.

30. Those interested in a criticism by Marx of Ricardian theorems of this kind, may be referred to Marx 1968 (a): Vol. 2, 199 sq.

31. Cf. the rather typical way of "understanding" Marx, which we find by Habermas, 1968, p. 73 sq.: "Auf der Grundlage einer Produktion, die über den elementaren Bedarf hinaus Güter erzeugt, entsteht das Problem der Verteilung des erarbeiteten Mehrprodukts. Dieses Problem wird durch *die Bildung sozialer Klassen*, die in verschiedenem Maße an den Lasten der Produktion und an den sozialen Entschädigungen beteiligt sind, gelöst."

32. Italics added. Connoisseurs will recognize the approach of Bortkiewicz' criticism (1906–1907) of Marx' alleged "transformation" of values to prices of production. I made a criticism of Bortkiewicz' articles in my essay "Transformasjonsproblem og verditeori" in Sandemose, 1973. Cf. also Sandemose, 1976. Besides, it may be mentioned that some remarks about the relation between Sraffa and Wittgenstein are made in that book, cf. pp. 197 and 369–371.

33. In Marxian terms, that would be something like (variable capital+surplus value)/constant capital, or $(v + s)/c$.

34. The text is from Appendix D: "References to the literature". In this Appendix, Sraffa shows himself prey to certain misunderstandings of Marxian texts. The reference mentioned goes to *Capital*, III, Ch. 15, Section 2 (1968 (b), Vol III, p. 257) where Marx is discussing the relation between a rising rate of surplus-value and a falling number of hands. The quotation is faulty. Marx is writing not of "the workers", as if it were a question of presupposing that capitalist production might go on without wage labour. Instead, he is for the sake of argument pointing to the fact that two men, each working 12 hours a day, could not possibly produce as much surplus value as 24 men, each working 2 hours a day, even if those two "could live on air".

35. The following clarification of the issue is appropriate (§23): "It is true that, as wages fell, such a commodity would be no less susceptible than any other to rise or fall in price relative to other individual commodities; but we should know for certain that any such fluctuation would originate exclusively in the peculiarities of production of the commodity which was being compared with it, and not in its own."

36. See Sandemose, 1976, p. 209. As for the last quotations from Sraffa's book (as well as the following one), they are all from §43. (It should be noted that Sraffa is here pointing at a purely latent "purchasing power" on side of the Standard net product. So no presupposition about changes in the quantity of population is relevant.)

37. Still, Marx uses categories like "paid labour" and "labour price" in *Capital*. But that, as one should know, is meant to reflect the fact that the value of labour power is being mystified into the category of "wage" (*Arbeitslohn*). To use hard, but fair language: Bourgeois "Marxists" are justified in employing the expression "labour price", but only because it adequately reflects their own mystification as well as the attempt to conceal it. (One should take note of how Marx consistently is using these "fetishist" categories in his description of the active forces of capital accumulation (1968 (b), Vol. I, Ch. 23). The point of that description is, according to him, to show the effect of the growth of capital on the situation of the working class. And no investigation of that situation is fully adequate if it fails to take into account the alienating way in which those phenomena present themselves to the consciousness of the worker.)

38. Here Sraffa says: "We suppose labour to be uniform in quality or, what amounts to the same thing, we assume any differences in quality to have been previously reduced to equivalent differences in quantity so that each unit of labour receives the same wage." This, needless to say, gives us no description of Marxian "abstract labour", but only (an adequate one) of what by Marx is called "simple, socially average labour", which in fact is a determination of *concrete* labour. See my book, mentioned above, pp. 277–279.

39. That is necessarily so, given the fact that w is an expression of the net product, which as far as values are concerned, resolve itself into equivalents for the wage + equivalents for the profits.

40. "The last remaining use of the Standard net product is as the medium in terms of which the wage is expressed – and in this case there seems to be no way of replacing it (§45)."

41. This seems to me to be the true reason why the theme is not being treated before the fourth chapter of the work. Sraffa claims (§45) that it could conveniently have been introduced earlier, but it seems clear that all important arguments bearing on the use of the wage as an independent variable would first have to be taken care of.

42. The reason why "labour" has got a lower exponent is, of course, that Sraffa presupposes that the wage is paid post factum. Further, Sraffa's text is characterised by blatant identifications of use value and exchange value, as would have been pointed out by Marx, who: (1) would have protested against giving *labour* a value at all, and (2) would have detested the jargon which allows for "multiplying" heterogeneous use values by rates.

43. As it is nicely summed up by J. A. Kregel (1971, p. 30).

44. See above, Section II. It seems fit to uphold the German original as against Anscombe's translation.

45. In Marx, 1968 (b), Vol III, Ch. 9.

46. By Marx, "v", unlike "c", does not represent values transferred (by concrete labour) during the production process.

47. One should note how E. K. Hunt and J. S. Schwartz, in the introduction to their influential antology (1972, p. 21), clearly presuppose that Sraffa's concept of capital, as developed in §48, is a vindication of Marx' theory of alienation. In fact, the authors nicely anticipate a standpoint close to the one represented by Mounce, above (I.1).

48. Even owners of "non-basic" industries would be dragged in, mediated through a participation of their employed workers in collective bargaining.

49. For references to the debate on these paragraphs, see Garver, 1994, p. 255 sq., and Baker and Hacker 1994, p. 238 sq.

50. "In englischen Schriften ist die Konfusion über Maß der Werte (measure of value) und Maßstab der Preise (standard of value) unsäglich. Die Funktionen und daher ihre Namen werden beständig verwechselt." These words by Marx (1968 (b), Vol. I, p. 113, note) have lost nothing of their validity and importance.

51. It is of importance to note a formulation by Mounce, who makes "fetishism" imply that people "treat the products of their own activity *as if* they were alien to them." (Mounce, 1981, p. 120, note, italics added.) That is definitely not Marx' way of looking at it. On the contrary, his point is that they *are* alien to them. The view advocated by Mounce was harshly criticised by Marx, who spotted it in the works of the progressive "proletarian" Ricardians at the time of Chartism. Here one might compare with a remark by Wittgenstein in *Zettel*, §143, where he is searching for "a something that distinguishes paper money from mere slips of paper and gives it its meaning, its life!" (Wittgenstein, 1967, p. 25.) The implicit answer is that one would have to search in the technical-empirical characteristics of paper money. Contrariwise, the Marxian view is that the possible "life" of paper money would consist in its being a representative of the "phantasmagoric" money-form of commodities, a stage in the development of what he calls the "capital fetish".

52. The text quoted above from *Remarks*, I, §130, is repeated in nearly identical form in *Philosophical Investigations*, §197 (Wittgenstein, 1953, p. 80). There is, then, a substantial parallel here to theories of social reproduction of the Ricardian stem. It was stressed by Marx that Ricardo represented a bourgeois economics so to speak of the *Sturm und Drang-period*, where massive weight was put on *production*, which was looked upon as an end in itself. (See, especially, Marx, 1968 (a), Vol. 2, p. 161 sq.) In my book *Ricardo, Marx og Sraffa*, especially Ch. 2, I try to show that this point of

view leads Ricardian economists to figure their models of social reproduction as just an aggregate of productive entities, without minding their interconnectedness in the market, that is, their circulation as money capital and as commodity capital. It is this last kind of capital circulation that forms Marx' starting-point in building up his model of social reproduction (the "reproduction schemes"). (Cf. Marx, 1968 (b), Vol II, p. 391.) According to Marx, the Ricardian procedure leads one to abstract from the concrete historical circumstances of capitalist production. Anyway, the Sraffian model, like the models of von Neumann and Leontief, is a clear-cut instance of a reproduction model of Ricardian type.

53. See Section III, above.

54. In his thought-provoking article, Øyvind Horverak (1988) makes some references to my book, for which I have to be grateful. There is, however, a source of mis-understanding to be found concerning the concept of the *numéraire*, which Horverak at one point (p. 286, note) refers to as "price measure". For the sake of clarity, one should stress the importance of using a term equivalent to the German "*Maßstab der Preise*", not to a possible term "*Maß der Preise*", which is both incorrect and easily confused with the correct term "measure of *value*". (One may note that Marx himself made such an error once in a published work, namely in the analysis of money in Marx, 1972, p. 59) There, it evidently is a mere slip. Further, the error is to be found in the preparatory *Grundrisse*. (Marx, 1953, pp. 104, 126, 680, 862). More importantly, possibly led astray by the dubious terminology, Horverak in the same connection says of the *numéraire* that it functions as such "in that all other commodities are measured against its value, i.e., against different *quantities*, of the commodity". The true relation would seem to be that the relative prices of all other commodities are measured in the *use value*, or mate-rial reality, of the commodity that functions as *numéraire*. The relative price differences among commodities come to the fore through a counting on that measuring rod. Further, strictly speaking the employed physical parts of the rod are not quantities of a "commodity", but simply of a material also functioning as a commodity.

55. As can be seen from his equations, Sraffa makes no such presupposition: He is not comparing use-values according to form at all. Consequently, seen from a Marxian stance, he scarcely should be taken as an advocate of a "labour theory of value", not even in his "Reduction", where the presupposition is just that it is analytically possible to resolve prices into labour terms. More significantly, those terms are not genuine terms of labour time, since they are expressed by and through the wage, that is, by sums of money. For this theme, see above, Section II, 3.

56. In Marx (1953, p. 216) it is expressed in the following way: "Those, then, who show that all the productive force which is ascribed to capital is a *Verrückung*, a *transposition* of the *productive force* of labour, are forgetting precisely that capital essentially is this *Verrückung*, this transposition, and that wage labour as such presupposes capital, and also for its own part consequently is this *transsubstansiation*" (p. 216). In the same manner, he writes in the analysis of the circulation of the total social capital: "Those who look upon the autonomisation (*Verselbständigung*) of value as an abstraction pure and simple, forget that the movement of industrial capital is this abstraction in actu" (1968 (b), Vol II, p. 109). (My own translations from the German.) In fact, it is the same theme that is taken up in note 51, above.

57. Cf. note 35 above. It is symptomatic of the dominating "performative" view of "the transformation problem" that Joan Robinson once said (1951, p. 149) that the whole argument was condemned to circularity, because the "values" which are to be transformed

into "prices" already are "values" derived from "prices", namely since the capitalists (and, so it seems, the scientists!) know only prices as points of reference. Against this, Pierangelo Garegnani (1960, p. 203) raised a most significant objection: "Ciò che l'argomentazione della Robinson . . . non tiene in considerazione è che mentre la quantità di lavoro incorporata in una merce è indipendente dal saggio del profitto, e può perciò essere usata quale *dato* per la determinazione dei profitti, il "prezzo" *dipende* dal saggio del profitto e non può perciò essere preso come dato quando si voglia determinare quel saggio. Di fatto ciò che è divenuto noto come "problema della trasformazione" tratta delle relazioni fondamentali della teoria della distribuzione (e dei rapporti di scambio) di Ricardo e di Marx." This is entirely correct, and in theory could have led Garegnani onto a Marxian way of looking at the problem. See also Sandemose, 1976, p. 203.

58. Frege, Grundgesetze der Arithmetik I, xviii, as quoted by Wittgenstein, 1956, p. 89. Of course, what is at issue is just a variant formulation of Leibniz' law of identity.

59. Cf. also Wittgenstein 1953, p. 84 sq (= §215 sq).

60. It is of importance that Sraffa in the introduction to his critical edition of Ricardo's writings tried to rehabilitate a way of thinking proposed by Ricardo in an essay from 1815, and later abandoned, to the effect that the rate of profits in society might be measured as a ratio between physical magnitudes (of corn). (Cf. Sraffa, 1951, Vol. I, p. xxx.) By giving up such a view for the more realistic, total approach of his main work, the *Principles*, Ricardo implicitly showed how "analysis" might be moving towards a more mature method. However, Sraffa's attraction to Ricardo's work of 1815 obviously is grounded in his predilection for systems with immediate material expressions of social relations, of which the Standard Commodity is so conspicuous an example. Maybe Sraffa should have listened more carefully to friendly advice. In a letter *dal carcere* to Tania Schucht, dated 1932, Antonio Gramsci proposes a different view on Ricardo's analytic method, requesting that Schucht make it known to Sraffa: "Che l'economia classica inglese abbia contribuito allo sviluppo della nuova filosofia è comunemente ammesso, ma si pensa di solito alla teoria ricardiana del valore. A me pare che si debba vedere piú oltre e identificare un apporto che direi sintetico, cioè che riguarda l'intuizione del mondo e il modo di pensare e non solo analitico, riguardante una dottrina particolare, sia pure fondamentale. Piero, nel suo lavoro per l'edizione critica delle opere del Ricardo, potrebbe raccogliere un materiale prezioso in proposito." Gramsci, 1965, p. 630. Cf. also Gramsci, 1966, pp. 90–104. (Sraffa's comment on Gramsci's letter is to be found in Sraffa, 1991. However, that text has no bearing upon the subject here treated.)

61. Cf. Gustav Bergmann 1966, p. 343–358, especially p. 354: "Not that the Investigations is a conventional scientific book. It is merely a medley of comments. Some are very keen; some others, more or less obvious; the rest, standard armchair psychology in the standard behaviouristic style."

62. §414. Cf. 1953, p. 79 (= §195): "Someone once told me that as a child he had been surprised that a tailor could "sew a dress" – he thought this meant that a dress was produced by sewing alone, by sewing one thread on to another."

ACKNOWLEDGMENTS

I would like to thank Olav Asheim and Riccardo Bellofiore for helpful suggestions, and for pointing out errors in drafts.

REFERENCES

Anscombe, G. E. M. (1981). The Question of Linguistic Idealism. In: *Collected Philosophical Papers* (pp. 112–133). Oxford: Blackwell.

Apostel, L. (1979). Logica e dialettica. In: D. Marconi (Ed.), *La formalizzazione della dialettica* (pp. 417–470). Turin: Rosenberg & Sellier.

Baker, G. P., & Hacker, P. M. S. (1994). *Wittgenstein: Rules, Grammar and Necessity*. Oxford: Blackwell.

Bambrough, R. (1960–1961). Universals and Family Resemblances. In: *Proceedings of the Aristotelian Society*, Vol. LXI (pp. 207–222).

Bergmann, G. (1966). The Glory and the Misery of Ludwig Wittgenstein. In: I. M. Copi & R. W. Beard (Eds), *Essays on Wittgenstein's Tractatus* (pp. 343–358). Bristol: Thoemmes Press.

Bloor, D. (1996). The Question of Linguistic Idealism Revisited. In: H. Sluga & D. G. Stern, (Eds), *The Cambridge Companion to Wittgenstein* (pp. 354–382). Cambridge: Cambridge University Press.

Bortkiewicz, L. v. (1906–1907). Wertrechnung und Preisrechnung im Marxschen System. *Archiv für Sozialwissenschaft und Sozialpolitik*, Vols. XXIII and XXV.

Bortkiewicz, L. v. (1907). Zur Berichtigung der grundlegenden theoretischen Konstruktion von Marx im dritten Band des Kapital. *Jahrbücher für Nationalökonomie und Statistik*, Vol. 89.

Eagleton, T. (1982). Wittgenstein's Friends. *New Left Review*, I(135), 64–90.

Gadamer, H.-G. (1972). Wahrheit ind Methode. Grundzüge einer philosophischen Hermeneutik. *J. C. B. Mohr*. Tübingen: (Paul Siebeck).

Garegnani, P. (1960). *Il capitale nelle teorie della distribuzione*. Milano: Dott. A. Giuffrè Editore.

Garver, N. (1994). *This Complicated Form of Life. Essays on Wittgenstein*. Chicago: Open Court.

Gramsci, A. (1965). *Lettere dal Carcere*. Turin: Einaudi.

Gramsci, A. (1966). *Il materialismo storico e la filosofia di Benedetto Croce*. Turin: Einaudi.

Guthrie, K. C. (1971). *Socrates*. Cambridge: Cambridge University Press.

Harcourt, G. C., & Laing, N. F. (Eds) (1971). *Capital and Growth*. Harmondsworth: Penguin Books.

Habermas, J. (1968). *Erkenntnis und Interesse*. Frankfurt am Main: Suhrkamp Verlag.

Hegel, G. W. F. (1970a). Wissenschaft der Logik. In: E. Moldenhauer & K. M. Michel (Eds), *Werke in zwanzig Bänden*, Vols 5–6. Frankfurt am Main: Suhrkamp.

Hegel, G. W. F. (1970b). Phänomenologie des Geistes. In: E. Moldenhauer & K. M. Michel (Eds), *Werke in zwanzig Bänden*, Vol. 3. Frankfurt am Main: Suhrkamp.

Horverak, Ø. (1988). Marx' View of Competition and Price Determination. In: *History of Political Economy*, vol. 20 (pp. 275–297).

Hunt, E. K., & Schwartz, J. S. (1972). Introduction. In: E. K. Hunt & J. S. Schwartz (Eds), *A Critique of Economic Theory* (pp. 7–35). Harmondsworth: Penguin Books.

Jones, W. T. (1975). *A History of Western Philosophy*, Vol. 5. San Diego: Harcourt Brace Jovanovich College Publishers.

Keynes, J. M. (1936). *The General Theory of Employment, Interest, and Money*. London, Macmillan.

Kregel, J. A. (1971). *Rate of Profit, Distribution and Growth: Two Views*. London: Macmillan.

Marx, K. (1969). Thesen über Feuerbach. In: *Marx-Engels Werke* (Vol. 3, p. 6). Berlin: Dietz.

Marx, K. (1953). *Grundrisse der Kritik der politischen Ökonomie*. Berlin: Dietz.

Marx, K. (1966). Ware und Geld (1867). In: I Fetscher (Ed.), *Marx-Engels II, Studienausgabe Politische Ökonomie* (pp. 216–246 (notes: pp. 272–278)). Frankfurt am Main: Fischer Bücherei.

Marx, K. (1968a). *Theorien über den Mehrwert*, Frankfurt am Main: Europäische Verlagsanstalt.

Marx, K. (1968b). *Das Kapital*, Vols. I, II, III. Frankfurt am Main: Europäische Verlagsanstalt.
Marx, K. (1972). Zur Kritik der politischen Ökonomie. In: *Marx-Engels Werke*, Vol. 13. Berlin: Dietz.
Monk, R. (1990). *Ludwig Wittgenstein: The Duty of Genius*. London: Vintage.
Mounce, H. O. (1981). *Wittgenstein's Tractatus. An Introduction*. Oxford: Blackwell.
Potier, J.-P. (1991). *Piero Sraffa – Unorthodox Economist (1898–1983)*. London: Routledge.
Rhees, R. (1958). Preface. In: *The Blue and Brown Books* (pp. i–xiv). Oxford: Blackwell.
Ricardo, D. (1969). *The Principles of Political Economy and Taxation*. London: Dent.
Robinson, J. (1951). *Collected Economic Papers*. London: Macmillan.
Robinson, J. (1971). *The Accumulation of Capital*. London: Macmillan.
Roncaglia, A. (1978). *Sraffa and the Theory of Prices*. Chichester: John Wiley & Sons.
Roncaglia, A. (2000). *Piero Sraffa. His life, thought and cultural heritage*. Routledge, London.
Rossvær, V. (1971). *Kant og Wittgenstein*. Dissertation: University of Oslo.
Salama, P. (1984). Value and Price of Production: A Differential Approach. In: E. Mandel & A. Freeman (Eds), *Ricardo, Marx, Sraffa* (pp. 165–176). London: Verso.
Sandemose, J. (1973a). Kapitalbegrep-Begrepsbegrep. Dissertation. University of Oslo.
Sandemose, J. (1973b). Transformasjonsproblem og verditeori. In: J. Elster (Ed.), *Marx i dag* (pp. 37–79). Oslo: Gyldendal.
Sandemose, J. (1976). *Ricardo, Marx og Sraffa*. Copenhagen: Rhodos, Oslo: Gyldendal, Lund: Bo Cavefors.
Sandemose, J. (1980). Positivisme, humanisme og materialisme. *Häften för Kritiska Studier*, 30–48.
Sandemose, J. (1982). Vareanalyse. *Kurasje*, *32*, 53–76.
Skidelsky, R. (1994). *John Maynard Keynes: The Economist as Saviour*. New York: Allen Lane.
Sraffa, P. (1925). Sulle relazioni fra costo e quantità prodotta. *Annali di Economia*, *II*, 277–328.
Sraffa, P. (1926). The Laws of Returns under Competitive Conditions. *Economic Journal*, *XXXVI*, 535–550.
Sraffa, P. (1951). Introduction. In: P. Sraffa (Ed.), *The Works and Correspondence of David Ricardo*, Cambridge: Cambridge University Press.
Sraffa, P. (1960). *Production of Commodities by Means of Commodities*. Cambridge: Cambridge University Press.
Sraffa, P. (1991). Letter of June 21, 1932, to Tatiana Schucht. In: V. Gerratana (Ed.), *Piero Sraffa: Lettere a Tania per Gramsci* (pp. 72–75). Roma: Editori Riuniti.
Stern, D. (1996). The Availability of Wittgenstein's Philosophy. In: H. Sluga & D. G. Stern (Eds), *The Cambridge Companion to Wittgenstein* (pp. 442–476). Cambridge: Cambridge University Press.
Wittgenstein, L. (1953). *Philosophical Investigations*. Oxford: Blackwell.
Wittgenstein, L. (1956). *Remarks on the Foundations of Mathematics*. Oxford: Blackwell.
Wittgenstein, L. (1963). *Logisch-philosophische Abhandlung (Tractatus Logico-Philosophicus)*. Frankfurt am Main: Suhrkamp.
Wittgenstein, L. (1967). *Zettel*. Oxford: Blackwell.
Wittgenstein, L. (1969). *On Certainty*. Oxford: Blackwell.
Wittgenstein, L. (1978). *Remarks on the Foundations of Mathematics*. Oxford: Blackwell.
Wittgenstein, L. (1980). *Culture and Value*. Oxford: Blackwell.

STALINIST IDEOLOGICAL FORMATION: ABSOLUTE GENERAL SECRETARY AND THE PROLETARIAN FETISH

Charles Bettelheim, translated by A. D. Bhogle

ABSTRACT

New official ideology in the USSR of the 1930s insisted on its being identical to Bolshevism and to Leninism, but in reality its distinctive traits are of such an importance as to constitute a new formation, describable as the Stalinist ideological formation. The General Secretary plays a decisive role in its formation, part of which includes "proletarianization" of the party, of the state apparatus and of culture. Although the influence of Stalinism operates quite beyond the frontiers of the USSR and beyond the years 1930–1953, this work focuses on that period in the USSR, particularly up to 1941.

Marx's *Capital* and Capitalism; Markets in a Socialist Alternative, Research in Political Economy, Volume 19, pages 233–289.
© 2001 Published by Elsevier Science Ltd.
ISBN: 0-7623-0838-9

SPONSOR'S PREFACE

Ranganayakamma

In 1982, when I read Charles Bettelheim's insightful book *China Since Mao*, I thought it was necessary to bring out a translation of the book into Telugu. I was convinced that it would help all those who are seriously and sincerely committed to the cause of revolution from a Marxist perspective. I received permission from Bettelheim who did not expect any remuneration. In that book, Bettelheim refers to his multi-volume work *Class Struggles in the USSR*. However, only the first two volumes of it were available in English translation, with the third and fourth available only in French.

Being in constant correspondence with Bettelheim since 1982, in 1984, we decided to translate into Telugu his *Cultural Revolution and Industrial Organization in China*. Although a first draft was prepared, we did not finalize it until I finished writing my Telugu *An Introduction to Marx's 'Capital'* (subsequently translated into English in three volumes and now available). I thought that readers would not be able to appreciate certain theoretical issues without reading Marx's *Capital*. We waited until 1994.

In the meantime, we were awaiting the English version of Volumes 3 and 4 of *Class Struggles*. When we had asked Bettelheim in 1982, he said it would soon be brought out by Monthly Review Press. Nothing materialized. When we again asked Bettelheim about it in 1993, he told us that the Monthly Review people expressed their inability to publish it, seemingly due to lack of funds. He also asked us if we could contact any Indian publisher who might be interested in it. We first asked Mr. M. Srihari Rao, a General Surgeon from India who had settled in USA, has been a reader of my books, and had provided funds for the publication in Telugu of my *An Introduction to Marx's 'Capital'*. He readily accepted the proposal to assist in publishing the English translation of Bettelheim's books.

The translation of Volume 3 into English (by J. N. Westwood) was purchased from the Monthly Review Press and Mr. Rao also agreed to provide funds for a limited-edition printing. Bettelheim was very pleased with the arrangement and permitted me to bring out that English version. Upon our suggestion, in June 1993 Bettelheim also wrote in French a 'Preface' to the English translation of the book; his student Mr. Ramnath Narayanaswamy, who is on the faculty of Indian Institute of Management, Bangalore, translated it into English. The limited edition then appeared in 1994 from T. R. Publications in Madras, circulating almost exclusively within India.

Bettelheim's 'Preface' to the English translation reflects the 'post-Soviet' period and is worth noting. In this 'Preface', referring to transformations then taking place as a supposed "failure of socialism", he replies:

> The present work stands opposed to this thesis since it reveals that the USSR and the other countries who had declared that they had "built socialism" had not actually accomplished any of the radical social transformations which could have permitted them to break away from this specific form of state capitalism which I have described as "party capitalism". In fact, it is the latter which has failed.
>
> This failure was brought about in the USSR through the aggravation of a general crisis born from the contradictions of the capitalist mode of production and particular forms reclothed by these contractions under conditions of party capitalism. All the so-called socialist countries have entered into a similar process. These have developed according to specific modalities determined by their own history.
>
> These countries had a number of similar characteristics: they were all, for example, subject to the leadership of a single party which upheld its legitimacy from Marx's works. Among other objectives, this book seeks to throw light on the usurped character of this "legitimacy".

Bettelheim then goes on to defend Marx's scientific work as "very much alive", including for "allegedly socialist models" which for him have been in fact party capitalism.

In 1995, we thought we should bring out the English version of the fourth volume as well. Bettelheim also agreed to this, again without expecting any monetary remuneration. Mr. A. D. Bhogle, a retired Professor of French language from Osmania University, Hyderabad, translated the work into English. Mr. Ramnath Narayanaswamy went through the translation and made some useful suggestions in view of his association with Bettelheim as his doctoral student. A limited edition appeared in 1996 circulating in India mostly to libraries, funding again provided by Mr. Srihari Rao. Bettelheim, who is now 88 and ill, has always appreciated and thanked us for our efforts regarding the English translations of his Volumes 3 and 4.

Now, in my capacity as the 'sponsor', that is, as someone who undertook the responsibility for the English translations of Bettelheim's Volumes 3 and 4, I permit and request Paul Zarembka and Elsevier/JAI Press to publish Bettelheim's first Part of his Volume 4, *Class Struggles in the USSR, Third Period: 1930–1941, Part Two: The Dominators*. It is this Part which best illuminates Charles Bettelheim's conclusions from his years of Marxist research on the character of the Soviet State. We hope that readers will benefit as much from Bettelheim's work as we have, and I take this opportunity to honor his achievements.

July 8, 2001

INTRODUCTION

Stalinism as a whole amounts to a system. The thirties deals with an especially complex and rapidly changing reality. It needed a type of investigation which cannot be seen in its manner of presentation. The results of our analysis of Stalinism and of its true nature are therefore given in two volumes: the first volume of *Class Struggles in the USSR, 1930–1941* was devoted to the dominated such as the peasants, the workers, the repression and mass terror to which they were exposed, and the accumulation of the capital of which they were the victims. The analyses *The Dominated* revealed that during the 1930s, a series of attacks were launched against the "Soviet" working class and peasantry (indeed, the peasantry had practically even ceased to exist as such once collectivization was brought about). We also notice the arrival in the world of a new form of capitalism where mass repression, terror and penal work on large scale in the concentration camps had played an extraordinary role. The rise of this capitalism is accompanied by crises of overproduction of a peculiar nature.

The second volume deals with *The Dominators,* their ideology and the changes that it underwent during 1930s, with the forms of existence of a new class, with the historical conditions leading to its formation, with the role of the party and with the international policy of the USSR. The general pattern of the work is thus as follows:

- First Period: 1917–1923;
- Second Period: 1923–1930;
- Third Period: 1930–1941, Part One: The Dominated;
- Third Period: 1930–1941, Part Two: The Dominators.

In this article, we focus upon the Stalinist ideological formation. The consolidation of positions by the new ruling class and its subjugation to a political direction comprising the leadership of the State and of the party (which had itself become an administrative apparatus) is accompanied by a new *official ideology*. It insists on its being identical to Bolshevism and to Leninism but in reality, its distinctive traits are of such an importance as to constitute a new formation which can be described as the *Stalinist ideological formation* because it takes its birth in the USSR during the period when Stalin occupied a dominant place on the Soviet political scene, while seeming to appear in the nature of a continuation of the Bolshevik ideological formation. Further, the *General Secretary* plays a decisive role in the formation of this new ideology.[1] We may conveniently denote by "Stalinism" this ideological formation and by the "Stalinist system" the system of social relationships in the countries where

"Stalinism" – with more or less "new" modalities – plays a major role in the dominant ideological and political practices.

The influence of Stalinism operates quite beyond the frontiers of the USSR and beyond the years 1930–1953. In changed forms, it is active even today [March 1883, Tr.], in the Soviet Union as also in other countries led by parties claiming to belong to the different variants of a "Marxism-Leninism" but reproducing some of the fundamental traits of Stalinist conceptions. This is in evidence in countries as different as those of Eastern Europe and Central Europe, from Poland to Albania, Romania, Cuba, Vietnam, Cambodia or China, etc. In these different countries the Stalinist ideological formation influences official ideology more or less profoundly even while it undergoes transformations linked to the political culture of these countries, to the internal social and political contradictions and to the more or less acute contradictions which exist between them and the Soviet Union. Furthermore, depending on each case, this official ideology can exert an effective influence on the decisions of the parties in power or can be used for waging of polemics which is only distantly related to the practical decisions of the leaders. Similarly, the response to this ideology in the different classes or strata of the population of these countries can be quite different and as an extreme case it can be almost inexistent. The role of this polemics is in no way less real: it serves to legitimize the practice of power and – with help from the repression – it stands in the way of a critical debate which gets marginalized as a result, pulverized and put down.

However, the Stalinist ideological formation also has an influence over parties (or over political groupings) in a struggle for power in order to set up an economic and social system more or less similar to the one obtaining in the USSR. These parties then claim to be one variety or the other of "Marxism-Leninism" by adopting certain traits of Stalinist theory, pretending at the same time to denounce the "abuses" or the "errors" committed in the USSR during the Stalinist era. Generally speaking, such parties put forth somewhat changed forms of the Stalinist formation. They often adapt and modify topical themes of the ideological discourses of the Soviet, Cuban, Chinese or Vietnamian parties. The impact of such variants of Stalinist ideology is mainly felt in the countries with little industrialization. They can influence strong movements of national liberation (which does not mean in any way that they always really help the liberation of these countries, indeed far from it).[2] These observations would show that the problems posed by the Stalinist ideological formation retain their relevance to our times. However, their non-Soviet and contemporary aspects are beyond the scope of this work.

We shall be mainly concerned here with the *Stalinist ideological formation of the period 1930–1953* (but mostly up to 1941). This ideological formation includes a partly theoretical discourse and practices sustained by specific discourses which we shall examine for their chief aspects without forgetting that they evolve over time when the dominant social and political relations in the USSR undergo a transformation, depending upon the periods and major contradictions that characterize them.[3]

An examination of these changes during the years 1928 to 1953 leads to a rough and provisional periodization; this periodization is based upon tracing the most visible displacements of certain ideological themes. It would thus appear that between 1928 and 1931, two ideological themes dominate, one of the destruction of the remnants and the bases of capitalism (collectivization, elimination of the private sector, "dekulakizing") and the other of the "proletarianization" of the party, of the state apparatus and of culture – denoted by the expression "cultural revolution". We shall later describe their characteristics and limits.[4]

This period sees the beginning of the 'setting up' of the working class, its subjection to an increasingly severe factory discipline and the strengthening of the authority and privileges of the managers. These traits of Stalinist ideology are reinforced during the period 1932–1934 which is characterized by the "struggle against egalitarianism" and by the accent that it places on acquisition of technical skills. From 1935 to 1938, there is a third period during which the dominant themes are the unity of the party (which in practice is subject to extremely brutal repression), the necessity of its "monolithism", struggle against saboteurs, plotters and traitors who have infiltrated within its ranks. It is the period when the glorification of the personality of Stalin takes a concrete shape. It is also the period which witnesses an open development of Russian nationalistic themes and the glorification of Russian traditional values. These years coincide with a sort of permanent *coup d'etat* by Stalin. He has most of the old leaders of the party arrested and replaced by men who appear to him to be more devoted to him personally. Lastly, from 1939 onwards begins a more conservative period where the glorification of Stalin and the glorification of national and traditional values tend to coalesce and get an edge over the references to "Marxism". This conservatism is further reinforced during the war. It is imposed by circumstances to some extent but it gets entrenched in the defense of the new social order and of the privileges that characterize it. It is fed on the assertion that the "socialist mode of production" is now established and henceforth it is a matter mostly of perfecting it. However, economic and political contradictions that arise in the aftermath of war lead to a new ideological thrust, radical in appearance, which points, for example, to the theme of "proletarian science".[5] The post-war period is beyond the scope of this work.

The above-mentioned indications point to certain aspects of the complexity of Stalinist ideology. This complexity is also related to two types of facts:

(1) With respect to the overwhelming mass of population it is essentially an official ideology and not merely the dominant ideology: *it functions more through constraints than through conviction* so much so that the degree of subordination of different classes and layers of society to this ideology is highly variable. This has its repercussions on the way it functions and the forms that it assumes.

(2) It is a peculiarly contradictory combination of *themes* some of which are borrowed from *Bolshevism* and others from *Russian political culture* and of *practices* that are in part refuted by ideological discourse.

I. IDEOLOGICAL THEMES AND PRACTICES OF STALINISM

A preliminary observation is necessary. The inability of the official ideology to function as the dominant ideology has resulted in the dominant ideology in the USSR in the 1930s (and this is true even now) being the same as the one dominating the rest of the capitalist world albeit with its specificities. This ideology tends to produce the same fundamental effects: they accept the social relationships and power such as they exist.

However, the dominant ideology is clothed in the USSR in very specific forms which would be discussed briefly when we deal with the Soviet ideological formation during the Stalin era. These forms are related to the very history of Russia and of the countries under its yoke, to the history of the class struggles witnessed in the USSR and to the interaction of official ideology and dominant ideology. The latter contributes to the growth of the influence of the former because both are ideologies of subjugation to power. However, the dominant ideology enters at the same time into contradiction with the official ideology and is an essential element of its weak influence, especially in so far as it carries individualist values while the official ideology leans towards a complete subordination of the individual before the decisions of the party which is presented as an instrument of history leading the proletariat from victory to victory.

This observation becomes highly meaningful when we examine the different areas in which discourse of the official ideology unfolds.

A. Political and Legal Ideology[6]

One of the dominant themes of Stalinist ideology is that of the *leading role of the party*. Its constant presence and the major place that it occupies make it the fundamental element of this ideology.

1. The "Leading Role of the Party"

Having identified the party with the proletariat, its dictatorship is postulated as essential for the "construction" and "consolidation" of socialism. Its role is presented as a *necessity* dictated by the "objective laws of history" because it is supposed to carry knowledge indispensable for the victory over capitalism and over the "enemies of the people".

The assertion of the leading role of the party was already at work in the Bolshevik ideological formation and in Leninism but it had a different appearance. On the one hand, it referred to a position of principle, to the identification of the proletariat and its vanguard. It is a matter of "substitutionism" which leads to the assertion that the proletariat exerts its dictatorship as soon as the party has captured power *(hence the founding myth of October.)* It tends to concentrate the power in the Bolshevik party by asserting that it *incarnates the historical mission of the proletariat* such as it was conceived in the entire Marxist tradition. On the other hand it was also a throwback on a certain interpretation of concrete history. It asserts the coincidence – simultaneity – of the vanguard of the proletariat and the leadership of the Bolshevik party. However, during the period of Lenin, this coincidence was not postulated as definitely achieved. The idea that the Bolshevik party can be seen incapable of assuming the role assigned to it by the official ideology, that it can cease to be the "vanguard of the proletariat" and that it may even be necessary to create another communist party was not theoretically excluded (as it was mentioned in 1918 or 1919, for example). On the contrary, such eventualities are not envisaged by Stalinist ideology which considers the party is implicitly, by *its very nature* capable and the only capable one, of propounding the correct political line based upon scientific principles.

The leading role of the party becomes increasingly the ideological formula which marks the emergence of a new *form of State*. This State is led not "by the party" but by a self-appointed politico-ideological oligarchy (very restricted in number and which can, at certain moments, be closely dependent on the person seen to be its chief). In this form of State, the "leading" lights of the party intervene essentially to ratify decisions of the dominant oligarchy on which they are dependent. The members of this group are named and dismissed by the small circle of top leaders. The party thus becomes an apparatus through which the oligarchy dominates the State. This oligarchy is answerable to none. It controls all the "mass organizations" and even the "private life" of each. It asserts itself as the only one knowing science and the only one to lay down law. The State that it leads tends to be totalitarian. Everything should be subordinate to it and whatever seeks to go against it can be termed as enemy activity (under the label of the "enemy of the people", "counter revolutionary" etc) punishable by death or deportation etc. This image of the party and its relationship to power, to law and to knowledge is in an embryonic state in the Bolshevik ideology but the totalitarian practice of the party has its full development in the Stalinist era when the top leadership seeks to control how anyone shall think, imposes his behavior on him and makes him a simple clog in the "machine" of the society and the State. This totalitarian practice *hides the real inability of the party in effectively mastering the social processes which it seeks to direct.* Such an inability only makes its attempts at "universal" control on the State apparatus, or social groups and on individuals more violent.

If the figure of the "leading party" is associated with a *new form of State,* it begins to assert itself only between October 1917 and the beginning of the 1930s. It is in the course of these last years that this State of a new type takes shape in real terms, thus giving an illusion that the Soviet formation of the 1930s is itself radically new, that it is based upon an "economic basis" of a non-capitalist type. We have seen that this illusion corresponds in no way to reality. It can, however, draw upon a postulate that seeks to establish a necessary link between the emergence of a new form of state and the development of an "economic base" which would also be so. Stalinism has widely used this illusion to assert the "socialist" character of the Soviet system.

The recourse to such a postulate may appear to justify certain passages of Marx, especially the one where he declares:

> It is always in the immediate relationships between the masters of the means of production and the direct producers that we must seek the close secret, the hidden basis of the entire social structure, as also the political form of the relationships of sovereignty and dependence, or, in short the form of the State at a given historical period.[7]

Concrete historical analysis leads to doubts being entertained about such a postulate and the conclusions which can be drawn from it by Bolshevism and Stalinism.

In USSR of the 1930s, the theme of the leading role of the party refers to a reality and a practice. It is an ideological symbolism under which *the dominant role of the leadership of the party* is represented and asserted in State structures as a whole. This theme tends to set up, without saying so, the leadership of the party into a higher organ of State power. It tends to legitimize implicitly the activity of the leadership of the party which prepares and in fact elaborates laws and decrees and which tries to control all the limbs of the State, which decides the appointment, promotion and dismissal of the highest cadres and which thus ensures through appropriate organs of the State, the manner in which these cadres fulfill the tasks which devolve upon them.

But the theme of the "leading role" of the party also hides at the same time this reality by letting it be understood that the party does not dominate the State and contents itself with merely guiding it. From it arise, for example, the themes developed in Chapters III to VIII of the constitution of 1936 which enumerate the different organs of power. These chapters announce that the Supreme Soviet is "the highest organ of State power" (article 30) that it concentrates all the rights of the Union, and that it has the "exclusive" exercise of legislative power (article 33). These chapters specify in detail the composition and the mode of election of the state organs; they even foresee the adoption of laws "by simple majority" (article 39) while in practice, "unanimity" is established since long.

The role as "highest organ of the State power" assigned by the constitution to the Supreme Soviet is pure fiction and is in contradiction with facts. In real practice, as pointed out, this "highest organ" is the leadership of the party. The constitution of 1936, in an indirect and camouflaged way, allows it to be so because its text contains, within brackets as it were, a proposition which practically gives full powers to the party. One may draw attention to a sentence in article 126, where it is said that the CP of USSR is "the vanguard of the workers" which "represents the directing core of all the organizations of workers, social as well as of the State". This amounts to saying that the Supreme Soviet, like any other organization, is governed by the party and should conform to its requirements.

Article 126 of the Constitution further makes it clear that the leading role of the party concerns not only the organs of power but all the activities of the citizens. It is under the ideological form that we see the generalized domination of the party on all the social organizations. (Komsomols, pioneers, trade unions, women's associations, writers' union, association for scientific knowledge, etc.)

During the 1930s, the theme of the "leading role of the party" is developed in a quasi obsessional manner because of the acuteness of the economic and political contradictions which the party was trying to confront.

The theme of the "leading role of the party" makes it possible to use the thesis of Marx on the historical mission of the proletariat which becomes the "mission" of the leadership of the party. The character of "historical necessity" attributed to this mission implied that it need not depend upon the risks inherent in the elections. Therefore, the elections can only be a symbolic gesture seeking a "ratification" of the decisions of the party by the "verdict of the ballot box". It does not even allow that a veritable popular check operate on it and on its decisions. If there is a check at all it can only be symbolic, it does not seek to limit the initiatives of the leadership but, in fact, reinforces its authority by a semblance of democracy.

The theme of the leadership role of the party seeks to justify the monopoly of the *leadership* [and, increasingly, that of *its chief (Vozhd) personally*] not only in political, economic and administrative decisions but in all the fields.

The role of the *Vozhd* extends also to the sciences, to literature and the arts. This extension of the role of the chief constitutes a specific trait of Stalinist ideology. The post-Stalinist ideology *tends* (but only tends) to limit the ideological "monopoly" of the party to enunciating the so-called "correct" formulation in the domain of policies and Marxist theory (although the present Communist Party of the Soviet Union does not hesitate either – in several cases – to decide what is "right" in the domain of literature and the arts).

2. The "Cult of the Party and its Chief"

By postulating that only the leadership of the party can lay down what is "true" and "just", Stalinist ideology raises it to a "higher entity" which should be respected by all. This obligatory respect soon changes into a "cult" in actual practice through an insistence on an absolute allegiance on the part of the members of the party to the decisions of its leadership and on a behavior in conformity to the directives of the party on the part of workers, peasants, scientists, writers, artists, film makers etc. This cultural practice in the beginning is placed at the level of guidelines for behavior. It is formally imposed through repetitions of the same phrases glorifying the "scientific" and "historical" character of the decisions of the party and, even more, through the watch on the population, the omnipresence of the police and through a general recourse to spying. At some moments, this practice tends to become obligatory to an extent because of the disarray and disquiet in the population which is reassured with the thought that there exists an authority which knows how to prepare for a better future.

The mode of functioning of the party, which is its extreme centralization, results in its authority appearing to be identified with that of the politburo and the general secretary. The more the leadership of the party is centralized the more the "cult" of its authority assumes a personal character. This cult is accepted by the group of leaders, by cadres of the party and by the dominating class, and so not only because it is imposed by the mode of functioning of the party and police repression but also because their domination can be consolidated only by chasing away all disagreements, by avoiding to the maximum, the risk of statements other than those certified as "correct" getting spread. Under these conditions, where "monolithism" becomes a principle, it becomes necessary that the supreme leader of the party monopolize the power to decide what is true and what is false. The *Vozhd* must, therefore, appear as the incarnation of wisdom, of science, and even of all knowledge, the one who solves all the problems without any dispute, in the light of "Marxism-Leninism" in the domain of "political economy of socialism", of biology or linguistics, of literature, of painting, of the theatre and cinema.[8]

For the new dominating class, it is not enough to avoid contradictory material from spreading, it was also to be ensured that the risk of an ideological decision is reduced to the maximum extent so that the myth of the infallibility of the leadership gets accepted. This aspect of Stalinist ideology brings it quite close to the nazi ideology which proclaims on its part the *Fuehrerprinzip,* the principle of the chief.

However, the cult of the chief is also fed by other non-official but popular manifestations. Thus the cult of the chief is rooted in forms of spontaneous manifestations which are born of the relationship of the workers and peasants themselves with the party as the organ of power. These relationships lend to the party an appearance as a higher power on which depends the daily life of each and even its survival. The respect accorded to it is above all an expression of fear. It is concentrated on him who is at top of the party, because the base of the party and the workers experience to a considerable extent the contradictions between the top and the cadres (out of which comes the arbitrariness and oppression of an immediate and everyday nature). They often look upon the top as a recourse against the "abuses" of local power. This recourse, more or less imaginary, used to function in old Russia where the "protector Czar" appeared as a means of defense against local authorities. During the 1930s, the situation becomes more contradictory because there is mistrust and even hate towards the top and a certain hope reposed in it. This hope is, furthermore, entertained by the official cult of the Supreme Chief which feeds populist politics. This politics produced all the more the effect desired by the power because the figure of the "protector" or ofthe "father of the people" is very much a part of the Czarist tradition of absolutism, that is to say of old Russian political culture.[9]

When the cult of the chief "interiorized" by the masses happens to add to the official cult practiced by the party, it becomes a real social force, at least for some time (during a part of the war years, for example).

3. The Fetishism of the State

Stalinist ideology developed state fetishism very systematically. This comes forth spontaneously in the exercise of power but by using it, Stalinist ideology functions, in this domain, as a veritable dominant ideology and thus contributes to making the authority of the party palatable as the apparatus situated at the top of the system of the state.

The real illusions which give substance to state fetishism function "conspicuously" because the abstract entity of the state appears as possessing a true power. It extracts this power from the very forces which the society gives to it on the basis of a division of work which makes it the foremost ideological power. This power is born of the dominant social relationship and the contradictions which these relationships strengthen. The development of social contradictions renders the nature of the State increasingly "independent" in appearance and makes it possible to bestow on this abstract power, and those that speak in its name, the apparatus that can intervene in the movement of the contradiction and in the class struggle. In this way is built an increasingly extended base of the "supernatural power" of the State.

Several passages from Marx and Engels (contrary to Stalinist ideology) deal with a critique of State fetishism and develop the thesis of the withering of the State with the disappearance of antagonistic classes.

The moment there are no longer any social classes to be held in oppression, the moment the collisions and the excesses resulting from it are eliminated along with the domination of class and the struggle for individual existence motivated by earlier anarchy of production, there is no longer anything to be put down which necessitates a power of repression or a State.

The thesis of the "disappearance" of all political power can, of course, be debated: one can cast doubt on the idea that in a complex society contradictions are not inevitable and that their mediation does not need institutional forms of the state. However, even if we doubt some of the conclusions of Marx and Engels, it is no less true that the sharpening or diminution of social contradictions should obviously be accompanied by a process of strengthening or of "withering" of the coercive role of the state. Therefore, the strengthening of this role in the "Soviet" social formation of the 1930s is undoubtedly the result of an increase in social contradictions and in particular of the struggle of the new dominant class for an increase of its authority and its privileges.[10]

Stalinist ideology does not pose the problem in these terms. It asserts that the (supposed) weakening of social contradictions should not lead to a corresponding weakening of the State, but, on the contrary, to its strengthening.[11]

a. The Stalinist Thesis of the Strengthening of the State   It is in the 1930s, at the XVI party congress, that Stalin enunciates the thesis that the withering of the state would occur through its reinforcement.[12]

This theoretical rupture is seen again in the report which Stalin presents in January 1933 in the "Balance Sheet of the First Five-year Plan" which he prepared. In this report, the general secretary of the party once again asserts that the "withering of the state will not come about by the weakening of the State power but by its strengthening to the maximum . . ."[13]

The fact that such an assertion is in contradiction to the classical theses upheld by Marx, Engels and Lenin renders the position of Stalin "theoretically uncomfortable" especially at a time when the USSR is supposed to have become a "socialist State". This undoubtedly explains why, in his report presented in 1936 on the new constitution, Stalin does not deal directly with the theoretical problem of the State in a society supposed to be socialist and therefore "freed from the antagonism of classes." The general secretary observes the same silence on this question in his 1938 work on *"Dialectical Materialism and Historical Materialism."*

However, at this time the theses of the withering of the State and the law (thesis accepted by the leaders of the party as not of a classical nature by imputing them to the old "official theoretician" on the problem of State and law, Pashukanis)[14] are condemned by official ideologues and denounced as the manifestations of "counter-revolutionary Trotskyism."[15]

Finally, Vyshinsky proclaims that Stalin has made a decisive advance in the theory of the State; thus he writes:

> Lenin has shared the idea of the withering of the State, but Stalin has introduced a correction and proved that under socialism the state should be strengthened. Consequently, the law should also follow and become socialist. Everywhere in the world, those who are in power violate the law and the rights of the individual. There is only one country where, like pure gold, justice shines. And that is the Soviet Union.[16]

Such a text, written when arbitrary arrests, convictions and deportations were ever on the increase, illustrates not only the glorification of the "new theory" but its function of mystification of reality.

Finally, in 1939, in his report of 10 March to the XVIII Congress, Stalin openly breaks away from "classical" theoretical positions. He declares on this occasion that the formulation of Engels, which was earlier cited, is a "general formula" which cannot be extended "to the special and concrete case of the victory of socialism in a single country", because, according to him, it "should have a sufficiently strong state" to be able to defend the conquests of socialism against attacks from outside."[17] But he lets it be understood that this withering could intervene if "the victory of socialism" were to be achieved on large scale than that of a single country.

b. Negation of the "Regressive Function" of the State   In the report cited above, Stalin implicitly distances himself from the question of the "function of repression" and does so in a paradoxical manner. He denies that the Soviet State exercises such a function; in fact, he declares: "because exploitation is suppressed, the exploiters no longer exist, *there is no one to be repressed."*

This assertion, enumerated when millions of men and women are deported, rests, if one may say so, on a "play on words" typical of the *code* used by the official language. In fact, Stalin specifies that "the function of *repression* is replaced by the function of *protection* of socialist property against the thieves and the misappropriators of public property" and by the" function of military defense." It is, therefore, these functions (and not the repression!) which requires the existence of a large police force, army and the "intelligence services necessary to capture and punish the spies, assassins, those engaged in sabotage . . ."[18]

Thanks to this code language, the activity of the police and corrective organisms, howsoever directed against innumerable workers and peasants, becomes a function of "protection of the people".

By identifying the State and people, Stalinist ideology justified the widest possible repression. Not yielding to the state, is not being one of the people, it is being its enemy so much so that one must logically conclude, in the words of Solzhenitsyn, that the people have become their own enemy."

State fetishism and the official negation of repression lead to another code language which brings forth the terms of *"education"* and *"reeducation"*. Vyshinsky – Chief Public Prosecutor of the USSR from 1935 to 1940 – explicitly cites these terms. He says that the State should "guide the large masses of the population" and goes on to add that this involves a task of educating where "an exceptional role devolves on organs such as the courts" and the institutions of "correctional work."[19]

This "educative" activity should "purify the conscience of the people". The class characteristic of the State said to be "socialist" becomes very clear here. One of the tasks is to enforce the people to be disciplined, by forging in them a "human conscience" that is respectful of "social and civic duties", aimed at a total subordination of all to work.[20]

The Stalinist Fetishism of the State and its apologia covers a theory and practice of total subordination of all workers to an authority which is quite external to them and on which they can exercise no control whatever. As for the "defense of socialist legality" also invoked by Vyshinsky, we notice that in practice it leads only to imposing "duties" to the individuals facing the all-powerful state and does not give them any right.

c. The State, the Rights of the Individual and the 1936 Constitution In Stalinist ideological discourse, things do not appear in this manner but in an inverted form: that of the defense of individuals against the arbitrariness of the State. The constitution of 1936 and official commentaries which accompany its discussion and promulgation yield a new typical example of an inversion of reality in Stalinist ideology. Let us allude to some facts.

On 5 December 1936, – while mass repression is already let loose in the country and while it engulfs the leading party itself –the VIII extraordinary congress of Soviets adopts a new constitution. This is supposed to incorporate "the balance-sheet of the conquests already made" and to ensure a "consequent and unfailing democratism."[21]

As far as the rights of individuals are concerned, Chapter IX of the constitution enunciates an apparently important discourse: it deals with tribunals and prosecution agencies and asserts that judges are independent and are answerable only to the law" (article 112), that "the right of defense is guaranteed to the accused" and that "the hearings in all the tribunals are public" (article 111).

Now, this constitutional provision is in contradiction not only with everyday practice but also with official legal doctrine. Thus, a Soviet jurist has asserted, in a comment on this doctrine:

> One shall remember that the independence of the judges and their subordinates only before the law does not mean independence from the State, or independence from the policies of the party and the government, because the Court is an organ of the power and its function is one of the functions of the State.[22]

Moreover, no legislative provision is likely to strengthen any kind of "independence" of the judges.

The official stand of the constitution is particularly mystifying insofar as civil liberties are concerned. These are enumerated in articles 124 to 128. They include the freedom of speech, press, gatherings, processions and demonstrations in the streets, the freedom to form social organizations, "the inviolability of person" (article 127), of "home" and of "correspondence" (article 128). Now, all these liberties are constantly trampled upon by the NKVD and the citizens can take no steps against its decisions.

The same mystification on the subject of elections. According to the text of the constitution (article 134) these are henceforth held under universal suffrage, equal and direct, and by "secret vote" (article 134), all the earlier restrictions stand abolished, especially those that hit peasants whose "votes counted" far less than of those earning salaries. According to article 141, all sorts of associations and organizations can present candidates and – on the "decisions" of the majority of voters" – members of the legislative bodies can be relieved of their mandate (article 142). These provisions have practically no importance whatever. In fact, candidates can only be set up with the agreement of the party, and it proposes only one candidate per constituency. Secrecy of voting is not respected. As there is only one candidate, he who enters the secret enclosure of the ballet box can be suspected to be doing so to strike off the name of the official candidate.[23] Moreover, those that are set up receive about 98%, of the votes cast.[24] This did not prevent a large number of legislators being eliminated, after the constitution came into force as "enemies of the people."

Such is especially the case of six of the seven presidents of the executive elected by the congress and almost all its members and alternate members. This "elimination" then resulted in execution or deportation.

The Stalinist ideology of the State and of its relationship with citizens thus enunciates a double discourse: a "democratic" discourse which is in contradiction with facts and an absolutist and repressive discourse which is a commentary on actual practice. This duality is an expression of a social schizophrenia. It reflects the deep contradictions of an economic and political system which pretends to act in the name of the working masses even as it oppresses these masses, subjects them to repression and exploits them with an intensity rarely attained in history.

d. The Specific Form of Stalinist State Fetishisism and Bolshevik Ideology   It is important to emphasize that the specific form of Stalinist State fetishism and the political relationship which this fetishization nourishes (and which it feeds on) has its roots not only in the Russian past. It is present in embryonic form in Bolshevik ideology: it is the concrete circumstances by which the formation of the "society" has passed which give to it its Stalinist and later its post-Stalinist historical form.

The Bolshevik ideological formation carries in it a *newsymbolism* which enables the face of the party to incarnate the proletariat, people, revolution, knowledge, practice etc.[25] The October insurrection gives a form to this symbolism and thus inaugurates a *new system of representation* which sets off the emergence of a new type of State where the face of the party asserts itself increasingly as social power: power over itself by the society whose contradictions are "abolished" in its imagination so much so that it is visualized as a totality which can only be doubted by the "enemies". This power visualizes itself as universal and with the gift of knowledge and the capability of laying down the law. Incapable of really controlling economic and social forces, the Stalinist party tries to break all that comes in the way of its decisions, whether these obstacles come from the people, cadres, concrete or theoretical data, or the rules of morality of whatever kind. The party exists as an *organization* which incarnates the unity of the people.

The democracy which presents itself as this kind of power is the dictatorship of the people. By its very nature, it asserts itself to be in the "service of the people" (because the official ideology mystifies the effective divisions of the society and of the State while the privileges and the powers which multiply within these divisions are denied). It is conceived as *democracy of the masses* (all are organized by the party and can be mobilized to bring forth the directives fixed by it). From it arises the concept of a *real democracy as against bourgeois democracy.* This real democracy has the peculiarity of not letting the people express themselves (except in order to approve the party). In concrete reality, it is negation of the freedom of the individual but Stalinist ideology maintains that it is the supreme form of this liberty because it lays down the rights and the duties of everyone to obey the party. Through obeying it, "they are only obeying themselves."

Such is the ideological matrix of Stalinist totalitarianism. It throws into "the waste basket of history" the previously acquired democratic gains that are likely to serve as the starting point of a veritable social emancipation, namely the freedom of association, freedom of information, the right to go on strike, universal adult suffrage, etc.

e. The Soviet State as the Successor of the Russian State   Stalinist ideology does not restrict itself to strengthening the fetishization of the state but gives up the notion of a transient state characterized by the role it would play in social transformation. In place of this transient state it substitutes a durable state which is identified with the *Russian State.*[26] This state is not born in 1917. It has behind it a long history, that of Russia whose citizens are called upon to study history in order to learn better to love it.[27]

From 1936 onwards, the strength and the role of the old Russian State are held out as positive elements of world history, because this State has "served as the bastion of Europe against great invasions". As a result of the glorification of the Russian State, the leaders of the great revolts of the past, such as Razin or Pugachev, or the Decemberists no longer appear in a favorable light because they have weakened a State which embodies "progress". Henceforth, the true heroes are those who contributed to the building of the Russian State such as Alexander Nevski, Dimitri Donskoi, Ivan the Terrible, Peter the Great. They were the heroes of the cinema of Eisenstein and precursors of Stalin. The State thus built is the one in which the Russian nation is forged and its revolutionary capabilities led to the victories of 1917 and of the civil war. This discourse tends to fortify the Soviet State by giving it a past and a geographical base (that of the Czarist empire) and to identify October with the heroism of the *Russian* people. On a historical plane, it subordinates the other nationalities whom the Russian people have protected from the fate of barbarians, placed them on the way to civilization and kept them along the path of the revolution.

Thus the idea of a *nation* is restored and grafted on to that of the State,[28] while the Russian people become *guides and mentors.*

Immediately after the war, a communist leader from Azerbaijan faithfully develops this ideology when he writes:

The leading force which unites, cements and guides the peoples of our country is our elder brother, the great Russian people . . . By their virtues, the Russian people deserve the confidence, respect and love of all the other peoples.[29]

Thus goes the official ideology which covers up violent national contradictions, hatred of other nations on the part of the chauvinists of Great Russia and the subordination of the party apparatus and the States of different republics by cadres of the guiding nation.

4. The Russian Nationalist Component of the Ideological Formation of Stalinism

The Stalinist ideological formation of the end of 1930s is thus characterized by a strong Russian nationalist component. This component is not foreign to Bolshevism which very quickly poses the problem of a reconstruction of the *national economy* and the place of *Russian* industry in the world economy. Moreover, a section of the Bolsheviks (Stalin among them) seek as early as in the 1920s to maintain the domination of Russia over the peoples incorporated in the Czarist empire (this they did through the domination of the party over the totality of Soviet Republics). During the 1930s, the nationalist component of the official ideology is reinforced and is seen in practices seeking to ensure the pre-eminence of the Russian language and culture over those of the other nationalities. This ideology also orders an "artistic policy" which holds up Russian literary works of earlier centuries as a model.

a. Stalinist Nationalism and the Czarist Imperial Past The face of Stalinist nationalism is turned towards the imperial and Czarist past. As against the Bolshevik position, Stalinism tends more and more towards glorifying the history of Russia. Thus, it plays a conservative and even a reactionary role in reproducing (in general by more or less disguising it) the large number of prejudices inherited from the past. This aspect of Stalinist ideology enables it to "produce a consensus" within important layers of the Russian people whose nationalism is flattered and this contributes to "legitimizing" the dominant place occupied by the Russian party and cadres all over the country.

This nationalism "which produces consensus" is one of the elements which gives a populist appearance to Stalinism. During the second world war, it becomes an essential element of the official discourse which seeks to mobilize in favor of the power the patriotism of the country invaded by the armies of Hitler. This discourse does not hesitate to evoke the defense of the fatherland to which is associated the name of its supreme leader. This appeal to nationalism is seen to be infinitely more effective than invoking the defense of "socialism" which has a bitter taste for the workers. After the war, this nationalism is used to flatter certain "popular" prejudices (on the other hand condemned in the official discourse). The most significant of these prejudices is anti-Semitism. It is officially fought, but the censor, which is always vigilant otherwise, turns a blind eye from time to time to anti-Semitic labels. At different times, the "struggle against cosmopolitanism" becomes an almost open form under which an anti-Semitic ideology is actually developed.[30]

Stalinist nationalism and its glorification of a certain Russian past fulfils yet another function because it presents the leaders of the party and the Soviet State as "continuers" of the "great men" of the past such as Ivan the Terrible and Peter the Great. From 1937, patriotic expressions are commonly used. Thus, we find in the *Izvestia*:

> The word "Fatherland" has become a fundamental political concept [. . .] The most important condition for success is the combatant patriotic spirit of our nation, the unlimited fidelity to the Fatherland. . . .[31]

Russian nationalism, furthermore, is known to assume the form of an "internationalism" when it presents Russia as the defender of other revolutions or as sustaining the struggle of the colonial peoples against oppression by "western" capitalism. At the same time, traditional internationalism becomes an expression to be used by various communist movements as instruments of Soviet foreign policy. This internationalism then appeals for "the defense of the land of the Soviet" or to express solidarity with Russia.

The rise of Stalinist nationalism is an expression of the victory of the national capitalist component of Bolshevism which calls upon the exploited people to participate in the "construction of the country". Thus, while nationalism pushes the dominant class to "build" a strong country, it holds out to the masses the illusion of a "radiant" and "prosperous future" for which they should pay with an increase in sacrifices and misery.[32]

b. The 1936 Constitution and Russian Nationalism Chapter II of the 1936 Constitution denotes a significant moment of the penetration of Russian nationalism in Stalinist ideology pertaining to law. This chapter shows the Soviet State not as an eminently transient and new political form but as an enduring reality. It enumerates the republics which form a part of the union and defines the powers and the tasks of the union and of the different republics (articles 10 to 16). However, it reaffirms the right of each republic to "freely secede from the USSR" (article 17).

This "right of secession", like many other provisions of the constitution, is a pure deception because no concrete possibility whatever existed for the population of a republic to assert openly its desire to leave the Union. In fact, the official leaders of any given republic are members of the Communist Party of the Soviet Union and were duty bound to apply the policy of the Central Committee of this party to which they were totally subordinate by virtue of the rules of "democratic centralism". Thus, it could be officially said:

> It is evident that the probability of a republic of the Soviet Union expressing its desire to secede, through the democratically elected Soviet organs is so infinitely small as to be practically equal to zero.[33]

In fact, those who exercise the real functions of directing communist parties of the different republics are, most often, the Greater Russians because the communist leaders with origins in these republics can easily be accused of "nationalist deviations". Such accusations, moreover, make their appearance soon enough. Thus, as early as in 1926, Shumsky, the commissar for education in the Ukraine is accused of wishing to "Ukrainise" too rapidly the cadres of the republic, and also of "fighting against Russian culture in general and its highest expression, Leninism".[34] At that time the first secretary of the Ukrainian party was Kaganovich who relieved Shumsky of his functions in 1927; in 1933 he was arrested. The same year, Skrypnik, who had succeeded Shumsky in the Commissariat of Education, committed suicide after being accused of becoming a tool in the hands of "nationalist bourgeois" elements. (Skrypnik was a member of the party since 1897). In the succeeding years, a large number of old members of the party in Ukraine and in other republics, had to face the same accusations and were eliminated.

As far as national demands which tend to be expressed through channels other than the "Soviet organs" they are condemned by article 58 of the criminal code of the RSFSR [Federated Socialist Republic of the Russian Soviets] (and the corresponding articles of the codes of other republics) under the heading of "counter-revolutionary agitation and propaganda, intended to undermine or weaken the Soviet regime by exploiting national prejudices of the masses", which is a specific *crime*.[35]

By officializing the enduring character of the Soviet State and by treating it as a continuation of the Russian State the "Stalinist Constitution" makes a break from the Bolshevik tradition. This rupture is seen more generally in Stalinist ideological discourse. In fact, till the end of the 1920s, it was officially recognized that the former Czarish empire was a "prison house of the people", worse than the British empire. Even in 1929, the as yet official historian Pokrovsky could say: "In the past, we Russians – and I am a 100% great Russian – we were the worst gangsters imaginable."[36]

In 1936 – when the new constitution was being written – a *positive role* is attributed to Russia, so much so that expansionism is soon looked upon as an *asset* because of the "civilizing role" of Russia whose work was considered to be continued by the Soviet Union, but with a new content – that of class – which makes it possible to associate the peoples of USSR in a "freely agreed union" (article 13 of the constitution).

c. Nationalism, Elitism and National Bolshevism   The rise of Stalinist nationalism acquires its full significance from its combination with other components of Stalinist ideology, namely, the cult of the chief, a certain populism and the respect of rigorous hierarchical distinctions leading to the establishment of an "elite" supposed to be of "another nature"[37] than the "ordinary people".

The insertion of nationalist and elitist elements in Stalinism and the role which they play, makes this ideology[38] increasingly *"national Bolshevism"*.[39]

This national Bolshevism has many traits in common with Italian fascism and especially with another "national-Bolshevism" which had grown in Germany from 1919 to 1922 and which was one of the ideological sources of the "national revolutionaries" and then of "national socialism".[40]

The existence of these common traits did not escape some ideologues of nazism and fascism.[41]

Among the former, we find even in 1927 (and so even before Stalinism had acquired its face of the 1930s) Erich Mahlmeister. After the exclusion of Trotsky from the Politburo of the Soviet party, he talks of a "Stalinist Bolshevism" and adds that it is, as an idea, "the national socialism of Russia".[42] This theme is taken up again in 1934 by Joseph Drexel in an article in the magazine *Wiederstand*. Drexel wrote at that time: "The new Russia is the Third Reich."[43] Of course, the fact that some nazi ideologues accept that there exist affinities between the ideology to which they claim to belong and Stalinism would not fail to eliminate specific traits which place these ideologies in opposition to one another nor the national contradictions that lead to the confrontation between the nazi Germany and the Russia of Stalin.

The problem of the ideological relationship between Stalinism, fascism and nazism is clearly far too wide to be dealt with here. One must, however, point out that these ideologies feed not only large scale repressive practices but also refer to an *ideological power of great similarity*. This was already emphasized with respect to elitism and the cult of the chief but can be extended to many other ideological themes. Thus the notion of a "correct" thought and discourse is found in nazi ideology.[44] The "abolition" of the proletariat in Stalinist discourses, about which Stalin had said in 1936 that it does not exist any more in USSR and that it has been replaced by a new type of working class is not only not without any analogy either with the opposition between "proletariat" and "worker" which we come across in Ernest Juenger for whom the second term puts in a nutshell a very great "positivity" because it has a connotation of technique. Nazi ideology like Stalinist ideology thus speaks of a "workerism" which makes it possible, to exert in the name of the "workers", the oppressive practices of which they are the main victims.[45]

It may also be noted that Stalinist workerism makes it possible to repress real workers and hence every time their behavior is far from that of the model worker in this discourse in official novels and films. In the eyes of the authorities these workers cease to be "true workers", they are lazy and egoist "petit bourgeois". Official discourse easily finds an explanation of such loss of values in the peasant origins of these workers.

The Stalinist workerism also draws on the *myth of origins* as does nazism. Thus when an important cadre of the party would want to eliminate someone whom he finds troublesome, he would have his background examined if his ancestors were not workers. In this case, his "bad origin" is enough to make him suspect, and therefore guilty.

These various remarks throw light on the specific nature of Stalinist ideology in the domain of politics and law. They also show how closely the most diverse elements are linked.[46] We may mention, among others:

(1) A largely dogmatic version of Marxism-Leninism. This version has evolved over time, as the "exigencies" of the moment demanded it. However, we can consider this version found its canonic form in Chapter IV of the History of the Communist Party of the USSR (Bolshevik).[47] The propositions advanced there are, furthermore, interpreted by the ideological authorities of the party as the need for them arose at that time and they were clarified by the *Vozhd*.

(2) A Russian nationalism which glorified the Czarist past of the country, its historic mission and the progressive role of its great men, including the bloodiest czars most indifferent to the fate of the workers.

(3) A "demonism" which bursts forth each time it is necessary to the power, Satanic enemies which only strive to harm. These are "monsters" and "demons:, the "lustful vipers" denounced by Vyshinsky and his collaborators during the Moscow trials. This "demonism" is not without influence on the popular layers who are still given to a large number of superstitions. Thus a large number of the "enemies of the people" can be denounced even though they come up from the people themselves.

(4) A Fetishism of the State which has multiple appearances such as the cult of the party and its chief, cult of the police as the "glorious sword of the

proletariat" and as "protector of the people", assertion of the mastery of the party and the State over social development.

(5) A discourse of socialist requirements and legalities, a discourse that is uttered – whenever it is possible – with a detailed legalism. This legalism does not exclude total arbitrariness, the "confessions" and "depositions" being extracted by every possible means.

This discourse on "legality" is chiefly developed in the second part of the 1930s and is used for several ends. Immediately, it enables the members of the party to be judged and found guilty by an assertion that the *law should be the same for all* (whereas, till the mid-1930s, the members of the party were relatively protected against the actions of the police who had to obtain a prior authorization of the higher members of the party to proceed against them). But this "legalism" also contains, *for the future*, a promise of stability and antici-pation, a promise to which the cadres of the party are especially sensitive at a time when the *legality of the State* is not respected and where they are constantly under the danger of a second legality, *political legality,* that of terror included in a legislation of exception.[48]

Thus, during the 1930s – at the political and legal level – the Stalinist ideological formation represents a mixture of extremely diverse elements which lends to this ideological formation the chance of justifying its highly contradictory actions and of generating a response in the very different layers of the population; here they can see themselves in reflexion as also their familiar "values" formed of a history of oppression over centuries.

B. Economic Ideology of Stalinism

The economic ideology of Stalinism has multiple dimensions. On the one hand, it has evolved with time: it assumes different aspects depending upon periods. It is not the same during the years of the "revolution from above" (1928–1933) when prevailed an open voluntarism (which leads to a denial of all "law" and even of all constraint) during the years of consolidation of the position of Stalin through the turn of the second half of the 1930s which sees the formation of the earliest outline of the political economy of socialism and during the exercise of consolidation of Stalinist dictatorship, from the 1940s till the death of the General Secretary when the political economy of socialism and the series of its "economic laws" assume their true form.

On the other hand, the complexity of Stalinist economic ideology gets further augmented by the multiple role that it plays. It enters not only as a system of representations which "reveals" the reality while hiding it through apologia. But it also pretends to be a guide to action especially when it assumes the form of a "political economy".

It is not necessary for us to engage in an analysis of the historical development of Stalinist economic ideology ,[49] but it will be useful to point out some of the major themes as they make their appearance mainly from 1936 without forgetting that some of them are borrowed from the authors of the 1920s.[50]

1. The Socialist Mode of Production

One of the central themes of the Stalinist economic ideology concerns the *socialist mode of production.* This notion is a major innovation of Stalinism. Thus one can develop a discourse which claims to be scientific, that of the "political economy of socialism" which is supposed to enunciate the "laws" of this mode of production.

By putting forth the notion of the socialist mode of production, Stalinism breaks away from earlier Marxist discourse where socialism is not a mode of production but a *transitory phase,* the first phase of communist society.

This understanding of socialism takes shape progressively in the writings of Stalin.[51] Its complete and definitive form is to be seen in the *Manual of Political Economy* of the Academy of Science of USSR (1954). Despite the late date of the publication of this work, one must refer to it because it systematically develops the major themes of the Stalinist economic ideology of the period of maturity. Bernard Chavance highlights the fact that the socialist mode of production is "defined (in the *Manual*) as an economic form of an entirely new society, *complete,* representing the outcome of the historic evolution of humanity. It has its specific laws and *it is reproduced and developed on its own foundation,* which sets it apart from all the earlier economic and social regimes (. . .) According to Soviet theory (. . .) it is an economic system which is based upon the *social ownership of the means of production* and which is rationally organized at the same time through *state planning.*[52]

In this understanding, two categories play a key role, that of "socialist ownership" and of "State planning". One must, therefore, spend some time over the significance of these categories and of their place in Stalinist economic ideology.

2. Socialist Ownership

In the 1936 constitution, "socialist ownership assumes the form either of State property (belonging to the entire people), or the form of kolkhoz co-operative (ownership of each kolkhoz, ownership of the cooperative union)".[53] Socialist ownership is also considered as "social property" according to a tradition which goes back to the 1920s and which can claim to be based on the interpretation of some of the writings of Lenin.[54]

The category of "socialist ownership" can be operative only at the price of a complete subversion of the analyses and categories of Marx. For him, *capitalist ownership* is not a *juridical Category*. It is a social category which denotes the *set of conditions of capitalist production*. Even in the *Poverty of Philosophy* Marx had denounced the juridical illusion which reduces ownership to an "independent relationship".[55] Nearly twenty years later, in a letter dated 24 January 1865, he returns to this theme and writes that "the modern bourgeois ownership" (that is to say, capitalist ownership) can only be understood "by an analysis (. . .) which encompasses the set (of) property relationships not in their *juridical expression* or *relation of will*, but in their real form, that is to say as relationship of production".[56]

Although the socialist "virtues" of state undertaking is a common point for most Marxisms[57] (where Stalinist ideology only repeats the assertions on this point), the belief in such a "virtue" is in contradiction to the theoretical thought of Marx and enables Stalinism to systematically develop its specific themes.

The identification of State ownership to a social property constitutes an anchor of a formalist reasoning which claims to change the significance of mercantile and capitalist categories by sticking to them the label of socialist. This procedure (which becomes systematic in the *Manual* but which had appeared much earlier) makes it possible to speak, for example, of a "socialist price" or of a "socialist wage" by asserting that only the *terms* of price and wages exist in "socialism" but that these "terms" have, henceforth, new "contents" which make them the "instruments" of planned economy.[58]

Such an affirmation leads to a rejection of a fundamental thesis of Marx, namely that the form of social relationships cannot be separated from their nature, that it is their social mode of manifestation which has determined effects. This excludes their reduction to the simple role of "instruments".

3. Planned Economy

The category of "planning" is mentioned by Marx a large number of times, particularly when he speaks of the possibility the "individuals associated with a control on the whole of their production" can have when exchange value and money will have disappeared.[59]

In Stalinist economic ideology, the category of planning denotes State activities tending, simultaneously, to "elaborate" economic plans and "applying" them. During 1930s the "defects" of this "application" does not prevent one from speaking henceforth of *"planned economy"* or *"socialist planned economy"*.

These expressions assume that economic development is "subject" to the state plan and that there exists thus a *"mastery over economy"* by the plan.

We all know that this "mastery" is an illusion because effective development fails to conform to the "objectives" of the plan. However, it corresponds to a *real appearance* born of the combination of State ownership, State fetishism, and forms of intervention that constitute economic plans. These exert an effective but blind action on the process of reproduction. They do not shield the process from the exigencies of capital accumulation and the contradictions resulting from them although they give specific forms to the development of these contradictions.[60]

4. The Economic Laws of Socialism

The notion of the "economic laws of socialism" appears only progressively in Stalinist ideology. During the 1920s it is generally accepted that there exist "economic laws of the period of transition," but this idea is practically rejected during the first two five-year plans and reemerges progressively from 1937. Thus, while in the initial phase an open voluntarism dominates, in a second phase, the stabilization of the system appears to call for a proclamation by the power of the existence of objective economic laws.

It will serve no purpose to retrace here the transformation which Stalinist ideology has undergone in this domain,[61] it will be enough to recall briefly some of the "theoretical" formulations corresponding to the final form of this ideology namely the one enunciated by Stalin in *the Economic Problems of Socialism in USSR*.

In this book, Stalin developed an "objectivist" conception of the economic laws of socialism. He proclaims that these "reflect objective processes which operate independently of human desire". He criticizes those who confused these laws with those "enacted by governments, created by the wishes of men and having only a juridical force".[62] However, the existence of these laws is affirmed and postulated, it is never demonstrated. Such is the case for what Stalin calls "the fundamental economic law of socialism" about which he says:

> The essential traits and the exigencies (of his law) could be formulated more or less as follows: ensuring the maximum satisfaction of the material and cultural needs which keep increasing all the time in the entire society by developing and perfecting ceaselessly the socialist production on the basis of a superior technique.[63]

It will be noticed that it is only apparently that the above-mentioned "fundamental law of socialism" proclaims the primacy of the "maximum satisfaction of the material and cultural needs" because it is immediately specified that this "satisfaction" calls for ceaseless perfecting of production. Moreover, the highly official *Manual of Political Economy* (which appeared two years after the text of Stalin, in 1954) says:

> The fundamental economic law of socialism is indissolubly linked with law of priority development, that is to say relatively quicker development, of the branches producing the means of production as compared to the one for the branches yielding articles of individual consumption.[64]

Thus, mainly during the days of Stalin, this law sought to justify the *primacy of accumulation* and a slower growth of real wages than that of work productivity. Thus it expresses some deep tendencies of capitalist production and accumulation.

Another "economic law of socialism" enunciated by Stalin in his writings of 1952 is the "harmonious development of the national economy" which, he asserts, has come forth in opposition to the law of competition and of anarchy of production (. . .) on the basis of socialization of the means of production. . . ."[65]

Stalin places this law in opposition to those which consider that there appears to exist a "law of planning" for socialist economy because, according to him, "the law of harmonious development of national economy" offers to our planning organization the *possibility* of correctly planning social production. But we should not confuse *possibility* and *reality*. These are two different things.[66]

Such a formulation makes it possible to develop the theme of more or less "correct" laws to be "applied". This theme is taken up again in the context of the "law of value" about which it is accepted that it exists "objectively" but about which it is said specifically that it should be "applied" in a just manner in order to avoid "confusion (. . .) in the price policies".[67]

As B. Chavance points out, the reasoning at work here contains a veritable rupture with the *form* of voluntarist theses of the beginning of 1930s. In fact, it postulates that the laws of socialism exist, to a certain extent, independently of the planning activity of the state which seeks to "apply" them.[68]

All in all, the Stalinist economic ideology is above all an apologia. Even in its "developed" form, *it only apparently gives up the voluntarism of the early 1930s* because the economic laws whose existence it proclaims essentially serve to "justify" the decisions of the power. However, in the form which it acquires from 1952–1954, Stalinist economic ideology plays a more complex role. In essence, it tends to render above discussion a political economy presented as "applying" objective laws which can only be enunciated and interpreted by the power. Thus no discussion can be possible. Under the cover of a "scientific nature" Stalinist economic ideology fortifies the absolutist practices of the leadership of the party. On the other hand, by invoking the notion of "application" of laws, it opens a field of justification to the errors which can affect this "application" – for example, in the domain of prices – and thus certain "gaps" between what takes place really and what "should have" taken place if the laws were correctly applied could be explained.

II. HOW THE STALINIST IDEOLOGICAL FORMATION WORKED

An analysis of the main themes constituting the Stalinist ideological formation, their development and their relationships with the political practice suggests – and justly – that this ideological formation represents a putting together of various and contradictory elements where role varies with the political and economic contingencies. Thus, Stalinist theories of the "revolution from above" are deeply different from those of consolidated Stalinism which takes over from the 1940s onwards.

However, the allegedly scientific and dogmatic form of the Stalinist discourse can hide the strange and shifting character of the Stalinist ideological formation. It unifies its mode of functioning. It lets its votaries to engage in ideological terrorism (based upon terror pure and simple) and to indulge in flight from reality: Stalinist discourse is given out as "scientific". It asserts itself to be truer than the facts themselves, than living reality.

A. Pseudo-Science and Dogmatism

The contradictory discourse of Stalinism is systematically ossified by two *corpus* which are brought to bear in a dogmatic manner: "Dialectical materialism" and "historical materialism" authored by Stalin. He gives them a canonic form when he publishes, in September 1938, *Dialectical Materialism and Historical Materialism.*[69]

The Stalinist conception of dialectical materialism (or *diamat*, for short) is highly speculative. The *diamat* is presented as a set of four "principles" in juxtaposition and without coherence. The first place is assigned to the general interdependence of all the phenomena. This interdependence is built in a reductionist manner, it really leaves no place to the notion of contradictions which affect the different levels of the real. The inter-dependence thus plays a role of metaphysical principle of totality. On the other hand, Stalinist ideological philosophy does not refer to any concrete analysis: the "motion" to which it alludes is posed as an abstract category, removed from all contradictions, from their relationships and from their complexity. Consequently, it appears to flow essentially from *quantitative* accumulations ending up in *qualitative* changes[70] which assume "the figure of an evolutionist conception" where the motion "goes from simple to complex, from the lower to the higher in a dull neo-Hegelian perspective."[71]

This metaphysical dialectical materialism plays several roles. On the one hand, its existence as a dogma shuts the door on all "unauthorized" public discussion of philosophical problems that are not restricted to a simple repetition or a simple commentary on a "theory" which has no critical importance whatsoever. On the other hand, it functions as a "theoretical *guaranty* of a political line"[72] and as justification of an historical materialism which itself is dogmatic. This historical materialism does not refer to concrete analyses and appears as the "application" to history of the "universal laws" of the dialectic. Consequently, real history is mentioned only to "illustrate" dogmatically presented theses of "historical materialism" and to "justify" the course of events such as it is presented in official discourse.

The role of these two "theoretical cores" of Stalinism is instrumental in essence. The *diamat* becomes a "science of the sciences" in whose name one settles what is true or false in the domain of the sciences, from outside, without any social experimentation. Thus, the theories of the biologist Lyssenko are announced as true because they are "justified" by dialectical materialism. The *diamat* is an impoverished *Hegelianism* where all that is proclaimed as real is declared rational. At the same time, historical materialism claims to show the "steps" (five, in all) through which humanity passes in the course of its history.[73] Such an evolutionism is based on an *underlying teleology* and plays the role of an apologia by presenting socialism as the "end of history".

This ideology retrospectively shows different steps of Czarist expansionism as "progress" that enabled the Russian people to bring socialism to the people who would not have attained it without his help. Under these conditions, what is judged to be in conformity with the historical role of the Russian people is considered as "going in the direction of history."

Here, we must emphasize two points.

(1) Stalinist ideology calls itself "scientific". What it proclaims as true is presented as the result of a scientific analysis, but it is only a case of presenting something without any justification by any concrete analysis or any social or historical experimentation. While scientific conclusions can be demonstrated and can be discussed and doubted, propositions advanced by Stalinist ideology should remain un-discussed (except when the leadership of the party wishes to put forth new propositions); thus, they constitute a *dogmatism claiming to be science* which collects undemonstrated assertions (often ones which cannot be demonstrated) and put forth these as "proofs" even when they happen to be in contradiction with what can be observed. These assertions are supposed to constitute "principles"

or "cases of knowledge" because of the *authority* bestowed upon the person who enunciates them. Whenever possible this authority seeks to fortify itself by a reference in its turn most often to another authority, namely the authority of the books of the "founders of Marxism" (in practice, Marx, Engels and Lenin). Hence the extraordinary importance which Stalinism bestows upon *citations*. These citations mostly have the role of doing away with demonstration of any kind and they give to Stalinism its dogmatic form.

A more general observation may be made at this point: the dogmatic character of the "theoretical" enunciations and the recourse to citations as "proofs" of the "truth" of what is being asserted is a characteristic common to the ideology of several so-called "Marxist-Leninist" parties. At the theoretical level, they are in fact used in varying degrees depending upon the norms that have taken shape in the USSR during 1930s and which, even in the Soviet Union, are very far from being totally given up after the death of Stalin (although the recourse to citations no longer plays the same role today). It can be assumed that this dogmatism is linked to the position occupied by ideology in the system of domination of the Soviet type in general as also of specific forms of centralized leadership which characterize the parties in power in such a system. The renewal of the organs of power takes place through cooption. This needs "legitimization" of the discourse of leaders which does not arise from specific opinions of the members of the party but from the supposed fidelity of the leaders to the theoretical core which they are supposed to guard and manage most faithfully. That too is one of the reasons for the dogmatic character of the ideology of these parties.

(2) The allegedly "scientific" form of Stalinist ideology thus tends to fortify the power of the party where the leadership is presented as the depository and interpreter of the laws of the history of the society and of the class struggles. The party claims to be the instrument of history created by history. All it does is to apply its laws and it even has the duty of applying these in an unrelenting way because they should liberate mankind and give birth to a superior "new man".

The allegedly scientific and teleological aspects of some of the concepts of Marx and the character of undebatable truth which Lenin attributes to them could open up the way to Stalinist pseudo-science but the implicit justification for terrorist practices which Stalin draws from it is foreign to the thought of the author of the *Capital.*

It will be seen, on the other hand, that the use which Stalinism makes of so-called science is similar to the one made by Hitlerism, although one claims to observe the laws of history while the other claims to observe the laws of nature. Both have before them a certain evolutionism which has its model in the work of Darwin.[74]

This model constitutes a theoretical substratum of two totalitarian systems which turn to terror by scoffing at any positive laws (even when these are promulgated by themselves) in order to ensure the fulfillment of "scientific" laws proclaimed by them. As Hannah Arendt points out:

In the political corps of the totalitarian regime (the) place of positive laws is taken up by total terror whose duty it becomes to give reality to the law of historical or natural movement (. . .) This movement (. . .) distinguishes in the human race the enemies against whom a free play is given to terror (. . .). Culpability and innocence become notions without any meaning: he is "culpable" who becomes an obstacle to the natural or historic progress (. . .)[75]

The structure and development of Stalinist ideology correspond to extremely diverse functions that this ideology fulfills (and to which we shall return presently). It puts forth, in a systematic form, some of the real appearances of the system including those on which the action of the party is based. It tends to hide the social contradictions in order to invest the party with the monopoly of power and to so fill the ideological field that no other discourse can be entertained.

In its development, the dogmatism of Stalinist discourse increasingly takes a form of religious dogma. More specifically, as Victor Serge points out, it shows up as an "over-devout" discourse which sustains a "religious order".[76]

In his later writings, Stalin even condemns those whose ideas he is driven to rejecting by asserting that they are "sinning against Marxism".[77]

B. The Flight Away from the Real and the Mystique of the Party

The Stalinist ideological formation very specifically combines a discourse which takes into account a certain level of reality and the constraints that are seen and a discourse which contradicts not only the real movement but even reality lived. The mode of operation of this combination directly hinges upon two *founding myths*: the myth that since October 1917 a "proletarian power" was set up and the myth of the "construction of socialism" a myth that becomes indispensable during the 1930s. These two myths not only announce that the working class has won great victories over the class enemy, they carry the promise of immediate and important successes for the workers. This promise is quite removed from the real movement which, in the 1930s, is characterized by a lowering of living standards of the workers and peasants, an hardening of factory discipline, punishments at work, etc.

Stalinist ideology is an alienated ideology incapable of holding together its promises and living reality. Its discourse develops along the mode of upsetting reality and hiding it. Thus a language is developed that is convenient, coded, where a part of what is said signifies the opposite of what is asserted (but the assertions have to be repeated all the same by each because that is the official truth and there cannot be any other). This coded language slowly assumes the form of a dead language from which all life is sapped because it has lost contact with reality.

If the mechanisms of inversion and ideological reversal are at work here, they are so in a precise way because the discourse of official ideology is carried out so as to go beyond the domain of a simple alienated ideology to operate on the terrain of potent counter-truths, pure and simple falsehoods. Such is the case of the discourse presenting "socialist emulation" as a "help between comrades" while in fact it was a case of veritable competition,[78] of the ones who assert, during a clear rise in prices, that "a Soviet money is the most stable in world" to say nothing of the talk of massive voluntary membership of the Kolkhozes or of the most democratic constitution in the world.

We are thus in the face of obvious examples of a flight from truth. It appears, however, impossible to make out, in each case which, of these flights, is a matter of ideological illusion, of a self-intoxication of the leaders who would wish that the things be the way they wish them to be, or of untruths skillfully enunciated.

We must emphasize here that the flight from the real which characterizes a large portion of Stalinist ideology cannot be separated from the mystique of the party. This tries to pose as true what is enunciated "by the party", thus hiding the question of errors and of untruths from the view of those who adhere to this mystique (and rendering increasingly difficult, the correction of mistakes and denunciation of lies).

One of the earliest declarations (which stands witness to the mystique of the party and to the beginning of a process of sticking "unanimously" to its assertion) belongs to a period much before the absolutist regime of the Gensek [General Secretary]. It goes back to the XIII Congress of the party (23–31 May 1924). This congress, meeting four months after the death of Lenin, opts for the "model of unanimity". Thus, not one of the spokesmen of the opposition present at this Congress participated in voting. It is on this occasion that Trotsky enunciated a proposition which was later to be imposed in an increasingly brutal manner:

> I know that one cannot be right against the party (. . .) because history has not created any other means of bringing about what is just.[79]

Thus begins the dawn of a new "criterion of truth", at any rate a "truth" with a practical political reach.

About a year and a half later, during the XIV Congress (18–31 December 1925), the way the debates unfold leads Bukharin to invoke, in his turn, the role of the party in the enunciation of "truth". He does so during a discourse in which he opposes Krupskaya who was defending an opinion different from that of the majority. Bukharin then declared:

> N. K. Krupskaya says that truth is what corresponds to reality, each can see and hear and answer by himself. But what happens to the party then? It has vanished by a stroke of the magic wand.[80]

One would rather say, in these days, that what is "true" is not what "conforms to the reality" but what the party states to be so.

It is true that these formulations of Trotsky and Bukharin in no way represent the "official doctrine". They stand, however, for the points of view quite widely accepted in the party and especially by its leadership.

From 1930, when Stalinist ideology begins to assert itself, the capacity which the party was supposed to possess for telling the "truth" and, therefore, to enunciate the "correct" ideology acquired an unprecedented dimension. Henceforth, the capacity of the party to distinguish between the true and the false corresponds no longer only to what such and such leaders of the party accept. Without being explicitly stated, it becomes a dogma which has to be "accepted" compulsorily and which ends in practice in a prohibition of any open discussion on an increasing number of problems.

However, the degree of effective adherence to the discourse of the party is evidently impossible to evaluate because it varies considerably as a function of the themes developed by the party, the moments and the social layers and the individuals.

Moreover, for those who conform to official discourse, the idea of dissociating from it appears criminal. The crux of the dogma is *to doubt is to betray*.[81] Thus whenever doubt raises its head, it cannot be entertained.

For those who wish to be with the party, or not go against it, official discourse had to be fundamentally "true" (whatever its relationship with the real) and, therefore, continued to be accepted by the members of the party who were arrested and deported. For them, to adhere to the dogma and to be identified with the party gives birth to the certainty that the party can only act for the good, and what turns out badly is only an "accident". Confronted with an evidence or with a reality of daily life which contradicts the discourse, what is heard or seen is declared to be outside Soviet reality. It is the exception necessary for the rule. Thus arise the sentences of this type.

That is an heritage of the old order. That is not true. Your witnesses are false witnesses. It is a matter of local bureaucratize. The fact is without any general application. The State which belongs to the workers cannot exploit them, nor oppress them. Bad is the opposite of good. Without violence or injustice the new state could not have survived.[82]

He who adheres to this ideology and who is arrested by the NKVD under false charges can continue to believe that he alone is the victim of judicial or police mistakes and that all other prisoners are really culprits.

By allowing the flight from the real, the discourse of Stalinist ideology carries a certain order but for this order to be maintained, the discourse has to be continually repeated.

And thus the *rituals* which surround the repetition. These rituals must contribute to masking of the contradictions. Repetitions and rituals give to the discourse, a "Semblance of reality" which it does not have itself.

III. THE PRACTICAL IDEOLOGY OF STALINISM AND ITS SOCIAL EFFECTS

The contradictions of real social movement in the 1930s and the dialectic which is developed between this movement and abstract Stalinist ideology give rise to political and ideological practices that exert powerful influences on different forms of social consciousness. Thus a process takes form whose effects react on its own conditions of existence. The complexity of this process is such that we can only imperfectly describe it by giving a detailed description of some of its moments and characteristics.

A. The Specter of a Conspiracy

The specter of a conspiracy is inherent in Stalinist ideology in practice. It is born of a sharp contradiction between the illusion of a mastery which is supposed to be exerted on development and social transformations and the real absence of such a mastery. This contradiction gives an extra-ordinary dimension to the *political illusion* which appears to constitute a State into "a power that is apparently autonomous"[83] and all powerful. Such an illusion had acquired a similar dimension during the French Revolution to the extent that at times any resistance to what the men in power desire appears to be due to hostile activities. As Engels points out, the fear of these hostile activities generated in France, in 1793 and till July 1794, what is known as " terror as a means of self-preservation".[84]

Stalinist ideology produces even more exacerbated forms of this political illusion. In fact, it arises while State power is concentrated within the leadership of a single party considered to be invested with a historical mission. Further, this party must accomplish its mission all the more because it is guided by a scientific vision of the world and of history and has at its head a person who is "the head of the world proletariat" and is gifted with an outstanding capacity (a "genius" in fact) for bringing into play the principles of a just policy.

Under these conditions, it is inevitable that the specters of a *conspiracy* and of *sabotage* should raise their head as an explanation for the non-realization of projects and the promises of a power that calls itself and believes itself to be all powerful. The belief in its strength lends the power to impute difficulties and failures to conspiracies and to revolts which prevent it from fulfilling its historic mission. That is the explanation for the fear and the repression that strikes at real resistances and at acts deemed to be criminal as soon as they are seen (for example, peasant resistance to collectivization). And also the repression which strikes at past activities that are more or less imaginary. Thus, we witness a multiplication of the spectacles of the Moscow trials and innumerable police actions and local trials, during the second half of the 1930s, ending in condemnation of hundreds of thousands of criminals without crimes. This repression is not the product only of objective social contradictions, of the struggle to eliminate the men supposed to be "incapable" or inadequately loyal or attempts seeking to pacify discontent of the workers (who are said to be "responsible" for a difficult material situation, even an unsupportable one). These trials and arrests and condemnations without trial are also the result of an ideological obsession. The power and its agents are convinced that if "things do not happen as they should happen, it is so neither because of the economic system nor of their own policy but because of a *subversive* activity of saboteurs and other agents of the enemy. Thus a whole set of "enemies" and "conspiracy" hatchers come up and they are consigned to death, to prison or to detention camps. The specter of multiplication of conspiracies becomes more menacing in periods of economic or political crises. It attacks most of the leaders and a part of the security services. This does not prevent agents of these services subjectively being in an ambivalent situation. They often know far too many concrete facts which prevent them really from believing in the culpability of those that are accused of conspiracy but they are not allowed to raise doubts for to doubt is to betray. Thus, they turn a blind eye, they consider the specter of conspiracy necessary for "explaining" difficulties and incoherences which cannot be accounted for by official ideology.

The leaders fear the past and the future at the same time. Thus, the repression after the Second World War, the one connected with accusations of "cosmopolitanism", a highly anti-Semitic accusation, seeks to eliminate thousands who have nothing to do with Zionism (but whom the power fear for their critical spirit) and to destroy those who are living witnesses to the anti-Semitism of the period of collaboration with Hitler.

The specter of conspiracies is not limited to ruling circles, it pervades a part of the workers and the peasants who are unable to account for difficulties in which they are struggling as not being at least partially due to sabotage and subversion. Thus, by unmasking "imaginary conspiracies" (their so-called perpetrators often finding themselves obliged to "confess") the power does not only not become weaker but is strengthened. The ghost of conspiracy becomes one of the elements of a "populist" policy and fortifies the "cult of the chief", who is strong, clairvoyant and without pity".[85]

Starting with the assassination of Kirov (December 1934) the specter of conspiracy plays an increasingly menacing role in Stalinist ideology in action. This assassination takes place at a time when there is a sharp turn to the crisis due to the behavior of some leaders who dare to raise doubts about Stalinist policy while Stalin and his supporters wish on the contrary to establish power without any sign of opposition. The assassination of Kirov marks the beginning of a new type of terror.[86]

Henceforth, conspiracies, treachery and sabotage become familiar demons of the practice of Stalinist ideology. They raise their heads not only because of the "maneuver" of the agents of security and of law (even though these maneuvers are necessary for "unmasking" the accused) but basically as a product of a particular form of political illusion. It is a creation of the very crisis of the Stalinist system.

As F. Furet points out, the exacerbated forms of the political illusion came up for the first time during the French Revolution. It "opened up a world where every social change is attributed to forces that are known, listed and living. Like mythology, it attributes to the objective universe subjective wishes (. . .) that is to say provides it with agents deemed to be responsible and with scapegoats. The action no longer meets with obstacles or limits but only with enemies, preferably traitors . . ."[87]

Bolshevism had already entertained such a Jacobin conception of history criticized by Marx and Engels.[88] It was taken up and exacerbated by Stalinism which gave to it an ideological edge without precedent by a fusion of state fetishism and pseudo-scientific dogmatism. At the practical level, there is an equally unprecedented obsession with "conspiracies" and "traitors". We may think that such an obsession is a part of a certain French ideological tradition and that the trials and Stalinist terror was accepted by many Frenchmen as a political practice "that is usual" and not as a sign of the disorder of a system afflicted with "ideological folly" and passing through a grave political crisis in which the consolidation of a new privileged class was at stake.

From the winter of 1936–1937, terror becomes a veritable ideological weapon. It was no longer a case only of eliminating the real or imaginary enemies of the past or of the future. In the absence of carrying conviction that the system was building a better world it became necessary to convince others that its existence was inevitable and that all must bow before it.

B. The Ideology of Terror and the Soviet Ideological Formation

The ideology of conspiracy and of treachery, the efforts of Stalinist leaders to establish a power which no one can risk opposing openly gave rise in the society as a whole to an ideology of terror. It tended to reduce any opposition and even any criticism to total silence. It paralyzed resistance of the workers and peasants to increased exploitation and oppression. It made it possible to impose on workers and cadres such constraints and requirements as would not have been possible in other conditions and which they sought to escape not by an organized resistance (which was rendered impossible by the reach of police repression) but by multiple acts of "disobedience" and "indiscipline" which made them all "guilty" of some infringement.

Under these conditions of terror, the Stalinist discourse on "iron discipline" had, as its counterpart, highly contradictory social practices: blind discipline, servility, personal "loyalism" but also indiscipline, disobedience, lying, hiding and cynicism. These practices were not simple "vestiges of the past", They were the product of the system and an integral part of the Soviet ideological formation of the Stalinist period. Not only were they bred by the system but it could not even survive without them because it has to partially cheat on the rules it had formally laid down if it was to function at all. Consequently, it entertained "misdemeanors" and "crimes" which yield "objective reasons" for the perpetration of terror and for multiplication of ideological practices to which it gave birth among those who implemented it or submitted to it.

It is evidently impossible to analyze here *the Soviet ideological formation of the Stalinist period* (even if we were to restrict ourselves to the 1930s) because it is characterized by extreme bursting of the forms of social consciousness.[89]

In the absence of an analysis of this ideological formation, it is indispensable to reveal some aspects of social practices entertained by it, particularly at the level of the new dominating class, that is to say those who manage the reproduction of fundamental social relationships. This exercise is necessary to understand some of the traits of Stalinist system in action.

One of these aspects is an "unconditional outer loyalism" from each functionary at each level with respect to their superiors. This loyalism and this unconditionality took care of various ideological relationships but their existence contributed to the reproduction of a formal respect of the hierarchy which was the source of a discipline built on servility that brings to mind the practices of oriental despotism from which Czarist society can hardly be separated. Initially, Bolshevism had attempted to promote a discipline of another kind, but having failed in this task, Stalinism imparted all its vigor to the old discipline founded on hierarchy. It conferred authority to each as a *function of his rank*. This rank is increasingly "materialized" by insignia, uniforms and other symbols of the place occupied in the social hierarchy and especially by a series of *material privileges*.

In his novel, *the Tulaev Affair*,[90] Victor Serge dramatically illustrates certain manifestations of authority. He shows how the behavior of a Soviet accountant changes – when this mediocre and rather stupid person is promoted as "the senior assistant" and receives the "external marks" of his rank. The description which he gives of this metamorphosis deserves to be summarized:

> "From his unremarkable table . . . Romashkin (that is the name of the person) goes up to a polished desk which faces another desk similar to his own but a trifle bigger, that of the director of rates and salaries of the trust. Romashkin got an internal telephone (. . .) which was an unbelievable symbol of authority". He now has a certain power and Romashkin – quite timid till then – begins to exercise it on his subordinates with a simple firmness without appeal". He "realizes" the authority that adds inches to a man's stature, holds the organization together, makes work fruitful, saves time, lowers general costs . . ." His conclusion: the principle which bestows worth on a man earlier worthless is the *"principle of hierarchy"*. This principle is his watchword in his reactions with his superiors, and especially with the chairman of the trust. When this Chairman would call him on the telephone, "Romashkin would experience some difficulty in answering the call seated, without bending, without smiling endearingly. Only, he would have certainly liked to rise from his seat to wear a respectful look . . .".[91]

These few lines throw light on the form of discipline spreading over all the arms of power while terror increasingly shapes the manner of their behavior.

A frantic *individualism* constitutes the other face of a rigid formal discipline. The development of this individualism accompanies the rapid expansion of the administrative, economic and ideological apparatus and has no patience with the spread of terror in the later half of the 1930s. In no time at all, the State apparatus is penetrated by managers and by *small and middle-level functionaries* who have nothing in common at all with the earlier militancy of the Bolshevik party (who are by and large removed from positions of responsibility between 1917 and 1930). In the middle of the 1930s, official publications increasingly denounce the "petit-bourgeois" mentality of the new administrators, managers and functionaires.[92]

Formal discipline and the chase for privileges forms a unity and favors the rise of cynical and mediocre cadres in the apparatus who prefer to be surrounded by servile elements even though they are incompetent. Thus the transformations already set off before the terror of the 1930s become more rapid and are consolidated. They lead to an hierarchy of persons despotic towards their subordinates and servile before their superiors, as Moshe Lewin has observed very justly.[93]

The hierarchy of privileges is not limited to its effects on the members of the dominating class. It also exerts an influence on some of the exploited and, especially, during the period of great *social mobility*. The promotions of workers and peasants to positions of some small importance with a little bit of "responsibility" of any kind and the alleviation of some small privileges (e.g. postings in less painful jobs) also affects a number of the exploited whose number is non-negligible. These promotions and privileges, or the hope of obtaining them, has an influence over the ideological links of a portion of the workers with power. They often lead to these workers "supporting" the power to some extent and enlarge its social base to an appreciable extent.

Similar is the case of campaigns of denunciation and spying. If some spies are moved by a spirit of "patriotism", others – and they are perhaps not fewer in number _ are moved by jealousy of their superiors or by plain arrivism. Thus, they are in solidarity with the power. During the time when the discovery of the "conspiracy" is ever on the rise, many of those who are generally servile are ready to pull down managers placed above them, often in the hope that they would occupy the post held by the disgraced should circumstances be favorable. During the period of repression of managers in the second half the 1930s, we see a "mine of young wolves" who denounce the "faults" and the "crimes" (real or imaginary) of their superiors. During the same period we also see the executives occupying a certain position wishing to protect themselves against possible accusations and to give evidence of their zeal, setting up a purely formal discipline which reduced the efficiency of the apparatus to its lowest. The executives achieve any task whatever and repeat the slogans of the time. Thus, we have – to use the expression of Claude Lefort – a "check on those who produce, whatever be their field of production, by professionals of incompetence."[94]

Thus, a brutal, quasi-military "style of command" is fashioned. This style has often been described, and even glorified, by Soviet leaders of those times. It seeks to attain objectives whatever the price (vo shto by to ne stalo), deal with severity with the leaders responsible at a lower level who do not "fulfill" targets fixed, accept neither any discussion nor reservations nor explanations. They "put pressure" *(nazha*t) on the lower ranks, have a "solid fist which organizes and controls", do not accept any objections and come down with a heavy hand in order to harm so that others learn the lesson *(bolno stuknut kogo sledue*t, *v primet i nauku drugim).*[95]

These social practices introduced in the ideological formation of the Stalinist period, are developed from contradictions of the system and characteristics of the official ideology which places the set of social transformations and relationships before a double code.

C. The Two Codes of Stalinist Ideology

One of the peculiarities of the Stalinist ideology such as it had asserted itself in the USSR in the 1930s arises from its status: it is the *official* ideology, it is not a dominant ideology whose influence would be *direct* upon the population (in the sense that the population would have appropriated it, would have made it its own even in a changed form). It is only very partly that official ideology coincides with the image that the population has of the real situation, of the policy followed and the history of the country. This coincidence shows up especially when official ideology incorporates spontaneous images of social consciousness, like those associated with state fetishism or of the currency or, for a part of the Russian population, those devoting a large part to the greatness of Russia and its historic mission. When such is the case, official ideology plays an active role in the backing which a part of the population gives to the system of domination.

If official ideology does not generally function as a *dominant ideology*, it is because there are strong contradictions between the real social movement and even the apparent reality and the discourse of official ideology. Hence, despite formal "respect" shown to it, the ideology of the party does not succeed in functioning as a system of representation, values and norms to which the dominant class would, in fact, be subject and so would the dominated class under differentiated forms.[96]

Official ideology, therefore, functions much more *"under constraint"* than in willing acceptance, or in appearances or as consensus. One of its functions can even be to help in discovering those who are not entirely subservient to the party because they express their disagreement with such or such proposition of official discourse. To fulfill this function well, it is not unnecessary that some of its propositions be more or less absurd.[97]

At the international level, that of the Communist Inter-national, parties affiliated to it and sections that these parties influence (that is to say, outside the USSR) official Soviet ideology plays another role and is likely to receive a much more real adhesion than what it obtains even in the Soviet Union. This ideology, in fact, plays an unquestionably active role beyond Soviet frontiers and cannot work there under constraint. Moreover, non-Soviets are more or less unaware of the extent of contradictions between the discourse of official ideology and the realities lived by the population of the USSR and forms of consciousness corresponding to these realities. However, even this external adhesion becomes possible only at the cost of a great "vigilance" by removing systematically from the top of the International and affiliated parties, those leaders who are not ready to accept without any discussion the discourse of Soviet official ideology. The history of the CI is one of multiple exclusions and elimination of "deviationist" elements, especially during the 1930s. This history is also one of physical elimination of a large number of those who could bear witness abroad to the profoundly fallacious character of official ideology and to what was the concrete reality of life in USSR. This, and the future annexation of a part of Poland explains the physical decimation, which took place in the USSR in 1938, of the old leadership of the Polish party.

To the massive functioning of official ideology "under constraint" corresponds the use of a double code written into this ideology, *a code of interpretation* and *a code of subjugation*. Both of them are indispensable for the reproduction of relationships of domination of the system.

1. The Code of Interpretation

To a large extent, Stalinist ideology constitutes *a system of myths*. This system is built around the founding myth of the October Revolution proclaimed to be a "proletarian" revolution. This myth itself hinges wholly upon a code of interpretation and identification. Stalinism tends to solidify this code and make a total system out of it. The official language is thus found *subverted* and impoverished. It produces a dead language, a *wooden language*, which is a vehicle of several myths. Thus, industrialization and collectivization which are supposed to bring an abundance of agricultural produce and well-being to the peasants and which brought poverty and lowering of the level of life of workers and peasants and even famine, is announced to be no less than the source of a "more joyful life". *By turning the back to the principle of reality and using a codified language which negates it, the discourse of the party sets itself on a path of "fiction-making". As it progresses, this fiction-making gives an increasingly mythical content to official discourse.*[98]

Similarly, the Stalinist ideology develops the myth of an economy which the plan has mastered, that of the Kolkhozians who "collectively take their destiny in their hands", that of the workers "who are enthusiastic about production" (symbolized successively by the Udarniki and the Stakhanovists), that of a

Soviet Union that would "give birth to progress" in all spheres, succeed in "transforming nature" and in "fashioning a new man".[99]

The reality incessantly giving a lie to these assertions led the party to an increasingly mendacious discourse to a *falsification ever more brazen of reality and of history*. Hence the rewriting of history which characterizes the Stalinist (and post-Stalinist) regime.

Once on the path of large scale falsification, the leadership of the party is led to encoding the quasi-totality of the field of expression and saturating to the maximum, the space of public discourse because any other discourse could be in violent contradiction with official ideology. When such a saturation is more or less achieved, spontaneous forms of social consciousness are seen to practically ban any coherent expression. This unleashes a process of inner shutting up[100] and blocks the enunciation of a systematic critical discourse. The different social classes are voiceless.

In conditions of the 1930s characterized by great social mobility and massive repression, official ideology in action is an element stabilizing the existing order. It produces a *specific de-socialization*, a *social pulverization* different from that which is produced in the countries of old style capitalism, but this de-socialization is at least as effective. To escape it, it is necessary to take the risk of negating official discourse[101] and developing social practices independent of it. This is possible only under certain conditions. In their absence official discourse also becomes the vector of a *code of allegiance*.

2. Code of Allegiance

The ideological monopoly claimed by the leadership of the party also fulfills the *function of allegiance*. By forcing each one to repeat *ad infinitum* what is said by the party (even when he knows that it is false) and acting, at least outwardly, according to directives, political, scientific, artistic, etc., the top leaders of the party change official discourse into a *code of allegiance* any lack of respect towards which is looked upon as "lack of loyalty" and "deviation". And the deviant quite easily becomes an *enemy*, a potential one at any rate.

The allegiance so obtained has all the more importance as official discourse is in contradiction with what is "thought" as "true", as "just" by a portion of those who "adhere" to it publicly. Thus, when the party asserts – at a time when there is a shortage of most common articles of consumption that "life has become more beautiful" or when it says that the citizens of the USSR (constantly in danger of being arrested arbitrarily) live under "the most democratic constitution in the world" and when it demands that each repeat it, it brings into play a specific practice of *enslavement*. Accepting what is evident does not imply any allegiance because you limit yourself to saying what you think is true. On the contrary, prostrating before a discourse you do not believe in, that is accepting the *authority* of the enunciator of the discourse. By functioning as it does, official discourse plays the role of an *instrument of social surrender* which it would not have if the discourse had spontaneously inspired acceptance.

The role of an instrument of social surrender to the code of allegiance which characterizes Stalinism is also formed of absurd and killing accusations that the organs of security and law make against real or imaginary "opponents." Those are made victims of senseless epithets like "trotskyists-Bukharinists" or "trotskyists-Hitlerites" (while Trotsky and Bukharin were the earliest to warn against the Nazi menace and proposing a policy of opposing it much better than Stalinist policy who made the social-democrats the chief enemy). They also hurled absurd and vulgar swear words as that of "lustful vipers". This dimension of official discourse does not aim only at "justifying" condemnation of those so accused, it seeks also to oblige each one to repeat these intemperate sentences which has apparently become an "act of faith" imposing a sort of *credo quia absurdum* ("I believe because it is absurd").

Of course, the fragments of an ideology based on evidence are not characteristic of Stalinist ideology. Only the elements of ideology are specific when functioning under constraint. They alone are the instruments of enslavement and social surrender.

The function of allegiance of official ideology requires, lastly, the intervention of the police, but this happens only in the boundary line cases (incidentally quite many in the Stalinist era). But even before the police intervenes, social surrender is obtained through the action of a closed network of ideological instruments. Each of them keeps a watch on a part of a particular population with which it is regularly in contact, whom it calls to order, "guides" its noticeable behavior, teaches it the day's "truth", repeats to him the "correct discourse", the one which should form a part of the conversation in public. (At that time, because of police action, nearly all conversation was potentially public). Ideological agencies obliged almost every single one to "participate" in meetings, explanatory campaigns, lectures and "discussions" where he had to speak and say what was expected of him. The agencies that are given this task of ideological subjugation are several. First, the party itself, then several administrative organs of the State (such as the school, the universities) and all kinds of "associations" (Komsomol, trade union, union of writers, of film makers, society for the spread of knowledge, etc.). All these organizations, having security police and informers, are placed under the "direction of the party". Almost no one can escape these agencies of ideological subjugation. Even the "unorganized", few in number, notice that they are under observation because of the network of spies and informers who were quite "ready" to report every incorrect behavior or statement for fear that if they did not do so they themselves could be denounced. The role of ideology as a code of allegiance implied, as a result, a strict watch on the population.

It was shown that the specificity of the system requires effectiveness of official ideology as an instrument of social surrender and enslavement is better ensured if the numerous aspects of this ideology are not spontaneously accepted. It is by openly bending before what is subjectively unaccepted that you acknowledge allegiance to the power.

It is necessary to emphasize that an important shift has taken place in the operation of this code of allegiance during the Stalinist era and the present period. Today, the power is generally satisfied with a *public allegiance* to official ideology (which appears to have lost much of its authority even over those who are the most "authorized" spokesman of it). During the Stalinist era power demanded a *private allegiance* too. It wanted that it should appear as if its ideology had indeed been *interiorized*. Therefore, *the effort made to discover what each person thought and to unmask those with a double face.*

Also, in the 1930s and till the death of Stalin, a constantly mentioned pre-occupation in speeches and in the press was of the fight against *men with a double face* in order that the party could become an "impregnable fortress" where none of these men could penetrate.

In the Stalin era, this fight against individuals with "a double face" had several aspects. It was inscribed in the "routine" of those innumerable meetings mentioned earlier and where each one was called upon to speak and publicly denounce such or such person (known militant or a comrade in the workplace) arrested by the security services as an "enemy" or a "saboteur". These meetings served to "police thought" and locate those who do not show enough "fervor" which too could bring them the accusation of "men with double face".

The political police played an essential role in the uncovering of these individuals suspected of "bad thinking". The *agents provocateurs* established a "relationship of confidence" with those on whom they had to report on their "secret thoughts". They would make these persons talk "open heartedly" and if the confidences made to them were against the thinking of the party, they would denounce these persons at an appropriate moment. The NKVD would know how to extract confessions of the "crimes" or "offences" they were supposed to have committed. To carry out this "work", the security services could depend upon provocateurs "maintained" by them and upon numerous casual informers who would denounce the "subversive" opinions they had heard (or imagined to have). The reasons for these denunciations were manifold: personal hostility, professional jealousy or again the hope of being promoted or have a house sanctioned (generally, one which the person so denounced used to occupy).[103]

The minuteness with which "policing of thought" was carried out in the Stalinist period would give the illusion that the dictatorship of the party was an "ideocracy". This illusion led to hiding the reality of relationships of exploitation and power. In fact, "respect" demanded by official ideas only seeks to subjugate all before the power. What is demanded is the constancy of this subjugation and not the "fidelity" to "ideas" which changed with times.

The metaphor "men with double face" denotes a reality which is pushed back by official ideology. The fact was that the discourse of Stalinist ideology was hardly and very badly interiorized so much so that it was frequently denied in private discourses that burst forth.

Official discourse thus "doubled" with various other discourses. These are in patches. They are discourses of peasants, middle layers, intelligentsia, etc. These multiple and atomized discourses incorporate *a part* of "explanations" of official discourse but in a *fragmentary form*. They do not have the same relationship to the real as the discourse of the party but they do not manage to form a unified social counter discourse which could help in the formation of an organized resistance to the power. However, those who privately have a discourse other than the power are innumerable and really have a "double face". Their personality tends to decompose. Thus, the new Soviet man is a "*double man*". This leads to a specific *social schizophrenia* which makes for a grave social dysfunctioning inherent to the set up of ideological domination.

However, the power does not give up having a full adherence to its own discourse. With this aim it seeks to mobilize literature, cinema and art to "transform the thought" of those it enslaves. Thus, it wants that writers be "the engineers of the souls", to use the words of Stalin.

The main effect of this slogan is to powerfully bring forth "a socialist realism" which must illustrate official discourse. The cultural section of the Central Committee keeps a watch on the respect of this "realism" and the "norms" fixed by the party.[104] One of the tasks of this "realism" very specifically is "to show our man in a true manner, to show him such as he *ought to be* ..." to quote the formula of Alexander Fadeev.[105]

"Socialist realism" of the 1930s has only a limited influence because the authors dear to the Soviet readers continue to be those of the XIX century as also some of the authors who manage to escape from these norms of realism. This realism is generally felt, and quite justly, as instituting a *ritual of falsification* not only of the present, constantly glorified, but also of a constantly rewritten past (conforming to the need of the hour).[106] This does not manage to change in any profound manner what the people think because the imaginary discourse of official "realism" is opposed markedly to the concrete reality. This has, therefore, no credibility, generally speaking.

All in all, the way Stalinist ideology operates (born as it is of the contradictions of the system) makes the leaders and the led live in a double world: that of real relationships and that of the official discourse. The latter seeks to order a set of behaviors that are partly inadapted to the real but *necessary to the* "respect" of power and to the leadership of the party. That is the source of a permanent and serious crisis of ideology. It contributes to giving its specific form to the movement of contradictions characteristic of the Stalinist system and it is a burden on the conditions of political battles. The post-Stalin period is much less rigid on the ideological plane but allows a massive pressure of official discourse to continue, with perverse effects indicated previously.

ANNEX:
ARE HUMAN RIGHTS MARXIST?

An analysis of the ideological formation of Stalinism brings out the cracks which marks its structure. These cracks clearly show the distinction between this ideological formation of Bolshevism, Leninism and the thinking of Marx. These cracks are found at several levels: the conception of the dialectics, conception of history, role of the development of productive forces and class struggles in history, conception of the State, its characteristics and its role, conception of economic laws, assertions about the existence of a "socialist mode of production", etc.

The observation of these cracks leads to a rejection of the simplistic thesis (of the evolutionist – Stalinist type) that would like Marx to have "caused" Lenin and Lenin, Stalin, and so the Gulag and the Soviet totalitarian system.

This observation goes much beyond the simple assertion that Marx would not have liked to set up a social formation similar to the Soviet formation and that, if he had been alive, he would reject it as foreign to all the aspirations expressed in his writings.

However, to admit the propositions enunciated just now does not enable us to consider as solved another problem, that of the perverse effects that some of the enunciations of Marx can exert when they are put into practice in a privileged and unilateral manner. Thus, it is not enough to reject the evolutionist idea of a "causation" of Stalin by Marx to be able to affirm that Marx's writings – particularly those having a utopian content – did not contribute to what was being done in his name in the Soviet Union. In reality, it is not without some reason that the General Secretary of the Bolshevik party and his successors could claim Marx on their side.

One must not forget that *there are several Marxes in Marx*. His texts are not always coherent between themselves. Thus, it is possible to develop discourses and practices conforming to some of his writings while being in contradiction with others. We can, for example, cite a text of Marx which does not express Marx's dominant ideas, namely the *Preface* in 1859 to the *Critique of Political Economy*. The class struggle is absent from this text, the productive forces here appear as the motive force of history and one comes across an outline of a sort of "General Theory of Revolutions".[107] Now, Stalin has largely delved into this *Preface* to justify the conceptions which he put into practice during 1930s. Hence one can see a certain *historical relationship* between the text of Marx and the Stalinist practice.

There are other examples of this "plurality" of Marx. The most significant – with respect to the question we are tackling –are from the writings of the younger days of Marx, like the *Jewish Question*.[108] In his writings, Marx mainly grapples with the ideological function of "human rights". To him, they aim essentially at the defense of the "egoist" man, man such as he is, member of the bourgeois society, that is to say an individual apart from the community (. . .) uniquely concerned with his personal interests and obeying his private inclinations."[109]

Enunciations of this kind, and the critique of human rights in general were exploited by Stalin and his partisans who dealt with contempt what they called "rotten liberalism" and who equated the rights of man with "bourgeois liberties", incompatible with "socialism" (although Stalin had proclaimed – in the 1936 constitution – that these rights would be respected in the USSR, even though he violated them systematically). This "Stalinist" manner of dealing with human rights – freedom of expression, freedom to oppose power in the saddle, the freedom to organize for the defense of one's interests and one's opinions – are characteristic even today of the Soviet system. It can certainly lay claim to following some isolated texts of Marx,[110] by interpreting them is a very particular manner, but it cannot lay claim to the general principles defended by Marx, either when he emphasizes the positive role of democratic rights in the struggle of the exploited and oppressed classes or, more generally, when he upholds that the democratic forms, especially universal franchise, are necessary for the "emancipation of work".[111]

To summarize, there is a "Stalinist way of using" the texts of Marx.[112] This usage makes it possible to establish practices, and the traits of the Soviet formation related to these practices. But this is a case of giving importance to isolated texts and to the letter of these texts in order to use them and aim at targets other than those Marx had in view. This amounts to turning them, in the final analysis, against the fundamental concepts of Marx.[113] Of course, such use of Marx could be forced, not only because some of his texts lent themselves to such an use but above all because of the accidents of class struggle which systematically placed a higher importance on some particular writings of Marx distorted with the aim of bestowing on the Soviet dominant class a state apparatus of an increasingly repressive nature.

NOTES

1. In *Class Struggles in the USSR, Second Period: 1923–1930*, I had partially anticipated the changes in the Bolshevik ideological formation during the 1930s. I will not repeat here the analysis which I have presented there. However, it now appears to me more correct to speak Stalinist ideological formation in order to account for the bearing of the changes undergone by official ideology from the 1930s.

2. In any case, they do not help such a liberation, when they let their country fall in the sphere of Soviet domination once they capture power.

3. Of course, I leave aside an examination of Soviet ideology of the post-1953 years. I will content myself with a few brief observations on this subject:

    a. The official ideology of these years has seen serious changes but they are nonetheless a product of the Stalinist formation because the main themes of Stalinism are still at work.

    b. The relationship of the Soviet leaders to this ideology has undergone a deep change. It hardly seems to dictate their decisions or it does so under other forms: thus contemporary Soviet expansionism is more directly related to the internal contradictions of the system and to Russian nationalism and its aspirations for a wider international hegemony based upon a relationship of military forces favorable to Russia rather than to an "international revolutionary" role which the USSR thought it played through the CI. However, in a changed form, Stalinist ideology can still be used to "legitimize" the policy adopted by the Soviet leaders.

    c. The credibility of the theoretical themes of Stalinist ideology among the workers of the USSR was always low. During the last two decades, it has almost vanished.

4. Sheila Fitzpatrick's book, *Cultural Revolution in Russia,*1928–1931, Bloomington – London, Indiana University, 1978, will be found especially instructive for this period.

5. cf. On this point the book of D. Lecourt on the development of this theme through the episode of "Lysenkoism" in 1948 (D. Lecourt, *Lyssenko,* Paris, Maspero, 1976).

6. In the following pages, the citations illustrating the various themes of Stalinist ideology have been kept limited as much as possible because many of them appear later in the pages devoted to the transformations of political relationships. A specific illustration of it can be found in the proceedings of the XVII and XVIII congress of the party and in the newspapers of that period, especially from 1935 and on the occasion of the great Moscow trials.

7. cf. K. Marx, *Capital,* Book III, Section 6, quoted from *Oeuvres Economie (Economic Works)*, Paris, Gallimard, "The Pleiade", 1960, Vol. 2, pp. 1400–1401.

8. Literature and cinema are especially held in respect as the means of shaping the spirit of the masses. During the first congress of the union of writers, the phrase of Stalin according to which the writers are the "engineers of the souls" is repeated *ad*

nauseum and the role of the leaders of the union (like the censor) is to keep a watch that the "engineers" fulfill their task in the manner the leadership of the party understands it. It will be borne in mind, furthermore, that in 1924, Stalin had repeated the idea of Lenin but had expressed it in harsher words: "The cinema is the most effective tool for stirring the masses. Our problem is to know how this tool should be handled". *(cf. Le Cinematographe, No. 55 – The Stalinist Cinema,* quotes Gay Leyda, Kino, p. 198 and p. 351). In the beginning of the 1930s (and also later) each film is examined in the Kremlin for an assurance that it is "ideologically correct" and "effective".

9. On this point, see the contribution of S. Cohen, "Bolshevism and Stalinism", in Robert C. Tucker (ed), *Stalinism"*, Essays in Historical Interpretation, New York, Marton & Co., 1977, p. 27.

10. cf. E. Engels, *Anti-Duehring,* Paris, ES, 1950, p. 319. See on this point *Class Struggles in the USSR, First Period: 1917–1923.*

11. The identification of the increase of the authority of the State to the development of liberty is a matter that haunts the Russian autocracy and despotism in general. Therefore, it is no chance that the in the *Legend of the Grand Inquisitor,* Dostoyevski makes him say that "the organization of total liberty passes by the setting up of an absolute dictatorship".

12. On this point see the article: "Stalin and the State" in No. 24 of *Communism,* especially the section on "the maximum reinforcement of the state" as the path of its withering, p. 33.

13. cf. Stalin, Balance Sheet of the First Five Year Plan presented to the Plenum of 7 January 1933, in *Questions of Leninism,* Paris, Publisher Norman Bethune, 1969, Vol. 2, p. 595 (in French).

14. cf. On this point *Sovietskoe gosudarstvoi Travo,* No. 4, 1936.

15. cf. N. Timasheff, *The Great Retreat,* New York, E. P. Dutton, 1946, p. 254; this author cites various Soviet periodicals.

16. Cited by N.Timasheff,. *ibid,* p. 256.

17. cf. Stalin, *QL,* Vol. 2, p. 877.

18. Ibid, p. 881, (Emphasis added by me, C.B.).

19. cf. A. Vyshinsky, *The Law of the Socialist State,* Russian edition of 1938, appeared in translation in London, Macmillan, 1948, p. 50. See also the preface to the collection, from *Prisons to the establishments for education,* Moscow, 1934.

20. cf. A. Vyshinsky, The Law . . ., *op. cit.,* p. 49 and p. 52.

21. cf. The report of Stalin on 25 December 1936 to the VIII Congress and the text of the constitution, in *the New Constitution of USSR,* Paris, BE, 1937 (citations of the speech by Stalin in *op. cit.* p. 24 and p. 28).

22. cf. M. V. Kozhnevnikov, *Istoriya Sovjetskogo Suda,* 1917–1956, *gody,* Moscow, 1957, p. 277, L. Schapiro, who cites this text, goes on to note further that since 1931 almost all the judges are members of the party *(The Communist Party of the Soviet Union,* London. Methuen and Co., Ed. 1970, pp. 458–459, and therefore subject to its discipline.

23. cf. On these points, the observation of L. Schapiro, in *The Communist Party. op. cit.,* p. 457–458.

24. During the 1937 elections to the Supreme Soviet, there was (officially) 98.6% voting and those elected received on an average 98% of the votes; 81% of those elected are members of the party (against 73.8% in the earlier Congress of Soviets, elected within the framework of the 1925 Constitution (cf. Nicolas S. Timasheff, *The Great Retreat, op. cit.* p. 99).

25. cf. Claude Lefort, *L'invention democratique,* (The Democratic Invention) Paris, Fayard, 1981, p. 95s.

26. cf. H. Carrere d'Encausse, *Staline, L'ordre par la terreur,* (Order through Terror) Paris, Flammarion, 1980, p. 78.

27. cf. Richard Pipes, Pierre Le Grand et le "Systeme Russe" (Peter the Great and the Russian System) in *'Histoire* No. 33, April 1981, pp. 37–46.

28. H. Carrere d'Encausse, *op. cit.,* pp. 80–84.

29. *Ibid.*

30. The assertion that there is "no anti-Semitism" in USSR allows it to be perpetrated. It is known that this assertion authorizes the tribunals to condemn as "anti Soviet propaganda" those who take the risk of denouncing discriminatory measures or anti-Semitic ragging.

31. Cited in N. Timasheff, *op. cit.,* p. 167.

32. B. Kerblay speaks of an "alliance brought about in the collective conscience between Marxism-Leninism and Patriotism" and a "drift from one to the other". (cf. *La Societe Sovietique Contemporaine,* Paris, A. Colin, 1977, p. 272.

33. *Sovietskoe gosudarstvoi Pravo,* Moscow, 1948, p. 254.

34. cf. Stalin, W, Vol. 8, p.157s.

35. This article 58 is replaced since 1958 by the law on the "crimes against the State" which makes similar actions punishable with a maximum of seven years in prison plus five years of deportation whenever necessary.

36. Cited by H. Carrere d'Encausse, *Staline',* *op. cit.,* p. 81.

37. The "elitist" character of Stalinism is obviously related to the Leninist notion of "vanguard" but Stalinist elitism has its own specific characteristics. It tends to justify the multiplication of privileges of the "elite", that is to say, in essence the members of the party apparatus and of the *nomenclatura.*

38. Its signs are chiefly the increasing role in official discourse played by the words "fatherland", "patriotism", and "the land of our forefathers".

39. cf. Mikhail Agursky, "An ideology for the new class in USSR: national Bolshevism" in *Les Nouveaux Patrons* (The New Employers), Geneva, Ed. Noires, 1980, pp. 81–90.

40. On these different ideologies, on their thematic studies and on their language, see Jean Pierre Faye, *Langages totalitaires* (Totalitarian Languages), Paris, Hermann, 1972, especially p. 5, p. 83, p. 91 and p. 760.

41. Such is the case especially of Renzo Bertoni, who published in 1934 a book titled: *Triomphe dur Fascisme en URSS* (Victory of Fascism in USSR) cited by M. Agursky, *art. cit.,* p. 88).

42. cf. Erich Mahlmeister, *Russland und der Bolschewismus,* Russland und wir (Russia and Bolshevism, Russia and Us) Friburg, 1927.

43. J. Drexel, *"Dostoiewskij -Stimme des Ostens"* (Dostoyevsky, Voice from the East), *Wiederstand,* Vol. 9, 1939, p. 84. This reference and the previous one is found in the work of J. P. Faye, already cited, p. 432, notes 99 and 100.

44. This adjective "correct" appears for the first time in a speech at Breslau by Himmler where he seeks to find out what can be considered as "acceptable in words, writings and deeds," (cf. on this point, the article of J. P. Faye, *L'archipel total.* (The Total Archipelago) in *Recherches,* No. 32–33, p. 27.)

45. cf. *ibid,* pp. 17–18 and pp. 27–29.

46. A part of the developments that follow were inspired by an intervention of Moshe

Lewin in the course of a round table discussion devoted to Soviet industrialization in the 1930s. This round table discussion was under the auspices of the EHESS at Paris on 10 and 11 December 1981 (EHESS: The School for Advanced Studies in the Social Sciences. *Tr*).

47. cf. The translation of this book at the Bureau d'Edition, Paris, 1939.

48. This point was particularly brought out by Helene Carrere d'Encausse in her contribution to the Round Table discussion of EHESS devoted to Soviet industrialization in the 1930s. (cf. her paper: *Permanences and Changes of Political Power in the Years of Industrialization, 1928–1941*.

49. This was recently done, and excellently, by Bernard Chavance, in the book *Le Capital Socialiste* (Socialist Capital), Paris, Le Sycomore, 1980. The reader will only have to refer to it.

50. On this point too the book of B. Chavance is highly illuminating. Among the authors developing themes treated by Stalinist ideology, even when driven out of the party and "liquidated", mention must be made of N. Bukharin who has published, among others, the *Economy of the Period of Transition* (published again, Paris, EDI, 1976) and of E. Preobrazhensky and his book *The New Economics* (published again in Paris, EDI, 1966). An interesting analysis of the development of Stalinist economic ideology can be found in the thesis of Louis Basle, *Elaboration of the Political Economy of Socialism in the Soviet Union* 1917–1957, thesis submitted for the award of a doctorate conferred by the State in economic sciences, Paris X, 1979.

51. It continues to be valid today in the USSR and in the countries of the Bloc, but also in China, in Vietnam, in Albania, in Cuba etc.

52. cf. B. Chavance, *Le Capital Socialiste, op. cit.*, p. 307 (the emphasis is added by me, C.B.)

53. cf. Article V of the Constitution.

54. cf. B. Chavance, *Le Capital Socialiste, op. cit.*, p. 64, particularly note 60.

55. cf. Karl Marx, *Oeuvres* (Works), Vol. 1, p. 118.

56. cf. *ibid*, pp. 1453–1454.

57. Especially of the Marxism of Kautsky (cf. K. Kautsky, *Das Erfurter Program* (published for the first time in 1892, Berlin, Dietz Verlag, 1965, p. 115).

58. cf. B. Chavance, *Le Capital Socialiste, op. cit.*, p. 221s and p. 308.

59. See, for example, K. Marx, "Principles of a critique of Political Economy", in *Oeuvre-Economie* (Economic Works) *op. cit.*, Vol. 2, p. 211.

60. On this point, see the last part of *Class Struggles in the USSR, Third Period: 1930–1941, Part One: The Dominated.*

61. The theses of the economic laws of transition such as they were generally accepted at the end of NEP can be found in the work of I.Lapidus and K.Ostrovitianov, *Precis d'economie politique* (French translation, Paris, ESI, 1929). The different conceptions which make their appearance later are expounded in the already cited works of B. Chavance (but especially in his thesis: *Les Bases de l'economie politique du socialism* (The Bases of the Political Economy of Socialism), Paris X, 1979, cyclostyled text) and of L. Basle. See also A. Smolar, "Utopia and Science: The Political Economy in the Marxist View of Communism and during Industrialization", *Revue de l'Est*, 4, 1974, and A. Miller, "A Political Economy of Socialism in the Making", *Soviet Studies*, April 1953.

62. cf. J. Stalin, *Economic Problems of Socialism in the USSR*, Paris, French Communist Party publication, 1952, p. 6

63. *Ibid*, p. 34.

64. cf. Manual . . ., *op. cit.*, p. 443.

65. cf. J. Stalin, *Les Problemes* (The Problems).. . .. *op. cit.*, p. 9.

66. *Ibid*, p. 10, The words are underlined in the original text of Stalin.

67. *Ibid*, p. 19.

68. cf. B. Chavance, *The Bases*. . . . (The Bases), *op. cit*, p. 461.

69. cf. Stalin, *QL*, Vol. 2, pp. 785–822.

70. cf. *ibid*, pp. 787–790.

71. cf. Dominique Lecourt, *La Philosophie Sans feinte* (Philosophy without pretence), Paris, Albin Michol, 1982, pp. 146–147.

72. *Ibid*, p. 145.

73. cf. *Ibid*, p. 811.

74. F. Engels had already established a parallel between Marx and Darwin in his introduction to *The Origin of the Family* . . . and in the introduction in 1890 to the *Communist Manifesto*; other authors too have done so. Marx did not refute them. cf. P. Thuiller, *Darwin & Co*, Brussels, Edition Complexe, 1981.

75. cf. H. Arendt, *Le Systeme Totalitaire* (The Totalitarian System), Paris, Seuil, "Points", 1972, pp. 209–210.

76. cf. Victor Serge, *Memoires d'un revolutionnaire*, (Memoirs of a Revolutionary), Paris, Seuils, "Points" 1979, pp. 294–296.

77. cf. J. Stalin, The Problems.. . .., *op. cit.*, 1952.

78. cf. The Second Part of *Class Struggles in the USSR, Third Period: 1930–1941, Part One: The Dominated*.

79. Cited by L. Schapiro, *The Communist Party* . . ., *op. cit.*, pp. 288–289.

80. cf. *ibid*, p. 298.

81. I draw inspiration here from the expression used by Moshe Lewin who writes to make the same observation: "doubt = treachery". He sees in this equation one of the most lethal instruments of the moral and cultural reaction which hits the country in the 1930s. (cf. M. Lewin, "Society, State and Ideology during the First Five Year Plan" in Sheila Fitzpatrick (ed), *Cultural Revolution in Russia* 1928–1931, *op. cit.*, p. 69.

82. cf. Claude Lefort, *Un homme en trop* (A man too many) Paris, Seuil, 1971, p. 171.

83. Marx notes to what extent this illusion had grown in Germany of the end of the XVIII Century. (cf. Marx, *German Ideology* in *Philosophical Works*, Paris, Edition Costes, 1938, p. 182s, especially p. 185.

84. cf. the Letter of 20 February 1889 from F. Engels to K. Kautsky, in Marx-Engels Werke (Dietz Verlag), Vol. 37, p. 156.

85. cf. Nicolas Werth, *Etre Communiste en URSS sous Staline* (To be a communist in USSR under Staline), Paris, Gallimard/Juillard, 1981, especially p. 269.

86. cf. on this point *Class Struggles in the USSR, Third Period: 1930–1941, Part One: The Dominated*.

87. F. Furet, *Penser la Revolution Francaise* (Thinking the French Revolution), Paris, Gallimard, 1978, p. 43.

88. This fact was revealed by Trotsky in 1904 in *Our Political Tasks* (republished in 1970 by Pierre Belfond); he mentioned then that this conception was foreign to Marx and analyzed the "dead-ends and the ideological follies of the Jacobin terrorism" (*op. cit.*, p. 189), cited by F. Furet, *op. cit.*, p. 119.

89. See *Class Struggles in the USSR, Third Period: 1930–1941, Part One: The Dominated* for some observations made on this question. We may add here the following observations: the manifestations of the various forms of social consciousness that burst forth are especially difficult to be located because they are generally pushed back and repressed. However, it is possible to note certain traits through memoirs and accounts in the Soviet Union and also through writings of foreigners who have lived for a considerable time in the USSR and who have had long contacts with the citizens of this country. Some of the traits of these forms that burst forth in the social consciousness appear also through the writings published in the USSR, chiefly between 1956 and 1965 at a time when the norms laid down on the contents of the literary works were somewhat less strict, particularly for those dealing with the pre-war period. Almost all these writings bring out how much the spontaneous forms of social consciousness are many-sided and diverse, and in contradiction with the official ideology. For an idea of it, it is enough to read some of the following works: Bielox, *Affaire d'habitude* (A matter of habit), Juillard, 1969; Ciliga, *Dix Ans au pays du mensonge deconcertant* (Ten years in the country of disturbing Lies), Paris,Champ Libre, 1977. Boris Mozhaiev, *Dans la Vie de Fedor Kuzmine* (In the life of Fedor Kuzmin) Paris, Gallimard, 1966; Emilio Guarnaschelli, *Une petite Pierre* (a small stone) (exile, deportation and death of an Italian Communist Worker in USSR, 1933–1939), Paris, Maspero, 1979, Valentin Rasputin, *L'Adieu a l'ile* (Farewell to the Island), Paris, Laffont, 1979; Moshe Zalcman, *Histoire Veridigne de Moshe* (Moshe's True Tale), Paris, Encres, 1977. A. Solzhenitsyn, *La Maison de Matriona* (Matriona's House), Paris, Juillard, 1965.

90. cf. V. Serge, *Les Revolutionnaires*, Paris, Seuil, 1980, p. 657s.

91. *Ibid*, pp. 938–939.

92. Complaints of this nature can be seen especially in the Soviet review *Za Sotsialisticheskuyu Zakonnost* for example, in Vol. 7 of 1936 where there is an article by Vyshinski (especially pp. 74–76).

93. cf. Moshe Lewin, "The Social Background of Stalinism", in Robert C. Tucker (ed), *Stalinism, Essays in Historical Interpretation*, New York, Morton & Co., 1977, p. 120.

94. cf. Claude Lefort, *Elements d'une critique de la bureaucratie* (Elements of a critique of Bureaucracy), Geneva, Librairie Droz, 1971, p. 158.

95. cf. M. Lewin, "L'Etat et les classes sociales as en URSS, 1925–1933" (The State and the Social Classes in URSS, 1925–1933) in *Actes de la Recherche en Science Sociales*, February 1976, p. 128. The author cites particularly a speech made in Kharkov by P. Postyshev and reproduced in No. 5 of PS, 1933. As Lewin points out, the expressions used summarize what was considered then as "the Bolshevik art of governing).

96. This becomes evident from volumes 1 and 2 of *Class Struggles in the USSR* that the Bolshevik ideology could not function either as dominant ideology of 1917 to 1930. This was not very explicitly formulated at that time. I think it necessary, therefore, to indicate it clearly here.

97. cf. *infra* the paragraph devoted to the "Code of allegiance".

98. cf. Stephen F. Cohen, "Bolshevism and Stalinism", in Robert C. Tucker (Ed). *Stalinism, op. cit.,* p. 26.

99. cf. Marc Ferro, *L'Occident devant la Revolution Sovietique et la dissidence" L'histoire et Ses mythe*s) (The West and the Soviet Revolution and dissidences, History and its Myths), Brussels, Editions Complexe, 1980, p. 88s.

100. In a paper *"Le regime ideologique sovietique et la dissidence"* (The Soviet ideological regime and Dissidence), Claude Orgini happens to deal with this theme. cf. his writing, in *Chronique des petites gens d'URSS* (Chronicle of the common people in USSR), Paris, Seuil, 1981, p. 165s.

101. At different times, the writers officially published in USSR manage it, but it is, generally by using the official discourse while altering the terms (cf. G. Svirski, *Les Ecrivain de la Liberte*, (Writers of Freedom), Paris, Gallimard, 1981).

102. cf. Stalin, *l'Homme, le capital le plus precieux* (Man, the most precious capital), Tirana, 1968, p. 26.

103. The accounts of these spyings and provocations as also the descriptions of the role of the repeated meetings are numberless. We do not generally find them in the "official" literature but in the memoirs of those who lived and worked in USSR and published abroad. We can also come across them in the Soviet literature published abroad. Thus, the book cited already by Yuri Dombrovski, *La Faculte de l'Invtile* (The Useless Faculty), Paris, Albin Michel, 1979, constituted a remarkable evidence on the way spying and provocation functioned. It seeks to suddenly come upon the "Secret thoughts". The book by N. Werth, already cited, *Etre Communiste . . .* (To be a Communist) provides a large number of examples of "The thought policing" at work in the Stalinist period. Its merit lies in basing itself on a deep study of important archival documents.

104. cf. Victor Serge, *Memoires . . . , op. cit.*, p. 280s.

105. Cited by G. Svirski, *Ecrivain de la Liberte* (Writers of Freedom), *op. cit.*, p. 76.

106. On the genesis of the Stalinist Concept of "Socialist realism", See the observations of S. Cohen in his work *"Bukharin and the Bolshevik Revolution*, New York, Alfred A. Knoff, 1974, pp. 355–356.

107. cf. On this point my remarks in Volume 2 of this work and the remarks of Dominique Lecourt, in *La Philosophie sans Feinte* (Philosophy without Sham), *op. cit.*, p. 140.

108. cf. Marx, *Philosophical Works*, Paris, Editions *Costes*, 1927, Vol. 1, p. 169s; cf. also, Marx, Works III – Philosophy, Paris, Gallimand, "La *Pleiade*" 1982, especially pp. 366–367.

109. cf. p. 195 of the Vol. I of the Editions Costes and p. 366s of Marx, Works III, *op. cit.*

110. See, for example, what Marx has written under the heading "Observations on the recent regulations of the Russian Censor", in *Philosophical Works*, Vol. 1, *op. cit*, p. 120s; cf. also *Works III -Philosophy*, *op. cit.*, p. 111s.

111. On this subject, see the plan of a work that Marx intended writing and which was to be a "critique of politics" in Marx-Engels Werke (Dietz Verlag), Vol. 3, p. 537; this text was reproduced by *Maximilien* Rubel in *Oeuvres-Economie* (Works, Economics, Vol. 2, p. LXVII/LXIX.

112. On this subject, see the remarks of Claude Lefort in *"Droits de l'homme et politique"* (Human Rights and Politics, in *L'invention democratique* (The Democratic Invention), *op. cit.*, p. 58s.

113. When Marx and Engels took part in the activities of the workers' movement, they had increasingly emphasized the importance of democratic liberties. In 1865, in a writing intended for the German Workers Party, Engels wrote: the workers movement is impossible without freedom of the press, without the rights of coalition and meeting" (Marx-Engels Werke (Dietz Verlag), Vol. 16, p. 73). In 1871, after the experience of

Paris Commune, Marx began insisting more than ever before on the rights of citizens and on the subordination required for the officials who should not be appointed but elected by citizens. [cf. K. Marx, *La Guerre Civile en France* (Civil War in France), Paris, ES, 1968.]